By the People

A History of Americans as Volunteers

New Century Edition

Susan J. Ellis and Katherine H. Campbell

Energize Inc.

Philadelphia • 2005

By the People: A History of Americans as Volunteers, New Century Edition

Energize, Inc.
5450 Wissahickon Avenue
Philadelphia, PA 19144 USA
www.energizeinc.com

Hardcover, ISBN-10: 0-940576-43-0, ISBN-13: 978-0-940576-43-0
Paperback, ISBN-10: 0-940576-41-4, ISBN-13: 978-0-940576-41-4
This edition is also available in electronic form, (ISBN 0-940576-42-2), at www.energizeinc.com

New Century Edition (Third): Energize, Inc., 2005
First Edition: Energize, Inc., 1978
Second Edition: Jossey-Bass Publishers, 1990

Library of Congress Cataloging-in-Publication Data

Ellis, Susan J.
By the people: a history of Americans as volunteers / by Susan J. Ellis and Katherine H. Campbell.--New century ed.
p. cm.
Includes bibliographical references and indexes.
ISBN 0-940576-43-0 -- ISBN 0-940576-41-4 (pbk.)
1. Voluntarism--UnitedStates--History. 2. Volunteers--United States--History. I. Campbell, Katherine Noyes. II Title.

HN90.V64E43 2005
302'.14--dc22

2005054673

Cover Design by Diane Jacobs

PRINTED IN THE UNITED STATES OF AMERICA

Once again...

To all the volunteers
we have known and respected

Photo/Image Credits:

"A Minute Man." Copyright, The Early American Digital Library.

"NAACP youth and student members marching with signs protesting Texas segregation laws." Library of Congress, Prints and Photographs Division, Visual Materials from the NAACP Records [LC-USZ62-84483].

"Young boy receiving pail of soup in kitchen of city mission. Dubuque, Iowa" by John Vachon, Library of Congress, Prints and Photographs Division, FSA-OWI Collection, [LC-USF34-060596-D].

"Barn erection. Gable panel at corn crib end is raised into place and nailed. Southeast Missouri Farms Project" by Russell Lee, Library of Congress, Prints and Photographs Division, FSA/OWI Collection, [LC-USF33-011577-M2].

"Fire department demonstration" by Harry M. Rhoads, Western History/Genealogy Department, Denver Public Library, [Rh-1200].

"Faith Hope Action" by Jolynn Desch, Director of Teams and Volunteers, Komen National Race for the Cure®. Special thanks to Eva Martorell and Edda Ashkenazi, present in the photograph, and the other ladies of the Latin Ladies Express team.

"Voter registration drive, Chinatown, San Francisco" by Russell Lowe.

Table of Contents

	Preface	vii
	Introduction: Volunteering in Perspective	1
	Part 1: Accomplishments in Our History	
1	Volunteers Found a Nation: 1607-1781	15
2	New Citizens and New Frontiers: 1782-1850	43
3	Facing Crisis and Civil War: 1851-1865	87
4	Rebuilding and Moving On: 1866-1899	113
5	The Progressive Spirit and World Conflict: 1900-1919	157
6	Volunteering amid Shifts of Fortune: 1920-1945	187
7	Protest and Change: 1946-1969	219
8	Volunteers Move into the Spotlight: 1970-1989	243
9	A Millennium Ends and a New One Begins	287
10	A Nation of Volunteers: The 21st Century	313
	Part 2: Implications for Our Future	
11	Volunteer Leadership as a Profession	335
12	The Past Is Prologue	353
	The Authors	363
	Name Index	365
	Organization Index	367
	Subject Index	379

Preface

What makes individuals worthy of historical note? Traditionally, it has been their political power; their literary, artistic, or scientific genius; their willingness to take unusual risks (which are usually only remembered if successful); or their creation of large and lasting enterprises. Fame comes from impact.

Our position is that the individual and combined volunteer actions of thousands of unnamed citizens have had an impact on American society. These actions were of citizens who became involved, not because of coercion or profit, but because they recognized a need and were willing to take responsibility for meeting that need. But because they assumed this responsibility in addition to their everyday duties, and because they did not seek monetary reward, the volunteers themselves may have underestimated the impact of their work. Traditional historians, too, have overlooked the magnitude and diversity of volunteer activities. However, the cumulative effect of many such voluntary actions, occurring as they do in every part of the country and in every decade, makes it apparent that our history has been shaped by everyone.

The historical chapters of this book present an overview of the involvement of volunteers in every area of American life and trace the effect of this involvement on American institutions, professions, and social events. We describe the accomplishments of group action rather than the singular efforts of famous individuals. Others have written comprehensive histories of the United States; *By the People* is meant as a companion volume that proposes a new frame of reference from which to view how things happened. It provides some of the between-the-lines material necessary to form a more complete appreciation of our democratic heritage.

Just about everyone, at one time or another, is a volunteer. Volunteering is so pervasive in the United States that it can be observed daily in almost every aspect of life. The problem is that volunteering, because it is so pervasive, often goes unrecognized. For instance:

Who donates blood?
Who runs the parent-teacher organizations in schools?
Who goes caroling in hospitals?
Who serves on school boards?
Who works to preserve historic landmarks?
Who appears on fundraising telethons?
Who passes out political campaign leaflets?
Who uses ham radios to relay calls for help?
Who leads 4-H Clubs? Scout troops? Youth sports teams?
Who supports community orchestras?
Who advocates for less violence on television?

The above list only touches the surface, but it serves to illustrate the diversity of possible volunteer activity. "To volunteer" does not mean only the formal commitment of being a Candy Striper or a Big Brother but includes all the ways people choose to become involved in their communities and help themselves.

Despite general acceptance of the activities of volunteers, the word *volunteer* has been associated with certain negative stereotypes. Volunteers have at times been perceived as do-gooders, meddlers, radicals, or those foolish enough to work for nothing. Volunteering has also often been perceived as "women's work" or as work done by untrained people. It is our premise that not only are such stereotypes unfair, they are historically and currently inaccurate.

Volunteerism is crucial to a functioning democracy because it mobilizes enormous energy. The more citizens involve themselves as volunteers in all areas, the closer they come to making the ideals of democracy real. Eleanor Roosevelt expressed this concept by identifying two sacrifices necessary to maintain a democracy: first, to give up selfishness, and second, "to give to our government an interested and intelligent participation."[1] Volunteerism is both an expression of patriotism in a pure sense and the means by which a democratic society remains "by the people."

Three Editions

When we began our research for the first edition of *By the People* in the fall of 1975, we had no idea how monumental the task would be nor that it would take two and a half years. At the time, we were employed as full-time directors of volunteers and had formed some strong opinions about the value of volunteer activity. We were challenged by the fact that no comprehensive history of volunteerism was available and set out to fill this gap in our field.

We energetically tackled the research necessary to the writing of our history of volunteers. Books and periodicals, current newspaper articles, and our own contacts (locally and across the country) provided much of the data. In addition, we conducted a questionnaire survey of 150 major volunteer organizations. Finally, we interviewed scores of people—some formally and some informally—about their personal volunteer experiences.

By the People was first published in 1978. For more than twenty-five years it has remained the only book to present the full scope and depth of volunteer activity throughout three centuries of American history. Because we felt that events of great importance to the development of volunteering occurred during the 1980s, and because we felt a personal commitment to keeping the book current, a second, updated edition seemed an especially worthwhile volume to produce. Further, our own professional growth and related experiences enabled us to bring new insight as well as additional knowledge to the revision. So we wrote the second edition of *By the People,* which was published by Jossey-Bass Publishers, Inc. in 1990.

It is now 2005. If we thought a great deal of new material was needed to bring the second edition up to date, we could hardly have imagined the events of the end of the century! The 1990s and early 2000s have been overflowing with critical world events and changes in the volunteer field. One tiny fact illuminates why a third edition of this book was necessary: the first Web site was created in 1991. As hard as that is to believe, the enormous changes in how we communicate across this country and around the world all started after the last edition of the book. So we had to return to our research and writing. You are reading the results.

It is also pertinent to note that the 1978 edition was written largely in longhand on paper and re-typed three times after cut-and-paste sessions requiring scissors and tape. The 1990 edition was written on the computer, but required us to mail things back and forth and to spend several intensive writing sessions together in the same spot. This 2004 edition, of course, has been created entirely in cyberspace. It becomes the first book fully published and sold by Energize in electronic and print-on-demand form.

Rediscovering American History

By the People does not claim to present totally unknown information about volunteer work. Rather, it draws together isolated citations in order to illustrate and emphasize the role of volunteers in United States history. We must stress that all the volunteer activities mentioned in this book are only examples—a sample of the massive achievements of volunteers, both past and present. We are frustrated by the impossibility of crediting everyone and hope our readers will add their own examples to what is cited here.

When we started writing, we realized that presenting history alone would not be enough. We needed, for example, to define terms and note how the past gives direction for the future. Increasingly, we began to feel that the ramifications of our historical data were important—not just the history itself. In fact, our perspective on the past gave us a way to address some concerns we have about the present:

- The ways in which volunteering is often misunderstood and therefore incorrectly stereotyped
- The frequent assumption that volunteering is only done by select segments of the population
- The tendency to credit volunteer work only in the social welfare area and not to see the many volunteer activities in other aspects of American life
- The assertion that volunteer involvement is a substitute for adequate funding

By the People puts these issues in historical perspective and suggests implications for the future.

Overview of the Contents

The Introduction tackles the critical task of definitions. It outlines the misconceptions and stereotypes about the word *volunteer* and shows how the word is often used too simplistically as "doing something for free." The chapter presents a step-by-step analysis of the concept of volunteering, identifying the elements that must be part of a meaningful definition such as choice, going beyond basic need, and not involving monetary profit. After suggesting a working definition of *volunteer*, we also define related concepts including *community service, voluntarism, voluntarily, pro bono publico work*, and other terms often used interchangeably with *volunteering*. The Introduction also raises some of the issues that will evolve in later chapters of the book, such as the concept of "mandated" volunteering connected to court-ordered community service or national youth service. Finally, we point out that the historical chapters in Part One contain examples of volunteerism that may not have been labeled as such when they occurred, but that we will place into their proper context as, in fact, the efforts of volunteers. This is particularly important in examining volunteer work done by men as well as women.

Part One contains ten chapters, arranged chronologically, that describe the contributions of volunteers to American history. A time line begins each chapter, in order to give readers a quick overview of the major historical events of each period (since we assume a majority of our readers will not be historians themselves). Each chapter presents examples of and anecdotes about the work of volunteers in various fields of endeavor. While the expected examples in the fields of health, human services, education, and religion are indeed given, equal attention is paid to volunteering in less recognized areas: agriculture, labor and industry, communications, the military, and scientific exploration—just to name a few. The impact of volunteers on the quality of life in such areas as cultural arts, recreation, and environmentalism is also catalogued.

Along with a conscious attempt to broaden the reader's perspective about the scope of volunteer interests is the goal of documenting volunteer work accomplished by the widest variety of people. *By the People* shows that both men and women have been active in community service. It demonstrates that the poor engage in self-help as effectively as the wealthy provide charity. It provides examples of volunteering by every religious, racial, and ethnic group, pointing out that volunteering is a *method* of accomplishing something that is quickly adopted by every new wave of immigrants to this country.

Though much of the text remains the same as in the second edition, we have inserted a few major items omitted the previous times, which were brought to our attention by supportive readers over the years. This third edition of course includes a new chapter focusing on the 1990s, during which major changes occurred (such as the World

Wide Web) and the field of volunteerism came in to its own professionally. The events of September 11, 2001 were shattering to the country, but—as always in a crisis—volunteers became the silver lining in that dark cloud. News events kept overtaking our manuscript drafts, as we tried to include new issues critical to current volunteer involvement as they continued to unfold in 2004.

Chapter Ten, "A Nation of Volunteers," is a unique attempt to catalogue the enormous diversity of work being done by volunteers today. It is a comprehensive inventory of hundreds of volunteer activities, arranged by fields of interest. It is expected that while every reader will know many of the things identified, the scope of volunteering shown is so large that each reader will discover new roles that volunteers fill. The chapter concludes with a brief "crystal ball" look at some of the innovative activities volunteers might well be doing by the *end* of the twenty-first century.

Part Two presents the "Future" of volunteering. Chapter Eleven, "Volunteer Leadership as a Profession," considers the development of volunteer management as a career field. This chapter also expands considerably upon the material in the previous two editions of *By the People*. First, it explains the historical evolution of the role of the "leader of volunteers." Then, it describes the emergence of volunteer administration as a profession, outlining what has happened in the last three decades to shape this active field. Chapter Eleven serves to document the key organizations and dates in the development of volunteer administration and to highlight the ethical challenges that face leaders of volunteers in today's changing agency environment.

In Chapter Twelve, "The Past Is Prologue," we consider some of the important social, economic, and demographic trends in the United States that will undoubtedly have an effect on the future of volunteering. These include changing work patterns, family configurations, ethnic population shifts, and other well-documented trends. However, we point out that the role of volunteers in the United Sates has always been that of *pioneer*—to recognize significant issues and needs well before government or other institutions do and to form services to address those needs. Volunteers will continue to be on the cutting edge, to innovate, to protest, and also to support the work of organizations meeting real needs. Understanding this history will make the reader aware of the sure future of volunteer activity in this country. The causes will change; the presence of volunteers will not.

Acknowledgments

As with any research effort, this book owes a debt of gratitude to a variety of individuals and sources. We sincerely thank all of our friends and colleagues who supported us psychologically and added to our knowledge with many fascinating clippings and anecdotes. We also want to recognize the contributions of such diverse sources as television shows, airline magazines, and small-town publications that we saw in our travels. Though unaware of their assistance, they all provided bits and pieces of the volunteer history puzzle by mentioning volunteer activities being done throughout the country. Continuing thanks go to Ivan Scheier and Winnie Brown, pioneers in our profession and friends whose vocal enthusiasm for the previous editions convinced many of the book's value.

The original project was a rare example of equally shared dedication and creativity. The way in which we harmonized our methods, thoughts, and words was truly unique, making the experience a very special one. To our delight, our style of collaboration remained intact despite the challenge of no longer living and working in the same city. The first revision process spanned more than two years and required marathon writing sessions during just about every major holiday weekend. This second revision took just as long, but now we had the Internet as an invaluable reference tool and e-mail to keep in touch.

For this third edition, we now add thanks to Lori Renner for her library and Internet sleuthing for additional references and Cara Thenot for her painstaking formatting for the best online and print reading.

Susan and Katie have both undergone many changes in our personal lives during the last twenty-five years, not to mention growing older! We gratefully recall the past assistance of Ann Ellis, whose volunteer participation in the preparation of the original book went far beyond the call of motherly duty. Alzheimer's Disease took her from us last year, but we know she's cheering us on from above. For their quiet but steady faith in this work, we thank the Gregg, Noyes, and Campbell families. Matthew (who was three when the first edition came out) and Amanda Noyes (who was only a pre-teen at the second edition) are now more than old enough to read this book fully for themselves!

Finally, we acknowledge the thousand-plus volunteers who provided special services at the Philadelphia Family Court and who inspired us to attempt this project in the first place—and to the countless other volunteers we have subsequently met. Their commitment deserves to be placed in the broader context of the contribution of volunteering to past, present, and future American society. *By the People* is their book.

October 2005

Susan J. Ellis
Philadelphia, Pennsylvania

Katherine H. Campbell
Richmond, Virginia

Endnotes for Preface

1. Eleanor Roosevelt, *The Moral Basis of Democracy* (New York: Howell, Soskin and Company, 1940), 74.

Introduction

VOLUNTEERING IN PERSPECTIVE

We are usually taught the history of the United States as a succession of events, enacted by key individuals who emerged as leaders. Though it is always understood that such individuals represented thousands of other citizens, the focus and recognition have been on the president and the general, the mayor and the minister. This book concerns itself with the multitude of citizens who fall between the lines of history books but who stood on the front lines when history was being made. It recounts how Americans affirmed their rights and responsibilities as citizens by becoming involved in shaping their own future.

> *Patriotism is informed public spirit. It is genuine concern for the conditions within our society that degrade and dehumanize and demean persons. It is concern that expresses itself in positive action—not words, but deeds . . . A patriot is a participant in democracy and does everything humanly possible to encourage the participation of others.*[1]

The above thought comes not from a campaigning politician nor from any well-known social historian. Rather, it appeared during the 1976 Bicentennial year as an unsigned editorial comment in an issue of the *Civil Air Patrol News*. It expresses a sentiment that is held by many volunteers and demonstrates some of the spirit that has made us a "nation of joiners." The American propensity to form volunteer groups for countless purposes has been noted to the point of becoming a cliché. Yet, as with all clichés, there is a good deal of truth in the observation that volunteering is a method of getting things done that Americans seem to adopt naturally. This same culture that is criticized for conspicuous consumption and preoccupation with making money also accepts without hesitation the need to collect clothes and food for flood victims, march on the state legislature to express strong opinion, and give one-on-one support to a lonely or troubled person.

How has volunteering come to be so accepted, and what exactly have volunteers contributed to the growth of this country? Why is there also controversy about the current and future role of volunteers in our society? The answers to these questions can only be found by reviewing history from a new perspective: the interconnection between citizen involvement and social progress. By crediting the historic contributions of volunteers, modern volunteering can be seen in its appropriate context.

Defining "Volunteer"

A book that discusses volunteering in the United States needs to define its use of the word *volunteer.* At first, the definition may seem self-evident. But there are actually differences of opinion, and as yet there is no consensus on a single definition, despite many attempts to discuss the term in depth.[2] The historic lack of agreement about what constitutes volunteering has led to the formation of misleading stereotypes and to ambivalence about the value and future of volunteers in modern American society.

Most definitions of volunteering are too simplistic, dealing only with the issue of payment. In fact, for most people, the definition of *volunteer* is limited to "serving without pay." Payment is one defining factor, but to rely on it solely inaccurately limits the concept. By using such a narrow definition of *volunteer*, many important contributions made in the volunteer spirit are never identified.

The test of a definition is whether it stands up to specific examples. The problems of the no-money definition are revealed when we pose questions such as: are youths who scrawl graffiti on a public wall volunteers? After all, they receive no payment for their act. Obviously, no one labels them volunteers, so there must be something missing from the nonpayment definition to explain why we exclude them. Some people would argue that the graffiti artists cannot be considered volunteers because they are doing something illegal. However, the legality of an action is actually irrelevant to our definition. After all, consider the many civil rights protesters who knowingly broke the laws of segregation but whom we acknowledge as courageous volunteers. So what *is* the issue?

The term *volunteer* connotes positive social action. However, is an act right or good because of how others view it or because of the motivation of the individual performing the act? What seems most pertinent to a discussion of volunteering is whether or not there is a goal of social responsibility. It can be fairly assumed that the graffiti artist is not deliberately working for the common good, while civil rights activists are motivated by their desire to improve society.

To further complicate the question of right and wrong we must deal with the fact that people who support opposing sides of an issue can all be labelled volunteers. It does not matter which side is perceived as being right, just that each believes its actions are socially responsible. Volunteering is actually an ethically neutral concept—a *methodology* for getting something done.

There is another reason why the no-money definition of volunteering is too restrictive. It is possible to receive some money and still be considered a volunteer. For example, Peace Corps members receive stipends to cover living expenses to support their full-time, two-year commitment of service abroad. Reimbursement for out-of-pocket expenses such as mileage, parking, meals, and supplies is offered to a wide variety of individuals doing community service tasks. Yet we feel comfortable in designating all of these people volunteers because the amount of money involved is clearly not meant to be a salary, but rather enables them to serve. They contribute their time without compensation. Stipends and reimbursements do not equal the real value of their services and there is no monetary profit.

The issues of payment and motive have other dimensions. Social responsibility and personal gain are often closely aligned. Helping others can tangibly improve life for oneself as well. As the historical chapters that follow will show, early volunteering was a response to mutual survival needs. Today's self-help groups are the modern equivalent of those early efforts.

The choice to become a volunteer can be motivated by desire for leadership training, academic credit, career exploration, social status, potential for eventual employment, or strong personal sympathies. There are some who see the gratification of these motives as a kind of payment that negates the concept of a volunteer. Such reasoning is shortsighted. Individuals can achieve their personal goals and still be volunteers as long as they are also working toward a social goal and derive no monetary profit.

There is one last argument against a simple no-money definition of *volunteer,* related to the element of will or choice. Implicit in the very word *volunteer* is the root concept of volition. In order to be voluntary, an act must be performed without coercion. This is why a slave, who obviously receives no salary, is just as obviously not a volunteer. Less extreme forms of coercion occur as well. There are times when social norms place enough pressure on individuals that they are forced into certain activities, regardless of their will to do so. This happens when one's employer makes it clear that participation in an outside activity is expected and to refuse would be to jeopardize one's job. Also, when people participate in a large group action that suddenly changes into a mob action, they can lose the ability to choose whether they wish to continue participating. Even when other aspects of the definition of *volunteer* may be present, if a person does not act out of choice, he or she is not a volunteer. Recently we have seen a proliferation of government-sponsored programs that "mandate" community service for students, law-breakers, and welfare recipients. Understandably, this has evoked much debate, which we'll explore further in a little while.

It's also important to note that not everything done voluntarily is volunteering as defined here. For example, most Americans voluntarily choose where they live and work, but these do not constitute acts of volunteerism.

Considering all these aspects, we now propose the following definition:

> *To* volunteer *is to choose to act in recognition of a need, with an attitude of social responsibility and without concern for monetary profit, going beyond one's basic obligations.*

This definition contains several key words and phrases:

- *Choose*: emphasizing the element of free will;
- *Social responsibility*: meaning purposeful action that benefits others, whether individuals, small groups, or society at large (allowing for possible benefits to oneself as well);
- *Without . . . monetary profit*: meaning no personal economic gain, but allowing for some form of reward or reimbursement (monetary or other) that is not meant to equal the value of the service given; and

- *Beyond . . . basic obligations*: meaning over and above what is necessary, unavoidable, required, or generally expected. Basic obligations include caring for one's own family, responsibilities of citizenship such as voting, or doing one's paid job.

A Different Perspective

Note that all of this discussion defines volunteering from the perspective of *the person doing the service*. As will soon become clear, there is a completely different way of identifying who is a volunteer, and that is from the perspective of *the recipient of the service*. From that point of view, an operative definition of a volunteer would be someone who is invited to become involved in the work to be done without wages or requirement from the recipient (even if a third party is paying or mandating). In terms of agency fundraising, all such contributions can be counted as *in-kind services*, or non-cash community resource development.

Critics of this definition express concern about the application of the word *volunteer* to people engaged in third-party payment situations and mandated or required service. An example of a third-party payment situation is employee work-release time. The argument is that the individual still receives his or her salary, even while doing the service activity, and therefore is not a volunteer. However, as just explained, from the perspective of the receiving agency, this worker is not on the agency's payroll and represents a non-cash community resource—and so is a volunteer. In addition, a case can be made that the employing company is itself a volunteer when offering its staff in this way.

The question of perspective also affects whether or not one considers mandated service such as alternative sentencing, or a prerequisite number of hours of service by students in order to graduate, to be volunteering. There is no choice for the person to do *something* under the requirement. But within the requirement, if there are options for selecting the type of assignment or setting, then the situation becomes more desired than forced. Further, studies show that a reasonable percentage of people who begin work through mandated service remain in their roles well beyond the required time—in which case they become volunteers under any definition. So the question "Is this a volunteer?" may be answered less by how a person enters service, and more by whether and why they stay.

The Problem with Labels

One of the challenges in doing research on the history of volunteering is that the majority of activities done in the past by citizens under the definition just proposed were and are not distinctly identified as *volunteering*. So it is necessary to take a broader approach, identifying activity that fits our definition regardless of what others call it. Not everyone is comfortable applying the label "volunteer" to some of the actions mentioned in these pages. For example, when the first edition of *By the People* came out, one reviewer criticized the inclusion of the early Ku Klux Klan. Also, some people draw a clear distinction between *activists* and *volunteers*, on the premise that volunteers are helpers or supporters, while activists are leaders, campaigners, protesters, objectors, militants, or advocates. The latter list is exactly what came up in a Microsoft Word® thesaurus search on "activist," while an electronic search for "volunteer" produces "unpaid helper, unpaid assistant, helper."

Yet, upon analysis, it is clear that *activism* refers to volunteering that works toward reform. Most activists are volunteers because their change-oriented work is not supported by institutions or funders, and because they usually do their protesting without expectation of financial pay. The logical extreme of political activism is reform at all costs, even to the point of rebellion (no one is paid to start a revolution). When public laws conflict seriously with private conscience or morality, the activist may choose to disobey the law. Once again, what determines whether an act is volunteering is not outside measures of right or wrong, good or bad, legal or illegal. What matters is that the person is acting on the basis of social responsibility to meet a perceived need, without personal monetary profit. Note, too, that whenever we refer to *historical movements*, we are describing the cumulative effect of the actions of countless citizens on behalf of a cause in which they believe—above and beyond what they do to earn a living.

For all sorts of reasons that will be examined in this book, the word *volunteer* is fraught with connotations, not all of them positive. In fact, the term repels as frequently as it attracts. The diverse accomplishments described in the pages to come counteract such stereotypes as all volunteers are women, or wealthy, or retired, or white. But such misconceptions have led various groups to apply different terminology to what might otherwise be called volunteering. An abundance of new words and phrases gained popularity during the 1990s and continue to cause debate today.

Perhaps the most popular alternative phrase is *community service,* referring to activities that meet community needs, generally without financial remuneration. In fact, this term has evolved into the label of choice for students and young adults, possibly as a way to disassociate themselves from what is perceived as old-fashioned volunteering. The federal Corporation for National and Community Service (ironically changing its name from the previous great term ACTION) has also helped to institutionalize the term. Further, some well-established forms of community service are mandated by government entities and not everyone is willing to call this volunteering nor label the participants as volunteers. As already noted, this includes offenders fulfilling a court order, employees on work-release time, students earning academic credit, and workfare participants. (See Chapter Eight for more details on these modern types of community service and their connection to volunteer work.)

One of the arguments against merging the concepts of community service and volunteering is that the former has the connotation of punishment, which is antithetical to volunteering. Alternative sentencing has been a practice for over thirty years, ordering offenders to do a certain number of hours of what is consistently called community service. Educators and the government confuse the public by appropriating this term in different ways, yet it is hard to come up with a word or phrase that conveys the activities of students or AmeriCorps participants yet satisfies those who insist on a "pure" definition of "volunteer" (implying selfless altruism and no personal gain at all).

Synonyms for Volunteer

There are other terms used as synonyms for volunteering.

Community involvement, civic engagement, neighborhood action, self-help group, and *mutual aid* are in common use.

The business world offers its own vocabulary, including *corporate social responsibility, donated professional services,* and *work-release time. Pro bono publico* work literally means "for the public good." *Pro bono publico* is used most frequently by those in established professions such as law, medicine, or accounting to refer to services rendered at reduced or no charge.

Service-learning or *experiential learning* are terms used by schools at all levels to refer to curriculum-based community service programs. This means that the students study something in the classroom and then work in the community to apply, experience, or otherwise test their learning in the real world. This is similar to the academic use of the words *internship* or *apprenticeship*, which usually refer to an intensive educational placement which may or may not be paid.

Faith communities have their expressions, too. Depending on the religion or denomination, terms in use include *lay ministry, social concerns, witness, tzedakah* and *mitzvot,* and *zakat (sadaqa).*

Volunteerism and Voluntarism

There are several concepts associated with the word *volunteer* that require clarification because of confusion about their definitions and uses. The study of volunteering and voluntary action is still comparatively new, and therefore accepted terminology continues to evolve. The distinction between the words *volunteerism* and *voluntarism* is a perfect example. As recently as the 1970s, most dictionaries did not contain the word *volunteerism.* In the early 1980s, *volunteerism*—if included at all—was most commonly followed by "see voluntarism." By the late 1980s, however, dictionaries had caught up to usage and distinctly defined each word.

It is still possible to find *volunteerism* and *voluntarism* used interchangeably, but this book adheres to the practice of distinguishing between them. (However, if *voluntarism* appears in a direct quotation from another source, it has been retained, whether or not that would be the appropriate word today.) In simple terms, these definitions apply:

> *Voluntarism*: The generic term for all that is done in a society voluntarily.
>
> *Volunteerism*: Anything relating specifically to volunteers and volunteering.

On the surface, these two terms may not look very different. But in practice, the distinction between them is important.

In the United States, voluntarism includes religion, since we do not have a state religion or mandated tithing. Further, voluntarism includes everything we consider part of the *voluntary sector,* which means voluntary, nonprofit agencies and foundations. *Philanthropy* is also an aspect of voluntarism, since one can contribute money voluntarily as well as time. However, while it can be argued philosophically that democracy is the most voluntary form of government, the term *voluntarism* does not include government or public institutions, since they are mandated by law and funded by taxes.

Voluntary agencies are called voluntary because of how they are formed, governed, and funded. They are founded by individuals who recognize a need or cause and form an organization with private funds. They are not created by acts of government or laws, though they may receive public funds through grants and contracts. Voluntary agencies are nonprofit in purpose and are usually incorporated under section 501(c) of the Internal Revenue Service Code, which allows them to be exempt from federal income taxes. (Revenue may exceed expenses, but there are no individual owners who receive such profits; excess funds are used to further the mission.) They are governed by boards of directors made up largely of volunteers. Because money is solicited from private and public sources, by law this volunteer board serves as "trustees" to ensure the accountability of the organization.

The *private sector* consists of all voluntary agencies, volunteer associations, and businesses as opposed to government (which is referred to as the *public sector*). Within the private sector, there are times that the nonprofit (or not-for-profit) segment is separated from the for-profit segment. Two additional terms have been applied only to the nonprofit world: the *third sector* and the *independent sector*.

Now consider where volunteers are involved. They work in many nonprofit organizations, but they also are active in government programs such as courts, schools, prisons, libraries, parks, and so on. Further, some volunteers actually work on behalf of profit-making businesses, such as counselors to new entrepreneurs, and others come from corporations, such as loaned executives. If we only use the word *voluntarism,* we exclude all these activities. The term *volunteerism*, on the other hand, allows us to include all volunteering, regardless of where it takes place.

Another reason for using the two terms accurately is that there are dimensions of *voluntarism* that have nothing to do with volunteers. For example, many nonprofit agencies have chosen not to involve volunteers (except on their boards of directors) in providing services to their clients; all work is done by paid employees. Therefore, while such agencies are indeed part of voluntarism, they have very little connection to volunteerism.

Related Concepts

Because volunteerism is a broad concept, other words and phrases help to define particular aspects of it.

Volunteer associations are membership groups developed by and comprised of volunteers. Some support staff may be employed by the organization, but the members themselves form the core. Volunteer associations may or may not be formally incorporated.

Membership means affiliation with a group or organization. It can be formal or informal, and it can be voluntary or involuntary. Voluntary membership is an aspect of volunteering, though each member can choose his or her degree of involvement. Volunteer participation in the group can range from the minimal paying of dues and attending meetings to holding office or working on a project. However, if initial membership is not voluntary (for example, mandatory union membership or assignment to a task force by one's employer), the member is not a volunteer merely because of the affiliation. If later the individual chooses a more active role in the organization, then that action is truly volunteering.

Philanthropy is the expression of benevolence, generally associated with the giving of money or goods to charitable causes. Volunteering is a philanthropic act, but in practice, the word philanthropy is often used as a synonym for fundraising or donating. A formalized level of philanthropy is the private *foundation.*

Public service includes activities on behalf of the public good. However, it should be noted that public service has the additional definition "employment by the government" (that is, in the public sector). This is why government workers are called "public servants." Another related term with multiple connotations is *citizen participation.* This book will refer to citizen participation as synonymous with volunteering. To the government, however, citizen participation has a more narrow meaning: it is the process by which citizens (voters) provide input to the work of government agencies. Though the government is on the receiving end of voluntary letter-writing campaigns, marches to the capitol, and individual lobbying of legislators, the citizen participation process is frequently mandated by law and takes the form of commissions, advisory councils, and public hearings. On the other hand, the people who are named to such bodies most often serve without compensation beyond expenses, and so are also volunteers.

Citizenship or *civic duty* refers to participation as a citizen in the functions of a democracy, which is always voluntary but not necessarily an act of volunteering as we have defined it. There are numerous ways in which an individual freely exercises rights and privileges available to all in a democratic society. Voting is a good example. It is nonpaid and noncoerced, but is expected of every American citizen. When

Americans choose to exercise their citizenship beyond this minimum through some sort of political or community participation, they become volunteers.

Amateur has several dictionary definitions. The first is usually "one who is not paid for what one does." This is why *volunteer* is often equated with *amateur* by those who apply only the no-money definition of volunteer. The additional definition of the amateur as being "unskilled" is not appropriate in all cases. Consider Olympic athletes. No one would deny their high level of training and expertise, yet they are technically "amateurs" because (until recently) they receive no salary or profit for their work. In the same light, it is inaccurate to label highly-skilled volunteers as amateurs, if this is meant as an indicator of training. It is interesting to recognize that the word amateur is derived from the French word for "one who loves" one's work—hardly a pejorative when applied to volunteers.

Professional, as opposed to amateur, refers to receiving a salary or to having had training. Since many people apply their professional skills to their volunteer work, it is incorrect to equate the word volunteer with "non-professional."

In the twenty-first century, the newly-defined concept of *civil society* has captured the attention of academics and politicians alike. Civil society encompasses a wide range of social interaction, from simple courtesy to voting and expressing political opinions. The presence of a high degree and wide range of volunteering is clearly an indicator of a strong civil society, although there are only infrequent references to volunteering by name in civil society literature.

Confusing Uses of the Word Volunteer

In addition to all the nuances of definition discussed above, one must recognize that the word *volunteer* is frequently misapplied. The problem usually is confusion between the concepts of *voluntary* and *volunteer*. Consider: When an airline calls for "volunteers" to give up their reserved seats on an overbooked flight in exchange for a free airplane ticket, is this an example of volunteering, or is it simply an act that is voluntary? The remuneration (cost of the ticket) can even be profitable.

Another visible example of a mixed message is the military use of the phrase "the Volunteer Army." In this context, *volunteer* simply means non-draft, rather than nonpaid. In the words of a high-ranking naval officer: "Perhaps the sense of true volunteering is connected to a cause . . . as in 1776, when men were really fighting because they were angry . . . I would not equate it with today's all-volunteer force."[3] He compared the motivation for present-day enlistments to a search for the best employment opportunity; the armed services compete with private industry for workers. Therefore, enlisting in the armed services today is voluntary, but it does not involve the same choices and commitments as volunteering.

Historically, the military drew a distinction between its "regulars" and its "volunteers." While the use of the term *volunteer* always meant not drafted or conscripted, it is not always possible to determine whether monetary compensation was offered or consistently provided in previous centuries.

Another misleading use of the word *volunteer* is connected to medical experimentation. Researchers frequently solicit volunteers to participate in scientific tests, but a large number of such projects actually pay individuals to be subjects. Patients also "volunteer" for experimental treatments that might work when nothing else is effective. Agreeing to take a medical risk or submit to some discomfort is certainly voluntary, but a person who does so is, by this book's definition, only a volunteer if no financial compensation is involved.

Just as this third edition was in its final stages, an example surfaced of how ludicrous the terminology can become. The June 17, 2004, *Beacon Journal* in Columbus, Ohio, ran the headline: "Second volunteer scheduled for execution in July." A concerned reading provided more details:

> *Mink, 40, who pleaded guilty at trial, is dropping his appeals and could be executed next month. If the execution proceeds on July 20, it would be the quickest an Ohio inmate's death sentence was carried out since the state re-enacted the death penalty in 1981 . . . It would also come a week after the scheduled execution of another volunteer, Stephen Vrabel of Youngstown . . . Wilford Berry, dubbed "The Volunteer" because he dropped his appeals, was executed in February 1999. He was the first inmate to die since Ohio re-enacted capital punishment and the only other volunteer to date to be executed.*

Clearly, anyone researching the history of volunteering sometimes has to decide to apply or reject the label *volunteer,* depending on the specific situation!

Categories of Service

Some researchers muddy the water further by attempting to classify volunteers into such categories as "direct service," "policy making," "fundraising," "administrative," or "advocacy." These labels simply describe the type of activity performed, not whether it is done on a volunteer basis. Furthermore, individuals are often simultaneously involved in more than one form of volunteering, blurring the lines between categories.

This classification system also sets up a hierarchy in which policy-making volunteers are on top and direct-service volunteers are on the bottom. The implication is that one type of volunteering is more valuable than another. This is why volunteers themselves sometimes resist the label volunteer, which is wrongly identified only with the lower levels of the hierarchy. It sounds better to be called a trustee. While there are undeniable variations in the skills and activities involved in each type of volunteer work, the definition of volunteer nevertheless applies equally to all. Classifications based on the type of work performed tend to distort rather than clarify what a volunteer is.

Too often classifications also perpetuate stereotypes about volunteering, such as the belief that most volunteer work is social work. Apart from the client-oriented sphere of social welfare, volunteers are also active on behalf of the arts, agriculture, conservation, and politics, among other arenas. The following chapters demonstrate that this has always been true.

Women's Work and Social Work

Any historical look at volunteering must pay attention to the issue of women as volunteers. Until the twentieth century, women had very limited opportunity for impact except through volunteering. What becomes overwhelmingly apparent through a closer look at the history of volunteering in the United States is that women have made vital contributions to every aspect of the country's growth, contributions that deserve permanent recognition.

The problematic vocabulary of voluntary action just described contributes to the misconceptions about women and men as volunteers. Unpaid work done on behalf of social welfare has most often been labelled "volunteering," while unpaid work on behalf of political change has instead been called "activism," "campaigning," "advocacy," or "community involvement." The use of such terminology has fragmented people's perceptions of voluntary action, limiting the concept of volunteering to social services. A perfect illustration of this problem is the fact that when the first edition of *By the People* was published in 1978, the Library of Congress catalogued it under "Social Work—History of." The catalogers judged the book's content by their misconception of the subtitle.

This is also why it is sometimes assumed that men have not volunteered. Since women were perceived as doing mainly social services, while men did the politicking, volunteering became typed as "women's work." Yet men have always been volunteers under different labels and, as such, have been instrumental in the formation of all types of professions and institutions. The volunteer nature of this involvement is often overlooked because men were traditionally expected to assume civic responsibilities as part of their political or business functions. What is recorded by most histories is a clear division of roles: we remember the men for their voluntary political reform and the women for their voluntary social welfare acts. The fact is that such a clear dichotomy rarely existed. Thousands of women were involved in local and national political movements, and thousands of men took part in humanitarian relief efforts. All were volunteers.

It is critical that the words used to describe the volunteering of Americans be understood by everyone. This book is committed to a broad definition of *volunteer*, with the goal of proving the validity of such a perspective. Historical evidence supports the more encompassing definition. Only by applying the concept of volunteering in its fullest sense is it possible to appreciate the extent to which volunteers have affected our society and continue to do so.

Endnotes for Introduction

1. *Civil Air Patrol News* 8, no. 2 (March 1976): 3.

2. For extensive and provocative discussion of volunteerism terminology, see Ivan H. Scheier, *Exploring Volunteer Space* (Washington, DC: Volunteer, 1980, today available only through Energize, Inc.) and Jon Van Til, *Mapping the Third Sector* (New York: The Foundation Center, 1988).

3. Statement by Rear Admiral Wycliffe David Toole, Jr., personal interview, May 3, 1977.

PART 1

Accomplishments in Our History

Chapter
1

Volunteers Found a Nation

1607-1781

1607	Jamestown, Virginia, is founded.
1620	Pilgrims arrive aboard the *Mayflower*; establish a colony at Plymouth, Massachusetts.
1636	Harvard, the first college in the colonies, is founded.
1664	British capture New Amsterdam and rename it New York.
1673	Marquette explores the Mississippi.
1681	Quaker William Penn founds Pennsylvania as the "Holy Experiment."
1755-1763	French and Indian War.
1770	Boston Massacre.
1773	Boston Tea Party.
1774	First Continental Congress.
1775	Battles of Lexington and Concord. Second Continental Congress.
1776	Declaration of Independence.
1781	Revolutionary War ends. Articles of Confederation adopted.

The European settlers of the new American colonies all had the same priority: survival. Physically, the land was a wilderness, and socially, most familiar organizational structures were missing. Food, shelter, and defense were the first concerns, and colonists struggled to make do with the resources at hand. Cooperation frequently meant the difference between life and death, for no single individual could overcome the hardships alone. As more colonists arrived from Europe, they brought with them institutions and beliefs that they quickly adapted to the unique situation they found in America. Because religious persecution in Europe was a major reason for immigration, religion was the force that molded the early colonial systems of social organization and self-government.

An expression of the New World's commitment to voluntary cooperation to achieve mutual goals was the Social Compact of 1620. In this document the Pilgrims affirmed the necessity for a government based upon the consent of the governed. They further joined in a covenant that bound them strictly "to all care of each others good and of the whole by everyone and so mutually." In the early development of the Massachusetts Bay Colony, the Compact served as the governing force for all activities. It was supported by the structure and doctrines of Puritanism, which had a pervasive influence on the lives of community members.

> *Puritanism in its various manifestations in New England had been a way of life, a part of the everyday existence of men, and not something put on on Sunday . . . The strict moral code of the Puritans implied an active concern of the churches for the behavior and welfare of their members and indeed for the whole community, whether within the bosom of the church or outside.*[1]

The tenets of Puritanism were both pessimistic and optimistic in their view of man. On the one hand, man was born evil and only a select few could hope for salvation. On the other hand, individuals were able to attain grace, largely by performing good deeds in the earthly sphere, a thesis articulated in Cotton Mather's *Essays to Do Good* (1710). It was therefore basic to Puritanism that each member of the community willingly assumed responsibilities for the common good, in addition to meeting basic personal needs. Where cooperative action was necessary to deal with a common problem, volunteers could be found to tackle the task.

Neighboring farmers frequently combined efforts to accomplish important work such as clearing land, building houses and barns, haying, harvesting, and other required tasks. The men did most of the more strenuous physical labor, while the women and children assisted and also prepared communal meals. Such cooperation not only finished hard work quickly but also provided social outlets and promoted a sense of community. In addition, the women aided each other with general household duties. Quilting parties and spinning bees were common occurrences, as were "whangs," or gatherings of women assisting each other with annual housecleaning.[2] These volunteer efforts by both men and women were often referred to as "changing works."[3]

Cooperative farm ventures began when common lands were designated for the grazing of all herds together. Farmers combined resources to hire a cowherd or "cow-keep" to care for their cattle collectively.

The government structure adopted in New England was the town meeting, an open forum in which voting was generally restricted to white, male property owners and merchants. However, all community members were welcome to discuss town problems and to propose solutions. Administrative officials were elected to supervise the implementation of plans decided upon by the town meeting. It is evident by a review of the titles and functions of such officials that most were unpaid and accepted the positions out of a sense of moral duty and a desire for local prestige. Some examples were: selectmen, surveyors of highways, fence viewers, and clerks of the market.

> *Besides these a long list of additional petty functionaries were chosen, such as hog reeves, field drivers, pound keepers, overseers of the poor, tithing men, town criers and many others. Not all of these were chosen by every town; but the list in each case was numerous enough to give a public position to a good proportion of the inhabitants.*[4]

Obviously, this system of self-government was dependent upon citizens willing to volunteer.

In the middle-Atlantic and southern colonies, the problems of great distance between settlements and of slow communication increased the importance of each family unit:

> *Colonial law assumed the integrity of the family and assigned to it large responsibilities for the control of morals, labor, education, and the care of the sick and poor. The colonists accomplished much within the limits of the neighborhood by mutual family self-help.*[5]

The dominant church in a particular area directed the social welfare activities to be undertaken by congregation members. For example, many Quaker meetings served both a religious and governmental function. Meeting day provided for discussion of both secular and holy matters. Uniquely, Quaker women were permitted a full though separate voice in decisions affecting the whole community. Once decisions were reached, the plans for poor relief, town maintenance, or whatever were implemented by appropriate volunteers.

In the South, each plantation was a self-contained and largely self-governing unit with less loyalty to a larger community. Social welfare volunteering was largely confined to the boundaries of each plantation. The local parish maintained a self-help system among small farm owners.

From the time of the early colonists onward, church buildings in America were built by the people. There are many references to donations of land, materials, communion services, and money— all given voluntarily in order that each community should have its own place of worship. For example, as early as 1698, the citizens of Delaware joined in the building of Old Swedes' Church:

> *Every member of the community helped. The stones were broken by the congregation and hauled on sleds in the winter, and after spring had set in, on carts. The boards were all sawed by hand and the nails used were forged by the community blacksmith.*[6]

And later, in Virginia:

> *The Church was erected in 1756 and tradition tells us that the women helped in the work of construction, going with the men, holding bags and scooping in the sand. Then they rode, each with a bag of sand across her horse.*[7]

Circuit-riding preachers, often self-appointed, served the more remote communities. They relied on the Lord and on public generosity to provide for them.

The colonial period was unique in its lack of organized charity. Alms for individual sufferers were viewed as a means of diverting capital to an unproductive portion of the community. In New England, the strong Puritan ethic maintained that people were responsible for saving their own souls. Those who gave handouts were considered fools who confused pity with justice, refusing to acknowledge that a person's poverty was largely the proof of failure to live correctly: "Cursed were the poor, for theirs was neither the patrimony of earth nor the kingdom of heaven."[8] In fact, many towns implemented a "warning-out" system to exclude or eject newcomers without assured means of support. Often, citizens who brought long-term guests into their homes were forced to notify authorities, to safeguard against an influx of dependent residents.

Despite this intolerance for almsgiving and public doles, the need for some charity was recognized. Families bore the primary burden of aiding indigent relatives and close friends, thus reducing the likelihood of any individual becoming dependent on the community at large. Such voluntary aid harmonized well with the religious concept of good deeds: "This form of charity was considered to be a virtue, and it was encouraged . . . It had an advantage . . . over institutional charity, for the person who helped his unfortunate neighbor had personal knowledge whether or not the case was a worthy one."[9]

There were instances however, when this type of aid was not available, and it was then that local authorities became involved. Sometimes the old and infirm were boarded in a private home, for which the host family was paid through tax money. Orphans and illegitimate children were apprenticed to some useful occupation until the age of twenty-one. Another form of relief was termed "taking in," in which each family in a community took its turn providing for a destitute person for a certain number of weeks each year.

As population increased, these individualized systems proved inadequate to meet welfare needs, and almshouses were established—as early as 1662 in Boston and 1732 in Philadelphia. The early ones were not specialized facilities, however, and were held in low regard because they allowed the poor to get something for nothing. Workhouses were a preferred alternative, especially for able-bodied men.

Such social welfare depended largely on volunteer participation. Before long, clubs, societies, and fraternal orders sprang up whose primary objective was benevolent service. Scot's Charitable Society of Boston (1657) and the St. Andrew's Society of Charleston, South Carolina (1730), were typical. Private legacies were also common, as in the case of the Virginian Matthew Godfrey, who, in 1716, bequeathed to Norfolk County his slaves and the income of his 100-acre estate for assistance to the poor.[10] On a broader scale, several mass calamities occurred that evoked widespread cooperation. The Charleston fire of 1740, for example, brought gifts for relief from as far away as Massachusetts. The only type of labor organization in this prosperous economic period was the "benevolent society," formed as self-help by workers to assist with such things as sick benefits and burial expenses.

Clearly, the early colonists were neither uncaring nor uncharitable people. They expressed their concern for each other through individual acts of kindness and volunteered to contribute to the welfare of those for whom they felt a sympathetic or empathetic bond. Relief efforts, for the most part, consisted of very personal actions, primarily because to be in a position of need was a very personal predicament. Ultimately, however, aid to one's neighbor meant aid to one's community, and citizen volunteers slowly came to recognize that, when private alternatives failed, the obligation lay on the taxpayer to help those who could not help themselves. This was the beginning of institutionalized social welfare.

Closely related to charity and social welfare was medical care, which left much to be desired in colonial America. "The letters which passed between New England settlers contain ample evidence of the prevalent dearth of medical skill. A layman who had any tincture of such knowledge was constantly consulted by his friends and neighbors."[11] Each community had its herb specialist for general ailments, and most often common sense substituted for medical knowledge when an injurious accident occurred. Neighbors helped each other when the need arose, as was especially evidenced by the self-help system of midwifery practiced by women. At the birth of a child, the women in the immediate area volunteered to assist the woman in labor and to care for the household while the mother recovered. Those women who devoted themselves full-time to midwifing were often paid some fee, at least in goods, but most assistance was freely given friend to friend. Of all areas of medicine, obstetrics received the least formal attention until well into the eighteenth century and therefore remained dependent on the informal volunteer efforts of women themselves.

The few doctors practicing in the colonies were, of course, greatly in demand both as physicians and as trainers for new doctors. After a three- to seven-year apprenticeship to an established doctor, a medical student could declare himself a doctor and set up practice. Quite obviously, there was a crying need to set medical standards, and by the mid-1700s, some doctors were actively seeking solutions to this problem through voluntary cooperation. In 1749, the Weekly Society of Gentlemen in New York was formed, later evolving into the Medical Society of the State of New York (1794). Associations of concerned physicians, such as the 1755 Faculty of Physic in Charleston, pressed for such reforms as the regulation of fees. Similarly, in 1766, the New Jersey Medical Society attempted for the first time to produce a list of standards for doctors and stressed the importance of good medical education. The 1765 Philadelphia Medical Society was a forum where doctors read scholarly papers for the benefit of the medical students in the audience. By 1770 the Philadelphia group had become the American Medical Society.

No colony had any type of permanent health organization. Epidemics did not occur often, but when such a medical crisis happened

> *a committee of citizens, usually with a physician as a member, was chosen to combat the epidemic . . . Usually these bodies were called "boards of health"—sometimes "health committees." In some instances the government paid a fee to the committee members, but they usually served voluntarily as a public duty. They were often given power to make expenditures and to employ personnel at community expense.*[12]

When the epidemic was over, the volunteer health board disbanded.

Epidemics generated widespread community concern, but isolated illnesses contracted by individuals or families were treated by colonial towns through the "pesthouse." Pesthouses were not hospitals. They were simple shelters built in remote areas for the purpose of quarantine. There "medical and nursing care, was often carried out on a voluntary basis . . . Clothing and food were donated by individuals or by the community."[13] The volunteer nurses and others who helped in the pesthouses were usually immune to the disease inside because they had previously survived the illness themselves. Hospitals as permanent facilities were unknown until 1751, when the Philadelphia Hospital was founded as a voluntary, philanthropic enterprise.

Although the issues of survival were naturally given priority, the colonists were concerned about education and established schools as soon as they could. When the colonies began there were few state-supported public schools in Europe; most instruction, directly or indirectly, was under the influence of the various churches. Accordingly, the first schools built in America were founded and supported by religious groups. Classes were often held in churches, and a good many of the earliest teachers were members of the clergy. In New England, the

Puritans established a basic philosophy toward education that has remained an important American ideal: "that the public school exists to secure and advance the public welfare."[14] This served as an incentive for active citizen participation in the development of an educational system.

Schoolhouses were usually built through cooperative efforts. One notable example of such volunteering can still be seen in the Old School House in Mount Holly, New Jersey. It was constructed in 1759 by a group of twenty-one citizens who pooled their resources to buy land and build a schoolhouse. The schoolmaster was paid by the parents who could afford it, while less fortunate children were allowed to attend for free. Later, in 1815, the heirs of the original builders deeded the school over to the Female Benevolent Society, whose members volunteered to teach gratis all the poor children of Mount Holly and its vicinity.[15]

In the plantation communities of the South, individual planters usually joined to hire a schoolmaster and to build a schoolhouse. In general, these schools collected fees from parents who were able to pay but subsidized orphans and poor children. This arrangement was made possible largely because wealthy members of the community made endowments to the local school in order to provide for this type of charitable education. In the more remote areas, where such contributions were not as common, the local parson would often volunteer to take in a few needy children and teach them to read and write.

There were no standard qualifications for teaching, and the role was filled by any individual stepping forward to accept the responsibility. Often, classes were conducted by widows, housewives, college graduates, and ministers simply out of willingness to provide a needed service. Even those who were full-time teachers were hardly in it for the profit:

> *Salaries were derived from tuitions, voluntary gifts, and incomes from rentals of town land. Many were paid in kind with food-stuffs and livestock. For practically all teachers the time and form of payment were uncertain, and the natural consequence was a large turnover with many teachers becoming virtual itinerants. To make a living some of them had to hold down two or more jobs—including preaching, bookkeeping and even grave-digging.*[16]

In accordance with their concern for providing basic educational services, the colonists placed an understandably high value on books.

The few volumes that had been brought to America were widely read, and "privately owned books circulated almost as freely as the gossip of the neighborhood."[17] James Logan of Philadelphia had one of the best collections of scientific works in North America and made it available to serious students. When he died, he left both house and books to the city to be used as a public library. Similar bequests dated back as far as 1656, when a prominent Boston merchant provided for a town library in his will.[18] In addition, many private collections of books were opened to the general citizenry, and societies were formed in order to facilitate exchanges of personally owned volumes. This type of voluntary sharing was important in maintaining the educational life of colonial society. In 1731, Benjamin Franklin organized the Library Company of Philadelphia, thus introducing the idea that individuals might volunteer to pool their resources to establish subscription libraries. The concept took hold, and such associations spread quickly throughout the colonies: "People got together, raised funds, paid fees, bought books, and enjoyed the privileges of a reading room with a much wider selection of books than they could afford individually in their own homes."[19] Functioning thus as a kind of joint-stock association, these early subscription libraries illustrate the way in which colonists took it upon themselves to create a viable means of meeting a common need.

The library companies did not limit their acquisitions to books. Many societies also collected historical artifacts and curiosities. In 1773, the Library Society of Charles-Town exhibited its collection on the history of South Carolina by opening a public museum, "the first in this hemisphere."[20] This volunteer-created exhibition was the forerunner of the twentieth-century Charleston Museum. Library societies in other colonies similarly provided their areas with local museums.

In the seventeenth century, anyone desiring an advanced degree was forced to turn to European universities. This was inconvenient and expensive, especially for ensuring a supply of well-trained church leaders. Therefore, in 1636, a group of Massachusetts clergy founded the first American college. In 1638, the future of this school was assured through the benevolence of John Harvard, in whose honor the school was named Harvard College. Upon his death he left to the struggling college a large sum of money and his private library of four hundred volumes.[21] Similarly, in 1700, ten of Connecticut's leading clergy established what was to become Yale College. The first step taken by the founders was to make volunteer contributions of books from their personal collections.[22]

As colonial citizens began to enjoy a greater degree of security and prosperity, the desire for institutions of higher learning increased, and more American colleges were established. From the outset, many individuals made donations to the cause of college education: books, equipment, tracts of land, money for buildings and scholarships, even food. Nearly all the books in the libraries of these early colleges were donated, new purchases being altogether too expensive except for occasional volumes. Historical curiosities were also given to colleges for study and display. This flow of philanthropic gifts continued throughout the seventeenth and eighteenth centuries, stimulated by the growth of a civic and humanitarian spirit and the emergence of a well-to-do element in the cities.

College promoters sought to advance the cause of higher education through affiliation with library companies, many of which offered popular lecture courses. Ministers were urged to act as recruiting agents for the college identified with their sect, while alumni also volunteered to help recruit, especially if they were schoolmasters or pastors.[23] As a result of this close association between colleges and communities, many of the early American colleges differed from their English counterparts in one important respect: they were governed by lay boards of trustees rather than by the privileged clergy. "The colonial colleges were created under difficult circumstances by community effort. Having invested its time and resources, the community controlled the institutions."[24] Thus, through their material support and participation as board members, community volunteers shaped the American college from the very beginning.

The dogma of work so strictly adhered to by the early Puritan colonists was a factor directly influencing their recreational activities. Any "mispense of time" was severely frowned upon as a frivolous creation of the devil, so many of the more popular forms of amusement were initially banned. Ironically, however, drinking was permitted and soon became the most common form of recreation.[25]

Social restraint lessened as lifestyles became more diversified. As previously mentioned, isolated families often combined work and pleasure whenever they came together for log rollings, sheep-shearing, square dances, or country fairs. Even the tasks of hunting and fishing became sports: "Farmers of Massachusetts and Connecticut enjoyed squirrel hunts, went out after raccoons and also banded together every autumn to beat up the swamps and kill these 'pernicious creatures.'"[26]

"Ring hunts" were also common, where men and boys from neighboring settlements would encircle a vast area in order to catch animals. Such rural pastimes reflected the cooperative volunteer spirit that was so evident during colonial times.

After 1710, there was evident growth in the number of clubs, fraternal orders, and other societies for which Americans were always enthusiastic. Philadelphia boasted of having a Masonic Lodge as early as 1715, and by 1770 the order was one of many represented in most of the principal seacoast towns.

> *Other clubs, formed along national, professional or craft lines and avowing the pursuit of knowledge as their aim, brought gregarious spirits together once a week for an evening's comradeship in taverns and private homes. Most of such clubs seem to have forsaken their high aims and to have yielded to the delights of conviviality and good fellowship.*[27]

Jockey clubs became prominent in the southern and middle colonies, composed of sportsmen who arranged rather elaborate programs. There were also select dancing clubs and epicure societies in most larger towns and cities, devoted to the tastes of the more elite members of colonial society. In short, citizens developed modes of amusement that were well suited to their particular community. Such voluntary associations were often durable, existing for many decades as a means of linking together men and women with common interests.

As time went on, the need for increased contact within and among the colonies became vital. Transportation and communication needed organization, but it would not be until after the Revolution that such networks would successfully span the new nation. In the meantime, local and individual efforts had to suffice.

In most areas, responsibility for building and maintaining public roadways was assigned to the residents whose farms lay alongside the route. The work was apportioned at various civic meetings throughout the year, such as "court day," when rural neighbors conducted necessary village business. Besides cooperating to build the roads, farmers voluntarily acted as "viewers" or "overseers" to enforce the satisfactory upkeep of local routes.[28] New England winters created the need for clearing the roads after snowstorms. Neighbors volunteered to team their oxen to accomplish this task of "breaking out."[29]

Lengthy travel was still inconvenient and difficult. Coaches were few, and most people traveled only when absolutely necessary. Lodgings along the way were rare and of very poor quality. Some southern travelers were lucky enough to stop off at a planter's home, while others spent the night in one of the many small farmhouses en route. Hospitality was the primary concern of the host, and frequently a poor farm couple would give up their bed for the comfort of the traveler. Even in commercial inns and taverns further north, "landlords considered it their duty to give hospitality to all who came, especially in bad weather."[30] Profit making was not as important as a warm welcome.

Of course, the traveler was expected to perform certain duties in exchange for the comforts of food and shelter. Because visitors from distant colonies were few and far between, firsthand news was hard to come by. Travelers knew that they would be providing the evening's entertainment by recounting the latest items of interest learned through their travels. Additionally, a traveler might be asked to deliver a message or a letter to someone at his or her destination. Such a personal postal system served the colonies in the seventeenth century, when letters were carried by "ship captains, merchants, friends, travelers, private messengers, Indians—in fact, by anyone going somewhere near the addressee."[31] Often a small fee was paid for this service, especially when the courier was traveling on business. However, friends and neighbors voluntarily delivered messages reciprocally.

One of the first moves toward a more formal postal service occurred in Massachusetts in 1639. The General Court authorized one Boston tavern keeper to handle all letters destined for Europe, at the rate of 1 penny per letter. This plan was not meant to be compulsory, and the court even stated that "no man shall be compelled to bring this letter thither except if he pleases."[32] Ship captains were entrusted with the actual delivery of letters to England and the Continent.

By 1670, public demand had created a network of postmasters and regularized mail delivery routes. It would take another eighty years before the organization was even near to completion. Many of the early postmasters were storekeepers whose places of business were community centers. Because there were no established hours or holidays, mail was sorted for delivery whenever it arrived and was accepted whenever received. As a result, "usually every member of a postmaster's family was involved in running his postal affairs as well as his business."[33]

The important role of postmaster was one frequently held by women. The reasons for this become clear when one learns that running the local post office also meant feeding and refreshing the horses and drivers and often providing overnight bed and board. Such kitchen and innkeeping work was part of a woman's domain. "Hence women automatically came into the postal picture almost from the dawn of the service."[34] Clearly, running the local post office involved volunteering beyond the obvious requirements of the job. Entrusting women with the vital duties of postmistress was one of the first forms of public recognition that women, too, could meet civic needs. From the start, women were appointed to administrative posts and often rose to the highest positions in the postal service.

Transportation and postal services were only two of a number of community management concerns. Following rural tradition, town and city householders at first assumed responsibility for essential public works on an individual basis. They voluntarily shared such basic tasks as building and cleaning the streets, disposing of garbage, and maintaining an adequate water supply.

> *Prior to 1677 the digging of wells was strictly a private matter . . . In this year the [New York City] Mayor ordered the inhabitants in each of six streets to dig public wells. No appropriation of city funds was made indicating that the individual citizens had to bear the full cost.*[35]

It was not until 1686 that the New York City Council allotted public monies to cover well-digging expenses, and even then it only covered half. Through the 1730s, homeowners were responsible for sweeping the dirt in the street in front of their houses into piles to be carted away later by the city.[36] Keeping the streets lit at night was another concern requiring citizen cooperation. Each householder had to keep a candle or lamp burning in the front window, especially during the dark winter months. In addition, some towns asked the owner of every seventh house to hang a lantern outside by the road.[37] Such maintenance activities assumed that an attitude of volunteerism would prevail.

In the southern colonies, the plantation owners maintained the roads connecting their plantations with each other and with the growing port cities. Since the plantations were self-sufficient, all construction, supplying of water, sanitation, and other such concerns were handled routinely as matters of self-interest. The southern coastal cities tended to follow the same patterns of voluntary cooperation as their northern counterparts.

As towns and cities grew in size and complexity, it became evident that individuals alone could no longer handle basic maintenance functions. Citizens expected local government to assume the responsibility of organizing and funding these tasks. There were times, however, when city officials failed to respond to certain needs and the colonists employed a forceful countermeasure: the voluntary organization. Such a group approach had a long history with religious dissenters in England, who acted where and when neither church nor state was effective. The Americans simply utilized the voluntary organization in more practical, everyday matters. Examples of the projects of voluntary societies were hospitals, libraries, and other civic and cultural institutions established solely through private contributions and cooperative efforts. By 1775, "the voluntary organization had become a standard way to deal with any civic problem the government refused to face."[38]

Another concern was safety. Paid constables generally kept the peace during the day, but at night larger patrols were needed.

> *The common problems of the towns called forth common efforts. In early times police protection was a community responsibility shared by all able-bodied men. The smaller New England towns utilized train-bands in which all males over sixteen were liable for guard duty at night. In Philadelphia, prior to 1751, all householders were required to serve in the night watch.*[39]

Lest it be thought that all citizens shared the same commitment to such unpaid effort in the town watch, it should be pointed out that some wealthy men paid as much as 6 shillings a year to the constable in order to be exempt from such duty![40]

There was no colonial police force as such, though in a crisis the constable or sheriff could raise a posse or call together the volunteer watch. Justice was meted out quickly and painfully through use of the public whipping post and stocks or the gallows. Building jails was another local function usually accomplished through the time and efforts of the townspeople.

The earliest vigilante movement of note occurred in colonial South Carolina with the 1767-1769 "regulator" organization. Later, during the Revolution, Colonel Charles Lynch led retaliatory actions against Virginia Tories and outlaws, giving his name to this breed of justice. Interestingly, the early meaning of "lynch law" was usually limited to corporal punishment, most often whipping. It was not until after the Civil War that *lynching* became synonymous with *killing*. After the war, the frontier families took vigilantism with them. From 1767 to 1910, at least 327 separate movements can be identified, despite later efforts to suppress the violence of these voluntary justice seekers.[41]

Some town maintenance burdens could easily be apportioned among the citizens, but others called for capital funds beyond the pockets of individual homeowners. Money was needed for building bridges, churches, schools, and lighthouses, just to name a few of the more pressing items. Because there was little ready cash and great reluctance to pay taxes, lotteries became extremely popular as a way to subsidize public works. Of the approximately 158 lotteries licensed before 1776, 132 benefited civic or state purposes.[42] It was considered natural to indulge the human instinct for gambling, and so at first there were few legal restrictions on lotteries. Many of the early managers of the lotteries were volunteers who agreed to supervise this form of fundraising:

> *it was not regarded at all as a kind of gambling; the most reputable citizens were engaged in these lotteries, either as selected managers or as liberal subscribers. It was looked upon as a kind of voluntary tax for paving streets, erecting wharves, buildings, etc., with a contingent profitable return for such subscribers as held the lucky number.*[43]

The economics of colonial America were in a formative stage, both dependent on, yet isolated from, England. Labor, currency, and mercantile systems adapted to the unique conditions of the new land. The colonial money system was far from stable, and commercial banking did not exist until after the Revolution. "One finds frequent references to 'banks' in the writings of [the Colonial] period, but the term was applied to issues of notes, which were secured, if at all, by a pledge of land or merchandise."[44] Such notes were circulated by subscriptions asking the signers to pledge themselves to accept that currency as payment for goods and services. There were few savings banks for the private citizen, except in Philadelphia, where Benjamin Franklin started one, and in a few other northern cities. "These dated, however, from a period of philanthropy, having been founded as 'mutual banks' by sponsors (whose profits were restricted to the amounts of interest paid to depositors), principally as a means of stabilizing their communities."[45] Such economic arrangements developed out of a volunteer spirit.

The growth of towns and cities increased the threat of fire, and effective firefighting required well-organized emergency action. It was Benjamin Franklin in Philadelphia who in 1736 pioneered the organization of "a company of thirty volunteers who equipped themselves with leather buckets and bags and baskets."[46] The concept of the volunteer fire company was an overwhelming success immediately. Within a few years, almost every property holder in Philadelphia belonged to such a company, and the idea spread rapidly up and down the coast. Each town was divided into wards, with the residents volunteering to fight blazes in their area.

Because of the danger involved, being a volunteer fireman carried social status. Rivalry was strong among the volunteers, and street fights frequently erupted as companies battled to reach fires first. Though such mob scenes ultimately brought an end to voluntary firefighting in the major cities, all fire emergencies were handled completely by volunteer fire companies until at least the 1780s. "New York in 1772 had eleven fire companies and engines, with a force of 163 men organized under a fire chief."[47] By 1775, in fact, the press was able to note that, thanks to the volunteers, the fire menace had been brought under control in New York and Philadelphia.

The pattern of dealing with community concerns through citizen cooperation continued as the frontier was pushed further inland. The first volunteers to brave the wilderness were woodsmen who blazed trails so that others could follow. As new settlements grew, voluntary civic responsibility was again called forth:

> *Devoted primarily to the development of their own land the settlers were possessed by the mingled vision and commonsense to recognize the necessity of devoting themselves as well to the affairs of their neighbors.*
>
> *Every interest on the frontier was perforce a common interest. Each was . . . called often from the plow to the public service.* [48]

The roles of judge, militia commander, surveyor, and other town officials were filled by matching qualified citizens to the job. Frontier settlers volunteered to accept the encumbrances of civic office in addition to their regular farm duties, thus transforming isolated homesteads into communities.

During the early 1700s, American newspapers were filled with gossip and with material copied from any available source. Even in the 1770s, "news was a haphazard thing. The papers printed information in the form in which it was received: actual stories, advertisements, proclamations and letters."[49] One important source of news eagerly sought by editors was private letters between friends in distant colonies or from abroad. Because the thirst for firsthand news accounts was never slaked, any mention of current events—no matter how casual—made a private letter worthy of public interest. It was accepted practice to give such letters voluntarily to the local newspaper for public dissemination. This sharing of personal correspondence made colonial newspapers a community responsibility.

From 1740 through the 1780s, American magazines were the product of club-like associations and had a very limited circulation restricted to subscribers.

> *Their . . . subscribers assumed the role rather of patrons than of customers. Their editors and publishers were more likely to be writers or professional men than business entrepreneurs. Their contributors resembled a loose, voluntary group of acquaintances and kindred spirits rather than paid employees.*[50]

The magazine clubs were not formed to make a profit, and members usually had some other way to make a living. Most authors contributed voluntarily, receiving no payment even for original work. The same was true for editors, who were usually

> *clergymen, professors, or lawyers filling editorial posts on a part-time basis or continuously for brief stretches away from their more regular occupations. Some magazines had multiple editors of this sort who described themselves as "a society of gentlemen."*[51]

Frequently, in fact, magazines were the outgrowth of actual local men's clubs in which no one wrote professionally. The magazines were a way to exercise one's avocation; the idea of making a career of writing was still far-fetched to most colonists.

Though the private-subscription magazines enjoyed a great vogue, all had disappeared by 1820. In their time they were a source of educated entertainment and commentary on affairs of the day. They all represented the work of interested volunteers. But of lasting impact were those papers, tracts, and pamphlets that fostered political awareness and sympathy for the upcoming revolutionary cause. Hunger for news became even more intense as the Revolution loomed near. Editors and publishers exchanged papers and shared news. It became evident that newspapers could stimulate patriotism and nationalism. The importance of colonial newspapers to the people was demonstrated concretely:

> *When the war opened, the supply of paper from England ceased, and the forty mills in the United States were unable to supply the demand. Rags could not be gathered. Again and again the newspapers were forced to suspend . . . The Massachusetts Spy besought "the fair daughters of Liberty" to save every scrap of rag and send it to some paper-mill.*[52]

Rag appeals were met by all patriots, and the newspapers kept up their circulation with such volunteer donations.

Beginning in the mid-1700s, politics increasingly became a daily concern for American colonists. The impending crisis necessitated a network to link town, county, and colonial assemblies. In 1764, during the early stages of the Stamp Act furor, this network took the form of the Committees of Correspondence. Their original aim was to communicate intelligence about hostile British activities. When the Stamp Act crisis passed, these ad hoc committees became dormant until 1768, when the Townshend Acts again aroused the more outspoken colonists. In 1772, Massachusetts had a standing Committee of Correspondence, and by 1773, so did Virginia. The other colonies soon followed suit.

The Committees of Correspondence actually were the culmination of years of colonial experience in bypassing the royal government. Committees had been a tool of civic management for decades. Further, by "blocking the legal, natural channels of protest and remonstrance, the royal governors and other crown officers virtually instigated cooperative protest: committees of protesters were the result."[53] The Committee system gave the growing protest movement structure and mobilized the voluntary action of citizens across the colonies.

There was danger in Committee membership, and those involved were sworn to secrecy. The main functions of the Committees of Correspondence and later the Committees of Safety were writing regularly to Committees in the other colonies and reporting local conditions, keeping watch over resolutions and violations, and initiating protests. Their most important psychological function was to be a symbol of colonial unity. Committees were either formed by election or by assembly appointment, and such volunteer service was patriotically accepted. Though the volunteers who made up the Committees of Correspondence and Safety were largely middle class and literate, their organization demonstrated "the practical working of a democracy at its best."[54]

The Committees fostered a new sense of united purpose among the colonies, shown in a variety of small and large actions. In 1774, when the Boston port was closed as punishment for the famous Tea Party, other colonists responded with generous aid:

> *Up and down the seaboard popular gatherings helped stimulate concern, and men went from door to door and from street to street to collect contributions. Soon great quantities of wheat, livestock, cheese, rice, and other foodstuffs poured in on the stricken town, as well as clothing, firewood, and gifts ofmoney . . . In this case to be sure, patriotism spurred charity, but basically the relief endeavors sprang from abiding wells of human compassion.*[55]

The patriot slogan of liberty affected many black slaves, especially in New England. Some slaves attempted to gain their personal independence through "freedom court suits" and petitions. Neither technique was very successful, though freedom suit verdicts often forced an owner to pay damage fines to the slave complainant. In 1773, a group of Massachusetts slaves

> *petitioned the legislature to liberate them, calling attention to the things they lacked: "We have no property! we have no wives! we have no children! no city! no country!" . . . the following year the Bay State slaves sent to Boston another petition, stating that, in common with all other men, they had a right to their freedom.*[56]

The legislature tabled both petitions, but this early example of volunteer organization by the slaves had a deep effect on some of the rising statesmen.

There were a number of ways that the average citizen could play an active part in the growing rebellion. Economic pressure on England was an important weapon. The Boston Tea Party was but one of many citizen efforts. Though the colonists had grown dependent upon the goods of the mother country, boycotts of British products were attempted, usually successfully, all over the colonies. In 1764, the Society for the Promotion of Arts, Agriculture, and Economy was formed in New York to foster local manufacturing of linens and woolens.

> *Large numbers of people agreed to abstain from the use of mourning at funerals, such as black cloth, scarfs, gloves, and rings, not of domestic manufacture . . . To keep up the supply of material for woollen manufactures, most of the inhabitants agreed not to eat any lamb or mutton, and not to deal with any butcher who should kill lambs.*[57]

To compensate for the loss of material from England, "the spinning-wheel came into renewed use in every household, and homespun was worn by the wealthiest. Spinning matches at neighbors' houses became a common occurrence, and an excellent outlet for patriotic ardor."[58] Though the term *boycott* was unknown until the 1880s, the colonists found the volunteer practice of "resolving to abstain" quite effective.

After the Stamp Act, colonists resolved to abstain from buying and using such diverse items as loaf sugar, coaches and carriages of all types, imported hats, gold and silver lace or buttons, diamonds, clocks and watches, muffs, starch, women's stays, velvet, gauze, silks, and many other luxury and basic articles imported from England. Colonial women were the natural participants in such boycotts and eagerly exercised their might in this arena of political activity. Abigail Adams, in her July 31, 1777, letter to her husband John, described one particularly vivid episode of the treatment given to a Boston merchant who tried to undermine the boycotts by hoarding already scarce products:

> *You must know that there is a great scarcity of sugar and coffee, articles which the female part of the State is very loath to give up, especially whilst they consider the scarcity occasioned*

by the merchants having secreted a large quantity . . . It was rumored that an eminent wealthy, stingy merchant (who is a bachelor) had a hogshead of coffee in his store, which he refused to sell to the committee under six shillings per pound. A number of females, some say a hundred, some say more, assembled with a cart and trucks, marched down to the warehouse, and demanded the keys, which he refused to deliver. Upon which one of them seized him by his neck, and tossed him into the cart. Upon his finding no quarter, he delivered the keys, when they tipped up the cart and discharged him; then opened the warehouse, hoisted out the coffee themselves, put it into the trucks, and drove off.

It was reported that he had personal chastisement among them; but this, I believe, was not true. A large concourse of men stood amazed, silent spectators of the whole transaction.

The women willingly boycotted, but made sure merchants did not take advantage of consumer patriots!

The need for nails, bullets, and other metal items was met domestically by the home industry system that had been growing before the war. Massachusetts farmers erected "small forges in their chimney corners, and in winter, or on evenings when little other work [could] be done, great quantities of nails [were] made, even by children."[59] Everyone pitched in to win the struggle for economic as well as governmental independence.

The military strength of the colonies was directly dependent upon voluntary action in the most basic sense. In the 1600s, there was no army to protect citizens from the dangers of the wilderness. This meant that all settlers protected their own families and property and assisted their neighbors when called upon. As the colonists began to develop a greater sense of community, they felt the need to create more unified defense measures. Laws were enacted in several colonies as early as the 1630s requiring all citizens to hold arms, to be called up as needed to carry out the governor's orders. As time went on, more permanent companies of those willing to volunteer for active duty were formed.

The "common militia" were the militia based on the principle of compulsory service; the "volunteer militia" were the formations whose recruits chose membership in them, generally with the understanding that they would respond first to calls for active service.[60]

As a result of this distinction, the volunteer militia often took on a kind of elite status. The cavalry and artillery units brought the most prestige and entailed greater expense for the individual volunteer. For example, the Ancient and Honorable Artillery Company of Boston was more of a social than a military unit, choosing its members with a degree of exclusiveness.[61] Another, more useful elite militia consisted of thirty Massachusetts volunteers who could be ready for service at a half-hour's warning; they were later to become the Minutemen of 1775.

Colonists had come to America, in part, to escape compulsory soldiering, and they did not wish to abandon their homes and farms for months at a time to fight for causes only remotely connected with their own aspirations or security. This attitude proved to be a problem for England during the French and Indian War, when the volunteer militias were asked to fight for lands extending far beyond the existing British settlements. Insufficient numbers of colonists volunteered for active duty, and the local assemblies were unwilling to impose a draft on the common militia. Thus, in 1757, eleven thousand men belonging to the regular British Army arrived to carry the major burden of the war.

Some twenty years later, however, the colonists proved that if the cause was right they would willingly come forward:

Especially after Lexington and Concord, large numbers of New Englanders evidently viewed the redcoats in Boston as a menace to their safety and their future . . . Individual volunteers and volunteer companies such as the Kentish Guards of Rhode Island . . . streamed to Boston. By late May the New England colonies believed they had gathered 24,500 men.[62]

On June 14, 1775, the Continental Congress authorized the muster of troops under its own sponsorship and appointed George Washington as commander. Intercolony military union resulted from cooperation on all levels.

At the beginning of the Revolution, slaves and free Negroes were barred from enlisting in the Continental Army. But later, in the face of possible defeat, they were allowed to volunteer. Two of the most well-known all-black units were the First Rhode Island Regiment and the

"Bucks of America" company from Massachusetts.[63]

Of course, there were problems created by this citizen army. Most soldiers enlisted for one year, after which time they felt they had done their share and could go home to their farms and families. Enthusiasm for the cause fluctuated partly because the pay promised by the emerging government was sporadic.

Citizens aided the war effort in ways other than joining the army or navy. Members of General Washington's spy organization—the Culper Ring—were civilian volunteers. They included a schoolteacher, a farmer, an ex-whaler, a tavern keeper, a Quaker merchant, and others whose only reward was the inner satisfaction of knowing they had served their country.[64] American whaleboats, privately owned and manned, contributed to the war effort by raiding British merchant vessels, though not always for purely altruistic reasons:

> *The efforts of the feeble Continental Navy were supplemented by practitioners of the lost wartime art of privateering. Today war is waged only by governments, but in the Revolutionary era the civilian volunteers, fighting for gain as well as from motives of patriotism, added another dimension to this nation's defense.*[65]

A large component of this civilian network consisted of women. From the very beginning, women contributed to every aspect of the war because the Revolutionary cause was one that affected them as well. Women organized the Daughters of Liberty (the female counterpart to the Sons of Liberty), boycotted British goods, wrote letters, and published newspapers in support of the colonist cause. They collected funds door-to-door for the army and made clothing and flags by the barrelful. Many upper-class women donated their property to quarter soldiers. They also exerted social pressures, even to the point of pledging themselves "not to receive addresses of any suitors who had not obeyed the country's call for military service."[66] They visited military hospitals and prisons daily, bringing food and comfort to those held there, and contributed greatly to the general morale of the soldiers. Some even found military service on behalf of their country so irresistible that they joined husbands and sweethearts in the fighting.

The Revolution, of all our wars, became the one war in which women played active roles in battle. The women who fought were, like the men, a varied crew. There was Deborah Sampson, actually a private in the Continental line. There were the Molly Pitchers who followed their husbands to war and, in desperate moments, manned the guns. There were frontier women, battling the twin evils of Tories and Indians. And finally there were passionate patriots like Nancy Hart.[67] Women also volunteered as spies.

Since the Revolution was, in large part, fought in skirmishes wherever small bands of Americans and redcoats met, virtually every acre was a potential battlefield. These small battles began and ended quickly, with action moving on to another site. This meant that women and children were often confronted with the unpaid and unrecognized task of burying the dead left by both sides.

Women also had a role to play in tending to the medical needs of wounded soldiers. Their biggest role was in keeping military hospitals supplied. One army doctor made an appeal to the citizens of New York and came away with piles of sheets, bandages, and other useful articles. A similar appeal worked in Philadelphia, where the ladies donated old sheets and shirts.[68]

Regimental surgeons often cared for ill soldiers in nearby private homes, and, even after hospitals were established, "arrangements for the wounded were necessarily extemporized . . . Many were taken by their friends to the barracks and tents, or to private houses."[69] Often, wealthy citizens opened their homes as medical centers. During the battle of Brandywine in Pennsylvania nursing care was volunteered by the brothers and sisters of the Ephrata Cloisters. When hospital conditions reached an all-time low near Charleston, South Carolina,

> *a subscription for the support of the sick was filled by people of every denomination with amazing rapidity. Several of the ladies of Charleston, laying aside the distraction of Whig and Tory, were instrumental and assiduous in procuring and preparing every necessity of clothing and proper nourishment for our poor, worn out, and desponding soldiers.*[70]

The Revolutionary soldiers owed whatever medical care they received to the generosity of local citizens.

> *In studying the history of our Revolutionary War, it is but natural that our attention should first be caught by the highlights and brilliant color of the exciting events of the military conflict, or the romance of the diplomatic scenes, to the exclusion of the commonplace, everyday efforts of the average citizen.*[71]

As the preceding pages demonstrate, the "average citizen" was critical not only to the success of the War of Independence but, more basically, to the formation of a new society. The simple cooperation among neighbors that made life in the early wilderness tolerable was succeeded by more structured forms of joint community effort. The scope of government responsibility increased as population grew, but on the frontier "pioneer conditions put a high premium upon personal work, skill, ingenuity, initiative and adaptability, and upon neighborly sociability."[72] In the cities, voluntary associations supplemented governmental action by making needs known and by organizing volunteers to implement solutions.

What is most important in this era is the pervasive attitude of cooperative volunteering. Individuals actively sought a role in their growing communities, beyond the basic demands of survival. Involvement on the local level expanded with a developing sense of common purpose with neighboring settlements. This, in turn, broadened into an emerging loyalty to the colonies as a whole. In this way, person-to-person volunteering was linked to actions supporting the cause of patriotism. As Nathan Hale said:

> *I am not influenced by the expectation of promotion or pecuniary reward; I wish to be useful, and every kind of service, necessary to the public good, becomes honorable by being necessary. If the exigencies of my country demand a peculiar service, its claims to perform that service are imperious.*[73]

ENDNOTES FOR CHAPTER 1

1. Louis B. Wright, *Culture on the Moving Frontier* (Bloomington: Indiana University Press, 1955), 171.

2. Alice Morse Earle, *Home Life in Colonial Days* (New York: Macmillan, 1923), 417.

3. Oscar Theodore Barck, Jr., and Hugh Talmage Lefler, *Colonial America* (New York: Macmillan, 1958), 297.

4. John A. Fairlie, *Local Government in Counties, Towns and Villages* (New York: Century, 1920), 23.

5. Bradley Chapin, *Early America* (New York: Free Press, 1968), 234.

6. Edward F. Rines, *Old Historic Churches of America* (New York: Macmillan, 1936), 163.

7. Ibid., 29.

8. William S. Sachs and Ari Hoogenboom, *The Enterprising Colonials: Society on the Eve of the Revolution* (Chicago: Argonaut, 1965), 84.

9. Gaillard Hunt, *Life in America One Hundred Years Ago* (New York: Harper and Brothers, 1914), 194–5.

10. Arthur M. Schlesinger, *The Birth of the Nation* (New York: Knopf, 1968), 115.

11. John Andrew Doyle, *The English in America* (Reprint of the 1882 edition: New York: A.M.S. Press, 1969), 3: 41.

12. Wilson G. Smillie, *Public Health, Its Promise for the Future* (New York: Macmillan, 1955), 62.

13. Ibid., 67.

14. Chapin, *Early America*, 75.

15. Roscoe L. West, *Elementary Education in New Jersey: A History* (Princeton, NJ: D. Van Nostrand, 1964), 10.

16. Carroll Atkinson and Eugene T. Maleska, *The Story of Education* (Philadelphia: Chilton, 1962), 96.

17. Curtis P. Nettels, *The Roots of American Civilization* (New York: Crofts, 1947), 504.

18. Louis B. Wright, *The Cultural Life of the American Colonies, 1607–1763* (New York: Harper and Brothers, 1957), 145–6.

19. Theodore C. Blegen, *Grass Roots History* (Minneapolis: University of Minnesota Press, 1947), 182.

20. Laurence Vail Coleman, *The Museum in America* (Washington, D.C.: The American Association of Museums, 1939), 1: 6–7.

21. Thomas A. Bailey, ed., *The American Spirit* (Lexington, Mass.: D.C. Heath, 1968), 70.

22. Doyle, *English in America*, 5: 218.

23. Beverly McAnear, "College Founding in the American Colonies, 1745–1775," in *Essays in American Colonial History*, ed. Paul Goodman (New York: Holt, Rinehart and Winston, 1967), 588–92.

24. Chapin, *Early America*, 219.

25. Foster Rhea Dulles, *A History of Recreation: America Learns to Play* (New York: Appleton-Century-Crofts, 1965), 1–21.

26. Ibid., 25.

27. Nettels, *Roots of American Civilization*, 459.

28. Parke Rouse, Jr., *The Great Wagon Road from Philadelphia to the South* (New York: McGraw-Hill, 1973), 197.

29. Earle, *Home Life*, 412–3.

30. Rouse, *Great Wagon Road*, 175.

31. Barck and Lefler, *Colonial America*, 359.

32. Ibid., 360.

33. Arthur E. Summerfield, as told to Charles Hurd, *U.S. Mail* (New York: Holt, Rinehart and Winston, 1960), 48.

34. Ibid., 48–9.

35. John Duffy, *A History of Public Health in New York City*, 1625–1866 (New York: Russell Sage Foundation, 1968), 30.

36. Ibid., 41.

37. Barck and Lefler, *Colonial America*, 435.

38. David Hawke, *The Colonial Experience (Indianapolis: Bobbs-Merrill, 1966)*, 439.

39. Nettels, *Roots of American Civilization*, 457.

40. Ibid., 457–8.

41. Richard Maxwell Brown, "Legal and Behavioral Perspectives on American Vigilantism," in "Law in American History," eds. Donald Fleming and Bernard Bailyn, *Perspectives in American History* (Harvard University, Charles Warren Center for Studies in American History), 5 (1971):100–1.

42. John Samuel Ezell, *Fortune's Merry Wheel, The Lottery in America* (Cambridge, MA: Harvard University Press, 1960), 272.

43. A. R. Spoffard, "Lotteries in American History," *American Historical Association Annual Report, 1892* (Washington, D.C.: Government Printing Office, 1893), 174.

44. George William Dowrie, *Money and Banking* (New York: Wiley, 1936), 180.

45. Summerfield, *U.S. Mail*, 89.

46. Nettels, *Roots of American Civilization*, 458.

47. Ibid.

48. Dale Van Every, *Forth to the Wilderness* (New York: Morrow, 1961), 307.

49. Laurence Greene, *America Goes to Press* (Indianapolis: Bobbs–Merrill, 1936), 26.

50. Ibid., 19.

51. Ibid., 25.

52. John Bach McMaster, *A History of the People of the United States* (New York Appleton, 1884), 2: 63–4.

53. John C. Fitzpatrick, *The Spirit of the Revolution* (Port Washington, NY: Kennikat Press, 1924, reissued 1970), 101.

54. Ibid., 116.

55. Schlesinger, *Birth of the Nation*, 116.

56. Benjamin Quarles, *The Negro in the Making of America*, rev. ed. (New York: Collier Books, 1969), 45.

57. J. Franklin Jameson, *The American Revolution Considered as a Social Movement* (Boston: Beacon Press, 1926), 54.

58. Ibid.

59. Ibid., 61.

60. Russell F. Weigley, *History of the United States Army* (New York: Macmillan, 1967), 8.

61. Ibid.

62. Ibid., 31.

63. Dorothy B. Porter, "The Black Role During the Era of the Revolution," *Smithsonian* (n.d.): 53–54.

64. Corey Ford, *A Peculiar Service* (Boston: Little, Brown, 1965), 28.

65. Fred J. Cook, *What Manner of Men* (New York: Morrow, 1959), 273.

66. Elizabeth F. Ellet, *The Women of the American Revolution*, 5th ed. (New York: Baher and Scribner, 1849), 1: 16.

67. Cook, *What Manner*, 216.

68. Louis C. Duneau, *Medical Men in the American Revolution, 1775–1783* (Carlisle Barracks, PA: Medical Field Service School, 1931), 66, 114, 170–1.

69. Ibid., 50.

70. Ibid., 320.

71. Fitzpatrick, *Spirit*, 116.

72. John Dewey, *The Public and Its Problems* (New York: Holt, Rinehart and Winston, 1927), cited in Frank Freidel and Norman Pollack, eds., *American Issues in the Twentieth Century* (Chicago: Rand McNally, 1966), 148.

73. Ford, *Peculiar Service*, flyleaf.

Chapter
2

New Citizens and New Frontiers
1782-1850

1787	Northwest Ordinance establishes procedures by which territories can become states.
1788	United States Constitution ratified.
1789	George Washington elected and inaugurated president.
1791	Bill of Rights ratified.
1803	Louisiana Purchase.
1812-1814	War of 1812.
1817-1825	The Erie Canal constructed.
1820	Missouri Compromise.
1823	Monroe Doctrine.
1845	Texas is annexed.
1846-1848	Mexican War.
1848	California gold rush.
	Seneca Falls Convention declares women's rights.

The close of the Revolutionary War brought the new American citizens face-to-face with the realities and responsibilities of self-government. The years of the new republic were filled with controversy and compromise, yet a unified government was formed. The original colonies grew in population, and cities evolved as true urban centers. More states joined the union, and the original frontier was pushed further west. The settlers who participated in this westward expansion faced common problems and challenges: Indian raids, the securing of land titles, the establishment of local law and order, and the acquisition of those essentials not produced by the frontier itself.

All these needs drew people together and fostered a continuation of the colonial spirit of mutual cooperation and volunteering.

By the start of the nineteenth century, the concepts of north and south, east and west represented distinct ways of life—yet all were undeniably American. Government on all levels was concerned with itself, with developing the working structure, legal procedures, and political foundations necessary for an effective, lasting government. In addition, the immediate pressures of economic instability and foreign relations could not be ignored. There was an obvious limit to how many areas of life the inexperienced government could devote attention. Therefore during the early days of the republic, social welfare, education, the arts, and other local issues continued to be handled by the citizens themselves.

The necessity for good communications within the growing country became increasingly crucial. The Postal Service, organized before the Revolution, underwent expansion and improvement as the years passed. The heart of the system was still the postmaster or, frequently, the postmistress, carrying out the duties of running the post office while at the same time keeping the family business going. Beginning in 1794, women also held courier jobs and often volunteered for routes considered hazardous, even for men. "Post day" was an important event, especially in small country towns. The mail rider was a source of news beyond the letters delivered and was expected to share his or her firsthand account of events with the community. Individual families often hosted the courier to dinner and enjoyed their payment of local and distant gossip.

The telegraph was a giant step forward in communications. Its inventor, Samuel Morse, dedicated himself to developing and promoting his telegraph and code. Beginning in 1832, he worked without pay for eleven years before the government recognized his invention as worthy of support. He always hoped for profit but suffered lengthy deprivation before receiving either profit or acclaim.[1]

The new country continued to rely on newspapers to bridge the geographical gap between cities, towns, and farms. As before the war, most small newspapers could not afford a staff of writers and reporters, and so citizens still shared private letters containing news items. Furthermore,

> *the newspaper was made up of contributions which came directly from the people or were copied from other Gazettes . . . Every gentleman of leisure who took an interest in manufactures, or had a taste for politics and could turn a neat essay was sure to send something to the press.*[2]

Newspaper editors were frequently looked upon as community leaders and became advocates for a variety of local improvement projects. They spent their own time helping to establish schools, libraries, lecture programs, and other progressive enterprises. Indirectly, the newspapers fostered such intellectual activities as historical and scientific societies by publishing their amateur findings in special columns. By seeking out the community's latent authors, the editor stimulated such volunteer groups to further research.

Some of the communities' latent authors contributed to periodicals as well:

> *If the statements of the projectors of our early periodicals may be trusted, they were moved by a spirit very different from that which animates their successors. It was (with) no idea of filling . . . their own pockets, or the coffers of a corporation, that they began to till this field of letters. They were moralists, philanthropists, censors whose high duty was to lead, not to follow.*[3]

This created a hodgepodge of articles on every conceivable topic. Of course, the general public rarely received the benefit of such instruction, as periodicals were primarily distributed by subscription until well into the 1800s.

Book publishing was often a private matter. For years literary piracy was an unfortunate fact of life in America. Foreign authors were especially open to the plagiarists' art. In the nineteenth century, the well-known writers of America voluntarily formed the Copyright League, which worked for many years to establish an international copyright law protecting foreign authors, at least for books printed in the United States.[4]

Progress in communication and progress in transportation were intimately connected. Before long, the bright future of the railroad was increasingly evident. Railroad building was carried out mostly by chartered companies organized with private capital, but there was still room for volunteering on the part of many. Initially, some citizens willingly gave the necessary rights of way across their land and even donated small amounts of acreage for the building of stations.[5] Furthermore, the conductors and porters who served on the trains performed many extra tasks on their own initiative, including assisting at births. They also ran a very reliable lost and found service that prided itself on its record of locating owners.

Some conductors carried small packages from destination to destination at the request of businesses and also ran errands in distant cities. This volunteer system eventually evolved into a profit-making express business.[6]

Volunteering could involve virtually every passenger on the train, especially in crisis situations:

> *Railroads did not offer to provide travelers with pistols if requested as did some stagecoach lines, but they did print on their tickets: "Passengers must assist the conductor on the line or road whenever called upon." This might mean helping to drive buffalo off the tracks, jacking the train back on the rails in case of a derail, and fighting off both Indians and train robbers.*[7]

Despite such potential hazards, long-distance travel by rail increased, as did the problem of stranded travelers. In response, the mayor of St. Louis mobilized volunteers to form the Travelers Aid Society in 1851. From this successful start, other Travelers Aid Societies were created in many cities.[8]

Until the 1850s, however, transportation primarily meant horses and wagons, either individually or in long wagon trains bound for the new frontiers. The individual traveler in the South, faced with long distances between plantations and notoriously awful southern inns, could rely on the abundant hospitality of the plantation owners. In fact, many hosts had slaves "stationed at the planter's gate where it opened on the post-road or turnpike, to hail travellers and assure them of a hearty welcome."[9] Such generosity was sometimes abused by tourists and curiosity seekers, who hoped to avoid the innkeeper's bill. Backwoodsmen also extended hospitality in their own way, as expressed in this firsthand account:

> *Enter this door, and tell him you are benighted, and wish the shelter of this cabin for the night. The welcome is indeed seemingly ungracious. . . . But this apparent ungraciousness is the harbinger of every kindness that he can bestow, and every comfort that his cabin can afford . . . You are shown to the*

best bed which the house can offer. When this kind of hospitality has been afforded you as long as you choose to stay, and when you depart, and speak about your bill, you are most commonly told with some slight mark of resentment, that they do not keep tavern. Even the flaxen-headed urchins will turn away from your money.[10]

More often than not the dangers of frontier roads induced travelers to set out together, forming mobile communities for the journey. Mutual need made strangers willing to share hardship and danger until they reached their destination. Wagon train leaders were faced with many responsibilities. They

had to create an "esprit de corps" quickly and preserve it among a miscellaneous crowd in the face of thirst, hunger, and disease, discouragement, mortal danger, and death . . . The leader was the persuader and the organizer."[11]

In many ways, these leaders were early directors of volunteers!

Community spirit was necessary to survival. Frontier families were dependent upon each other first to reach their destination and then to form productive settlements.

Knowing they were moving where jurisdiction was uncertain or nonexistent, they dared not wait for government to establish its machinery. If the services that elsewhere were performed by governments were to be performed at all, it would have to be by private initiative.[12]

The boundaries between public and private interests blurred for a time as the new communities grew their roots. Settlers "obligate[d] themselves to aid each other, so as to make the individual interest of each member the common concern of the whole company."[13] Following the early colonial pattern, neighborliness was an expected part of frontier life. For example, the arrival of a new family brought the settlement together for a cabin raising. Describing the Ohio and Mississippi valley settlements of 1815, Timothy Flint remarked, "The people more naturally unite themselves into corporate unions, and concentrate their strength for public works and purposes."[14] Because everyone had a community role, Flint also observed "a more familiar, and seemingly a more cheerful intercourse between the two sexes, than in other western states."[15]

In the new settlements, people often organized themselves politically long before Congress established formal procedures for the territories. Based on voluntary cooperation for mutual protection of the rights of homesteaders, the land clubs and claim associations began to develop written agreements governing their areas democratically.[16] During the 1830s and 1840s these associations also provided relief to poor farm families and helped protect them against foreclosures. This vital form of voluntary action was rooted in the American concept of self-help.

The westward expansion was certainly not the only example of growth in young America. As the urban population multiplied, it was no longer possible to maintain public services in the same ways that had worked before. The need for government control of town maintenance projects was increasingly felt. For example, by 1844 a report in New York City urged a comprehensive sewage plan and

> *mentioned several streets in which the residents had united to build private sewers. While [the author] commended the citizens and considered their efforts beneficial, he felt that an integrated sewerage system could not be built piece-meal.*[17]

Similarly, though volunteer fire departments filled a critical need, they also had some disturbing side effects:

> *In some of the large cities the volunteer fire companies were abolished. Of all causes of disorder they were the worst. Around their houses hung gangs of loafers, "runners" who, when an alarm was rung, ran with the engines and took part in the fight almost certain to occur.*[18]

The fights sometimes lasted for days, and there is even evidence that a few companies actually set fires to create some excitement. As such uncontrollable activities continued, a number of cities were determined to end the problem by establishing a paid lire department. Boston and Cincinnati led the way, and other cities followed in the late 1840s. While such negative aspects of volunteer firefighting were characteristic of the cities, volunteer companies continued to grow in numbers and importance throughout the rural countryside and the frontier.

The major concern of city governments was raising revenue to pay for vital projects, and many again fixed upon legal lotteries for fundraising. As before, the early managers of these lotteries were volunteers; when the programs became larger and more profitable, lottery management became a business. The increasing dishonesty, fraud, negative social effects, and lowered public profit all took their toll on the popularity of lotteries. It was obvious that what had started as a good idea was souring fast. Beginning in the early 1800s and taking form around 1830 was a growing movement to abolish the lotteries. Early labor groups were among the first to protest this form of disguised taxation, seeing it as hurting most those least able to pay, the poor.[19] By 1894, citizen pressure of several decades finally resulted in a federal law banning all lotteries.

Lottery proceeds were often used to build and maintain jails. But the mere warehousing of offenders was not the only justice concern. It soon became evident to those who cared that conditions for prisoners were intolerable. As early as 1787, a group formed in Philadelphia to focus on such mistreatment. The Philadelphia Society for Alleviating the Miseries of Public Prisons (still in existence today under the name of the Pennsylvania Prison Society) led the way for similar humane societies in caring for the physical needs of prisoners. Though the state provided some care for other offenders, the many imprisoned debtors were completely dependent on volunteer help. In 1808 for example, the Philadelphia Society for Alleviating the Miseries of Public Prisons fed and clothed thirteen hundred debtors alone.[20] In New York, the Society for the Relief of Distressed Debtors was also founded in 1787, later changing its name to the New York City Humane Society. Besides helping hundreds of imprisoned debtors each year, by 1811 the Society was maintaining a soup house to feed residents of poor neighborhoods.[21]

There was also no public money to support religious services or visiting clergy in the prisons, and so "now and then some society, or some individual, shocked at this state of affairs, would see to it that the Bible was read a few times and a few sermons preached."[22]

The concept of probation for minor offenders was developed during this period. In 1841 a Boston shoemaker, John Augustus, put up bail for a drunkard neighbor and offered to supervise him in the community. By 1859 Augustus had worked with over two thousand probationers, on a strictly volunteer basis. His efforts were soon duplicated across the nation.[23] This humane attitude extended to other justice issues. In 1842, volunteers gained support for an anti-capital punishment movement, or at least for the abolition of public executions.[24]

The problems of juvenile delinquency were apparent even in early times. In 1821, a group of Philadelphia citizens, determined to "save young children from falling into vicious ways," called a meeting in the mayor's office to form an association for this cause. Unfortunately the turnout was so poor that another plan had to be devised. The original civic-minded committee studied the problem and concluded that the cause of youthful crime was lack of education. It proposed the establishment of training schools as a long-range solution, but for immediate action it tried again to mobilize volunteer interest:

> *The young men had a public meeting and chose seven of their number for each city ward and assigned to them the duty of rousing the people to take vigorous measures to suppress the alarming nightly depredations on the persons and property of our citizens.*[25]

The above is a quote from the February 18, 1822, *American Daily Advertiser* and is a prime example of urban volunteering. Assisting in the effort to control crime were black citizens, such as the members of the Philadelphia African Methodist Church, who pledged themselves to assist the mayor's anti-delinquency campaign.[26] In fact, most cities and towns continued to rely upon volunteer peace officers until just before the Civil War, when larger cities hired specially trained full-time police.[27]

The approach of using citizen patrols to maintain law and order developed much more fully outside of the cities. The history of justice on the frontier is a history of vigilantism, largely because the lack of existing courts and governmental structures forced citizens to fill the vacuum. From the early nineteenth century into present times, Americans supported both a legal and an extralegal justice system, the latter devoted to suppressing crime without concern for judicial procedure. Vigilantes considered themselves public spirited–even when their actions became extreme. In brief, "Americans felt that there were certain functions in preserving public order that the legal authorities would not, could not, or should not be expected to perform. These functions the people themselves assumed as vigilantes."[28] This method of dealing with crime soon became a problem itself. What began as volunteer patrols got out of hand with violent results:

No survey of their work has yet proved that as citizens they consciously betrayed their city and state to violence and corruption. But when the laws they had created failed to protect them from the onslaughts of criminals, they put the immediate welfare of the community above their allegiance to the formulated laws, and did to the outlaws among them the things that seemed right in their own eyes.[29]

In 1847, farmers in Montgomery County, Pennsylvania formed the Abington Horse Association. This group and others like it served both as vigilante groups and as mutual insurance societies. Members patrolled each other's pastures to guard horses, rode in pursuit of rustlers, and posted rewards for the apprehension of horse thieves. If a stolen horse was not recovered, the owner was reimbursed out of the Association's treasury. Such organizations were common until the advent of the automobile.

Vigilantism was not limited to the sparsely populated settlements. San Francisco, faced with mounting pressure in favor of a citizens' protective organization against crime, formed the Committee of Vigilance of 1851. The Committee was formally organized, with a written compact, and members were assessed $5 apiece, with fines for absence from duty. Rooted in the tradition of self-protection and frontier self-organization, the Committee of Vigilance was very popular. It was able to raise $4,700 for a new county jail and enjoyed the financial support of many merchants, even of some who were not themselves Committee members. The San Francisco group had hopes for a statewide movement and did, indeed, gather support from all over. "It was not surprising that the scheme of protective committees was approved in the old mining centers, where men were already accustomed to volunteer associations."[30]

Accused lawbreakers who were brought to trial on the frontier found rather informal conditions, such as in this 1826 account:

Trials in those days were held in somebody's log cabin or in the bar-room of a tavern, and when the jury retired to deliberate it was to the shade of some near-by tree or to a log especially prepared for them.[31]

Justice was a community affair. Posses, juries, and court officials contributed their time voluntarily, and court day was seen as a form of communal entertainment.

One segment of the frontier, the mining camps, expanded the court day concept into a broader form of self-government. When gold was first discovered at Sutter's Mill in January 1848, no one could predict the ensuing mania. Despite the clear profit motive of the miners, the mining camps were generally outstanding models of a voluntary society.

> *The California mining camp . . . informed by a spirit consciously or unconsciously socialistic, watered and tended the early shoots of our democratic process a good deal more significantly than most of us realize . . . for instance . . . it was common for such organizations to require members to set aside a certain percentage of gains as a security fund to be drawn upon when any man fell ill or found that his claim had petered out.*[32]

By the end of 1848, hundreds of mining companies or associations had been formed back East, with carefully developed codes of behavior agreed upon before departure.

> *In circumstances where no exterior force could impose regulations each little concourse of miners voluntarily imposed upon itself laws which determined the adjustment of claims with the will of the majority.*[33]

Mining camps were governed by a special brand of town meeting, often referred to as "mining courts." These gatherings settled disputes and determined laws so sensibly that many of these laws were later adopted by the territorial and state governments. At first, the mining courts were simply a series of votes on issues presented to the assembly, with every free man present having one vote. If the case was particularly important, the miners "elected a presiding officer and a judge, impaneled a jury of six or twelve persons, summoned witnesses, and proceeded to trial forthwith."[34] Since all involved were volunteers, such due process cost nothing but time, and the sentences were carried out immediately.

As the population of the camps increased, the miners' meetings became more formalized. Often one official, called by the Spanish title *alcalde*, was elected to supervise claim allotments, preside at trials, and generally keep order. The alcaldes never totally replaced the more impromptu courts, but *the authority of the miners' alcaldes rested solely on the consent of the governed, who recognized the necessity of some form of social control, and gave voluntary obedience to these extraordinary magistrates.*[35]

The miners of 1848 "believed with all their hearts that there was gold enough for all; that the turn of the poorest miner would come."[36] This belief made it easier to share and share alike. Most mining companies had rules that included equal sharing of expenses, common tools, mutual protection, and rotating stints as camp cook. However, while some camps also divided up the profits equally, most miners preferred each man to keep whatever gold he himself found. Since most shelters were cloth tents or fragile wooden shacks, the danger of fire was constant. The miners soon formed volunteer fire companies to meet this need.[37]

There was, of course, another side of the gold rush: greed. The rivalry of some of the miners went to great lengths. There were anecdotes of travelers spoiling food rather than leaving it for others and of various violent endings to claim disputes. Once it became apparent that not everyone would strike it rich, dangerous jealousy plagued the camps. But seen in the broader picture, such incidents were not common.

When the rush of '48 finally subsided, most of the hastily formed mining companies disbanded, leaving only the most determined miners behind. The important legacy of the camps was their democratic and volunteer spirit, which was carried back home and reappeared in countless local governments across the nation.

America was still predominantly an agricultural society. Just as the towns were competing with the cosmopolitan flavor of the cities of Europe, so also did the farmers wish to keep up with modern techniques:

The Revolution brought the American farmers into more intimate association with Europeans, and especially with Frenchmen, and thus gave them a chance to learn more of the recent agricultural improvements . . . The organizing habit which was bred in the American mind by this period of political and social reorganization gave an impetus to the much needed formation of agricultural societies.[38]

Volunteer groups such as the Society for the Promotion of Agriculture began after 1785. They conducted agricultural experiments and disseminated helpful information. The 1786 Patriotic Society in Virginia blended an interest in politics with such concerns as new methods of fencing to save timber. Members pledged themselves to "a spirited exercise of industry, . . . enlarging the production of the land, and . . . practicing a strict frugality."[39]

Because of the early emphasis on farming, business and trade associations developed only sporadically until after 1850. However, notable exceptions such as the New York Chamber of Commerce, established in 1768, and the New York Stock Exchange, established in 1792, set the precedent for later business organizations. Concerned mainly with economic profit, these associations also sponsored civic improvement projects. All in all, the American businessman took such a volunteer interest in local affairs as a matter of course He was "a peculiarly American type of community maker and community leader. His starting belief was in the interfusing of public and private prosperity."[40]

It is illuminating to uncover the fact that American banking had volunteer roots. In 1780 a committee of Philadelphia citizens sought a way to furnish supplies to the destitute Revolutionary Army. This resulted in the first organized bank in the United States, the Bank of North America. This, of course, was a patriotic breaking away from foreign banking houses, and certainly carried financial risk for the organizers.[41] On a more informal level, the role of banker was handled voluntarily by diverse individuals in unlikely situations.

> *There was a good deal of trading by flat boats and keel boats between . . . places on the Ohio River, and . . . keel-boat owners, in addition to being public carriers, were sometimes accustomed to act as bankers and collectors on their three months' voyage.*[42]

Later, when paper currency was first introduced and many reticent merchants continued to trade only in coin, groups of other businessmen banded together in support of the new money. In Charleston, a secret committee was formed as part of the "Hint Club." The members sought out those planters and merchants who favored hard money and conveyed to them

> *a forcible hint that it would be well to desist. When the hint failed the club was notified. A meeting was called, a night and*

> *a rendezvous chosen, and, when the time came, three rockets let off. Then the members hastened to the appointed place and went thence in a body to hurl down, as it was said, public vengeance on the destroyers of the commonwealth.*[43]

Hardly the nicest example of volunteering, but an example nevertheless!

As towns grew into small cities and then into larger ones, and as industrialization spread, a labor class identity developed for the first time. Prior to the nineteenth century, working men and women rarely organized. Rather, they enjoyed comparatively personal relationships with their employers due to the small size of the work sites. As factories and industrial trades expanded, however, a new psychological distance was created between the many workers and the few owners.

At first, labor organizations were formed only for benevolent functions such as sick benefits or voluntary assistance to widows and orphans of deceased members. Between 1800 and 1810, twenty-four benevolent societies sprang up in New York alone.[44] One of their early crusades was for free education for working children. Some groups were "mechanical societies" made up of artisans in many trades within the same city, while others were developed purely for journeymen in the same trade. These groups generally advocated better wages and conditions.

By the 1830s, strikes and boycotts became publicized, and the benevolent associations were increasingly looked upon as "protective combinations."

> *What appears to be the first boycott in the country connected entirely with a labor dispute was organized by the Baltimore hatters in 1833 . . . The Master Hatters of Baltimore . . . had reduced the wages of the journeymen hatters about 25%, and labor throughout the city was justly indignant. The Journeymen Hatters had issued an appeal to the other Mechanics of the town and to the citizens generally, asking them to have no more dealings with the combination of employers.*[45]

In the 1830s, the movement for a ten-hour workday reached its peak, and public demonstrations occurred in every major city. Another cause of the Workingmen's Party—by now a political movement—was abolition of imprisonment for debt. Clearly, volunteerism had entered the labor scene.

In their early efforts to secure reforms, workers were joined by an unusual group of non-laboring-class reformers called Free Enquirers. This somewhat radical group had its roots in the religious commune movement of 1805-1829, during which time numerous short-lived idealistic experiments in cooperative agrarian living dotted the country. Along with supporting working-class issues, the Free Enquirers backed other causes such as free public education.[46]

Child labor was not yet a major issue, but the Manumission Society, dedicated to freeing slaves, took on a crusade against the horrible working conditions of young chimney sweeps. From 1811 to 1816 the volunteers of the Society tried to have legislation enacted that would limit and license the chimney sweep business. No other child labor cause was championed during this period.[47]

At this time most children were put to work, either at home or in developing industries. There was no consistency to the manner or amount of education they received. Learning took place in log cabins, in covered wagons along the trail, in seacoast churches, and in sod houses on the prairie. In many cases the apprentice system and the school of experience, rather than the school of books, served to educate and train young American citizens.

Toward the end of the eighteenth century, however, there were a few individuals who sought to improve the American educational system. In 1785-1786, Noah Webster went on a self-supported lecture tour around the country, crusading for a reform of English spelling. He was generally well received, and can be viewed as laying the groundwork for new types of educational materials that were to appear a few decides later. Similarly, in 1794, the Society of Associated Teachers was formed in New York City, leading a movement to improve the education of teachers. This concern by individuals in the field for voluntarily setting professional standards eventually led to the development of the first teacher-training courses in the early 1800s.

Before the turn of the century no free schools existed in which a poor child could obtain an education. This problem was especially prominent in the urban areas, where hundreds of children labored in factories with neither the time nor the money to obtain private schooling. Back in England, this situation began to receive attention in the 1780s, when the first Sunday schools were established. Classes in reading and religion were held on Sunday, that being the only day on which the children did not have to work. The idea soon spread to

America, and in 1791 "some earnest gentlemen at Philadelphia, who had the welfare of the poor much at heart, formed the design of educating the children of laborers and mechanics."[48] They created the "First Day" or "Sunday School Society" and proceeded voluntarily to teach hundreds of children with no funds other than their members' subscriptions of $1 a year. After the turn of the century, many other so-called school societies were formed in the cities along the East Coast, providing instruction to poor children and supported primarily by volunteer subscriptions.

Such societies ultimately were the basis for tax-supported public schools, which began appearing in the 1840s—but not before many concerned citizens had taken the matter into their own hands and had addressed the educational needs of a less fortunate segment of the new American population.

It should be noted that another way of dealing with the limited funds for education was to utilize the Lancastrian method of teaching, developed in London by Joseph Lancaster in the late 1770s and brought to America by 1800. Under the Lancastrian system, the teacher first taught a lesson to the older children who would, in turn, teach what they had just learned to the younger pupils. The system made it possible for large numbers of children to be enrolled in a school at little cost to the supporters. The Lancastrian movement flourished between 1800 and 1825, making use of students as resources for self-help.

Independent efforts such as these stimulated a broader concern for the education of all America's young, and towns began to authorize the raising of money specifically for educational purposes. However, the cooperation and generosity of local citizens was still vital:

> *Sometimes the people of a community built a schoolhouse and then permitted a teacher to conduct a private school in it, and later on the school was taken over and made a public school. In still other cases the first schools were distinctively voluntary community undertakings, owing their origins and maintenance to the voluntary action and contributions of the parents who sent their children to them.*[49]

As a unit for school organization, the community district was well suited to the needs of the time. Wherever half a dozen families lived near enough together to make organization possible, they were permitted by the early laws to vote to form a school district. Members of the community, usually three in number, were elected by the citizens to serve as school trustees; guided by the people in annual and special school district meetings, they managed the schools as well as they could. These early school boards, totally volunteer in nature, were very involved in the day-to-day activities of the schools:

> *Since there were no trained superintendents, principals, or supervisors, and few trained classroom teachers, the board members visited classes, heard the children read and spell, questioned them about their work, and examined the writing and ciphering books.*[50]

Later, of course, these duties became the responsibility of paid school personnel. But it was the initial dedication of these concerned citizens that established a solid tradition of public education responsive to the local popular will.

The education of slaves was another concern to be handled initially by volunteers. Though all the slave states forbade teaching a slave to read or write, many people were willing to risk personal safety by defying the law.

> *Some slaves were fortunate enough to belong to masters who offered them the skills of writing and reading. A few benevolent individuals established Sunday schools for the instruction of such as might be permitted by their master to learn . . . Naturally . . . when the news of this activity spread, community pressure forced most masters to abandon the scheme.*[51]

Wives and children of the masters would sometimes teach slave children, but as the years went on there were increasing examples of educated slaves teaching other slaves to read and write.

The early 1800s also witnessed an increased interest in adult education. The Lyceum movement began in the 1820s as a somewhat formal way of enlightening the adult populace. By the late 1830s, there were over three thousand local lyceums. Philanthropic and humanitarian agencies promoted this idea of spreading knowledge to all classes of people, contributing to the founding of the Boston Mechanics Institute in 1826 and the Society for the Diffusion of Useful Knowledge in 1829. Many such volunteer organizations sponsored libraries, early museum collections, lectures, discussions, and debates, while employers and philanthropically minded members of the wealthier classes also promoted adult education in such forms as the Lowell Institute (Massachusetts, 1836) and the New York City Cooper Union (1859). Urban free blacks also established library companies and literary societies for self-improvement, such as Baltimore's ambitiously titled Young Men's Mental Improvement Society for the Discussion of Moral and Philosophical Questions of all Kinds.[52]

Directly related to this movement was an increase in the number of adults interested in scientific study as an avocation. "Inquiry" and "observation" were much-used words during this period, and institutions such as the Philadelphia Academy of Natural Sciences (1812) were established.

> *These societies and their counterparts in other cities were primarily organizations of amateurs interested in promoting research and preserving data. Through the efforts of resident and corresponding members they financed expeditions to collect specimens, established libraries and museums, sponsored courses of popular lectures and published voluminous proceedings.*[53]

Later, this amateur scientific volunteering became professionalized as the more specialized sciences were carved out of general knowledge and applied to the practical needs of an expanding industrial society.

During the first decades of the new republic, medicine remained relatively informal and unstandardized, practiced by a variety of trained and untrained citizens Since there was no supporting team of specialists, each doctor became surgeon, druggist, and visiting nurse as well. In many areas, the first medical care was provided by women, who combined nursing with the prescribing and compounding of remedies: "Country women on the successive American frontiers, heirs of the age-old mother lore, likewise served their communities in times of illness and continued to do so until medical colleges and licenses transferred the art of healing to other hands."[54] And as pioneers moved westward, most wagon train leaders became volunteer surgeons, removing bullets and amputating mangled limbs, there being no doctors along on the journey.

Quarantine was one of the oldest public health practices, and was one of the first to be recognized as a governmental responsibility.

Obviously, quarantine required voluntary cooperation, and yet early efforts were often stymied when neighbors insisted on making sympathetic sick calls against the doctor's orders! Eventually the need for a more authoritative public health agency was felt.

One of the more well-known quarantines of this period occurred during the yellow fever epidemic that struck Philadelphia in 1793. This crisis called forth many volunteer efforts, most of which were documented by Stephen Girard's medical accounts of that summer. Almost immediately, a citizens' committee was formed to take charge of the emergency. Before long, a "town" of sufferers had sprung up along the banks of the Schuylkill River, where over twelve hundred people had been quarantined.

> *A call for aid, for money, tents, boards, clothes, meat, food, anything that could help the sufferers, went out. The response was immediate. Philadelphians who had fled to Germantown ordered thirty thousand dollars to be raised in their name. Provisions poured in from New Jersey.*[55]

The Philadelphia Free African Society also became deeply involved in assisting the stricken of both races. These black volunteers nursed the sick and gathered corpses and carted them away for burial.[56] The accounts of similar aid go on and on, as the entire surrounding area offered whatever help it could.

The epidemic virtually emptied Philadelphia and left the deserted city defenseless against thieves and looters. "Alarmed at the depredations nightly committed, the men of Southwark, of Northern Liberties, and of the city, formed bands to protect the town."[57] There being no available police force, these men took it upon themselves to meet the need that confronted them.

In reaction to the epidemic in Philadelphia, New Yorkers were also called into action, forming a volunteer citizens' committee to enforce strong measures to keep the disease out of New York. Called the Health Committee, it imposed a rigid quarantine on the New York harbor to keep Philadelphians out. "When it became evident that refugees from Philadelphia were still eluding the quarantine the Committee organized citizens' night watches consisting of seven men in each ward to patrol all landing areas."[58] Having thus proven its ability to protect New York from disease, by 1794,

> *the Health Committee had developed into an agency of the municipal government. In the process, it had established the*

> *principle of civic responsibility and had demonstrated the feasibility of governmental action in the public health sphere.*[59]

During this period there emerged a new concept of public health, which has been appropriately defined as:

> *that responsibility which rests upon the community for the protection of life and the promotion of the health of its people. It is one of the basic community functions . . . recognition of the necessity for community action in promotion of individual and community health and welfare.*[60]

In 1797, a system of local boards of health was established in Massachusetts, with Connecticut following soon after. And although the movement did not gain full momentum until after the Civil War, many towns and villages were authorized during this period to organize boards of health and to employ health officers. In the southern and southwestern states, where the unit of local government was the county, county boards of health were provided for, or the county governing board was authorized to perform the functions of the board of health and to employ a health officer. These boards were all made up of willing, concerned citizens who monitored the health of the community as a whole.

One result of this growing concern for public health was the formation of free vaccination clinics. New York established a Vaccination Institute in 1802, as did Boston in 1803, both staffed by volunteer doctors.[61] Another result was a demand for vital statistics, especially after the epidemics of the 1790s. One individual, John Pintard, began in 1802 to collect statistics on deaths in New York City and to advocate the registering of births and marriages. Due to the preliminary work of Pintard, on his own initiative, doctors were soon ordered to turn in death certificates, and the city began to issue a weekly list of deaths.[62] Another citizen to pioneer in this area was Lemuel Shattuck, who waged "a personal and almost solitary campaign to obtain the official recording of vital data in Massachusetts."[63] He finally succeeded in getting a model piece of public health legislation passed in 1842.

Very few hospitals existed during the 1700s. The poor received medical care in the almshouse, and the rich were usually cared for in their own homes. However, as public health awareness grew, dispensaries were established to provide better treatment.

In Boston the physicians were accustomed to dispense medicines freely from their offices to the indigent, but in 1790 they agreed that it would be more efficient to establish a central free dispensary and consultation service for the poor, each physician in town to take his turn as dispensary physician.[64]

Thus the Boston Dispensary was organized, along with those in Philadelphia and New York, becoming the forerunners of today's outpatient services in hospitals. Although the city usually appropriated some money for the dispensary, most funds came from private contributions, and the trustees were constantly appealing to the public for financial help. Furthermore, they called upon clergy, charitable associations, and "intelligent persons" to help educate the public in general to the necessity of vaccination when epidemics threatened.[65]

Charleston, South Carolina, can be credited with establishing the first visiting nurse service in America. In 1813, the Ladies' Benevolent Society of that city organized a volunteer nursing service for the sick poor: "A severe epidemic of yellow fever had devastated the community, and a group of charitable minded ladies assumed the task of providing for home nursing care of the victims."[66] Later, in 1839, a Nurses' Society of Philadelphia was founded to pay for needed nursing services: "Its purpose was to train 'pious and prudent' women who would then be paid by the society to give nursing care to the sick poor, particularly in childbirth."[67] By 1850, fifty nurses were employed and housed by the Society, and a graduating certificate was given upon completion of training.

These volunteer organizations were among the first to provide benevolent nursing services under the auspices of a community agency and signified the beginning of more standardized training in medicine.

During the same period, a small counter-approach to the professionalization of medical care appeared. Early in the 1800s Samuel Thompson promoted a "Botanic System" of medical care that completely ignored the doctors of the time and relied on traditional neighborliness:

He developed a plan, on a local community voluntary basis, for prepayment of medical care, with the formation of "Friendly Societies" in each community. These groups provided for the exchange of home nursing care, the interchange of therapeutic information, and also the exchange of actual remedies.[68]

Thompson had no medical training, believing instead in the power of herbs and folk medicine, and his temporary success in several communities brought him the enmity of many a local doctor!

A committee of citizens became concerned about the quality of care being given to child-bearing women and reported in 1823 that the number of stillbirths was higher than the state of obstetrical knowledge warranted. This led to the establishment of a system of "Out-Door Lying-ln Charity."[69] All expectant mothers who the physicians knew were unable to pay or who were recommended by the authorities were to be provided with free medical care. How long this system remained in effect is not clear, but this would appear to be one of the first attempts in the United Sates to establish a maternal and child health program.

Due to the tireless efforts of many interested New York citizens, progress was made in additional medical areas. Specialized institutions were established with volunteer support, such as the Asylum for the Deaf and Dumb (1827), the New York Institution for the Blind (1831), and the New York Ophthalmic Hospital (1852). For large-scale medical care, the dispensaries became the most effective charitable organizations. By 1866 there were ten in New York City alone, treating over one hundred fifty thousand patients, and, although the doctors were paid subsistence wages only, they flocked to the job because of the practical experience gained.

The earlier-established medical societies continued to play a part in the professionalization of the field. Although they usually represented only a small percentage of the practicing physicians, their members were influential enough to secure some licensure laws and to organize the first medical schools. These early schools were faced with the serious problem of securing cadavers for study; not a few students found a solution by engaging in grave-robbing.[70]

There were problems in trying to reform American medicine, as evidenced by the stormy early history of the American Medical Association. Established In 1847, its ideals and stated purpose were to improve the quality of licensure throughout America and to promote better medical teaching. This was perceived as a direct threat to traditional medical methods entrenched across the nation, and so it was not until the late 1800s that the American Medical Association began to be recognized as a representative medical group.

Prior to the mid-nineteenth century, philanthropy and charity remained a predominantly private affair in America. Among the rich, it was common practice to leave part of their fortunes to charitable institutions; while they lived, their leisure time allowed them to participate as individuals in many worthwhile societies and causes on a volunteer bases. Middle-class and even lower-class citizens were also active in welfare organizations, contributing much of their time and whatever funds they could afford. True, with prevailing religious beliefs, such generosity may have been a form of self-interest: "For many it was a way of putting themselves right with the Almighty—a form of investment, with the returns paid in the next world."[71] However, such motivation did not negate the volunteer accomplishments on behalf of social welfare in the new nation. Examples of such activities were everywhere.

The Society for the Relief of Poor Widows with Small Children was formed in New York in 1797. It established an orphan asylum and provided services to families without a breadwinner. Initially, the Society did its work on an inadequate income of volunteer contributions, but in 1807 it successfully incorporated its orphan asylum and was able to get state aid to supplement private subscriptions.[72]

Also in New York, the 1809 Assistance Society began to provide food and medical care for the poor. "In summarizing its activities for 1812 the Society stated that it had visited and relieved 3499 individuals at a cost of $965.85."[73] Similarly, in 1843, the Association for Improving the Condition of the Poor began an active program aimed at alleviating all aspects of slum conditions.

As the new nation grew and the industrialized areas became more dense, there was a large increase in the number of paupers, criminals, and beggars who depended on more affluent citizens to support them. But it was not until 1816, when economic hardship caused much general misery, that people began to seek out the causes of pauperism. Part of the cause, they suggested, was ill-regulated and ill-advised charity by a myriad of well-meaning organizations and individuals.

> *They found that a radical change m the mode of administering charitable relief was most imperative. The number and variety of benevolent associations which Philadelphia supported were so great that, when joined to the provision made by law for the care of the poor, they made the city a veritable "emporium of beggars."*[74]

So began the first efforts to coordinate charity and to develop some semblance of a social welfare plan. In Pennsylvania, it took the form of the Pennsylvania Society for the Promotion of Public Economy, while in New York a similar body became known as the Society for the Prevention of Pauperism in the City of New York (1817). These groups were managed by willing citizens who, though their recommendations were not always readily accepted, at least formed the beginnings of a centralized welfare system.

Had the times improved, this public interest in the reformation of society's dependents would probably have subsided. But the times grew worse, and with succeeding winters the people in the cities were required over and over again to make contributions for the relief of the destitute.

> *These reported drains upon their pockets kept them ever mindful of the suffering of their less fortunate fellow-men, and did not a little convert what might have been a temporary effort on the part of a few kind hearted gentlemen into an important part of a great humanitarian movement.*[75]

The hard winter of 1820-1821 brought an abundance of soup societies and fuel-saving societies into existence throughout the country. The search for the causes of social ills brought many citizens to the conclusion that drunkenness was at the root of it all. To correct this vice, the American temperance societies were organized. The temperance movement is thought by most to have begun in Boston in 1824, though one author claims otherwise:

> *In view of the possibly libelous yet generally accepted charge—namely, that loggers would eat hay if you sprinkled it with whiskey—it is worth knowing that the very first temperance society in the United States was organized in the small logging town of Moreau, Saratoga County, New York . . . when [the] local physician became alarmed at the all-consuming thirst thereabout. On April 30, 1808, he instigated a gathering at which the Union Temperance Society of Moreau and Northumberland came into being, and forty-three men . . . signed the Cold Water pledge.*[76]

In any event, by the end of 1829, more than one thousand such societies had been formed, and the importation of spirits into the United

States had fallen from over $5 million in 1824 to $1.1 million in 1830. More than fifty distilleries were closed, hundreds of merchants renounced the traffic, and in 1836 Canadian and United States societies joined to form the American Temperance Union. Through these organized volunteer efforts, a visible change in drinking habits occurred.

The social problems of the new republic increased with the arrival of large numbers of immigrants. It was almost impossible for so many newcomers to find employment, especially in a time of general business depression. Although some returned to their homelands when their dreams of prosperity were not instantly realized, most did not. Yet stranded as they were, they did not let their despair overwhelm them, and most refugee groups began to form their own self-help societies to meet their financial, social, medical, and vocational needs. The functions of these fraternal associations were extremely diverse but all sought to support immigrant families as they entered American life through such activities as classes for teaching English; reading clubs; folk-dance circles; maintenance of orphanages and homes for the aged; support to schools and scholarships to worthy students; publishing of newspapers and historical research; and provision of financial insurance to aid members and their families in cases of sickness, injury, or death.

In addition, during the years after 1825, these associations helped to find employment for immigrants who had recently arrived. Some associations were patronized by foreign consuls residing in America, and at least one even received some aid from the head of a European state.[77] A few native philanthropic agencies also grappled with the employment problems of alien workers, as exemplified by the Society for the Encouragement of Faithful Domestic Servants, founded in 1825. However, it was not until after mid-century that the mainstream of American charity began seriously to help the immigrants. Thus, in the beginning, the newcomers' survival depended on their own code of mutual aid and cooperative solidarity.

The cities began to see a large increase in the number of dependent children. In colonial times and in the early years of the nation, homeless children were taken in by a neighboring family who assumed responsibility for raising them, while the children themselves often earned their keep through some type of indentured service. However, as the nation grew, and the problems of the urban areas became more intense, public ways of providing for these children had to be found.

The first institutions to be established for this purpose were linked with the religious community, the members of which felt obligated to save the homeless waifs. The devastation of the Indian Wars, the War of 1812, and the war with Mexico brought a number of such institutions into being. In addition, the outbreaks of yellow fever and cholera between 1790 and 1835 made many children homeless and led to the establishment of secular orphan asylums in the large cities:

> *A group of women in New Orleans became interested in the children of immigrants whose parents had died of yellow fever en route to Louisiana. Arrangements were first made to provide for the children by taking them into the homes of members of this group and in 1817 the Poydras Female Orphan Asylum was founded.*[78]

And in New York,

> *prostitution was so rife that the women formed a society and opened a home for girls, between five and ten years of age, whose parents were drunkards, taught them to read, write, and sew, and when old enough, sent them to service with respectable families, or bound them to a tradesman.*[79]

The above examples are typical of the way in which many of these institutions were founded during this period. A specific case of distress would come to the attention of an individual who then proceeded to organize a group of volunteers to assist the children in need.

About the same time as these institutions were coming into being, some cities were dealing with the problem in another way. Public officials were given permission to commit to almshouses any child found "in a state of want or suffering, or abandonment, or improperly exposed or neglected by its parents or soliciting charity from door to door, or whose mother was a notoriously immoral woman."[80] This practice was continued for several years, no doubt because of its convenience and low cost. Public authorities were slow to recognize the disgraceful conditions of these places, but eventually an effort was launched by concerned volunteers to establish better care facilities. The Boston Society for the Care of Girls worked actively for this cause during the first decade of the nineteenth century, as did the Orphan Asylum Society of New York. Such cooperative societies as these established alternatives to the almshouse that became prototypes for the many institutions that were to follow.

Individuals launched personal crusades when they saw a societal problem that needed solving. A typical example can be found in Samuel Gridley Howe and his fight for the blind. He began unpretentiously by caring for blind patients in his father's home and later, in 1832, established the Perkins Institute for the Blind in Boston. His efforts inspired the local ladies of that city, who sponsored fairs on his behalf and collected thousands of dollars for the Institute.[81]

Dorothea Lynde Dix came to the forefront during the 1840s with her crusade against harsh treatment of the insane.

> *In the course of eight years Miss Dix travelled sixty thousand miles, went over every State in the Union save North Carolina, Florida, and Texas, and came into contact with more than nine thousand idiots, epileptics and insane, all destitute of proper care and protection.*[82]

In 1850 she reported her findings to Congress, which appreciated her efforts but extended no funds. Yet her public education campaign eventually affected American attitudes, bringing sympathy and better treatment for the mentally ill and the disabled.

Clearly, social welfare in this era was dominated by volunteers acting individually and in groups. Government involvement to any great degree was yet to come.

Religion played a large role in the lives of early Americans, and the church continued as a voluntary association whose members were active and committed. Toward the end of the eighteenth century, America was becoming increasingly secular, and the so-called New England Establishment no longer dictated the "true" faith. Nevertheless, many felt that the Protestant influence on society should be maintained through cooperative participation in common causes. Interdenominational voluntary societies were expanded. The Connecticut Moral Society of 1813 was the first of many such groups that spread from New England to New York and the Midwest. These moral societies were then supplemented by organizations for allied purposes: tract societies, missionary societies, Sabbath school societies.

Many were eager to participate in missionary societies, which, up until 1812, served the American frontier. Among the first were the Jesuit missionaries, who received no salaries and depended largely on private donations to get started. The San Diego Mission was established in 1769 as the first white settlement in California, and by 1823 a chain of twenty missions reached as far north as San Francisco. Although many volunteered for this dangerous and strenuous work, they often returned home embittered and frustrated by their lack of impact on the Indian natives. Progress of any real substance did not appear until 1819, when Congress authorized $10 million to support volunteer religious groups who were working with Indians. This type of government aid continued until 1900 and represented one of the earliest efforts to work with Native Americans.

One interesting group of volunteers associated with the early southwest missions were the soldiers who defended them:

> *In employing their own defensive force the missionaries had the opportunity of selecting as soldiers and captains only the better type of available men who were without disease. In fact, the type of soldiers the missionaries themselves selected and commanded became equally involved with the mission spirit and purpose and frequently consented to serve without pay when the missions had no money to pay them.*[83]

In addition to working to convert the Indians to Christianity, many of the eastern missionary societies sent volunteers into the frontier communities to preach and to establish Bible societies. They found little religion there, but continued vigorously to distribute Bibles. In 1815, the American Bible Society was founded. Its members attempted to reach all parts of the new nation, and in five years managed to establish 229 local chapters. A total of 140,000 Bibles were given away.[84]

Another type of religious growth occurred within the slave population of the South. Initially, it was customary for a white minister to preach to the slaves on Sunday afternoon, after the morning service for the slaveholder and his family. Often, if no preacher was available, the master himself would fill the role.[85] Later on, however, individuals among the plantation slaves emerged as religious leaders, and a more organized black church began to develop:

> *In the religious meetings the people of the slave quarters gathered together to discuss the events of the day, to gain new strength . . . to celebrate the maintenance of life in the midst of adversity, and to determine the communal strategies and tactics. Out of these meetings came the modern black church and the many black lodges which play an important role in the modern Afro-American community.*[86]

Similarly, the religious life of urban slaves was very active, as blacks increasingly took over more and more of the responsibility for their churches. Of course, the law vested formal supervision and control in white leaders. But the fundamental tasks of recruiting members, locating and supporting ministers, paying rents, and staffing the Sunday schools fell to volunteers among the blacks themselves.

> *Though not ministers in the conventional sense, the preachers and class leaders were something more than mere slaves. And the formal connection with white ministers and lay boards gave them some prestige, at least among the congregation. In the life of these churches the first signs of traditional Negro leadership were visible in the cities even before the abolition of slavery.*[87]

The success of these churches was directly related to the enthusiasm and dedication of both slave and free blacks, making this segment of America's religious life a truly voluntary effort.

Free blacks actively organized self-help groups, often begun under religious leadership. Richard Allen and Absalom Jones spearheaded the formation of the already-mentioned Free African Society in 1787 in Philadelphia. Other groups followed in other cities: the Brown Fellowship Society in Charleston, South Carolina (1790); the African Society in Boston (1798); and Masonic and similar secret groups.[88] By 1835, Baltimore blacks alone had formed thirty-five benevolent societies.[89]

Although provision for religious freedom was written into the new state constitutions, prejudice was evident, especially against atheists and Jews. Politics sometimes reflected this intolerance and bigotry. A good example was the Native American Party of the mid-1830s, which reacted to increased immigration from Europe with a popular movement to deny full citizenship to foreigners. A corollary of this political mood was the anti-Mason sentiment prevalent in many areas during this time.

Early Americans had little leisure time, and so there were few forms of organized recreation. There was even disapproval of using spare time for fun. A nationwide cultural reawakening affected all classes of society, emphasizing the importance of self-education. Even labor law demands were based on giving workers more time for self-improvement, not simply more idle time.[90]

Because of this widespread interest in intellectual matters, a great vogue developed for public lectures. The lyceum movement brought public speakers to every town throughout the country. These lectures were attended by a large working-class audience, and the topics ranged from serious debate to entertaining fads. But the underlying purpose was always self-improvement.

As for the arts, adequate patronage was slow to come into being in America, especially because there was neither a royal court nor an established church to assume this responsibility. Some prosperous merchants and political leaders volunteered support to literature, science, and the arts. Those who could afford it were fond of commissioning portraits of themselves. Others contributed materials and equipment necessary to maintain studios and laboratories.

As the nineteenth century progressed, a new American playfulness sprang into being. Holidays were eagerly celebrated, partly because they were so infrequent, and partly because of growing patriotism:

> *A parade almost invariably led off the day's festivities. Everyone turned out—the militia companies in their handsome uniforms, the patriotic societies and political clubs, the volunteer firemen in glistening helmets and flaming red shirts. The generation of the 1850's was fascinated by parades . . . At election time—and there was no more exciting holiday—the streets of every town and city would be filled with rival marchers . . . There was no artificiality, no regimentation, about the public demonstrations of the young democracy.*[91]

In the cities, these parades were followed by mass meetings or public banquets, whereas country folk joined together for picnics and barbecues. Such celebrations formed the roots of many cherished American holiday traditions.

In this period, the organized sport of baseball emerged, beginning under the name of "town-ball." A group of New York business and professional men began playing it about 1842 at the Elysian Fields in Hoboken, New Jersey. They then formally organized the

Knickerbocker Club and adopted a code of rules, printed in 1845. Initially the various clubs who participated in the game attempted to keep baseball as an exclusive recreation, but its popularity spread, and it became necessary to adopt a more democratic attitude. By 1858, there was a National Association of Base Ball Players, with twenty-five clubs as charter members.[92] From these first volunteer teams, the sport grew to its professional status of today.

The victorious close of the Revolution did not mean an end to the need for national defense. Indian attacks were still of great concern, but the government's new involvement in foreign politics brought other threats. The question of the best way to maintain an adequate fighting force caused debate over the advantages of a citizen militia versus a professional army.

The next test of the American military system was the War of 1812. Initial overt action against England was nonviolent and required the voluntary cooperation of all citizens. As early as 1807, the Chesapeake Bay Resolution called for a halt to communications with Britain and a refusal to supply British ships. It further

> *named a committee to invite the people of the seaports to join them in refusing supplies. How determined they were to keep these resolutions was soon made evident. Not a pound of meat, not a drop of water went to the fleet.*[93]

The embargoes passed by Congress expanded these initially volunteer boycotts.

When it became evident that war was unavoidable, there was much confusion as to the constitutionality of the government ordering militias into such fighting. The only way out at the time was compromise: members of the volunteer militia were invited to join the regular army for one year. Because of the heroism of all the troops, the War of 1812 demonstrated no clear superiority of the regular army over volunteer militia. However, it was concluded that

> *state volunteering, despite its defects in competitive bounties, untrained officers and soldiers hard to mobilize, affords, after all, the best available means of working out the military resources of the whole nation.*[94]

America as a nation was peace-loving but willing to engage in war when pushed to the brink of it. Yet there were some citizen organizations that stressed pacifism regardless of the cause. The earliest conscientious objectors to military service were the Quakers, Mennonites, Shakers, Brethren, and similar pacifist religious sects. These groups were recognized by colonial legislatures and were exempt from militia duty, though they were often required to pay special taxes or hire substitutes. But the peace movement really began in the early 1800s; in 1815 the New York Peace Society became the first pacifist organization not church affiliated. By 1828, the group was able, with justification, to rename itself the American Peace Society. The Society was concerned with the broader concept of world peace and sought to gain international cooperation. This volunteer effort was not supported by Congress, but the crusade was the beginning of a persistent pacifist thread through later history.

When the Mexican War began in 1846, the federal government again turned to the established volunteer militia companies. As before, there was the obstacle of state militias being limited to domestic fighting, but the legislators soon found a semantic solution:

> *The militia are the soldiers of the state, and their duties lie wholly within its limits, unless called out by the President of the United States in an emergency . . . The volunteers on the other hand, enlist directly into the service of the United States, and it becomes the duty of the National Government to provide for them from the very date of their enlistment.*[95]

Meanwhile, among the civilian population, the Mexican invasion of Texas brought forth much volunteer activity:

> *Wherever the invasion was known the people were aflame. At Galveston the women moulded bullets and made cartridges. At a public meeting in that city, when it was decided to collect money to fit out vessels to cut off the enemies' transports, the sum needed was raised on the spot. Some gave money, some houses, others lots, horses, cows, negroes, wood, guns, or head rights, which were put up at auction.*[96]

In fact, sympathetic meetings were held all over the South, and many men volunteered to emigrate to Texas to join the fight. The end of the Mexican War brought the discharge of the volunteers and also the disbanding of many of the new regular regiments. But the leadership of the professional officers during the war caused them to consider their skills superior to those of the volunteers. This was a rift that would widen in future military engagements.

The 1830s were characterized by an overwhelming variety of "isms," each in vogue for several months to a few years. Many were religiously based, but all demonstrated a basically positive outlook, optimistic as to the future of America and of humanity. These fad groups included spiritualism, animal magnetism, phrenology, atheism, Noyesian free love, vegetarianism, Fourierism, Owenism, and transcendentalism. The list goes on and on, covering every conceivable area of life. The members of these movements sometimes had leaders as eloquent as Emerson and Thoreau. The thrust was to find utopia, and short-lived voluntary communities governed by consensus and love sprang up around the country. By the end of the decade, Emerson could describe the 1840 Boston meeting of the Friends of Universal Reform as

> *perhaps rather disorganized, but in any case rather colorful: crazed men and women, bearded men, Muggletonians, Agrarians, Adventists, Quakers, Abolitionists, Calvinists, Unitarians, Philosophers spoke in turn, tirelessly thundering, praying, preaching, protesting.*[97]

The mania for reform was well illustrated in such famous experiments in utopian communal living as Brook Farm and the Oneida Group. In 1843, the Fourierites sought to reform what they considered to be a defective society by replacing individualism with voluntary association:

> *An association, or Phalanx, was an assemblage of not less than three hundred nor more than eighteen hundred persons, voluntarily united for the purpose of carrying on, with order and unity, the various branches of industry, art, and science.*[98]

They held the premises that labor should be attractive to be accomplished gladly and that there should be no restrictions on dress or amusement. They governed themselves by a hierarchical structure of committees all based on voluntary cooperation to achieve economic goals.

Such communities spread fast and died fast, though here and there economic success was achieved at the expense of some of the utopian philosophies. The average duration of a phalanx was two years, yet the impact of these extreme philosophic organizations was pervasive. Perhaps because so many writers joined such communities, the general population knew of the experiments and—even if disdain was the common reaction—had the chance to think about the ideals expressed.

Probably one of the few unifying movements of the period was temperance. It cut across the boundaries of geography and philosophy to gather adherents from all sides. People who were in opposition on other issues found common ground in the volunteer crusade against the bottle. Drink was considered white slavery and so was an obvious starting point to condemn other forms of slavery:

> *Temperance served the cause of abolition directly in many ways. It helped give respectability to its agitators, who might have been called fanatical, but not corrupt. The demand for "immediate" temperance added an argument to abolitionist appeals for "immediate" abolition.*[99]

Women took up the banner and found a platform in both the temperance and the abolition crusades.

There is no question but that the political activist movement of overriding importance toward the end of this period was abolitionism. The abolition movement, culminating as it did in the outbreak of the Civil War, is too frequently thought of as a fervor developed in the years immediately preceding the southern secession. But in reality, antislavery sentiment was as old as the nation itself. Abolition began as early as the 1760s, when the members of the Pennsylvania Society of Friends freed their slaves in recognition of the fact that slavery contradicted their religious principles. Vermont proclaimed abolition in 1777, and by then records listed thousands of freed Quaker and other slaves. However,

> *to seize upon these, run them off and sell them again into slavery, soon became so common a crime that a few men of heart determined it should stop. A score of gentlemen, therefore, gathered, five days before the battle of Lexington, in the old Sun Tavern at Philadelphia. There they framed a constitution, and organized a body which they named "The Society For The Relief Of Free Negroes Unlawfully Held in Bondage."*[100]

The Society met four times, and then the Revolutionary War intervened. For nine years the Society lay dormant, until in 1784 the members reassembled and began a long period of activity.

By 1790, the antislavery forces were urging congressional action but repeatedly met with defeat. After 1794, abolition groups sprang up all over, especially in the South. Though these organizations met irregularly and did not coordinate their actions in any way at first, they formed a continuum of concern leading to the 1830s, when the extremist factions gained the spotlight. The early antislavery volunteers held meetings, published addresses and information, and saw to the legal defense of blacks accused of being fugitives and to the prosecution of cruel masters. They also led the opposition to both the foreign and domestic slave trades, labored to bring education to blacks, and supported legislative candidates who were in favor of antislavery laws. Until the 1830s the antislavery societies were predominantly concerned with altering public opinion.

At times, the abolition groups turned to more aggressive methods, but not all members supported such action. A good example was the attempt in 1800 to organize a mass uprising of slaves, later called Gabriel's Rebellion. It failed because

> *an elite initiated, planned and dominated . . . In the four months before the insurrection they lived and were sustained by it . . . Meanwhile, the rank and file simply raised their hands at meetings, a few personalized their commitment by volunteering for specific responsibilities and acquiring weapons. Enlisting in the most inauthentic manner, they did not share the leaders' distinctive revolutionary awareness. Thus their commitment was fragile at best; and in the end, Gabriel and his men stood alone.*[101]

Abolitionism clearly demonstrated the impact of individual volunteers on history:

> *It gave to individuals supporting it a scope for their talents, ambitions, and theories, which ultimately shaped events. There were, to be sure, impersonal forces at work in the economics of cotton and slavery, the politics of sectionalism, and the social forces of large groups. Yet a small group of willful men and women made an imprint on nonslaveholding America in the antebellum years not to be underestimated.*[102]

This small group of leaders effectively mobilized large numbers of society members, though exactly how many societies or members the American Anti-Slavery Society possessed was never recorded.

> *It would misconstrue the abolitionist crusade not to appreciate its roots in ordinary people. The most famous reformers were merely elements of an advance guard of anti-slavery workers, made notable by accident or peculiarities.*[103]

If the leaders gained the notoriety, it "was the people who furnished their audiences, who purchased their printed materials and signed their petitions, who joined their societies, contributed their support, or helped uphold the underground railroad."[104]

Abolitionism had its strongest support In New England, geographically the farthest removed from real slavery. But there were many southern antislavery societies, and, in fact, out of 130 known groups in 1827, 106 were southern. "The actual influence of these societies was small, their strength an illusion."[105] Because the South effectively smothered organized abolition groups, it was left to courageous individuals to overcome the risks involved.

The renowned Underground Railroad had its roots in these early southern organizations. There is also much evidence that giving assistance was not limited to the white population. Blacks were involved from the very beginning, and Native Americans played a role as well:

> *In the early days running slaves sometimes sought and received aid from Indians. This fact is evidenced by the introduction of fugitive recovery clauses into a number of the treaties made between colonies and Indian tribes. Seven out of the eight treaties between 1784 and 1786 contained clauses for the return of . . . "negroes and other property."*[106]

Though the colonists sometimes even offered rewards to Indians returning fugitive slaves, the record shows that runaways often found shelter and protection with Indian tribes already hostile to the white settlers.

The first step toward creating an organized system to aid fugitive slaves developed as the numbers of runaways increased. New protective organizations sprang up until a chain of sorts was formed from the South to Canada. "The system is said to have extended from Kentucky and Virginia across Ohio, and from Maryland, through

Pennsylvania and New York, to New England and Canada."[107] Some whites openly aided fugitive slaves by hiring them, or giving them a pass "signed by a white man." Often whites, sometimes fugitives themselves, posed as gentlemen waited on by the black runaway. The methods of escape were many and ranged from such open, under-their-noses tactics to more covert smuggling of slaves in hay wagons and other conveyances. Many citizens who had legitimate reasons for being on the road a lot had specially built wagons or carriages that allowed them to transport runaways at the same time. The list of ingenious volunteers in the movement is endless. For example:

> *It was said that two market women in Baltimore were their best helpers. They had come into possession of a number of passports, or "freedoms" which were used by slaves for part of the distance, and then were returned to serve the same purpose again.*[108]

Once the Underground Railroad became formalized in the 1830s, more elaborate techniques were developed by the volunteers:

> *Much of the communication relating to fugitive slaves was held in guarded language. Special signals, whispered conversations, passwords, messages couched in figurative phrases, were the common modes of conveying information about underground passengers, or about parties in pursuit of fugitives. These modes of communication constituted what abolitionists knew as the "grape-vine telegraph."*[109]

Many of the people who aided the Underground Railroad took part only in scouting and information gathering. But

> *despite such relatively routine activities by individuals who had no bizarre aims or desires to be offensive to their neighbors, the anti-slavery movement demanded that some of its partisans jeopardize their livelihoods, their personal relations, and even their lives.*[110]

Mob violence and riots against the abolitionists were common occurrences. The extreme tactics of the opposition were so harsh that the antislavery advocates found themselves battling for their right of free speech. In this way, abolitionism broadened into a campaign for all civil rights.

The underground Virginia communities of free and quasi-free blacks in Petersburg, Richmond, and Williamsburg were especially active in aiding runaway slaves. In addition, blacks worked side by side with white Underground Railroad workers in many towns and cities. It is true, however, that despite such cooperative action, many abolitionists feared and even despised blacks. "Anti-Slavery forces North and South failed signally to utilize the free Negro, despite the fact that his own efforts in behalf of slaves probably exceeded those of all others."[111]

The self-help nature of slave efforts was in evidence from as far back as colonial days. For decades,

> *the plantation slaves' organized and systematic schemes to obstruct the plantation's workings—their persistent acts of attrition against crops and stores, and cooperative night-time robberies that sustained the black markets—were more "political" in their consequences and represented resistance to slavery itself.*[112]

The more acculturated the slaves became, the more outwardly rebellious their acts grew. The slaves with artisan skills were the most difficult for their masters to control. As early as 1727, the royal governor of Virginia reported that "fifteen Africans" left their plantation and attempted to form a new settlement near Lexington, Virginia. They were, of course, recaptured, but the incident demonstrated the ever-present possibility of overthrow of control.[113]

Generally, field slaves were not violent in their rebellion. Though some murders and suicides could be viewed as psychological rebellions to slavery, most subterfuge was accomplished in more quiet, cooperative ways. Techniques included

> *deliberate laziness, feigned illness, and truancy. While this type of behavior on the part of one slave was ineffectual, slaves understood that if together they did a "little leaning" the overall effect on the plantation's efficiency could be considerable.*[114]

It was not until the late 1820s and early 1830s that black insurrections gained attention. The most famous event was what became known as Nat Turner's Rebellion, in 1831. Nat Turner succeeded in mobilizing seventy Virginia slaves to march on the county seat: "The insurrectionists were met by a volunteer corps of whites and were forced to give ground."[115] Later, the uprising was suppressed by heavy reinforcements of troops and militia. In the end, fifty-seven slaves were killed as one group of volunteers proved stronger than the other. The Nat Turner Rebellion and other similar incidents galvanized the abolitionist to seek better ways to organize themselves. With the abolition conference of October 29, 1833, the movement gained new structure and succeeded in forming a coalition of the various threads of evangelicalism, New England ideals, and antislavery sentiments.

Free blacks sometimes earned enough money to actually buy their brothers as slaves and allow them to work themselves free. In 1834, 75 percent of the thirty thousand blacks in Cincinnati had worked themselves free in this way. Others made public tours and door-to-door appeals to raise money.[116] There was also concern for Canadian blacks, about which several "conventions of colored men" were held. These were to arrange

> *some plan of operation by which the more prosperous of the race could aid the colony in Canada, which was suffering great distress. Nearly all had gone there from Ohio, after the enforcement of expulsory laws; and their number was increased from time to time by fugitive slaves from the states. For a considerable number of years they received assistance from the United States, presumably from their own race. Conventions for the purpose were held in at least three successive years: 1830, 1831, and 1832.*[117]

Even at this time, a large number of antislavery advocates were in favor of deporting blacks, or rather of aiding them to return to Africa. This group of volunteers, known as "colonizationists," was quite vocal in advocating that freed slaves return to their roots and form new colonies in Africa. A few boatloads actually left to cross the ocean, but ultimately the colonizationists broke from the abolitionist movement and were countered by effective organization by blacks who wished to remain in America.

Certainly the most flamboyant abolitionist was William Lloyd Garrison, whose aggressive style soon polarized the movement and took the limelight away from the larger but more peaceful faction. Garrison advocated immediate action. One of his first targets was the colonizationists, and his fervent oratory defeated much of their rhetoric. Before long he was also involved in women's rights, although *his first view of their role in the anti-slavery crusade had been conventional; his female coworkers had organized auxiliaries; had knitted, prayed, signed petitions, held Liberty Fairs and Bazaars for raising money.*[118]

Eventually, the role of women in all aspects of the movement became a major issue:

The question of female participation in anti-slavery actions, which, while personally offending many of the abolitionists, especially in strategic New York, also seemed to them basic to a practical campaign for northern support.[119]

Despite the ongoing controversy, after 1836 women played key roles in the abolition crusade. Partly this resulted from the basic need for more hands at work, but the women themselves divided into those favoring "seemly" feminine activities and those seizing the platform as a first step toward a suffrage movement.

One of the popular approaches of abolitionism was the circulation of petitions by volunteers gathering signatures protesting slavery. "The battle for petitions brought women to the fore as partners in the work of drawing them up and soliciting signatures."[120] Children were also drawn into the struggle. A letter in Garrison's *The Liberator* in 1837 exhorted members to: "Begin with the Children." It was considered valuable to lecture children on the evils of slavery and so bring them up to be abolitionists. In the same year, *The Liberator* reprinted "Petitions for Minors":

The Boston Juvenile Anti-Slavery Society has procured to be printed a large number of the following forms of petitions for minors. Members of that society are now engaged in circulating them for signatures in this city, and we hope that measures will be taken to circulate them in every town and state. Abolitionists should aid and encourage children in this good work. The petitions are designed for both boys and girls.[121]

Ultimately, the abolitionists realized that their only real power would lie in political control of the legislatures, and so abolition emerged as a political force.

The period from after the Revolution to around 1850 involved the opening of many frontiers as the United States established its visible identity. Geographic expansion resulted from the courage of pioneer families who dared to leave the security of the eastern settlements. Despite the lack of formal laws in the newly opened territories, these citizens were able to develop democratic governing codes that functioned so well they later formed the basis of new state constitutions. These codes presupposed volunteer initiative for self-help and mutual aid, such as that witnessed by a foreigner who visited America in this period:

> *Americans are interested in the human race, and in each other . . . There is a general helpfulness, which I have not found in the same degree elsewhere. A homesteader in Dakota will accompany a traveller for miles to set him on the right road. The neighbors will rally around one of their members in distress with the loyalty of a Highland clan. This friendliness is not a self-conscious duty so much as an instinct . . . Waves of mass emotion may sweep the country , but they are transient things and do not submerge for long the stubborn rock of individualism . . . With them the sense of a common humanity is a warm and constant instinct.*[122]

Many other frontiers were crossed through the volunteer efforts of individuals. Social welfare, education, medicine, justice—almost every aspect of life progressed because of the vocal societies and movements formed to advocate a spectrum of causes. It seemed an age of experiment with approaches to new problems, especially those associated with urbanization; as solutions were tested, the push toward institutionalization gained momentum. Slowly volunteer activities attracted the involvement of government and fostered the development of new professions.

Soon however, abolition and the divisive passions of North and South threatened the newly gained unity of the young republic. The momentum of social progress was to be interrupted by these causes and loyalties, which came to overshadow all others.

Endnotes for Chapter 2

1. Robert Luther Thompson, *Wiring a Continent* (Princeton, NJ: Princeton University Press, 1947), 10–9.

2. John Bach McMaster, *A History of the People of the United States* (New York Appleton, 1884), 2: 58.

3. Ibid., 5: 269.

4. Henry Van Dyke, *The Spirit of America* (New York: Macmillan, 1910), 181–2.

5. Charles Frederick Carter, *When Railroads Were New* (New York: Simmons-Boardman, 1926), 41.

6. Robert Selph Henry, *This Fascinating Railroad Business* (Indianapolis: Bobbs-Merrill, 1942), 325.

7. Richard Dunlop, *Doctors of the American Frontier* (Garden City, N.Y.: Doubleday, 1965), 158.

8. John R. Seeley, Buford H. Junker and R. Wallace Jones, Jr., et al., *Community Chest: A Case Study in Philanthropy* (Toronto: University of Toronto Press, 1957), 15.

9. Alice Morse Earle, *Home Life in Colonial Days* (New York: Macmillan, 1923), 396.

10. Timothy Flint, "Recollections of the Last Ten Years," cited by Rebecca Brooks Gruver, *American Nationalism 1783–1830: A Self-Portrait* (New York: Putnam's, 1970), 84.

11. Daniel J. Boorstin, *The Americans: The National Experience* (New York: Random House, 1965), 57.

12. Ibid., 66.

13. Ibid., 69.

14. Flint, in Gruver, *American Nationalism,* 81.

15. Ibid.

16. Mary Floyd Williams, "History of the San Francisco Committee of Vigilance of 1851," in *University of California Publications in History,* ed. Herbert E. Bolton, 12 (1915): 11.

17. John Duffy, *A History of Public Health in New York City*, 1625–1866 (New York: Russell Sage Foundation, 1968), 411.

18. McMaster, *History of the People,* 7: 70–1.

19. John Samuel Ezell, *Fortune's Merry Wheel, The Lottery in America* (Cambridge, MA: Harvard University Press, 1960), 272–3.

20. McMaster, *History of the People,* 4: 544.

21. Duffy, *History of Public Health,* 262.

22. McMaster, *History of the People,* 4: 549.

23. National Information Center on Volunteerism, *Volunteers in Social Justice,* 5, no. 4 (November 1972): 5.

24. McMaster, *History of the People,* 4: 146–51.

25. Ibid., 540.

26. Ibid.

27. Statement by Gerald S. Arenberg, Executive Director of American Federation of Police, in response to authors' questionnaire, March 30, 1976.

28. Richard Maxwell Brown, "Legal and Behavioral Perspectives on American Vigilantism," in "Law in American History," eds. Donald Fleming and Bernard Bailyn, *Perspectives in American History* (Harvard University, Charles Warren Center for Studies in American History), 5 (1971):100.

29. Williams, *San Francisco Committee,* 436.

30. Ibid., p. 375.

31. McMaster, *History of the People,* 5: 157.

32. Joseph Henry Jackson, introduction to *Mining Camps* by Charles Howard Shinn(New York: Knopf, 1948), x.

33. Williams, *San Francisco Committee,* 73.

34. Charles Howard Shinn, *Mining Camps* (New York: Knopf, 1948), 119.
35. Williams, *San Francisco Committee,* 83.
36. Shinn, *Mining Camps,* 107.
37. Robert Lacour-Gayet, *Everyday Life in the United States Before the Civil War, 1830–1860* (New York: Ungar, 1969), 162.
38. J. Franklin Jameson, *The American Revolution Considered as a Social Movement* (Boston: Beacon Press, 1926), 51.
39. McMaster, *History of the People,* 1: 290.
40. Boorstin, *The Americans,* 115.
41. Jameson, *American Revolution Considered,* 63.
42. John Jay Knox, *A History of Banking in the United States* (New York: Rhodes, 1900), 780.
43. McMaster, *History of the People,* 1: 287.
44. Ibid., 510–1.
45. Harry W. Laidler, *Boycotts and the Labor Struggle* (New York: Russell and Russell, 1968), 69.
46. McMaster, *History of the People,* 5: 88–9.
47. Duffy, *History of Public Health,* 263.
48. McMaster, *History of the People,* 2: 83.
49. Ellwood P. Cubberly, *Public School Administration* (New York: Houghton Mifflin, 1944), 4.
50. John W. Diefendorf, *The School Board and the School Board Member* (Albuquerque: University of New Mexico, 1947), 2.
51. Stanley Feldstein, *Once A Slave* (New York: Morrow, 1971), 65.
52. Benjamin Quarles, *The Negro in the Making of America,* rev. ed. (New York: Collier Books, 1969), 98.
53. John Allen Krout and Dixon Ryan Fox, *The Completion of Independence, 1790–1830.* vol. 5, *A History of American Life in Twelve Volumes,* eds. Arthur M. Schlesinger and Dixon Ryan Fox (New York: Macmillan, 1943), 322.
54. Mary R. Beard, ed., *America Through Women's Eyes* (New York: Macmillan, 1933), 366.
55. McMaster, *History of the People,* 2: 412.
56. Quarles, *The Negro,* 97–8.
57. McMaster, *History of the People,* 2: 413.
58. Duffy, *History of Public Health,* 125.
59. Ibid., 128.
60. Wilson G. Smillie, *Public Health, Its Promise for the Future* (New York: Macmillan, 1955), 1.
61. Ibid., 31.
62. Duffy, *History of Public Health,* 146.
63. Smillie, *Public Health,* 246.
64. Ibid., 91.
65. Duffy, *History of Public Health,* 247–8.
66. Smillie, *Public Health,* 406.
67. Ibid., 407.
68. Ibid., 195.
69. Duffy, *History of Public Health,* 236–7.
70. Ibid., 65, 87.
71. Author unknown, "The Spirit of Reform" (n.p.: n.d.), 274.
72. Duffy, *History of Public Health,* 262.
74. McMaster, *History of the People,* 4: 526.
75. Ibid., 532.

76. Stewart H. Holbrook, *Yankee Loggers* (New York: International Paper Company, 1961), 43–4.

77. Robert Ernst, *Immigrant Life in New York City, 1825–1863* (New York: Columbia University, King's Crown Press, 1949), 65.

78. Emma Octavia Lundberg, *Unto the Least of These: Social Services for Children* (New York: Appleton-Century-Crofts, 1947), 102.

79. McMaster, *History of the People,* 4: 540.

80. Lundberg, *Unto the Least,* 102.

81. Carl Russell Fish, *The Rise of the Common Man, 1830–1850.* vol. 6, *A History of American Life in Twelve Volumes,* eds. Arthur M. Schlesinger and Dixon Ryan Fox (New York: Macmillan, 1943), 256–7.

82. McMaster, *History of the People,* 7: 152.

83. William Christie MacLeod, *The American Indian Frontier* (New York: Knopf, 1928), 344.

84. McMaster, *History of the People,* 4: 554–5.

85. Feldstein, *Once a Slave,* 69.

86. George P. Rawick, *The American Slave: A Composite Autobiography* (Westport, CT.: Greenwood, 1972), 37.

87. Richard C. Wade, *Slavery in the Cities: The South, 1820–1860* (New York: Oxford University Press, 1964), 172.

88. Dorothy B. Porter, "The Black Role During the Era of the Revolution," *Smithsonian* (n.d.): 55.

89. Quarles, *The Negro,* 91.

90. Foster Rhea Dulles, *A History of Recreation: America Learns to Play* (New York: Appleton-Century-Crofts, 1965), 89–92.

91. Ibid., 63.

92. Ibid., 186.

93. McMaster, *History of the People,* 3: 259–60.

94. James Schouler, *History of the United States of America, Under the Constitution* (New York: Dodd, Mead, 1882), 2: 438.

95. Philip Van Doren Stern, *Soldier Life in the Union and Confederate Armies* (Bloomington: Indiana University Press, 1912), 21

96. McMaster, *History of the People,* 7: 306–7.

97. "The Spirit of Reform," 266.

98. McMaster, *History of the People,* 7: 143.

99. Louis Filler, *The Crusade Against Slavery* (New York: Harper and Brothers, 1960), 40.

100. McMaster, *History of the People,* 2: 20.

101. Gerald W. Mullin, *Flight and Rebellion: Slave Resistance in Eighteenth Century Virginia* (New York: Oxford University Press, 1972), 161.

102. Jane H. Pease and William H. Pease, *Bound with Them in Chains* (Westport, Conn., Greenwood, 1972), 6–7.

103. Filler, *Crusade Against Slavery,* 70.

104. Ibid., 279.

105. Ibid., 19.

106. Wilbur H. Siebert, *The Underground Railroad from Slavery to Freedom* (New York: Russell and Russell, 1898), 91.

107. Albert Bushnell Hart, *Fugitive Slaves (1619–1865)* (New York: Bergman, 1969), 60–1.

108. Ibid., 63.

109. Siebert, *Underground Railroad,* 56.

110. Filler, *Crusade Against Slavery,* 70–1.

111. Ibid., 15.

112. Mullin, *Flight and Rebellion,* 35.
113. Ibid., 43.
114. Ibid., 81.
115. Filler, *Crusade Against Slavery,* 53.
116. Ibid., 16.
117.Alice Dana Adams, *The Neglected Period of Anti-Slavery in America (1808–1831)* (Gloucester, MA: Peter Smith, 1964), 92–3.
118. Filler, *Crusade Against Slavery,* 129.
119. Ibid., 130.
120. Ibid., 101.
121. Louis Ruchames, *The Abolitionists* (New York: Putnam's, 1963), 112–3.
122. Lord Tweedsmeier, "The American Character," in Alan Nevins, ed., *America Through British Eyes* (New York: Oxford University Press, 1948), 497–8.

Chapter 3

Facing Crisis and Civil War

1851-1865

1857	Dred Scott decision.
1860	Abraham Lincoln elected president.
1861	Confederate States of America Organized.
	Civil War Begins.
1862	Emancipation Proclamation issued.
1863	Battle of Gettysburg.
1865	Civil War ends.
	Lincoln assassinated.

By the 1850s the young republic was entering a period of paradox. A visible nationalism accompanied the devotion to "manifest destiny," while at the same time irreconcilable rifts between northern and southern states widened. Though proudly claiming to be a world model for democracy and freedom, a major portion of American society was based upon slave labor. In addition, America was factionalized by activism and many reform movements. This splintering of loyalties and energy was ultimately overshadowed by a far greater polarization: civil war.

The period just before the outbreak of the Civil War was characterized by a high degree of citizen involvement in the concerns of the day. Membership in various societies and participation in political causes reached an emotional pitch that contributed to the readiness of the nation to go to war. Feelings ran strong on both sides of many fences: for and against the annexation of Texas and the following Mexican War; for and against the slaveholding status of Kansas and

Oregon; for and against John Brown's Harpers Ferry raid; and, of course, for and against temperance, women's rights, and abolition. Federal leadership seemed incapable of responding to the moral appeals made by the often fiery and frenzied leaders of these opposing forces. Thus factions grew further and further apart in the absence of any unifying or neutral voices. The general populace had chosen sides well before the call to arms. Fighting in battle was not the only way to demonstrate loyalty to one's side; the Civil War called upon those at home to support the military efforts with service in countless ways.

This turbulent period saw political activity on many fronts. The women's rights movement launched itself formally with the Seneca Falls Convention in 1848, acquiring enough solidarity and fiery spokeswomen to assure a continuing effort thereafter. A short-lived and unique protest movement sprang up in 1851 when one of the leaders, Amelia Bloomer, exhorted women across the nation to defiantly wear her shocking new form of underwear. Bloomerism gained notoriety if not lasting impact. Most of the more serious volunteer efforts at gaining civil rights for women were channeled in those years into hard work for the growing temperance movement and, of course, for abolitionism.

As jobs in the cities grew scarce, immigrants were looked upon increasingly as unwanted competition. In 1850, a secret society calling itself the Order of the Star Spangled Banner formed in New York to spread anti-foreign and anti-Catholic sentiment. Similar groups all over began to use politics as a way to enforce their prejudices, but they did not support their own candidates openly. Instead, they preferred to deal in backroom schemes and alley violence.

> *This new intruder into the field of politics, it was whispered about, was a political secret society, whose suspected members declared they knew nothing about it. No sooner therefore had the result of elections made manifest that some hidden influence had been working against certain candidates than the unknown party was dubbed the Know Nothing, a name it never lost.*[1]

The Know Nothings, also called the American Party, became a potent force in the elections beginning in 1854, especially in the new states disputing the slavery issue. They were always proslavery and rooted in such secret volunteer societies as the Blue Lodge, the Social Band, and

Sons of the South. They were strongest in Missouri, Kansas, and the southern states. The tactics of the Know Nothings were even used by some Massachusetts abolitionists who supported the use of illegal acts to attain political victory.[2]

Meanwhile, the passing of the Fugitive Slave Law in 1850 gave the abolitionists the rallying point they needed. Though the abolition movement was still a loosely organized conglomerate of local groups, its numbers were growing daily. The abolitionists' primary goal was to aid escaping slaves threatened by the new law. Many northern cities formed volunteer vigilance committees to prevent fugitive slaves from being arrested and to assist in any possible way with resistance to the Fugitive Slave Law. "Of such importance did it become, that at the beginning of the Civil War one of the chief complaints of the southern states was the injury received through the aid given their escaping slaves by the North."[3]

As already noted, the antislavery crusade attracted men and women of all types. "To free themselves and to free the slaves, they gave significant energy, time, talent, and funds to the cause, which was often the only thing that tied them together."[4] Leadership always centered in New England, but spontaneous action took place everywhere; thousands of ordinary people found extraordinary ways to aid the antislavery cause.

The Underground Railroad grew in size and impact as the war approached. Volunteers, engaged in what was called the "forwarding business," became involved in the Railroad as a chance to defy what they considered unconscionable laws. Sympathetic directors of railroads gave out free passes to fugitives riding on their trains. Similarly, abolitionist boat captains were an integral part of the system, transporting fugitives by waterway to Canadian safety. Those contributing money rather than service came to be known as "stockholders" and included many distinguished philanthropists and politicians.[5] In the West, former Southerners were willingly involved in the struggle too.

In a few neighborhoods settlers from the southern states were helpers. These persons had left the South on account of slavery . . . they pitied the slave. It was easy for them to give shelter to the self-freed negro.[6] The role of blacks, both free and slave, continued to be crucial. On the plantations, slaves conducted day-to-day resistance, limited strikes, and acts of sabotage, requiring the voluntary cooperation of all. A code of silence protected those who committed individual acts of violence or who took the dangerous steps toward freedom. There were also scattered open revolts.

As already mentioned, free blacks were a part of many abolition activities. Also "abolitionist lecturers were usually lodged in black homes, spoke in black churches, ate food prepared by black women, and traveled on monies in part donated by blacks with little money themselves."[7] Black "vigilance committees" supplemented the work of the Underground Railroad by providing shelter, protection, and employment for ex-slaves who had reached their destination.

Despite all of the heated pro- and antislavery activity that seemed to make a war unavoidable, there was also a determined and visible group of pacifists. Still organized after their struggle against the Mexican War, many of the peace advocates of the 1840s had been transformed into ardent and even violent abolitionists, but

> *those in the Ohio Valley tended to hold firm. Indeed, they found that thousands of their neighbors were developing a passionate interest in preventing war or more accurately, a passionate interest in preventing war between the North and South. This ground swell of popular sentiment was to make the Ohio Valley the backbone of the American Civil War peace movement.*[8]

The Ohio volunteers found allies in the New York and Massachusetts peace societies, and together they determinedly formed a political coalition known as the Peace Democrats.

The political turmoil preceding the Civil War was not the only factor of influence in the daily activities of Americans. The cities had grown rapidly in both population and area, resulting in problems that residents were poorly prepared to handle. Drunkenness and poverty, vice and crime, riots and disorders had always existed, but the proportions they now assumed made them uncontrollable by the simple methods so long in use. Better means of transportation, more efficient police, more orderly and better trained firefighters, and cleaner streets were badly needed. But not all citizens were in favor of changes brought by progress. When in 1853 the New York City Council decided to build a new horsecar line up Broadway, there was so much citizen protest that its construction ultimately stopped. In the same year, New York decided that all city police must wear a uniform symbolizing their professional departure from the earlier volunteer peace patrols. However, this was opposed by many patrolmen and citizens on the grounds that it created an unnecessary barrier between the public and the police. The law was finally enforced in 1854.[9]

The cities were also experiencing the problem of rampant unemployment. Mass meetings of unemployed persons were held to demand public loans and other relief services. By 1854, many volunteers had rallied to help:

> *Doctors offered their services free, women held fairs, merchants and bankers subscribed to the relief fund, and shopkeepers offered to contribute a tenth of a quarter of their gross receipts for a week or a month.*[10]

Relief associations sprang up everywhere. Some workers lucky enough to be employed agreed to work half time or for half pay so that more people could be hired.

The intense interest in education and self-improvement that had begun during the preceding decades continued to exist right up to the beginning of the Civil War. Philanthropists such as Thaddeus Stevens opened their large private libraries to the citizens of their communities, contributed to private academies that had run into debt, founded new colleges, subsidized teachers, and lent their books to local schools. At the same time, on a smaller but just as impressive scale, education and culture were spread throughout the new frontier by women's volunteer associations. For example, the Ladies' Library Association of Kalamazoo, Michigan, was established in 1852 for the purpose of maintaining a public library and analyzing and discussing books. The Minerva Club (1857) was similarly organized by women who wanted to bring European culture to the Midwest. During the 1850s, women in the Iowa prairie communities organized reading circles in their homes.[11]

Closely related to this fascination with culture and self-improvement was the continuation of a strong humanitarian movement throughout the country. In New England almost any idea for bettering the community soon resulted in a group competing for enthusiasm, money, and members:

> *The sick, the infirm, the blind, indigent boys, fallen women, orphans, widows, children, seamen, were now the objects of a benevolent care quite unknown thirty years before. In truth, there was scarcely a worthy object of any sort that was not furthered by a society.*[12]

City newspapers took up the crusade for social improvement. Their readers, composed largely of the middle and upper classes, were influenced by what they read, and editors drew their attention to the problems of the day.

> *The excellent work of the New York newspapers in arousing public concern can scarcely be overstated. Their editorials constantly hammered away at the corruption in the City Inspector's Department, while news stories and articles repeatedly exposed the grim living conditions to be found in slum areas.*[13]

Such journalism fostered the volunteer spirit necessary to the solving of social ills.

Foster home placement of homeless children began at this time through agencies such as the New York Children's Aid Society, founded in 1853. The children were sent to other parts of New York State and to cities in the Midwest, where they were given homes with farmers or townspeople who agreed to accept them. The practice of reimbursing such foster families did not begin until 1866, but even after that many opened their homes on a completely volunteer basis.[14]

The large immigrant population continued to catch the attention of many welfare-minded citizens. Private American philanthropy addressed the task of finding jobs for newcomers, as demonstrated by the formation of the American and Foreign Emigrant Protective and Employment Society in 1854.

Other social welfare concerns such as housing conditions were targets of much public activity. The Association for Improving the Condition of the Poor (AICP) led a major campaign for housing reform. In 1854 it founded the Working Men's Home Association to build model tenements. Twelve years after the first was constructed, it, too, had become a slum, and the AICP began to recognize the need for treating the *causes* of poverty, rather than the symptoms.

In 1851, Thomas V. Sullivan, a retired American sea captain, gathered together young men in Boston and established the first Young Men's Christian Association (YMCA). The organization served many boys who came to work in the cities from rural areas or from abroad and provided a home away from home of good moral influence. The idea spread quickly into many communities, where Protestant volunteers were responsible for carrying out all YMCA activities, maintaining the organizational structure, and handling business affairs. By the late 1850s, Young Women's Christian Associations (YWCAs) were developing as female counterparts. In 1858, student YMCAs began on college campuses. Other denominations had already begun to establish similar organizations, such as the Jewish Independent Order of B'nai B'rith (1843) and the Catholic Society of Saint Vincent de Paul (1845).

Developments occurred in the field of medicine. For instance, occupational therapy began with the individual efforts of Thomas Eddy, who convinced the New York Hospital Board to include programs of exercise and employment in plans for the new Bloomingdale Asylum for the Insane. To look at the health and welfare services of the country as a whole, Dr. John Griscom proposed a Hygiological Society in 1854. It was a joint association of volunteer lay people and physicians.

> *It would take under its keeping and guidance the sanitary interest of the whole people in all their aspects and relations, and as a medium of communication between the people and the profession would exert a powerful influence for the good of both.*[15]

General health care improvement, at least in large cities such as New York, was the goal of many public health groups. Because doctors were in a position to see the daily effects of poverty, they often volunteered to serve in the dispensaries and clinics, making the medical profession active in the reform effort:

> *In a democratic society, support for any reform movement must have a broad base, and the ranks of health reformers invariably included responsible citizens from many walks of life. Yet there can be little question the individual New York physicians supplied leadership which brought sanitary reform to the city.*[16]

The years prior to the Civil War were marked by continuous growth in the physical boundaries of America, and there were many citizens who devoted much of their lives to adventure and exploration. Typical of such citizens was Eli Thayer, who founded the Massachusetts Emigrant Aid Company in 1854. This company proposed to settle the West in an organized manner, beginning with Kansas. The public was skeptical about the project, but several wealthy and influential citizens took an interest in it. Aided by volunteer contributions, it slowly attracted the attention of many who were willing to move westward.

> *The inspirational force of Thayer and his parent company led presently to the formation of hundreds of Kansas leagues and Kansas committees in our Northern States, all loyal to one another, all combined for a common purpose . . . the secret of success in such an emigration was cooperative sympathy.*[17]

For the most part, the frontier consisted of individual homesteads, scattered lumber and mining camps, and isolated cattle ranches. Volunteer cooperation was evident but did not change the essential independence of each. There were, however, some groups that consciously transplanted themselves into the new territories as ready-made communities. A major example was the Mormon migration to Utah beginning in 1847 to escape religious persecution in the Midwest. The Mormons were governed by a strict moral code dictating proper behavior in all aspects of life and placing primary emphasis on the good of the community. The essence of Mormon life was voluntary cooperation, as evidenced by collective farms and stores, boycotts of non-Mormon businesses, aid to local Indians, and numerous societies aimed at enforcing Mormon rules. Utah was not blessed with enough water for farming, and so the Mormons ingeniously developed an extensive irrigation system in the 1860s. These canals "were built by farmers, owned by farmers, and operated by farmers. In fact they constitute one of the greatest and most successful community or cooperative undertakings in the history of America."[18] An even more impressive example of Mormon volunteering was the construction of thirty-seven miles of railroad between Salt Lake City and Ogden. At the dedication of the Utah Central Railroad in 1870, Brigham Young acknowledged the volunteers who built the line entirely without government subsidies: "I also thank the brethren who have aided to build this, our first railroad . . . They have worked on the road, they have graded the track, they have laid the rails, they have finished the line, and have done it cheerfully 'without purse or scrip.'"[19]

One of the problems confronting early western settlers was slow communication across a vast geographic area. The Pony Express, active in most of the frontier territories beginning in 1860, was a successful attempt to expand and speed mail service. The salaries of Express riders in no way compensated for the danger and effort involved on hazardous routes. "That no Pony Express rider ever turned back stands as one of the finest examples of courage in American history."[20] Only a year and a half after it began, the Pony Express ended operation because of the completion of the first transcontinental telegraph line. Yet the fame of those daring riders who chose to go beyond normal expectations to prove the possibility of faster communication lives on today:

> *The history of this organization should be a lasting monument to the physical sacrifice of man and beast in an effort to accomplish something worthwhile. Its history should be an enduring tribute to American courage and American organizing genius.*[21]

During this pre-Civil War period, there were many contributions to the scientific knowledge of America through volunteer exploration and observation. Arctic and Alaskan expeditions were plentiful during the mid-nineteenth century and were carried out under the auspices of individual explorers, the army, the federal government, telegraph companies, newspapers, and the Smithsonian Institution. Regardless of the sponsor, all depended on donations of money, goods, and transportation.[22] Although profit and personal ambition were often the primary motives behind such expeditions, many volunteer contributions to science were also made. Additional studies were conducted by the explorers in their leisure time, going beyond the specific purpose of their particular expedition. For instance:

> *For the Western Union expedition, Kennicott requested permission to engage a few other naturalists, organized as a "Scientific Corps" designed to gather data and specimens as official duty permitted. Professional opportunity in lieu of fabulous pay induced half a dozen men to enlist.*[23]

Similarly, one northern trader supplied the Canadian Geological Survey with the remains of a mammoth, later used in a study of that extinct animal. And American traders volunteered to monitor meteorological instruments for the Signal Service, to collect specimens, to take census figures, and to map remote areas.[24] Thus, in ways such as these, the less immediate needs of science were often met because of the curiosity of individuals with special interests, who willingly collected data without being paid to do so.

Obviously there were many dimensions to the pre-Civil War decade. When war came, such activities gave way temporarily to the priorities of the civil struggle. The hostilities dominated life with immediacy and totality, demanding the involvement of all citizens on both sides.

The enthusiastic participation of volunteer soldiers in the 1846 Mexican War was a foreshadowing of the capability of American citizens to wage serious war on each other. As the Civil War began, both sides set out to muster mass armies, capitalizing on the patriotic enthusiasm that followed the Fort Sumter battle:

> *The sense of a "cause" (vital to any war) was not to be imposed by remote authority. The cause had to be something whose effectiveness, from both without and within the individual citizen, depended to a remarkable degree on its being voluntarily assumed. The moral coercions flowed not from the fiat of the state but from consensus in the community.*[25]

Two days after Lincoln's inauguration, the Confederacy voted to enlist an army of one hundred thousand volunteers for one year. Almost one-third this number came forward within one month of the call.[26] But as it became evident that this war would take a good deal longer than a year to finish, the Confederacy faced a crisis in maintaining troop strength. By 1862, "in what was the last great volunteer war in history, the South . . . could not muster volunteer support in sufficient quantity."[27] Increasing casualties, martinet military leadership, and long dependence on slaves to do hard work caused the Confederacy to pass a conscription act just one year into the war. This made it obligatory for white men between the ages of eighteen and thirty-five to enlist.

The North, benefiting from an already-established military structure, was able to take less extreme measures. At first the federal government could rely on the state militias to meet individual quotas:

> *The active militia of each loyal State was hurriedly put in readiness, and companies sprang up besides, organized in town-meetings, to tender patriotic services to the President . . . The quotas assigned under the proclamation did not begin to comprehend the volunteers freely raised and freely offered through the several State Governors to the War Department.*[28]

However, in 1862, for much the same reasons as the South, the North was forced to consider conscription at least in those states not meeting their troop quotas. But despite the draft proclamation that year, the practice was never actually implemented. As soon as the draft measure was announced, the state governors protested the unreasonable pressures on them to muster high quotas, and draft riots broke out in various places. Four days of mob violence in the cities caused one thousand casualties and a general destruction of property. This had a sharp impact on the middle and upper classes by emphasizing the terrible tenement conditions and overcrowding, as well as resistance to the draft.

In view of this massive protest against conscription, the Secretary of War, Edwin Stanton, agreed to postpone the draft for a month, and finally indefinitely. The 1863 Enrollment Act did obligate able-bodied men to serve, but it permitted both substitution (hiring another man to fill one's slot) and commutation (paying $300 to be relieved from duty outright). As it turned out, only about 6 percent of the federal army was drafted. Otherwise:

> *The main practical use of the draft proved to be to stimulate volunteering. Districts could still avoid the draft by meeting their quotas through volunteering, and so the Enrollment Act stimulated recruiting campaigns and helped perpetuate the hope that the United States could still wage its wars mainly with volunteers.*[29]

The methods of substitution and commutation were also intended to be appeasement for conscientious objectors, especially as the $300 waiver of service fee was meant to care for the sick and wounded soldiers. But there were still pacifists who refused this plan and continued the struggle to win legislative exemption from military duty.

> *As a result of energetic petitions by the pacifist churches, Congress in 1864 granted exemption from combatant military service to "members of religious denominations who . . . are conscientiously opposed to the bearing of arms . . ." Those qualifying . . . however, were to be drafted into military service as noncombatants and assigned to duty in hospitals or to care for freedmen.*[30]

Despite pacifist groups, most citizens were willing to take up arms for their cause. The war was made possible by the military strength of the citizen militias, but as the fighting dragged on it became evident that there was a limit to the nation's supply of volunteer soldiers:

> *It proved to be the last major war both of state-affiliated and of volunteer armies. After reviewing the problems . . . the United States would never again attempt to raise a wartime army by that method. Federal conscription would be the principal legacy of the Civil War experience to future American war armies.*[31]

The Civil War divided the country but unified the citizens of each side as never before. Volunteer efforts permeated every aspect of the war-torn society. It was considered a matter of duty and honor for all able-bodied males to take up arms, while women played an extensive voluntary role at home.

> *At the outbreak of war, women in every station in life vied with one another in giving to their cause and country. If the individual were wealthy, she gave all she had, her services and herself; if she were in humbler circumstances, the sacrifice was the same.*[32]

In fact, a British journalist who observed the American people at war concluded that there was probably no conflict in history up until that time that was as much "a woman's war" as that of 1861-1865.[33]

It was not unusual for women anywhere to work for those suffering because of war. But the American women were different in that they organized relief "not in the spasmodic and sentimental way which had become common elsewhere, but with a self-controlled and national consideration of the wisest and best means of accomplishing their purpose."[34] Soon after the outbreak of fighting, northern women began to organize themselves in Ladies' Aid Societies for the purpose of making bandages, shirts, drawers, towels, bedclothes, uniforms, and tents. Ladies who had never worked before transformed their gay silk dresses into banners and flags, and many wealthy women acted individually to outfit an entire military company or to endow soldier-aid institutions. In addition, there were frequent accounts of farm women who traveled miles to the nearest Ladies' Aid Society headquarters to obtain cloth from which they made clothing; many an impoverished woman shared her scant supply of food with passing troops or individual soldiers.

Fundraising fairs and bazaars were also common, and although attention was often focused on obtaining the moral and financial support of men, most of these affairs were planned and managed entirely by women:

> *They sparked the movement, provided the initiative, gave freely of their time, energy and talents, and contributed material possessions ranging from a priceless family heirloom to a jar of pickles.*[35]

Some women also volunteered to serve in a more dangerous way, acting as spies, couriers, guides, scouts, saboteurs, smugglers, and informers. They sometimes actually participated in the battles fought by the northern army, and some of the most effective espionage was conducted by women in their own neighborhoods. Such activities on the part of women served to stimulate male enlistments by humiliating men who hesitated to fight.

Another visible way in which northern women aided the cause was by operating "refreshment saloons" for transient soldiers passing through their communities. At such places the men could rest and obtain food, drink, and medical care—all services having been donated by citizens in the area. One of the most outstanding examples was the Cooper Shop Volunteer Refreshment Saloon, established in Philadelphia.

The Saloon began in April 1861, when the women of Southwark observed the trainloads of troops who gathered in Philadelphia to await transportation south. In response, the women immediately formed a committee and began to distribute coffee and refreshments to the hungry men. Soon their efforts attracted the attention of others, among them Messrs. Cooper, Pearce, and Simpson, who loaned them the use of the fireplace in the nearby Cooper Shop. These men then began a drive to collect provisions, and their example was quickly imitated as the citizens turned out en masse with donations. Storekeepers, butchers, and milk dealers responded cheerfully and generously, "as though the salvation of the Union depended on their individual efforts."[36] Before long, the Cooper Shop Saloon had become a massive institution.

The excitement among the people increased. Everybody seemed to make common cause—their hearts beat with patriotic impulses, and it was not an unusual scene in the early mornings . . . to observe a hundred women—women who sew and work hard at various pursuits to maintain an honest livelihood—arranging themselves along the railroad track, and happy, indeed, in handing cups of homemade coffee through the windows of the cars to the soldiers, who received the same with grateful consideration.[37]

The public was welcome to visit the Saloon, day or night, and there was always a committee on duty to prepare for expected troops. Arrangements were made with the railroad company transporting the men so that the Saloon had several hours' notice before they arrived. Another group, the Union Volunteer Refreshment Saloon, cooperated fully with the Cooper Shop group, sharing the work to be done. Together they ultimately distributed food and supplies to over six hundred thousand federal soldiers during the course of the war.

Another immediate result of this effort was the creation of the Cooper Shop Volunteer Hospital, which was dedicated on November 6, 1861. It was operated by a doctor who served for three years without pay and was staffed by a volunteer committee of women. This was no army hospital, however, for strict military discipline was replaced by the freedom of a home:

All was voluntary and free from restraint. It was a labor of love which sought no compensation; for, excepting perhaps a single case, everything was done gratuitously . . . all sought their reward in the luxury of doing good.[38]

The hospital was kept going by many generous supporters, among them Dorothea Dix, who sent a donation of books. Later, another need was recognized, and in December 1863, the Cooper Shop Soldiers' Home was opened. It was built by funds raised by local women and provided a home for discharged and homeless soldiers. It served as an example for many other soldiers' homes throughout the country.

The medical needs of the northern army evoked perhaps the most massive type of citizen involvement: the U.S. Sanitary Commission. Immediately at the start of the Civil War, Dr. Elizabeth Blackwell formed the Women's Central Relief Association for the Sick and

Wounded of the Army. This group consolidated several Ladies' Aid Societies, and on May 16, 1861, delegates of this organization descended upon the War Department in an effort to secure official recognition from the federal government for a voluntary relief association. At first, their request was refused: "The War Cabinet supposed that some clergymen, sensitive women, and a few physicians had concocted a sentimental scheme."[39] But the toll of war changed the legislators' minds, and on June 9, 1861, the U.S. Sanitary Commission was created. It was to receive no financial aid from the government but was to depend entirely on voluntary contributions.

As the largest private relief organization of the war, the Commission involved itself in a multitude of activities. Collections of food, clothing, and medical supplies were stockpiled in huge warehouses in the major northern cities, to be distributed by a small army of several hundred volunteer field agents. Sanitary arrangements in the army camps were policed. Approximately twenty-five soldiers' homes were maintained throughout the North and South, where passing federal soldiers could receive meals, lodging, rest, advice, and comfort. "Sanitary fairs" were held to raise money, and a drive was launched to obtain a steady supply of fresh fruits and vegetables to fight scurvy. Many farm women cultivated a "Sanitary potato patch" or an "onion patch for the Commission," and children pledged their July 4th firecracker money to buy vegetables for soldiers. Later on, the Commission was also involved in finding jobs for partially disabled men and for the wives and mothers of soldiers, in treating the permanently crippled, and in securing pensions and arrears of pay.

Nursing was another great service rendered by the Sanitary Commission. Prior to the Civil War, most nurses in the general hospitals were males who were paid. The only women involved were Catholic and Protestant sisters, whose training was in immediate demand at the start of the fighting in 1861. When, therefore, Dorothea Dix approached the Secretary of War in 1861 and offered to lead—without pay—the vital searches for nurses, her services were accepted immediately. She was authorized to recruit suitable female volunteers and to supervise their placement in general hospitals, where heretofore men only had served. This change in hospital staff freed many men either to enlist in the army or to serve as nurses in the military hospitals.

Citizen doctors were fairly plentiful in the field hospitals, due to patriotism as well as to the opportunity to gain experience. But the supply of nurses was never sufficient, and before long it seemed as though just about anyone who could apply a lint bandage was put to work. During the early years of the war, these nurses included undesirable soldiers, convalescents, invalids, and even prisoners. However, as the war progressed, the Sanitary Commission increased its effectiveness and improved volunteer nursing care in the field. A system of ambulances was devised for rapid removal of the wounded from the field of battle. At Gettysburg, where twenty thousand wounded were left on the field with little or no official medical care, they were attended and evacuated almost totally by volunteers of the Sanitary Commission.

In summary, the U.S. Sanitary Commission was loosely organized, and in some cases, poorly administered, while its achievements in the field of sanitation were negligible. Yet, despite its faults, the Commission met a great need, monitored the government's fulfillment of its obligations to soldiers, and accomplished its goals to a remarkably successful degree, largely because of the enthusiasm and dedication of its volunteers. Furthermore, the Commission not only demonstrated "that a citizens' group could affect governmental action, but also showed the value and power of organization on promotion of public welfare."[40]

Another project vying for citizen support during the war was the Christian Commission, formed in 1861 for the purpose of performing evangelical work among the soldiers. Most regiments of the army had no chaplain at all, and so the call went out for volunteers, bringing a large response from the home churches:

> *Few northern pastors failed at some period of the war, for a few weeks or a few months at a time, to visit the army camps for Christian work, loaned temporarily by their churches and commissioned for the occasion as delegates of the Christian Commission.*[41]

Many northern women also participated actively in the Commission's work, though they were more concerned with the physical and material needs of the soldiers. They collected Bibles and religious tracts to be distributed, and prepared hundreds of thread-and-needle cases, called "house-wifes," to help the men in the field. They also established a system of special diet kitchens that eventually extended throughout the entire army. The purpose of these kitchens was to supply the sick soldier with food "as nearly resembling as possible that which his mother and sisters would have furnished him at home."[42] The establishment of such a system required extremely careful coordination, not to mention the volunteer cooperation of many women throughout the North. As one author asserts: "The Christian Commission . . . owed its efficiency mainly to the zeal, the patience, and the generosity with which it was sustained by the loyal ladies of the country."[43]

Volunteers from the North were also involved in helping Southerners during the war. For instance, the citizens of both New York and Boston donated clothing and money to keep the Confederate inmates of nearby prison camps well-clad.[44] Another charity was that given to those southern whites who remained loyal to the Union, whether they escaped north or remained in the South:

> *The wretches were mostly women and children, poor and forlorn in the extreme, in need of clothing, rations, hospital service, and direction in finding employment. In the frequented places refugee committees sprang up among the loyal people and finally the American Union Commission was formed to harmonize the work of the local societies.*[45]

The contributions of black volunteers, free and slave, were many and valuable. The war reversed, at least temporarily, the enforced passivity of blacks in white America, for it was recognized that their assistance was needed in order to preserve the Union. Though there were many examples of slaves who aided the Confederate cause and remained loyal to beloved masters well after the Emancipation Proclamation, the record shows that thousands of slaves actively helped the Union.

> *Some one hundred thirty thousand fought in the Union armies, another half-million fled from bondage and entered Union lines, where they performed support services for the military, and countless others aided the Union by serving as scouts or spies or by withholding much of their labor on Confederate farms and plantations.*[46]

By engaging in work slowdowns and by not fighting in the southern army, "the slaves systematically sabotaged the war effort by refusing to produce."[47] This was one factor in the inability of the Confederacy to create a sufficient food yield. Other, more open sabotage included arson and physical violence against slaves loyal to the South.

Already having an underground organization, the slaves aided the northern troops by providing food and shelter for federal patrols and escaping prisoners. "Without assistance, shelter and food given them by scores of Negroes along the way, these Union soldiers and many others could not have made good their escape."[48] The blacks even guided the soldiers toward the main army encampments. Groups such as the Loyal League helped runaway slaves and spied for the Union army. The mechanism of the Underground Railroad, extending as it did well into southern territory, made it the only plausible escape route from Confederate prisons: "The time never came during the war when prisoners trying to escape were not safe for the time being in trusting themselves to the guidance of Negroes."[49]

Like their white counterparts black women volunteered to sew for and aid the Union troops. Black spokespeople tried to influence public officials to support the war effort and urged President Lincoln to act on behalf of Negroes. Toward the end of the war, the issue of equal suffrage in addition to emancipation roused much activity. In 1864, a group of blacks in New Orleans sent a suffrage petition to Washington that bore a thousand signatures, and later that year, 144 black delegates from eighteen states attended a national Negro convention in Syracuse, New York. The convention drew up an "Address to the People of the United States" containing an impassioned plea for the right to vote.[50]

The Civil War was fought predominantly on southern soil, and so the war affected the daily lives of every Southerner in an often brutal and direct way.

> *With armies in their backyard subsisting off the civilians and with battlefield casualties having to be cared for on the spot, Southerners were in the midst of the war's anguish . . . Nothing brought the war home so indelibly as this personal involvement with death and dying.*[51]

The Confederacy, never centralized in the way the North was, faced overwhelming problems in managing the demands of a standing army and a new government. One primary need was for increased production of food. No longer able to depend upon northern supplies, southern planters could only survive by converting from cotton to food crops. At first this conversion was approached as a voluntary effort to aid the Confederate cause.

> *The Confederate Congress, dominated by "laissez-faire" ideas, did not prohibit the raising of cotton; but the effects of the blockade, a campaign of appeal to patriotism, and state laws drastically reduced the planting of this crop. Under the voluntary system vigilance committees enforced the restriction of cotton growing.*[52]

However, voluntary controls began to lose effect when some planters sought illegal profits from trading with the advancing Yankees, and so some states passed laws limiting cotton production. Between 1860 and 1863, "the combined effect of voluntarism and state coercion . . . was to double the acreage in the Confederacy devoted to corn, wheat, and potatoes."[53] Ultimately, however, this success was insufficient to meet the need for food, and everyone in the South simply learned to do without many items. Even cooking implements soon became scarce, but cooperative spirit prevailed: "Suffice it to mention the fact that metal pots and pans were much handed about in a community wherever distances did not make borrowing an impossibility."[54]

The only word descriptive of the efforts of southern civilians during the war was sacrifice. All work centered around maintaining the fighting forces. Precious carpets, table linens, curtains, and other home furnishings were donated to supply makeshift hospitals. Blankets were made and collected for distribution to the troops. Some mill owners provided sheeting, shirting, and other clothing material to be sewn up by eager volunteer hands for the soldiers. Theater managers gave benefit performances for the cause. Some citizens in Pulaski, Tennessee, even attempted to provide shoes for the Tennessee men.[55]

> *Meanwhile, plantations were becoming miniature factories turning out clothing and blankets on hand looms. Without this household industry the supplying of the army would have been an insurmountable problem.*[56]

The pressing need for arms and ammunition was also met by private volunteer efforts, and at times during the war there was actually a surplus of these items. "Indeed, the energies of the entire people were employed in the production of every description of small-arms, and the enthusiasm displayed . . . pervaded all classes."[57] Vast amounts of money were raised, often from donated jewelry, to buy and construct gunboats and other necessary fortifications. Ladies' Gunboat Societies were popular, and the women of Alabama actually contributed approximately two hundred thousand dollars for the construction of a gunboat to protect the Alabama River.[58]

Confederate women were plunged into the war through the horror of watching it take place around them. Their men were all engaged in protecting the South from the federal troops, and so southern women were left to supervise the large plantations and the far more numerous non-slaveholding farms. These farm women

> *plowed the fields, cut the firewood, slaughtered the hogs, nursed the sick, and buried the dead, while their husbands, fathers, and sons, too far away to render assistance and comfort, provided moral support.*[59]

These were the same supposedly fragile ladies protected from the real world before the war by a romantic, male-dominated society.

Some women were angry at the injustice of not being allowed to fight alongside the men. At times this frustration worked itself out in humorous ways:

> *A Georgia girl wrote in 1861 that she and her female friends had organized a unit for local defense. "The name of our company is the Bascom Home Guards," she stated; "We are all delighted with the idea of learning to shoot."*[60]

But there were far more serious and important ways to help the military.

> *There were brave and patriotic women with a flair for adventure . . . who risked their lives to spy for the Confederacy. There were women who smuggled medicines, other products, and even military supplies through the lines beneath their voluminous crinoline skirts.*[61]

One such volunteer exploit was described in *The Star* newspaper of June 12, 1861:

> *An exchange says: "A lady who has just reached Memphis from Cincinnati, writes to her sister that she carried through, upon her person, forty pounds of powder, 10,000 percussion caps, and eight revolvers." What a "person" she must have!*[62]

While some accepted the dangers of spying and smuggling, many more women set up wayside stops for Confederate soldiers passing through the South by road. The soldiers received food, drink, nursing, and a place to rest. As in the North, southern women also aided the men travelling by train. One account describes the attention received:

> *We proceeded leisurely from station to station, stopping long enough to receive provisions for all on board from the citizens on the line of the road, which were freely and gratuitously furnished. Whenever we stopped long enough to give people time to assemble, crowds came to offer relief—ladies with flowers, jellies, and cakes, for the poor fellows, and men with the more substantial provisions . . . This exuberance of supplies thus voluntarily furnished, is an index of the feeling of the masses in the South as to the cause in which they have embarked their all.*[63]

Uniforms were sewn and repaired by volunteers, first with material provided by the government and then with whatever could be found. Socks, scarves, and gloves were continuously being knitted for shipment to the front with boxes of food and small goods. One Confederate veteran asserted: "General Lee's army was mainly supplied with clothing by the women of the South."[64]

Further, citizen efforts aided the men during the actual battles. "The mobile canteen may have had its start in 1862 at the Battle of Fredericksburg, when one organization furnished a horse-drawn wagon with three wood fired boilers that could produce ninety gallons of coffee an hour."[65] Volunteer ambulance corps sprang up to aid the wounded.

The southern army was also aided by the psychological effects of feminine "pout and sulk" campaigns aimed at increasing the number of volunteer enlistments. One incident in Selma, Alabama, illustrated a particularly fine example of this technique:

> *The unmarried ladies were so patriotic, that every able-bodied young man was constrained to enlist. Some months previous to this, a gentleman was known to be engaged for an early marriage, and hence declined to volunteer. When his betrothed, a charming girl and a devoted lover, heard of his refusal, she sent him by the hand of a slave, a package inclosing a note. The package contained a lady's skirt and crinoline, and the note these terse words: "Wear these or volunteer." He volunteered.*[66]

It was generally agreed that "southern women were the best recruiting officers, absolutely refusing to tolerate or admit to their society any young man who refuse[d] to enlist."[67] There were innumerable fundraising campaigns, bazaars, and fairs. No stone was left unturned by the women in searching for new ways to secure funds:

> *The suggestion publicly made . . . late in the war that all southern women cut off their hair and sell it to Europe, where it was believed it might bring $40,000,000, failed of execution only because it was impossible to run the federal blockade.*[68]

The most extensive service performed by volunteer women was unquestionably their nursing of wounded Confederate soldiers. Though "the romantic conception of ladyhood tabooed their attending to the bodily needs of the wounded . . . energetic and practical women . . . became hospital matrons and managers."[69] And in crises, women handled any and all nursing responsibilities. The women, along with the men and even children left at home, did everything possible to ease the lot of the wounded men.

Hospitals were created out of any unused public building or church. Early in the war, before the number of wounded men grew unmanageable, private homes were recruited to shelter and care for the soldiers in a personal way. After the battle of First Manassas in July 1861, "there was hardly a gentleman in or about Richmond who had not from one to four patients in his house, upon whom the utmost attention was bestowed."[70] That winter Nashville women and local medical students aided the wounded in General Bragg's forces, but by the summer of 1862 the enormity of the casualty lists became apparent all through the South. Medical care became a constant and more public concern.

Wounded men were transported to nearby cities whenever possible. At some depots, such as in Mobile, Alabama, the trains were met by women with their carriages and servants, ready to take the men to the makeshift hospitals. Besides helping as nurses, the women prepared food, rolled bandages, wrote letters for the men, read the Bible out loud, and provided whatever small touches of flowers and delicacies they could muster. They formed Soldiers Aid and other relief societies and devoted themselves to their cause.

It should be noted that occasionally Confederate ideals were subordinated to the more universal concerns of human aid to sufferers. Memphis, Tennessee, had long been known as the "Good Samaritan

City" because of its generous treatment of riverboat disaster survivors. During the war, the northern wounded were so crowded into the few nearby facilities that some Memphis citizens were moved to invite the Yankees into private homes to convalesce under southern care.[71]

The Civil War experience left both sides mourning their dead. The magnitude of human loss was staggering—six times the proportionate losses in World War II. "The people had to be convinced, and to convince themselves, that the cause for which their sons were fighting was worth the sacrifices that would go well beyond the experience of any generation of Americans, before or since."[72] Commitment had been total, and therefore the end of active fighting could not bring immediate reconciliation of Yankee and Confederate sentiments.

Despite the difference between the North and the South, it is evident that there were also many similarities in the way they rallied to their causes. The volunteer spirit manifested itself on both sides in the call to arms and the accompanying support efforts by civilians. This parallel reliance on citizen involvement would prove useful in the subsequent challenges of Reconstruction and the regaining of a united national identity.

Endnotes for Chapter 3

1. John Bach McMaster, *A History of the People of the United States* (New York Appleton, 1884), 8: 85.
2. Norma L. Peterson, *Freedom and Franchise* (Columbia: University of Missouri Press, 1965), 36–7.
3. Albert Bushnell Hart, *Fugitive Slaves (1619–1865)* (New York: Bergman, 1969), 64.
4. Jane H. Pease and William H. Pease, *Bound with Them in Chains* (Westport, Conn., Greenwood, 1972), 5–6.
5. Eber M. Pettit, *Sketches in the History of the Underground Railroad* (Freeport, NY: Books for Libraries Press, 1971), 34.
6. Wilbur H. Siebert, *The Underground Railroad from Slavery to Freedom* (New York: Russell and Russell, 1898), 31.
7. George P. Rawick, *The American Slave: A Composite Autobiography* (Westport, CT.: Greenwood, 1972), 111.
8. James R. Flynn, *American Politics: A Radical View* (Auckland: Blackwood and Janet Paul, 1967), 102.
9. McMaster, *History of the People,* 8: 70–2.
10. Ibid., 287–8.
11. Louis B. Wright, *Culture on the Moving Frontier* (Bloomington: Indiana University Press, 1955), 228–9.
12. McMaster, *History of the People,* 8: 86.

13. John Duffy, *A History of Public Health in New York City*, 1625–1866 (New York: Russell Sage Foundation, 1968), 566.

14. Hazel Frederickson, *The Child and His Welfare,* 2d ed. (San Francisco: Freeman, 1975), 22.

15. Wilson G. Smillie, *Public Health, Its Promise for the Future* (New York: Macmillan, 1955), 452.

16. Duffy, *History of Public Health,* 566.

17. James Schouler, *History of the United States of America, Under the Constitution* (New York: Dodd, Mead, 1882), 5: 325–6.

18. George Thomas, *The Development of Institutions Under Irrigation: With Special Reference to Early Utah Conditions (1920),* 27, quoted in John A. Hawgood, *America's Western Frontiers* (New York: Knopf, 1967), 376.

19. *The Deseret News,* January 11, 1870, quoted in John A. Hawgood, *America's Western Frontiers* (New York: Knopf, 1967), 379.

20. Ralph Moody, *The Old Trails West* (New York: Crowell, 1963), 297.

21. Waddell F. Smith, ed., *The Story of the Pony Express* (San Francisco: Hesperian House, 1960), 28.

22. J. E. Nourse, U.S.N., ed., *Narrative of the Second Arctic Expedition Made by Charles F. Hall* (Washington, DC: U.S. Naval Observatory, Government Printing Office, 1879), 40–2.

23. Morgan B. Sherwood, *Exploration of Alaska, 1865 –1900* (New Haven: Yale University Press, 1965), 18.

24. Ibid., 151.

25. Eric Louis McKitrick, *Andrew Johnson and Reconstruction* (Chicago: University of Chicago Press, 1960), 24–5.

26. Russell F. Weigley, *History of the United States Army* (New York: Macmillan, 1967), 198.

27. Rawick, *American Slave,* 117.

28. Schouler, *History of the United States,* 6: 35.

29. Weigley, *United States Army,* 210.

30. Richard J. Regan, *Private Conscience and Public Law* (New York: Fordham University Press, 1972), 22.

31. Weigley, *United States Army,* 216.

32. Matthew Page Andrews, *The Women of the South in War Times* (Baltimore, MD: The Norman, Remington Company, 1920), 127.

33. Mary Elizabeth Massey, *Bonnet Brigades* (New York: Knopf, 1966), 25.

34. Phebe A. Hanaford, *Daughters of America; or Women of the Century* (Augusta, ME: True and Company, 1909),166.

35. Massey, *Bonnet Brigades,* 37–8.

36. James Moore, *History of the Cooper Shop Volunteer Refreshment Saloon* (Philadelphia: Jas. B. Rodgers, 1866), 18.

37. Ibid., 16–7.

38. Ibid., 37.

39. Smillie, *Public Health,* 278.

40. Ibid., 283.

41. Emerson David Fite, *Social and Industrial Conditions in the North During the Civil War* (New York: Peter Smith, 1930), 285.

42. Frank Moore, *Women of the War; Their Heroism and Self-Sacrifice* (Hartford, CT: S.S. Scranton, 1867), 579.

43. Ibid.

44. William Best Hesseltine, *Civil War Prisons* (New York: Ungar, 1930), 42.

45. Fite, *Social and Industrial Conditions,* 296.
46. William L. Barney, *Flawed Victory: A New Perspective on the Civil War* (New York: Praeger, 1975), 141.
47. Rawick, *American Slave,* 116.
48. Ibid., 114.
49. Pettit, *Sketches,* 153.
50. Benjamin Quarles, *The Negro in the Making of America,* rev. ed. (New York: Collier Books, 1969), 122–3.
51. Barney, *op. cit.,* pp. 29–30.
52. Clement Eaton, *The History of the Southern Confederacy* (New York: Macmillan, 1954), pp. 240–241.
53. Barney, *Flawed Victory,* 97.
54. Andrews, *Women of the South,* 24.
55. H. H. Cunningham, *Doctors in Gray: The Confederate Medical Service* (Baton Rouge: Louisiana State University Press, 1958), 140–1.
56. Barney, *Flawed Victory,* 108.
57. William G. Stevenson, *Thirteen Months in the Rebel Army* (New York: A.S. Barnes and Company, 1862, reprinted 1959), 65.
58. Ibid.
59. Bell Irvin Wiley, *Confederate Women* (Westport, CT: Greenwood, 1975), xi–xii.
60. Ibid., 142.
61. Eaton, *Southern Confederacy,* 214.
62. John W. Stepp and William I. Hill, *Mirror of War* (Englewood Cliffs, NJ: Prentice-Hall, 1961), 48.
63. Stevenson, *Thirteen Months,* 129–30.
64. Cunningham, *Doctors in Gray,* 142.
65. *Twenty-five Years: Keeping Faith with Our Armed Forces Since 1941, U.S.O.* (New York: United Service Organizations, Inc., 1966), 8.
66. Stevenson, *Thirteen Months,* 135.
67. Massey, *Bonnet Brigades,* 30.
68. Arthur M. Schlesinger, *New Viewpoints in American History* (New York: Macmillan, 1925), 144–5.
69. Eaton, *Southern Confederacy,* 213.
70. Cunningham, *Doctors in Gray,* 45–6.
71. James W. Elliott, *Transport to Disaster* (New York: Holt, Rinehart and Winston, 1962), 186–8.
72. McKitrick, *Andrew Johnson,* 27.

Chapter 4

Rebuilding and Moving On

1866-1899

1867	Alaska purchased.
1868	Fourteenth Amendment, extending civil rights to all citizens, ratified.
1869	Completion of first transcontinental railroad.
1876	Newly invented telephone demonstrated at nation's Centennial Exposition in Philadelphia.
1877	End of Reconstruction.
1879	Invention of light bulb.
1886	End of western Indian Wars with surrender of Chief Geronimo.
1887	Interstate Commerce Act passed.
1890	Sherman Anti-Trust Act passed.
1896	Supreme Court upholds "separate but equal" doctrine in *Plessy v. Ferguson.*

The turbulent period following the end of the Civil War brought rapid and sweeping changes in the ways in which Americans dealt with each other and with the rest of the world. Immediate attention was given to the rebuilding of the devastated South, during what is commonly known as Reconstruction. But how this was to take place was an issue that continued to divide North and South.

Not all activity was focused on the South, however. The country's population was increasing, both naturally and from immigration, and the settlement of the West finally became a reality. At the same time the older cities of the North grew rapidly as they industrialized. The lure of urban factory jobs soon led to the frustrations of overcrowding and harsh working and living conditions.

The period was an odd blending of sordid political corruption on both local and national levels and of truly altruistic efforts to better the lot of those falling victim to the changing times. In addition, the American political sphere widened during this period to assume a world view, and for the first time the United States realized its potential for affecting foreign events. The earlier notion of manifest destiny was revitalized, but in the hands of dishonest politicians and greedy new capitalists the term became an excuse for imperialist ventures.

All in all, this era would be one of transition, preparing the nation for the complexities of the modern age.

Both the northern and southern armies were virtually dissolved at the war's end. Southern soldiers returned home to rebuild ravaged farms and lives and to face the ignominy of occupation by federal troops. The southern women showed admirable strength in the face of defeat and tried to rally the spirits of their returning men: "Popular were the 'starvation parties,' where no refreshments were served, and picnics where young folk danced to music of fiddles."[1] But the occupying troops were treated with total contempt. The women refused even minimal social courtesies to Union soldiers, despite cases on record when occupying troops "performed acts of charity and kindness for citizens."[2]

Occupation was compounded by the problem of determining who was actually a rebel, for the purpose of prosecution and legal status. In 1867 the attorney general decided that rebellious acts

> *had to be voluntary and deliberate and, hence, that serving in the Rebel army as a conscript did not qualify. Acts of charity or kindness to individual Rebel soldiers did not qualify either, but participating in contributions of food or supplies did.*[3]

Thus rebellion, as defined by the federal government, had to be voluntary in the most basic sense, and only volunteers were held accountable as rebels.

Once the southern occupation had ended, the federal army was mainly dispatched to fight Indians in the West. Most of the southern states were able to regroup their volunteer militia companies, including their Negro militia. The latter troops were used for

> *general police duty and especially to watch over electioneering and voting, to ensure that freedmen could and would vote and that ineligible ex-Confederates stayed away. Sometimes the militiamen interpreted these duties aggressively.*[4]

The black volunteers' aggression often provoked retaliation by whites who resented the new voting policies. Whites harassed the militias, thereby cooling the enthusiasm of blacks for enlistment. By the early 1870s the Negro militia was disintegrating, and with it much of the remaining military support for Reconstruction policies.

The Freedmen's Bureau, established in 1865, supervised massive relief efforts on behalf of the ex-slaves. The Bureau was especially concerned with education, labor arrangements between whites and blacks, and acquisition of available farm land by freedmen. Its main purpose was to make emancipation a reality.

The "Yankee teacher" entered the South on the heels of the occupying troops. Volunteers of all types came forth out of New England and the midwestern states—schoolmarms and masters, college presidents, Christian zealots, inexperienced idealists. Driven by a sense of divine mission and a degree of political realism, they swarmed southward, "generally flying over the mountains and alighting beyond wherever there was a job, often trusting to the future to develop a salary."[5] Northern sympathy was aroused for the freed blacks, and many local societies formed, uniting in 1865 to create the American Freedmen's Aid Commission. The American Missionary Association, the Freedmen's Aid Society of the Methodist Episcopal Church, and similar volunteer benevolence groups sent missionaries, teachers, and preachers to the South. The philanthropy of the Peabody Education Fund and others established many schools.

Although the teachers volunteered to go South, most were eventually paid a stipend by the northern benevolent societies that sent them, while the Freedmen's Bureau usually supplied transportation and school buildings. "Within a year after the war, 366 assorted societies and auxiliaries for Negro education were active; each of them would send from one to ten teachers to the South."[6] The exact number of teachers supported by such groups and the Freedmen's Bureau is unknown. One estimate is that in 1866, 1,300 teachers taught in about a thousand schools, with an approximate enrollment of ninety thousand young and old illiterates. By 1869, nearly ten thousand teachers were working at the task, and it is particularly important to note that only half of these were white Northerners or white Southerners; the rest were northern and southern blacks.[7]

After 1870, however, enrollment in these schools dropped drastically. Southern whites opposed them because politics were taught along with reading and writing. Blacks, too, began to feel that the schools were of limited use to them. Many of the benevolent societies also began to lose interest, as they saw that all their efforts and money had done little to ease the problem of mass illiteracy. Moreover, most of the southern states had adopted constitutions calling for equal educational opportunities for blacks at state expense. So the volunteers withdrew, hopeful that the states would now carry on the task themselves.

Reconstruction had a decidedly political purpose: securing the black vote. Northerners waged their campaign to sever whatever old allegiances might remain between ex-slaves and their former masters. Southerners played upon these old loyalties. And the southern blacks were caught in the middle.

The major tool of the northern radicals was the Union League. During the war, the League had been a pro-North propaganda dissemination device. With peace, the Union League moved south, called itself the Loyal League, and shifted emphasis toward winning black support for the Republicans. Every attempt was made to instill in the freedmen mistrust and suspicion of the former slaveowners. "To make the League the more appealing to the blacks, it was converted into a kind of lodge, with an elaborate ritual and much ostentatious ceremony."[8] Agents of the Freedmen's Bureau and occupying federal soldiers assisted Loyal League organizers. Before long, the League had succeeded in gaining control of the majority of blacks and assuring their registration and votes as Republicans.

One unique aspect of the Civil War was that hardly any women were raped during the open hostilities. Whether this was actually an indication of the soldiers' mutual respect for the families of their "brothers" is unproven, but for the duration of the war, the women were generally unmolested. Then came Reconstruction, and with it the influx of the corrupt northern profiteers who riled up the freed slave and changed the South into a crime-ridden area. For the first time, women were not safe from rape, "the foul daughter of Reconstruction."[9]

One evening in 1866, a group of young men in Tennessee, angry at the recent attacks on their female relations and bored into seeking novel amusement, decided to go scare the nearby encampment of freed slaves. Masquerades were in vogue at the time, so the young men dressed up in sheets and rode out. They immediately discovered that the freedmen were terrified by the shouting "ghosts," and what began as a lark ended up as a strategy.

> *From the intimidation of the Negroes it was an easy step to the challenging of the carpetbaggers and agitators who were lustily instilling into the black men's minds a hatred and distrust of native whites.*[10]

The rides became more frequent, and the group chose a name: the Ku Klux Klan. In the beginning, the Klan's concern as a volunteer group was to control crime, not to punish people with unpopular political views. And "it was not until the original Klan began to ride that white women felt some sense of security."[11]

But politics soon entered the picture. As Reconstruction progressed, more and more Southerners grew to hate the domineering and interfering Northerners who promised to give blacks political control of the South. Klans were often formed in retaliation to the Union Leagues created by the carpetbaggers. In 1868, the Klan held a national convention that gave an important boost to the organization.

> *By the end of 1868 the Klans practically dominated many large portions of the South. Of its total membership we have no knowledge . . . but it must have been . . . several hundred thousand at least. One writer of the time declares that the Klan numbered at the crest of its power and influence more than 600,000 men, many of whom were former Confederate soldiers and officers.*[12]

Originally, Klansmen did not discriminate against Jews and Catholics, many of whom joined the Klan as former Confederate soldiers. Blacks, of course, were denied membership from the start.

Documents of the early Klan show that the initiation oath required support of the United States Constitution, dedication to justice and humanity, and protection of widows and orphans. Volunteer groups rivaling the Ku Klux Klan sprang up after 1868. These groups, all of which dealt with local affairs, included

> *"Knights of the White Camelia," for a time a powerful federated society having its largest membership in Louisiana. The "Constitutional Union Guards," the "White Brotherhood," the "Council of Safety," the "'76 Association," and the "Pale Faces"*

were others. After 1868 all these organizations were societies of armed whites actually struggling for control of government in the South and for white supremacy.[13]

Other extralegal groups were Mississippi's White Line, Louisiana's White League, and South Carolina's Rifle Clubs.

Real police power was exercised by white sheriffs in rural areas who were supported by paramilitary organizations along the lines of the Ku Klux Klan. These organizations, instruments of community violence and intimidation, were an almost spontaneous Southern reinstatement of police control over the blacks.[14]

After the 1870 election, when the feared black governing class failed to materialize and the Act of 1870 gave political leaders broad power to suppress extralegal groups, the Klans began to disperse. By 1872, the various vigilante organizations had disbanded; it would not be until the next century that the Ku Klux Klan would again terrorize the countryside.

A fair evaluation of the Klan and similar groups in this period would have to list both positive and negative actions. The scales tipped irrevocably to the negative side because the name of the Klan was used as a cover for personal vengeance, pure lawlessness and racism. But it must be noted that Reconstruction was a harsh and chaotic time for the South. The laws were often bad and the administrators worse. The Ku Klux Klan

made life and property safe, protected womanhood, stopped incendiarism, and in a great many sections terrorized the agents of the Freedmen's Bureau, many of whom would have become without some sort of check, the most despicable local tyrants.[15]

Within a short span of years the South experienced both northern benevolence and exploitation. It would take several decades to recover from the destruction of the war, but ultimately the rebuilding came from efforts within the South itself. For the country as a whole, Reconstruction was an issue of little interest by the early 1870s. Although few believed that the angry division of the Civil War had healed, the approaching twentieth century brought incentives for renewed cooperation.

Despite the interruption of war, manufacturing continued to progress at a steady pace. Workers could be found in more than sufficient numbers from the returning soldiers and from the continuous flow of European immigrants. New production techniques for steel and oil created increased jobs and consumer demand, while the growth of the railroads could only be described as a boom. As the number of industrial workers increased, so did the inevitability of labor reform efforts and stronger unions. The undeniable realities of harsh and unsafe working conditions, exploitative salaries, and almost no protective benefits were the issues brewing during the second half of the nineteenth century. But regardless of the fervor for labor reform, unions had to recognize that their members were, at the same time, citizens in an open and complex society:

> *In this pluralistic society, men thought of themselves not only as workers, but as Catholics, Republicans, Odd Fellows, and much else besides. Trade unionism could not contradict those other loyalties, nor could it pursue goals other than those of concern to its members . . . Voluntary associations that they were, trade unions could lead only where the rank and file would follow—a narrow channel indeed.*[16]

So in the years just after the Civil War the unions emphasized economic actions rather than political ones, because their memberships were interested only in the immediacy of wage and working condition improvements.

Union organizations developed in almost every area of work. Because there was no national leadership at first, unions were local volunteer affairs, often with limited goals. Railroad workers began their organizing as early as 1855 with generally short-lived protective associations. By 1863, the Brotherhood of the Footboard was organized, later becoming the Brotherhood of Locomotive Engineers. It started, as nearly all the unions did, as a small meeting of volunteers in a private home. The lead taken by the engineers gave impetus to subsequent organizing efforts by the railroad conductors, firemen, telegraphers, and others.

> *Organization in 1873 of the Brotherhood of Locomotive Firemen . . . grew out of the incident of taking up a collection for the widow of a fellow-worker killed in a wreck.*[17]

Workers continued to organize themselves into mutual benefit associations for the purpose of providing protection in case of sickness, accident, or death. Employees agreed, on their own initiative, to pay weekly dues into a central fund, which was then available whenever a member needed relief. As the forerunner of worker's compensation laws, these activities further unified the working class. The scattered local groups needed only the right leadership to join forces and have an impact far beyond the imagination of the original organizers. Such unity and national scope were soon to come, as the size of industrial firms diminished the extent to which individual workers could bargain for themselves.

The newest and potentially most important weapon of this period's labor movement was the strike. Beginning around 1870, strikes, frequently accompanied by violence, became the favored tactic of virtually every union. In 1871 the Pennsylvania coal riots between union and non-union workers brought out the militia to restore peace. Strikes of trade mechanics also occurred in various states, and, in September 1871, twenty-five thousand workingmen met in New York City to demand an eight-hour labor law. Strikes were reactions not only to low pay and long hours but also to the increased use of cheap immigrant labor at the expense of benefits to the native worker. The increasingly violent demonstrations against Chinese miners and railroad workers in the West were examples of such nativist protest. The unrest and strike actions came to a head following the panic of 1873 when employers faced the threat of business failure. The employers' counterattack to the unions was blacklisting, with the ultimate effect of driving the organizing activity underground into secret labor societies.

By the late 1870s and early 1880s, union activism was reorganized and more regional in scope. National leadership was not far off for groups such as Sovereigns of Industry, the Industrial Brotherhood, and the important Knights of Labor. These groups tripled the number of work stoppages and doubled the number of workers involved in strikes. Furthermore, during that same decade, labor organizations began to use the technique of the boycott widely.

Some unions welcomed all types of workers into their ranks and joined forces with other volunteer social reform groups to advocate temperance, women's rights, improved education, and eradication of city slums. Other unions limited themselves to the pragmatic goal of gaining economic advantages for their members. As confrontations between labor and management grew more threatening, the unions changed their initial hostile attitude toward the immigrant worker. The unskilled foreigner still had trouble gaining union membership, but the need for strong numbers forced the groups to accept the support of at least the skilled newcomers. With the formation of the American Federation of Labor in 1881 and dissemination of Samuel Gompers' "doctrine of voluntarism," the union movement had come of age. By the late 1880s labor milestones such as the formation of the National Labor Union, the 1886 May Day strikes across the country, and the Haymarket Riot were history. Even the economic slump of the 1890s did not diminish union growth.

Some support for the labor movement came from the religious community. Out of concern for the plight of women in eastern city sweatshops, churchwomen founded more YWCAs in various cities to provide housing, recreation, and training for working women. Several other volunteer organizations were established that combined the interests of the churches and the workers. Examples were: the Church Organization for the Advancement of the Interests of Labor (1887); the Society of Christian Socialists (1889); and a variety of groups in the 1880s that opposed labor on the Sabbath, such as the American Sabbath Union, the International Sabbath Association, and the Sunday League of America.

One subgroup of laborers that was particularly active was the miners.

> *Despite the miner's indulgences and vices, he was generally a responsible citizen who took an active part in his community. He delighted in political debate, exercised his vote at nearly every opportunity, elected his fellow miners to such local offices as alderman, justice of the peace, and county sheriff . . . He also gave financial support to the schools, the church, charities, and his union.*[18]

The miner's unions took care of their own, as exemplified by the Gold Hill Union (1867), whose members paid 25-50 cents a month and received such benefits as medical and burial expenses. They also fought for safety procedures and loaned out prospecting equipment to members. There is even record of a Miner's Union Library, containing books selected by a board of directors elected by the union, with the union's financial secretary dutifully serving as librarian.[19] In terms of community service, the miners were involved in planning social events, such as July 4th celebrations, and served on "citizen committees" to aid public officials in keeping the peace during riots and violent strikes. Their volunteer spirit and generosity to those in need were exemplified in a letter submitted in a miner to the *Pittsburgh Chronicle* in 1865:

> *He asserted that miners of the district would be glad to dig coal without pay one day each month during the winter season, if arrangements would be made to deliver it free to the needy of Pittsburgh. Whether this offer was accepted, is not known, but it evidently was not a new suggestion. It had been made by miners during previous winters, but the mine owners had, in some instances, refused to cooperate.*[20]

Another labor subgroup was the mill factory worker. Most of the southern mills developed along paternalistic lines, with owners assuming responsibility for providing the necessities of life for their workers. Beginning in the late 1880s, the mill owners and their families offered religious leadership, housing, and material goods to their employees. Later these concerns were frequently taken over by citizen volunteers from the surrounding community, with the support of the mill management. Education was a major area of volunteer involvement, often because of the special interest of one teacher or one mill supervisor.

> *Sometimes, particularly in the early years, a night class for boys and girls or for adults was the hobby of some citizen in an adjoining community or of an organization such as a woman's club or a church society.*[21]

Some areas had paid daytime teachers who volunteered to hold night classes. For such efforts, many mills donated the space, fuel, and supplies. Thus the workers were given opportunities that many had never known before.

Loggers in lumber camps were also the focus of volunteer activity. Ministers occasionally traveled to the remote wood camps, as did many missionaries. A special committee of the YWCA sent reading matter to the lumbermen, and the American Home Missionary Society furnished religious tracts, all of which served to relieve the monotony of camp life.[22]

One historian noted that the period from 1853 through 1917 could be called "the age of cooperation":

> *Men are doing collectively the things which are not feasible to do alone. They are everywhere, in increasing numbers, uniting their efforts for the protection of a common cause. Nowhere is the spirit of cooperation better exemplified than in the modern trade association movement.*[23]

The earliest recorded trade association was the American Brass Association, founded in Connecticut in 1853. It was organized out of necessity by several mills located so close to one another that competition for raw materials and customers was counterproductive. Within three years, the Association had fixed prices and discounts and apportioned production.[24] Most trade associations had similar voluntary origins.

Eventually, the business community faced the same reality as did the labor force: individual and local efforts were not enough to confront the complex problems of an industrializing society. In response, trade associations slowly created national ties and took on diverse service tasks for their combined memberships. In 1868 a federation of local Chambers of Commerce formed the National Board of Trade to represent the interests of their member businesses nationally and even internationally. The 1855 predecessor of the American Iron and Steel Institute kept statistics on trade, supported exchange of scientific and practical information, encouraged the establishment of training schools, and collected samples. One of the volunteer activities of the 1862 United States Brewers Foundation was to help the federal government collect taxes on liquor.[25] The American Bankers Association, formed in 1875, promoted the general welfare of banks, ensured uniformity of action, provided for discussion of important banking subjects, and even served a social function: "for better acquaintance, for pleasure, for amusement, to get us away from home for a holiday—for a good time generally."[26]

Business leaders soon found that it was not only labor that could exert pressure on them. The consumer public, too, had its case to make against the excesses and injustices of business; it found its voice in the 1890s through consumer leagues. By 1899, the National Consumers League was formed and led the volunteer fight for economic justice, minimum wage laws, improved working conditions and hours, industrial safety, child labor laws, abolition of sweatshops, and aid to migrant workers. The major weapon of the Consumers League was the boycott of products produced in sweatshops through the exploitation of women and children. The League was comprised mainly of women, and soon the business world was well aware of feminine buying—or non-buying—power. When the League chapters were forbidden by law to blacklist products, "they ingeniously evaded this obstacle by publishing a *white list* of those which treated their people decently and kindly."[27] Later the League put out a "white label" for products produced under fair conditions.

The combined pressure of labor unions and consumer groups, plus new restrictive legislation, had its effect. By the end of the century, there was a noticeable change in the activities of many business organizations. Increased interest was shown in accountability to the pubic and establishment of training schools. For example, the American Association of Public Accountants, begun in 1887, developed a code of ethics for accountants, helped to open an accounting college, and obtained legal recognition of the title "C.P.A." (certified public accountant). Similarly, in 1890, 105 delegates of fourteen local societies formed the National Association of Life Underwriters, with the goal of ending abuses in the life insurance industry and improving the image of its agents. The underwriters voluntarily adopted standards and worked to eliminate unethical practices in their field. Also indicative of the impulse to organize and improve was the National Fire Protection Association, started by a Boston committee of concerned insurance and industrial representatives in 1895. They faced the problem of increased fire hazards in factories and the faulty or inconsistent installation of water sprinklers. The volunteer group set up standards and rules and a system for inspection. In their own words:

> *NFPA is a voluntary, nonprofit organization formed to promote the science and improve the methods of fire protection and prevention . . . it is fundamentally a cause; something of worth; something to be believed in and to be supported because it works for the good of society.*[28]

By the turn of the century, the United States was irrevocably committed to becoming an industrial power, but vast segments of the nation were still fundamentally agricultural. It was clear that farmers, too, had to organize regionally and even nationally in order to protect their interests. The best known of the rural farm associations was the Grange, which was founded in 1867 as the Patrons of Husbandry. It ultimately was most popular in the midwestern states but grew in the South as a way to regroup after the losses of the Civil War. The Grange was headquartered in Washington, D.C., and was supported by the Department of Agriculture, facts that made initial development efforts in the South suspect. Nonetheless, within six years there were fifteen thousand local Granges in the Midwest and South. In 1872, Mississippi and South Carolina boasted state Granges, and by 1873 practically every southern state was similarly organized. The high point of development was reached between 1873 and 1875. "Available information indicates that it was largely the small white farmer, rather than the large planter, who was the driving force behind the Grange."[29]

Cooperative Grange economic activities soon took on added social dimensions. Farmers were geographically isolated, and Grange meetings provided group reaction as well as important forums for new scientific agricultural techniques. The Grange also created an outlet for rural women:

> *One of its proudest boasts was that it admitted women to full membership, and this was one of the features which did most to give the Granges vitality . . . From the presence of this feminine element grew a wealth of general lectures and the provision of libraries. What would otherwise have been a rough business organization . . . became the means of lighting up the drab life of lonely farm communities.*[30]

Grange volunteers kept alive such traditions as festive Fourth of July celebrations and the enjoyable competitions of the county fairs.

While women were accepted as Grange members, the question of admitting blacks was far more controversial. The northern groups generally favored extending membership to black farmers, but the majority of groups around the country supported the formation of a separate but cooperating black organization:

> *This plan seems to have taken organic form with the creation of the Council of Laborers, a relatively unknown group closely identified with the Patrons of Husbandry. Even though the two bodies were separate and distinct, their aims were the same . . . the theory [was] that the interests of the colored farmers were intimately bound up with those of the whites, that the honorable white farmer was the best friend the Negro farmer had.*[31]

The Council of Laborers was originated by white farmers but operated as a black version of the Grange. Despite occasional accusations that the Council of Laborers was a Ku Klux Klan plot to keep black farmers down, the evidence was to the contrary, and the Council did provide black farmers with a viable volunteer organization.

The Grange groups had diversified interests. They dealt with farm labor questions, credit systems, railroad regulations, profits of middlemen, cotton output and price controls, and other farming concerns. In the Northwest, the Grange mobilized protest against the railroads during the early 1870s. In addition: "The educational efforts of the order represent one of the least emphasized, yet one of the most important, phases of its activities."[32] These educational opportunities were both formal and informal and were part of the larger self-help tradition of the Granges. On the informal level, groups encouraged reading of all types, especially current magazines and newspapers. To this end they endorsed newspapers for subscription and held "literary hours" after Grange business meetings. The larger Granges established libraries.

Granges had an impact on formal education by supporting the construction of more public schools and then demanding curricula relevant to farming communities. Educators were beginning to introduce nature study into the curricula of town and city schools, while rural areas increased the emphasis placed on appreciation of rural life and its opportunities. In an effort to provide farm children with training in practical subjects, some Grange groups opened their own schools. Corn-growing and other contests for youth were held as early as 1856 and continued after the Civil War in order to motivate future farmers.

Despite the enthusiasm of these volunteer activities, the Grange declined by the mid 1870s. The need for cooperative action had been clearly demonstrated, however, and farmers watched with interest as urban labor groups unionized:

> *Impressed with the occasional effectiveness of labor unions and eager to win comparable victories for agriculture, the farmers of both sections began to band themselves together into farm orders of various names and natures. Most important of these organizations were two great sectional "Alliances," the National Farmers' Alliance representing the Northwest, and the Farmers' Alliance and Industrial Union representing the South.*[33]

By 1878, the Grange was all but replaced by these Alliances, which were far more radical in nature.

The Alliances began locally, moved to state level, and ultimately regionalized or nationalized. The 1880 Texas Farmers' State Alliance merged in 1887 with the Louisiana protective groups to begin the National Farmers' Alliance and Cooperative Union of America. Soon after, the rest of the South and Southwest joined as well. At the same time, an organization known as the Agricultural Wheel developed. This was

> *a genuine "dirt-farmer" organization. It used the rural church and country schoolhouse as a convenient beginning point; and appealed chiefly to the destitute tenants and small landowners who felt insecure and found it difficult to adjust themselves to capitalistic methods of farming.*[34]

By 1889, the Wheel and the National Alliance had made yet another merger to become the Farmers' and Laborers' Union of America, or the Southern Alliance, as it came to be called.

The Southern Alliance, rooted in early efforts to ward off land sharks, cattle kings, and horse thieves, and to work cooperatively to the benefit of local farmers, had potential to be the first real alliance. The strategy of creating an affiliated but separate black farmers' group was maintained through the Colored Alliance. A Northern Alliance was founded in 1880 by the editor of a Chicago farm paper but never became more than a loose confederation of state orders.

Northern and southern farmers were now faced with the question of merger, but there were too many differences to make such a national group practical. However, by the end of the 1880s, each Alliance had concluded that political measures were the only way to assure lasting agricultural policy changes, and both began to look for candidates who supported their views. The Alliances formed the People's Party, or the Populists, and in their very first election (1890) secured twenty-one out of 144 electoral votes and elected five senators, ten congressmen, fifty state officials, and 1,500 country officials.[35] By so effectively voting into office those candidates with pro-agricultural views, the farmers had made their point. By 1896 the Populist party could dissolve, having met its goal. Through volunteer effort, government had been made responsive to its rural electorate.

In 1898, a Cornell University professor inaugurated a system of junior naturalist leaflets for use in rural schools and helped organize nature study clubs. These activities eventually consolidated into the 4-H Club after the turn of the century. A widespread campaign was launched by farmers to improve agricultural education on the college level, resulting in the opening of the "A & M" (Agricultural and Mechanical) schools. Also:

> *In the late 19th and early 20th centuries, agricultural college professors in nearly all States were organizing "Farmers' Institutes" meetings to bring the latest scientific agricultural information to farmers and their wives.*[36]

During this period cattle ranchers, too, found the need to organize:

> *The law of the range, like the law of the mining camps, was to a great extent invented to meet the needs of the situation. Stock-growers' associations were formed, at first for mutual protection, but later to work out rules for users of the range that actually had the effect of law. Indeed, the Wyoming Stock-Growers' Association, formed in 1873, came to have more power than the territorial government.*[37]

The stock-growers' groups encouraged community roundups, regulated and recorded the use of brands, tried to limit the overstocking of range land, guarded against the spread of cattle diseases, and organized to prevent cattle rustling. In 1884,

> *the cattlemen of the further West, finding difficulties in driving their herds from Texas to Wyoming and Montana, suddenly convoked a great convention in Chicago which presented a plan for the establishment of a broad route from South to North, and resolved on the steps proper for obtaining the necessary legislation.*[38]

In order for each cattle ranger to benefit economically, such voluntary cooperation was the most effective strategy.

The last quarter of the nineteenth century saw the rise of secret fraternities. Many developed out of the old concept of the mutual benefit association, providing illness and death benefits and caring for deceased members' families. The fraternities also combated urban anonymity and met the need for social outlets for men. These volunteer groups had elaborate secret rituals and often gave themselves medieval names. The period of 1880 to 1900 was the heyday of such fraternities, who could boast of a combined membership exceeding 6 million men. By 1890, over 124 secret fraternities had been developed; by 1901, an additional 366 societies had been formed.[39]

> *America possessed more secret societies and a larger number of "joiners" than all other nations. The "big four" were the Odd Fellows, the Freemasons, the Knights of Pythias, and the Ancient Order of United Workmen which collectively embraced more than one third of the entire lodge membership. Nor did students of religion fail to note that in all the large cities the lodges outnumbered the churches, Brooklyn and Boston each having twice and St. Louis and Chicago three times as many.*[40]

In addition to the urban fraternities, there were similar groups founded among western farmers and southern blacks.

The secret fraternities were a males-only world. But women's associations of one type or another had existed for a long time, and women had become accustomed to working together:

> *To thousands of women the club movement of the seventies opened new vistas of activity and usefulness. These women, busy during the war with innumerable tasks, could not go back to the sheltered idleness of the fifties. At first, the clubs were conservative in aim, emphasizing study and cultural pursuits, but . . . they soon annexed large provinces of civic and philanthropic activity.*[41]

Two pioneer groups were the New England Women's Club of Boston and the Sorosis of New York, both formed in 1868. As the initial literary and social programs lost their novelty, and as homemakers found new leisure because of increased household conveniences, the focus of the clubs shifted to serious matters. Child welfare, public education, divorce reform, food adulteration, and civic concerns received emphasis.

Attention was given to issues specific to women, such as equal suffrage and revolt against restrictive clothing. Clubwomen rebelled against corsets and other unhealthy garments. The 1891 Washington meeting of the National Council of Women of the United States challenged the clothing industry with some success. The diversity of problems tackled by the women's groups was determined by local needs. "In some communities the woman's club was the only organization devoted to civic improvement."[42] Also, the Woman's Christian Temperance Union had increased in volunteer strength after the Civil War. In 1873, "the country was startled to hear that in city after city squads of women were singing hymns before the saloon doors and even entering to hold prayers at the bar."[43] There were all sorts of such local outbursts, which combined to affect the progress of the temperance crusade.

Women's clubs increased in importance as the century wore on.

> *They proved to be an indispensable training school for countless women who became civic and humanitarian leaders in their respective communities. By 1889 the clubs were so numerous and influential that they became linked together in a great national system under the name of the "General Federation of Women's Clubs."*[44]

In 1890, the General Federation of Women's Clubs adopted its constitution, embracing "all women's clubs throughout the world."[45] Their scope was permanently enlarged. Between 1898 and 1914, membership swelled from fifty thousand to over 1 million women.

In 1896, the National Association of Colored Women was formed by the merger of the Colored Women's League of Washington, D.C., and the Boston-based National Federation of Afro-American Women. The National Council of Jewish Women and more localized Hebrew Benevolent Ladies Aid Societies, formed in the 1870s, also continued to expand, as did similar Catholic women's groups.

It was inevitable that the issue of female suffrage would gain importance in this era. After the Civil War, women abolitionists were dismayed to discover that the antislavery movement was deserting the female cause. The wording of the proposed Fourteenth Amendment clearly limited the right to vote to male citizens only. Feminists themselves were divided over support for the amendment, since many felt that the rights of the freed blacks were of paramount importance at that time. The American Women's Equal Rights Association, therefore, came out in favor of the Fourteenth Amendment despite the angry protests of such leaders as Elizabeth Cady Stanton and Sojourner Truth (who spoke out on behalf of black women). The passage of the amendment in 1868 split the women further, and in 1870 two opposing feminist groups were established. The National Woman Suffrage

Association, headed by Stanton, devoted itself to women's rights at all costs, while the American Woman Suffrage Association became the conservative faction. For twenty years volunteers in the two groups conducted a variety of equal suffrage activities and held annual congresses. By 1890, though differences still existed, the organizations determined to present a united front in their still unsuccessful battle for the vote and formed the combined National American Woman Suffrage Association.

The movement for equal rights was especially relevant to the plight of working-class women. At first, women attempted to join forces with the developing male unions, some of which were sympathetic to the special concerns of female laborers. But some feminist leaders, notably Susan B. Anthony, urged the formation of independent unions such as the Working Women's Association and the Protective Association for Women. These concentrated on legal aid and employment services. Early in the 1870s female as well as male workers in many trades organized themselves, but all unions succumbed to the business depression of 1873. The women's unions were not revived immediately, and for several decades female laborers worked to support male unions. Women labor leaders volunteered to join the 1877 railroad and mining strikes and enlisted in the 1890s cause of the debt-ridden midwestern farmers. By 1903, a National Women's Trade Union League was finally possible through the cooperative actions of working women, social workers, and women's clubs.

The period of the 1850s through the 1870s has been called the "metamorphic era in American history."[46] Public opinion on every critical issue from slavery to women's rights to foreign involvement was in transition. Groups representing all viewpoints sprang up, some to disappear as quickly as they arose, but others to grow stronger and effect lasting change. The major political parties underwent constant redefinition in response to the pressure of many factions. At no other time in the nation's history were there so many unofficial parties. In 1872, a convention of "Liberal Republicans" drew seven thousand delegates to Cincinnati:

> *Since the people gathered in the hall represented no definite state party organization, but were, for the most part, volunteers, the first task of the convention of "Liberal Republicans" drew 7,000 delegations.*[47]

Citizens were voluntarily involved on all levels of the local political process, from staffing voter registration boards to running for office.

However, this was also the period when political corruption in the cities became a fine art. In fact, "the period from the end of the Civil War to 1900 has been termed . . . the 'dark ages of American municipal history.'"[48] By the late 1880s, political machines, epitomized by the New York City Tammany Society, were so notorious that the British Ambassador, James Bryce, was moved to call the American city "the worst-governed political unit in the democratic world."[49] Inevitably, a reform movement grew.

> *During the 1890's dozens of citizens' committees had been organized throughout the nation for the purpose of reforming city government. Made up largely of solid middle-class businessmen, members of the professions, and assorted reforming spirits, these groups, usually non-partisan, objected not only to the professional politicians then in control but also to the nature of their operations and to the results, or lack of them, in service for the general citizenry.*[50]

The approach to reform became more permanent and scientific with the formation of municipal research bureaus and such volunteer groups as reform leagues, citizens' unions, and civic clubs. Because of the attention given to local corruption, it was not long before state and federal officials were forced into similar housecleaning. This process was aided by the Civil Service Reform Association, a volunteer group that began a vigorous campaign to convince the public of the need for screening and protecting federal job applicants. This eventually turned the tide in favor of lasting government employment reforms.

The beginning of public sanitation had occurred before the Civil War, as doctors and lay people alike began to recognize the relationship of squalid living conditions to disease. After 1865, public health became a movement all its own.

> *An awakening insight concerning those matters resulted in an aroused public consciousness. The newspapers, the church, businessmen, and the local sanitary services that were rapidly being formed educated the people in the simple laws of community sanitation. Energetic efforts were undertaken to clean up the cities and to promote wholesome surroundings . . . In truth . . . it was common-sense, down-to-earth community*

housekeeping which led the way out of the wilderness of disease and disaster. The period of great epidemics was over.[51]

In the 1860s, a committee of New York City doctors conducted a methodical and thorough sanitary survey that helped them take the control of health matters out of the hands of politicians; in 1866, a Metropolitan Board of Health was established. Eventually, this same group of medical volunteers formed the American Public Health Association, which quickly developed a broad base of support and membership among doctors and lay people.

One concern of such health organizations was the lack of public bath facilities. In 1870, two "floating" baths were built in New York City, but they were only usable in warm weather. To remedy this situation, the New York Association for Improving the Condition of the Poor ultimately opened the first truly adequate bathhouse in the United States in 1891.[52]

One of the most well-known volunteer efforts to come out of the post-Civil War era was the American Red Cross. Although the idea began in Europe while the United States was engaged in the war, the American organization was based on the work of the United States Sanitary Commission and one battleground nurse in particular. Clara Barton pushed for American participation in the Red Cross, and in 1881 she and a group of friends met to organize "the greatest venture of voluntary service in the world."[53] By 1900 the American National Red Cross had been granted a congressional charter.

From the beginning, Clara Barton felt that if the Red Cross societies were to be of use in time of war, they should train volunteers to handle natural disasters in time of peace. Thus, their first tests came in the form of devastating forest fires in Michigan (1881) and floods along the Ohio and Mississippi rivers (1882, 1884). Red Cross relief was given to victims in these and other cases. "The idea of an organized program of voluntary relief for disaster victims was the unique contribution of Clara Barton to the Red Cross movement world wide."[54]

Stimulated by the volunteer efforts of Lawrence Flick, tuberculosis was brought to public attention. After years of single-handed clinical research, he began to advocate the reporting and registration of active cases of tuberculosis. In 1892 he founded the Pennsylvania Society for the Prevention of Tuberculosis—the first American association of lay and medical persons devoted to the conquest of a specific disease.

This concern with the cure of tuberculosis produced a mass migration of health seekers into southern California during the late nineteenth century. Concurrently, many volunteer service groups were established to aid these newcomers.[55] The Christian Scientists and other religious sects located lodging for the convalescents. For example, Santa Barbara's Saint Cecilia Club supplied medical care and shelter. In addition, many individual Californians took sick, homeless migrants and stranded widows into their own homes and cared for them. The Pasadena YMCA had a male Committee on Visitation of the Sick, while many local women visited the hospitals and raised money under the auspices of the Charity Organization Society. The job could not be financed by churches alone, so other fundraising events, such as flower shows, were devised.

Of course, there were those who did not welcome these health seekers quite so enthusiastically and participated in the movement to "keep consumptives home." Their objections drew attention to the fact that there were not adequate sanatorium facilities anywhere in the country to provide local care. One good solution came in the form of the Adirondack Cottage Sanatorium, Saranac Lake, New York:

> *an institution built philanthropically by New York donors, staffed gratuitously by some of the state's most prominent physicians, and superintended voluntarily by "gentlemen residing in the Adirondack region for health."*[56]

It was an instant success. This approach was slow to be duplicated, but eventually other sanatoriums and open-air camps were established by religious and private interest groups.

Another illness receiving attention toward the end of the nineteenth century was epilepsy. As a result of the volunteer initiative of a New York lawyer and doctor, a public meeting was called in May 1898 for the purpose of discussing epilepsy openly for the first time. Seventy-five people attended, and before the meeting ended they had organized the National Association for the Study of Epilepsy and the Care and Treatment of the Epileptic.[57] At its height it involved some 270 volunteer members who visited and reported on the newly-opened epilepsy colonies around the country. It was the forerunner of the modern epilepsy organizations.

The latter part of the nineteenth century brought renewed attention to all aspects of poverty and human misery. Much of this concern was voiced by middle-class reformers and was primarily focused on urban rather than rural problems. Early efforts were largely volunteer, although increasingly the reformers looked to government intervention as the only means of attaining their ends.

Contributing to the social justice movement was the doctrine of the "social gospel" as introduced by several forward-looking clergy. They stressed the importance of a good environment and of making life more bearable in this world rather than simply anticipating future rewards in the hereafter. The social gospel gained most of its popularity in the cities, where the institutionalized churches began to develop many philanthropic enterprises—organized charities, paid welfare workers, athletic clubs, study classes, forums, social halls, and hospitals:

> *The failure of city governments and private organizations to perform these services threw them on the shoulders of men of God and goodwill. Later, when city governments entered more actively into welfare services and when other private organizations took up the work, the importance of the churches in social work declined. But the social gospel . . . colored the entire reform movement, lending it the moral urgency which was to be so characteristic of progressivism.*[58]

One result of the work of the institutionalized churches was the founding of settlement houses. At least three settlement houses had been established before 1890, supported by private funds. Organized and administered by educated women, and staffed by a volunteer corps of both sexes, the settlement house was defined as

> *a colony of members of the upper classes, formed in a poor neighborhood, with the double purpose of getting to know the local conditions of life from personal observation and of helping where help is needed.*[59]

The houses organized clubs and classes, operated day nurseries and diet kitchens, encouraged talent in the arts, and agitated for statutes prohibiting or regulating prostitution, horse racing, gambling, and the mistreatment of prisoners, children, and animals. In fact, *many of the roots of today's multitudinous social welfare organizations go back to adventurous middle-class women like Jane Addams, Florence Kelley, and Lillian Wald, who broke precedent and braved the scorn of their contemporaries by leaving their comfortable homes to live and work in the slums of large cities.*[60]

By 1900, there were over one hundred settlements, and ten years later there were more than four hundred. As their work and influence spread, they became involved with all economic classes, with the defense of labor unions, and with the needs of neighborhood ethnic groups. The peak of their influence probably came during the first decade of the twentieth century. But in the long run, the kind of volunteer effort exemplified by the settlements proved inadequate to meet the ever-increasing demand for a greater variety of social services.

Philanthropy was undergoing change. By the latter part of the nineteenth century, philanthropic giving had reached monumental proportions, but it was uncoordinated, competitive, and often impulsive. Many a rich person was taught that it was a disgrace to die with one's wealth intact, and therefore gave help to everyone who applied—never investigating the claims of poverty. Even the poor were volunteering to help others in distress. One author of this period stated:

Thousands of dollars are given away in the tenement districts every year by the inhabitants of the tenements, of which no charitable society makes a record . . . The children of our City Mission School, who come from the tenement houses, contribute every Thanksgiving-Day from $80 to $100 for the poor in our immediate neighborhood.[61]

Eventually this unsystematic situation led to more scientific methods of dispensing charity, and the "charity organization" came into being. Patterned after an English example, the first American Charity Organization Society was established in Buffalo in 1877. By 1893, there were almost one hundred such organizations throughout the cities of America.

Naturally these societies began their work as a crusade against indiscriminate charity. They brought together, as far as practicable, all the benevolent agencies which were at work in a given community, they introduced the scientific and system-

atic visitation of the poor, they sought out and exposed the iniquitous frauds which had been fostered by neglect, and in various ways decreased the growing volume of pauperism.[62]

With larger funds at their disposal, these societies were able to maintain elaborate filing systems under which all dependent persons were catalogued. Furthermore, they were able to recruit and train "friendly visitors" to investigate applications for aid and to separate the "worthy and upright poor" from the "willing paupers" and "voluntary dependents." Most friendly visitors were unpaid.

Eventually the role of the friendly visitor evolved into the new profession of social work, as attempts were made to codify techniques of investigation and to understand the causes of poverty. As early as 1892, the New York Charity Organization Society had established an experimental class for friendly visitors. The following year, in response to the demands for a "Training School in Applied Philanthropy," many societies began to accept the responsibility of training their workers. This step toward professionalization also meant a shift toward paid workers in addition to trained volunteers—a professional corps of reformers able to judge the needs of the poor and raise supporting funds in a systematic way. There were many who opposed the coming of paid workers, clinging to the traditional altruism of volunteered charity:

A willingness to work for nothing, it was considered, was the hallmark of a sincere charity worker . . . But despite this feeling against the paid worker, it was becoming increasingly obvious that in many communities there were not enough well-to-do and leisured folk who were able to give their time to friendly visiting, and so, as in England, volunteers retreated to advisory and fund-raising committees, and actual casework was left in the hands of paid, trained agents.[63]

So it was that scientific philanthropy evolved and with it the now common institution known as the foundation. Coming as they did, as part of the institutionalization and more effective administration of social reform, the foundations demonstrated that a social use could be found for the vast surplus of wealth accumulated by industrialists, financiers, and speculators. Business executives demanded efficiency and accountability from charity; foundations provided both while still allowing the donor a degree of personal involvement in meeting society's needs:

The private foundation is also an attempt to project the theory of individualism into the social sphere: those who accumulated large fortunes wished also to determine how this wealth was to be redistributed and what social effects it was intended to bring about. The foundation is, therefore, a symbol of individualism.[64]

Cooperative fundraising was conducted by the YMCA and the Jewish Federation. In 1887, the first successful plan for area-wide federated fundraising was begun in Denver as the Charity Organization Society. Under the leadership of four male clergy of different faiths and local female activist Frances Wisebar Jacobs, teams of volunteers solicited people in various lines of business and other citizens to raise a set sum. In 1888 the Society raised $21,700 for twenty-two Denver charities. This effort was the forerunner of the present-day United Way of America.[65]

A vast variety of voluntary organizations sprang up to attend to all types of social problems. The Salvation Army, a direct manifestation of the social gospel doctrine, was actively bringing evangelism into the homes of the poor. By the 1890s, however, it became apparent that preaching the gospel was not enough, and the Salvation Army's funds and volunteer energy were increasingly directed toward the maintenance of lodging houses, food depots, rescue homes, and employment agencies.

The National Association of the Deaf was founded in 1880 as a completely voluntary organization, remaining so until 1949. Supported by memberships and contributions, it sought to assist deaf people by interpreting for them, running clubs, and improving educational and other services for deaf people in local communities.

The Needlework Guild of Philadelphia was established in 1885, patterned on the English example. Members were asked to contribute household linens and practical garments for infants, children, and adults, "made plainly and of strong materials."[66] During that first year, the volunteers collected 921 articles for distribution to the needy. The Guild idea spread rapidly, and by 1896 there were 306 branches within a national organization. Though concerned primarily with local needs, members also gave aid to disaster and overseas relief.

The Volunteers of America was conceived by Ballington and Maud Booth in New York's Bowery section in 1896. The group began to organize a network of helpers, enlisting the advice and aid of such prominent figures of the day as Theodore Roosevelt, John Wanamaker, Bishop Manning, and Rabbi Stephen Wise. Slowly this national, religious, social welfare organization took shape. Among its activities were and still are: maternity and adoption services; aid to workers with disabilities and to prisoners and their families; day care centers; disaster relief services and emergency shelters; homes and clubs for the aging; girl's residences; and youth programs.

During the 1860s and 1870s, Henry Bergh had carried on his fight against cruelty to animals—specifically misuse of horses, cock fights, inhumane killing of cattle, and the like. In 1873, the Society for the Prevention of Cruelty to Animals was formed, and SPCA volunteers distributed millions of pamphlets throughout the country to spread word of their cause. This movement led directly to one that fought the abuse of children. In 1874, a beaten child was brought to court by the SPCA as an animal in need of protection; this dramatic act drove concerned citizens into action.[67] The first Society for the Prevention of Cruelty to Children was established in New York in 1875, beginning the crusade for the enforcement of state laws protecting children from abuse and neglect.

Another type of aid for children came in the form of day nurseries, which began to appear in the 1800s. Reform groups such as the Children's Aid Society and the National Conference of Charities and Correction searched for ways in which to provide good child care. They were aided by a number of philanthropically inclined women.

> *The day nursery women were usually married, the wives of wealthy men, with the leisure time to attend board meetings, to supervise the matron and staff of the day nursery, to plan fundraising events like balls, fairs, and concerts, and to cajole their peers into donating food, bedding and toys. At a time when the upper and upper-middle classes were the chief dispensers of charity . . . it seemed only natural that these women, mothers themselves, felt some special calling to deal with the children of the poor.*[68]

Day nurseries were usually located in large cities, in the neighborhood of industries employing a large number of women. Sometimes the nurseries were operated as part of settlement houses or churches, while others were adjuncts of family welfare agencies. Very few were publicly supported; instead, most charged a nominal fee based on the mother's ability to pay. Most were staffed, at least in part, by volunteers.[69]

Day nurseries offered a broad range of services, including employment, training, and child care. They kept the names of mothers looking for domestic work and matched them to requests for service from upper-class families. Since many mothers were not adequately skilled, they were trained by working in the nursery under the supervision of the matron or by one of the women on the board of managers who did the training in her own home. The day nursery volunteers could be criticized for the tendency to impose their own values on the poor, but "it is nonetheless remarkable that, given their limited class interests and narrow experience, these women managed to create the American day nursery."[70]

Also in this period concern grew over the separation of juvenile justice from the adult court process. Volunteers began to crusade for the formation of juvenile courts. In Illinois, when the Cook County Woman's Club approached a lobbyist with the plan to hire his services on behalf of the juvenile court cause, he counseled them instead to rely on the power of their volunteer numbers. Parent-teacher associations were also involved in the struggle. In 1899 both Chicago and Denver established juvenile courts, staffed almost totally by volunteers until 1925.[71] One other type of social welfare volunteering was aid to Indians, though the first schools and missions established on behalf of the Indians made little attempt to reconcile tradition with new lifestyles. Hostilities between Indians and white settlers increased between 1862 and 1877, causing the federal government to respond with troops and hard-line legislation. Popular opinion supported the takeover of Indian lands and the isolation of tribes onto reservations. Some whites, however, were moved by the plight of Native Americans and formed volunteer organizations for relief and advocacy. The Indian Rights Association was established in 1882, and the same decade saw several annual Lake Mohonk Conferences of Friends of the Indians. In addition, the Women's National Indian Association had chapters throughout the country. Together, these organizations formed a powerful legislative lobby and watchdog on behalf of Indians. Individuals also acted voluntarily to better the Indians' situation:

> *Better planned schooling began when young Lieutenant Pratt, after the revolt of the southern Plains Indians in 1874, was told to pick up some Cheyenne and Kiowa captives for confinement at Fort Marion, Florida. Pratt decided to make the experience worthwhile to the young warriors, so he trained them industrially. Under this stimulating attention the Indians blossomed and wanted more education. From this*

start grew the Indian school at Carlisle, Pennsylvania, a fort lent by the army and serving, in 1900, 1200 pupils from seventy-nine tribes.[72]

Following this example, government appropriations were made for Indian education, and boarding schools were instituted on most reservations. At first they were run by missionaries on contract, then gradually government employees were substituted. An unpaid Board of Indian Commissioners was named by the government to be responsible for inspecting the reservations and checking on contractors. Toward the end of the nineteenth century, most doctors and trading-post staff were put on the civil service payroll, thus replacing the original volunteer helpers.

Self-help among reservation Indians was a way of life. "The bands tended to be egalitarian . . . Band members shared food and assisted each other as they might."[73] Generally there was little authoritarian leadership to galvanize either protest or action. Group discussion and consensus governed the tribes. While tribe members were totally committed to each other, their sense of cooperation did not extend to tribes of other Indian nations. Occasional joint actions were take against enemy whites, but it would not be until well into the twentieth century that Indians would recognize and utilize their racial unity.

Mexican-Americans also formed mutual aid organizations, such as the 1894 Alianza Hispano Americana. As with other immigrant groups before them, Chicanos volunteered to help one another learn English, find jobs, and still preserve their Mexican cultural ties.

As early as 1878, Chinese immigrants formed an organization called the Six Companies to represent them both to the American government and in communication with the emperor in China. While San Francisco became the cultural center of Chinese-American life, similar organizations were established wherever Chinese immigrants settled. While under the umbrella of the Chinese Consolidated Benevolent Association, these local volunteer groups enjoyed great autonomy. The groups attempted to maintain Chinese language, ethnicity, and values while also fighting discrimination. These were sometimes conflicting goals.[74]

The welfare of people in foreign nations grew as a concern of many Americans.

During the Civil War the ordinary charitable and missionary activities [to those abroad] were not only kept up; they actually expanded . . . Both during and after the war the adminis-

tration of charity also shifted increasingly from local groups to national organizations. In view of the scope of benevolence on the home front the wonder is that distress in foreign lands aroused the interest and sympathy of so many American donors.[75]

Examples of voluntary foreign relief efforts were numerous. Supplies and funds were collected and sent to aid the French during their cotton famine, and the exploited English textile workers were assisted through the American International Relief Committee for Suffering Operatives of Great Britain. The victims of the Franco-Prussian War were also aided with funds and supplies. Among the most well-known activities were campaigns to help the victims of the famines in Ireland. New York and other cities with large Irish-American populations established effective relief funds. Donations were augmented with benefits, theatricals, concerts, boxing matches, and bicycle tournaments.

At the Stock Exchanges public auctions of donated poultry, Irish greyhounds, and other items swelled the treasury. Approximately $1000 came in from a sale of paintings donated by American artists. Mayo's Olympic Theater contributed 10% of gross receipts from each evening performance over a considerable period. Managers of theaters arranged special benefit performances on St. Patrick's Day.[76]

During the Civil War, the lack of government contributions to overseas relief efforts was understandable. But even in the years after the war, the government assumed no responsibility. Moreover, not all Americans favored foreign aid. Anti-foreign groups gained popularity, merging in 1887 to form the highly intolerant American Protective Association.

Early foreign aid efforts were organized by Americans with strong personal and ethnic ties to the countries in need. As travel abroad began to increase in the 1860s, Americans in general gained a greater understanding of European affairs. Both sides benefited:

The increased travel of Americans . . . was a natural accompaniment to our growing overseas interests, manifested in economic and naval expansion, the spread of foreign missions, and our deepening diplomatic involvement. American

> *tourists, students, technicians, explorers and humanitarians probably contributed more to the foreigner's image of the United States than did our diplomats. Contact with the outer world, in turn, changed American attitudes.*[77]

Americans not only directed charitable efforts overseas but met needs in neighboring Canada, too. In times of disaster, a variety of independent volunteer groups organized Canadian relief programs.[78]

The American missionary movement grew impressively after the Civil War. Missionaries contributed far more than evangelical fervor. They made diplomatic and humanitarian gains and opened up previously uncontacted areas to new commerce. Missions were developed through the 1880s and 1890s in Latin America, the Middle East, Africa, Hawaii, and the Far East.

> *The missions were also vital in the civilizing process—in translating material, in organizing schools and educational systems, and in developing science and art. Many of the American dollars earned in the business expansion of the age were channeled into institutions sponsored by a missionary board.*[79]

All in all, by the turn of the century the United States had determined a new adult role for itself as a young nation in a changing world.

> *The 1890s brought a subtle sense of change, a feeling that national unity was at last a reality . . . Many Americans sought a larger "civilizing" mission beyond material success to sustain national vitality.*[80]

A significant educational renaissance began in the 1870s. For the first time, public high schools outnumbered private academies, though universal free education was still more of an idea than a reality.

The Chautauqua Movement of adult education began in 1874 as a summer enrichment program for Sunday school teachers. It then enlarged to become the Literary and Scientific Circle, with a four-year study program. By 1892, one hundred thousand students were enrolled, half of them between the ages of thirty and forty.[81] This program led to other similar self-improvement movements, especially in

Michigan and Iowa: "Outdoor assemblies of one or two weeks' duration were conducted in various localities until about seventy were in operation at the close of the century, representing nearly every state in the Union."[82] In winter, lectures and "star courses" were offered—descendants of the earlier lyceum movement.

A direct result of this interest in adult education was a growing demand for well-run public libraries. In 1876, the American Library Association was formed in Philadelphia by librarians who sought to foster the establishment of free libraries. The Association's volunteer members developed the cataloguing and circulation systems that are still in use today and solicited philanthropic funds to supplement the tax dollars needed to build new libraries. Progress was slow but steady, and by 1900, over nine thousand libraries with more than three hundred books each were established throughout the country.[83]

Prior to 1870, museums were largely devoted to historical collections preserved by lyceums, academies, and various volunteer societies. Such collections usually became the responsibility of local libraries. Most art collecting was done by wealthy individuals; the paintings and sculpture were put on public display only at the owner's discretion. In 1870, however, both Boston and New York opened art museums and began the tradition of public ownership of art and artifacts. Volunteer donors, trustees, and docents were instrumental in the founding and management of these and subsequent museums.

Various other educational reforms took place during this period. The kindergarten movement was active in the 1860s and 1870s relying heavily on philanthropic societies for support. In 1897, the National Congress of Mothers was formed to represent the interests of school-age children; this organization later became the Parent-Teacher Association, and fathers were then admitted as well.

Higher education also underwent a transformation, largely due to a small volunteer group of university presidents who sought to revise the American system of higher education so that it would meet the needs of a more complex society. The presidents' individual and collective efforts helped to bring about changes in curriculum and the establishment of state-supported universities, the elective system, technical and professional schools, graduate education, coeducation, and education for blacks. Laboratories, instruments of precision, libraries, museums, and other necessary tools of research were secured through donations and philanthropic gifts. Furthermore, the leading scholars formed nationwide associations in all branches of research; for example, the American Chemical Society (1876); the American

Ornithologists' Union (1883); the American Catholic Historical Association (1884); the American Climatological Society (1884); the Association of Economic Entomologists (1890); the American Psychological Association (1892); and so on.[84] Never before had America witnessed such a banding together for the advancement of knowledge.

In 1882, some of the first college-educated women joined forces to advocate their position that, contrary to popular belief, schooling was not harmful to young females. They supported other women who sought higher education and fought to make colleges coeducational. This volunteer group later became the American Association of University Women.

Recreation was becoming more spectator-oriented and commercialized. A volunteer-led "play-movement" that sought to bring about a reorganization of social activities was launched after the Civil War. The result was a plethora of model playgrounds, recreation centers, and community centers; community music and drama groups; and municipal theaters, bands and orchestras.

Recreation increasingly found its way into the institutional church, as well. Although Puritan traditions still dictated disapproval of many of the new urban entertainments, the social gospel doctrine forced churches to become more realistic:

> *Provision was made in the new institutional or socialized churches of the 1880's and 1890's for libraries, gymnasiums, and assemblies; for games, concerts, and amusements . . . The YMCA had already become a leader in the promotion of sports . . . and other religious organizations vied with the churches themselves in providing social activities of all kinds. It was the era of sociables, fairs, suppers, and strawberry festivals.*[85]

These voluntary activities had the secondary function of fundraising. Though some frowned upon such church-sponsored recreation, it almost certainly contributed to the dramatic increase in church membership during this period.

The first Boys' Clubs were started in the late 1860s when organizations in various New England and New York communities opened their doors to give local boys a place to play, safely and out of trouble. The early volunteer staff consisted of affluent, concerned citizens, and interested friends contributed chairs, tables, and games. By 1906, some fifty clubs had banded together to form the national Boys' Clubs of America. At the same time, track and field events were promoted with the widespread organization of amateur clubs. Gymnastic games were sponsored by the German Turnverein (gymnastic society) and the YMCA. Further, the cause of bicycle riding was advanced as the League of American Wheelmen carried on a vigorous campaign for better roads, which finally bore fruit in the 1890s.[86]

Concern over the lack of adequate recreation facilities for city children brought forth two major developments during the late 1800s. The first was the idea of a "country week" or "fresh-air fund," begun in 1877 by a pastor of a small church in Sherman, Pennsylvania. Under his direction, parishioners opened their homes to children from New York City for two weeks, for which the hosts received no monetary compensation. The program expanded quickly through many towns in several states. Money was always forthcoming in the way of voluntary contributions, and food and facilities were also donated. Many city missionaries, physicians, and clergy volunteered to solicit these temporary homes for the children; such recruiters were usually reimbursed only for their travel costs. In addition, various transportation companies willingly made large reductions in their fares to enable the Fresh-Air Fund to take children on one-day excursions out of the city.[87]

The second development in the area of recreation for urban children involved the creation of "sand gardens." In 1885, a Boston society tried the experiment of setting aside specific areas in which children could play, consisting mainly of sandboxes. During the first years, there would have been no supervision for these areas had not the women living in the respective neighborhoods volunteered to watch the groups of children. The success of the undertaking led eventually to more public parks and playgrounds, supported by philanthropists and maintained by local residents.

Another marked reaction to the industrial, urban lifestyle was the development of a serious interest in camping and outdoor life. This desire among individuals and groups to return to nature resulted in the establishment of organized camping. Camping for children began as part of a Connecticut private boys' school curriculum, and later a physician established a camp in Pennsylvania to improve the health of "weakly" boys.[88] Between 1881 and 1900, organized camping gained momentum as many more camps were founded by YMCAs, settlement houses, and private individuals. However, there were no camps especially for girls until 1902, although a few early camps were coed.

A natural counterpart to this growing interest in the great outdoors was the conservation movement. In 1875, a small group of horticulturists and other interested citizens formed the American Forestry Association in Chicago. This was the first organized effort to protect the forest of the United States from fire and wasteful cutting and to promote the propagation and planting of new trees. Industrial exploitation of the nation's forests caused some citizens to fear the possibility of timber shortages. These conservationists were unable to enlist the support of federal executives or members of Congress and so directed their volunteer energies toward public education. They wrote and spoke about the need for reforestation and for community beautification. Locally, thousands of communities took up the custom of Arbor Day, with tree-planting ceremonies and speeches. In Washington and Oregon, mountaineering clubs sponsored campaigns for the preservation of the watershed areas that served their communities. In Colorado, petitions from civic, professional, and business organizations helped secure the establishment of the first federal land reserves in 1891 and 1892.

In 1892, the writer John Muir founded the Sierra Club, whose volunteers sought to preserve California's wilderness areas. As they battled to save the Yosemite park lands, the Club discovered there were limits on what local action could achieve. Eventually it was necessary to make conservation a national political issue. Laws were needed to protect woodlands, and the American Forestry Association continued to pressure Congress and the state legislatures. In 1896, a volunteer National Forest Commission was formed and given a small amount of money from Congress for public education campaigns. At the same time, the Audubon Society and various rifle and sport associations became actively concerned with the conservation of wildlife. Colleges and universities were urged to offer technical education in forestry to prepare students for professional careers in this field. Cornell and Yale were the first to do so, around the turn of the century.

In these ways, the citizens of America became defendants of the land, voluntarily putting forth their energy and time in order to ensure that valuable resources were not lost. Much conservation activity was large scale and national. However, one aspect of the movement was aimed at local beautification and was carried on predominantly by children. Here is how a visiting Frenchman described it:

> *Americans start frankly with the proposition that cleanliness is not to be expected from grown-up people in general, and they have hit upon the idea of utilizing the spirit of emulation among children, by putting them in a forefront of a crusade against dirt.*[89]

By 1899 there were forty-seven Children's Leagues, and by 1901 the number had doubled. Children were instructed by health committees, and municipal councils instituted "cleaning days."

> *Americans who used to spit freely, have dropped the habit . . . In addition to all the leagues for municipal improvement . . . there are more than 700 associations of women of women for city beautifying all over the country. If the municipal government objects, they get another elected instead. They . . . see that workshops and public places are decorated with flowers. They handle the broom themselves, as do the children, and tell them to show their parents how to use the implement. They remind the tradesmen that a well-kept town means money in its inhabitants' pockets.*[90]

To some, improving society meant ensuring law and order. Dissatisfied with the job being done by local law enforcement officials, citizens took matters into their own hands. The southern Klans were not the first vigilante group to go beyond the law, and certainly not the last.

> *Another extralegal movement in the interest of community order involved the "White Caps" who first appeared in 1887 in Indiana as violent local enforcers of morality and then quickly sprang up all over the country before beginning to wane after the turn of the century.*[91]

Vigilante groups during this period attracted lawyers and others who acted against what was to them an unsatisfactory American legal system. Desire for law and order led to impatience with the slow process of American justice and a shift toward speedier repression of crime. After the Civil War, private detective agencies and private police flourished. Vigilantes justified their actions by claiming popular sovereignty—the democratic right of the people to monitor and control their local communities. Furthermore, lynch-law proponents proudly stressed that their volunteer services were at no expense to the taxpayer—an especially effective argument in light of the cost to small towns of maintaining courts, jails, and related services.

Up until the 1890s, involvement in the vigilante groups was considered something of which to be proud and was even romanticized in novels of the day. One reason for such approval was that the lynch groups were regulators of morality. The White Caps, for example, whipped such offenders as drunkards, shiftless persons, and wife beaters, thereby operating "in the realm of human behavior where the authority of the law was either not clear or nonexistent."[92] But the problem was that vigilantes became more and more violent, ultimately executing approximately six thousand victims. Eventually, however, vigilantism led to movements to update and streamline the judicial process, as well as to campaigns to legalize castration and whipping as sentences. In the 1880s several states did reinstate whipping, in response to citizens' demands.

The industrial growth and social tension in the urban areas soon involved the federal army in policing strikes. But this surveillance of fellow citizens was very unpopular among the volunteer soldiers and contributed to the steady weakening of the militias. In 1877 a national meeting of organized militia officers planned to devise a way to represent the volunteer soldiers' interests to state and federal government and to the public. The result was the National Guard Association.[93] Although the National Guard was vocal, Congress was pressured by the War Department's professional officers to expand the regular army and place the volunteer forces under its control. A compromise was finally reached:

> *The Regular army would be supplemented by means of a Presidential call for volunteers for federal service, but any militia organization which volunteered in a body would be accepted as a unit . . . Not more than one regular officer could be appointed to any volunteer regiment, and efficiency boards composed of volunteers, not Regulars, would review the capacity of the volunteer officers.*[94]

This plan appeared to give the regular officers their desired federal army but built upon the existing volunteer state militia. At the same time Congress authorized special units such as volunteer engineers and volunteer medical corps of soldiers immune to tropical diseases.[95]

The next test of the American military forces came with the short but volatile 1898 Spanish-American War. The National Guard was eager to serve in this war. They were sworn in as individuals to circumvent the old constitutional provision limiting militias to domestic matters. The Cuban expeditionary forces included 7,743 volunteers, among whom the Rough Riders were conspicuously heroic. Volunteers were also instrumental in the Philippine engagements.

When the Spanish-American War was proclaimed, thousands came forward immediately. These volunteers showed remarkable devotion to their mission:

> *The volunteers were not concerned about the financial matters involved. Many paid their own railway fares to the places of enlistment and bore the greatest portion of their immediate expenses. One volunteer, when questioned about the scant pay he received in exchange for his services, replied, "we did not enlist for money, but to fight for our country."*[96]

One notable group was the Cowboy Volunteers, a cavalry troop from the frontier states. "In a period of nine months the regiments were organized, fulfilled their mission, and passed into oblivion."[97]

Volunteering to fight was not the only way citizens tried to help. In Buffalo, Wyoming, one hundred townspeople each donated between one and five hundred pounds of flour, plus free transportation of it to the railroad. The flour was meant for the starving Cubans. As in the Civil War, trainloads of soldiers were met at depots all along the way to Florida by women with food, coffee, and words of cheer. Women conducted countless assistance projects and formed Volunteer Aid Societies. They sewed items ranging from abdominal protectors to needle cases. In several states and territories, women sewed troop flags. Further:

> *A bill had been introduced in the Senate which provided for matrons to be sent with the volunteer army—"women to mend and wash clothing and see to the sanitary conditions of the men"—but it did not materialize.*[98]

The Spanish-American War provided the American Red Cross with its first war-related victims.

From New York to San Francisco Red Cross women were creating the substance if not the formal organization of the subsequent Gray Ladies, Recreation Services, and Canteen Corps, among others, by entertaining embarking troops and establishing rest and recreation tents.[99]

Meanwhile, the 76-year-old Clara Barton was in Cuba providing nursing care, medical supplies, food, and other necessities for civilians and the military forces. The war made the American Red Cross a truly national effort, and its members and nurses received much praise.

Some women, however, preferred a more active role in the actual fighting:

In Nebraska, enthusiastic women under the leadership of Miss "Girlie" Adams organized a complete cavalry of one hundred, every member of which was a "crackshot and excellent horsewoman," and notified the Governor that they were prepared to fight . . . In Denver, Mrs. Shute of the State Horticultural Society informed the Governor that 200 women were ready to form a cavalry. The news that a female brigade would, in all probability, not be a reality did not dim the ardor of some members of the fair sex. If they could not serve, their horses could.[100]

The women therefore donated their mounts to the male soldiers.

The Spanish-American War gave new impetus to the peace movements that had been present since colonial days. Volunteer peace organizations founded earlier now grew in number and membership. Among the active groups were the Universal Peace Union (1866), the Peace Association of the Friends (1869), the National Arbitration League (1881), the Christian Arbitration and Peace Society (1886), and the Peace Department of the Woman's Christian Temperance Union (1887). As is evident from these names, some peace groups advocated arbitration as an approach to settling international disputes. They were quite vocal, but it would not be until the first decade of the new century that the scattered local groups would become a real movement, led by the old American Peace Society.

Also at this time anti-imperialism began in Boston with the New England Anti-Imperialist League.

Most of the men who stepped forward to organize the anti-imperialism movement . . . had been ardent supporters of the

> *anti-slavery struggle and the Union cause in the years before . . . When they saw the U.S., so recently made secure by military victory over black slavery at home, pushed into a foreign war to enslave another colored people, they felt the nation, and themselves betrayed.*[101]

The movement was galvanized by the Battle of Manila Bay and by the McKinley administration's intent to annex the Philippines. This attitude of colonialism and complete disregard of the will of the Philippine people gave the anti-imperialists grounds for common action. League members included reformers, intellectuals, business and industrial group members, and some laborers. This volunteer movement spread west, and by 1889 the Midwest had its own anti-imperialist headquarters in Chicago. But ultimately the anti-imperialism leagues had little impact on the course of the war.

The dissent over the war personally affected the retuning soldiers. Although the fighting lasted only three and a half months, the men came home to

> *a country battered by homefront politicians debating the fate of what the men had conquered and even derogating the very real sacrifices they had made. The veterans of that era had no organization to plead their case before the government whose policies they had fought to support. The North's Grand Army of the Republic had no place for them, nor did the South's United Confederate Veterans.*[102]

Just as the Civil War veterans had formed these self-help organizations, the Spanish War veterans developed the forerunners of the Veterans of Foreign Wars. In 1899 they established an eastern and a western group, which would merge in 1914 to become the VFW.

The last thirty-five years of the nineteenth century bridged the gap between the frontier tradition of America and the modern demands of an industrialized nation. Volunteers played an active role in this transition with their contributions to fields as diverse as labor and conservation, education and foreign aid. Furthermore, the struggle to end slavery had launched an irreversible desire for the civil rights of blacks, women, Indians—all Americans who had been denied full citizenship.

The period was disorganized but critical, culminating in the frenzied activity of the Spanish-American War. With the war's end, the United States was catapulted into the twentieth century.

Endnotes for Chapter 4

1. Claude Gernode Bowers, *The Tragic Era* (Cambridge, MA: The Riverside Press, 1929), 54.
2. James E. Sefton, *The United States Army and Reconstruction, 1865–1877* (Baton Rouge: Louisiana State University Press, 1967), 53.
3. Ibid., 131.
4. Russell F. Weigley, *History of the United States Army* (New York: Macmillan, 1967), 263.
5. Carl Russell Fish, *The Rise of the Common Man, 1830–1850.* vol. 6, *A History of American Life in Twelve Volumes,* eds. Arthur M. Schlesinger and Dixon Ryan Fox (New York: Macmillan, 1943), 225.
6. Hodding Carter, *The Angry Scar* (Garden City, NY: Doubleday, 1959), 186.
7. Ibid.
8. John D. Hicks, *The American Nation: A History of the United States From 1865 to the Present* (Cambridge, MA: The Riverside Press, 1941), 34.
9. Bowers, *Tragic Era,* 307.
10. Ibid.
11. Ibid., 308.
12. Col. Winfield Jones, *Knights of the Ku Klux Klan* (n.p., n.d.), 28.
13. Ibid., 38–9.
14. William L. Barney, *Flawed Victory: A New Perspective on the Civil War* (New York: Praeger, 1975), 188.
15. Jones, *Knights,* 40.
16. David Brody, "The Expansion of the American Labor Movement: Institutional Sources of Stimulus and Restraint," in Stephen E. Ambrose, ed., *Institutions in Modern America* (Baltimore, MD: The Johns Hopkins Press, 1967), 12.
17. Robert Selph Henry, *This Fascinating Railroad Business* (Indianapolis: Bobbs-Merrill, 1942), 399.
18. Richard F. Lingenfelter, *The Hardrock Miners* (Berkeley: University of California Press, 1974), 11–2.
19. Ibid., 53.
20. Edward A. Wieck, *The American Miners' Association* (New York: Russell Sage Foundation, 1940), 158.
21. Harriet L. Herring, *Welfare Work in Mill Villages* (Chapel Hill: The University of North Carolina Press, 1929), 65.
22. Agnes M. Larson, *History of the White Pine Industry in Minnesota* (Minneapolis: University of Minneapolis Press, 1949), 85.
23. Joseph Henry Foth, *Trade Associations* (New York: Ronald Press, 1930), 3.
24. Ibid., 8.
25. Joseph F. Bradley, *The Role of Trade Associations and Professional Business Societies* (University Park: Pennsylvania State University Press, 1965), 20–2, 42.

26. Ibid., 22.

27. Henry Van Dyke, *The Spirit of America* (New York: Macmillan, 1910), 178.

28. Descriptive brochure of the National Fire Protection Association (Boston: n.d.), 1.

29. Theodore Saloutos, *Farmer Movements in the South, 1865–1933,* vol. 64, *University of California Publications in History,* ed. Theodore Saloutos (Berkeley: University of California Press, 1960), 33.

30. Allan Nevins, *The Emergence of Modern America, 1865–1878,* vol. 8, *A History of American Life in Twelve Volumes,* eds. Arthur M. Schlesinger and Dixon Ryan Fox (New York: Macmillan, 1927), 170–1.

31. Saloutos, *Farmer Movements,* 35.

32. Ibid., 40.

33. Hicks, *American Nation,* 245.

34. Saloutos, *Farmer Movements,* 68.

35. Ida M. Tarbell, *The Nationalizing of Business, 1878–1898,* vol. 9, *A History of American Life in Twelve Volumes,* eds. Arthur M. Schlesinger and Dixon Ryan Fox (New York: Macmillan, 1936), 145.

36. Extension Service, U.S. Department of Agriculture, *Early Development of 4-H* (Washington, D.C.: Government Printing Office, n.d.), 1.

37. Hicks, *American Nation,* 136.

38. James Bryce, *The American Commonwealth* (New York: Macmillan, 1914), 2: 281–2.

39. Arthur M. Schlesinger, *The Rise of the City, 1878–1898,* vol. 10, *A History of American Life in Twelve Volumes,* eds. Arthur M. Schlesinger and Dixon Ryan Fox (New York: Macmillan, 1933), 288–9.

40. Ibid., 290.

41. Nevins, *Emergence,* 342–3.

42. Harold Underwood Faulkner, *The Quest for Social Justice, 1898–1914,* vol. 11, *A History of American Life in Twelve Volumes,* eds. Arthur M. Schlesinger and Dixon Ryan Fox (New York: Macmillan, 1931), 171.

43. Nevins, *Emergence,* 338.

44. Schlesinger, *Rise of the City,* 144.

45. Anne David, *Help Yourself by Helping Others: A Guide to Volunteer Services* (New York: Simon and Schuster, Cornerstone Library, 1970), 119.

46. Norma L. Peterson, *Freedom and Franchise* (Columbia: University of Missouri Press, 1965), preface.

47. Ibid., 214.

48. Harold F. Alderfer, *American Local Government and Administration* (New York: Macmillan, 1956), 72.

49. George E. Mowry, *The Progressive Era, 1900–1920: The Reform Persuasion,* no. 212, American Historical Association pamphlets (Washington, DC: AHA, 1958, reprinted 1972), 14.

50. Ibid.

51. Wilson G. Smillie, *Public Health, Its Promise for the Future* (New York: Macmillan, 1955), 129.

52. J. J. Cosgrove, *History of Sanitation* (Pittsburgh: Standard Sanitary Manufacturing Company, 1909), 122.

53. Charles Hurd, *The Compact History of the American Red Cross* (New York: Hawthorn Books, 1959), 41.

54. Descriptive material of the American National Red Cross (Washington, D.C.: n.d.).

55. John E. Baur, *The Health Seekers of Southern California, 1870–1900* (San Marino, CA: The Huntington Library, 1959), 94–8.

56. Billy Mac Jones, *Health-Seekers in the Southwest, 1817–1900* (Norman: University of Oklahoma Press, 1967), 195.

57. *History of the Epilepsy Movement in the United States* (Washington, DC: Epilepsy Foundation of America, 1974), 3.

58. Harold U. Faulkner, *Politics, Reform and Expansion, 1890–1900* (New York: Harper and Brothers, 1959), 29.

59. Louis M. Hacker and Benjamin B. Kendrick, *The United States Since 1865* (New York: Crofts, 1939), 245.

60. Mowry, *Progressive Era,* 7–8.

61. Robert A. Woods and others, *The Poor in Great Cities : Their Problems and What Is Doing to Solve Them* (New York: C. Scribner's Sons, 1895, reprinted Garrett Press, 1970), 71.

62. Ibid., 179–80.

63. Kathleen Woodroofe, "Scientific Philanthropy in the Gilded Age," in *Pacific Circle, Proceedings of the Second Biennial Conference of the Australian and New Zealand Studies Association,* ed. Norman Harper (St. Lucia: University of Queensland Press, 1968), 177.

64. Eduard C. Lindeman, *Wealth and Culture* (New York: Harcourt, Brace and Company, 1936), 5.

65. M. Pellegrini (vice-president for communications, United Way of America), in response to authors' questionnaire, March 30, 1976. Also "United Way of America Fact Sheet" (UWA, n.d.).

66. *Facts for You from the Needlework Guild* (Philadelphia: Needlework Guild of America, n.d.).

67. Nevins, *Emergence,* 333–5.

68. Margaret O'Brien Stainfels, *Who's Minding the Children? The History and Politics of Day Care in America* (New York: Simon and Schuster, n.d.), 41.

69. Emma Octavia Lundberg, *Unto the Least of These: Social Services for Children* (New York: Appleton-Century-Crofts, 1947), 287.

70. Stainfels, *Who's Minding,* 41–2.

71. National Information Center on Volunteerism, *Volunteers in Social Justice,* 5, no. 4 (1972) and 6, no. 1 (1973).

72. Ruth Murray Underhill, *Red Man's America* (Chicago: University of Chicago Press, 1953), 329.

73. Murray L. Wax, *Indian Americans: Unity and Diversity* (Englewood Cliffs, NJ: Prentice-Hall, 1971), 75.

74. Shih-Shan Henry Tsai, *The Chinese Experience in America* (Bloomington: Indiana University Press, 1986), 50–5.

75. Merle Curti, *American Philanthropy Abroad: A History* (New Brunswick, NJ: Rutgers University Press, 1963), 65.

76. Ibid., 91.

77. Milton Plesur, *America's Outward Thrust* (De Kalb: Northern Illinois University Press, 1971), 125.

78. Curti, *American Philanthropy,* 80.

79. Plesur, *America's Outward Thrust,* 75–6.

80. H. Wayne Morgan, *Unity and Culture: The United States, 1877–1900* (London: Allen Lane, The Penguin Press, 1971), 120–1.

81. Schlesinger, *Rise of the City,* 172–3.

82. Ibid., 173.

83. Ibid., 177.

84. Ibid., 220–1.

85. Foster Rhea Dulles, *A History of Recreation: America Learns to Play* (New York: Appleton-Century-Crofts, 1965), 205–6.

86. Schlesinger, *Rise of the City,* 314.

87. Woods, *Poor in Great Cities,* 133–5.

88. *Camping at Mid-Century* (American Camping Association, January 1953), 1.

89. Paul H. B. D'Estournelles de Constant, *America and Her Problems* (New York: Macmillan, 1915), 294.

90. Ibid., 294–5.

91. Richard Maxwell Brown, "Legal and Behavioral Perspectives on American Vigilantism," in "Law in American History," eds. Donald Fleming and Bernard Bailyn, *Perspectives in American History* (Harvard University, Charles Warren Center for Studies in American History), 5 (1971): 101.

92. Ibid., p. 104.

93. Weigley, *United States Army,* 282.

94. Ibid., 296.

95. Ibid.

96. Clifford P. Westermeier, *Who Rush to Glory: The Cowboy Volunteers of 1898* (Caldwell, ID: Caxton Printers, 1958), 55.

97. Ibid., 10.

98. Ibid., 143.

99. Hurd, *Compact History,* 93.

100. Westermeier, *Who Rush to Glory,* 136–7.

101. Daniel B. Schirmer, *Republic or Empire: American Resistance to the Philippine War* (Cambridge, MA: Schenkman, 1972), 7.

102. James K. Anderson, "75 Years of Achievement," *V.F.W. Magazine,* September 1973 and August 1974.

Chapter 5

THE PROGRESSIVE SPIRIT AND WORLD CONFLICT

1900-1919

1901	President William McKinley assassinated; Theodore Roosevelt becomes president.
1903	First successful airplane flight.
1904-1921	Panama Canal built.
1906	San Francisco earthquake.
1912	*Titanic* sinks.
1914	Assembly-line method of mass production introduced.
1917-1918	United States fights in World War I.

America rushed headlong into the twentieth century. The depression of the 1890s proved to be only a temporary setback, and business was soon booming again. By 1900 the United States had established itself as a leading industrial nation, increasing its responsibilities domestically and abroad.

While the problems of the working class and urban poor persisted, reformers were joined by a new group of allies: the Progressives. From the start, Progressive social reform depended upon the successful collaboration between reformers from the urban lower and middle classes and, occasionally, organized labor. However, Progressivism was not limited to urban concerns and flourished in rural areas as well. The leaders tended to be lawyers, journalists, clergy, teachers, and businesspeople, whose professional training gave the reform activities a "respectable and rather benign character."[1] These middle-class reformers stressed organization, cooperation, efficiency, and data-gathering, but the common thread was humanitarianism.

It was becoming clear that if the American way of life was to be preserved, economics had to be tempered by moral principles. Property rights had to yield to human rights, as the democracy rediscovered its social function.

> *This promise of social progress was not to be realized by sitting and praying, but by using the active powers—by the exposure of evils through the spreading of information and the exhortation of the citizenry; by using the possibilities inherent in the ballot to find new and vigorous popular leaders; in short by a revivification of democracy.*[2]

There was a basic faith in the ability of organized citizens to effect meaningful change. The Progressives advocated direct participation in government, relying upon the public's civic alertness and will to do battle.

Progressivism concerned itself with every area of American life: education, conservation, trust busting, banking reform, food and drug control, wage and hour regulation, child welfare. The supporters of one type of reform were not necessarily advocates of other Progressive campaigns, though key leaders helped to connect the factions. The period was characterized by optimism and a belief in the basic goodness of the individual, and personal expression of these feelings took the form of active volunteer involvement and social change. The Progressive movement was

> *[an] amorphous mixture of reformers and ideas and uplift . . . Reform . . . [was] not primarily a social or institutional phenomenon, but the collective result of many individual efforts.*[3]

Reform leader Louis Brandeis epitomized this concept of the "collective result" by stressing the tactic of involving large numbers of people in his causes. His genius for organization, especially of public pressure groups, became a model for future reformers. For example:

> *The Savings Bank Insurance League and the Anti-Merger League had memberships numbering into the tens of thousands, yet their function was more than that of securing well-signed petitions; they carried the battle down to the level of each citizen.*[4]

These two Leagues utilized their many members as a personnel pool to handle numerous tasks—writing letters to legislators, holding public meetings, making personal contacts. Brandeis did not personally hold office in his organizations and made sure that others testified with him or instead of him at legislative hearings. He understood that only a large group of volunteers could realistically devote the time and energy needed to win success for a cause. Even his emphasis on gathering information as a critical fighting tool demanded volunteer research time. Brandeis operated on two beliefs:

> *If the common man assumed even a small share of civic responsibility, the future progress of society would be assured; if he did not, all would be lost . . . [and] the more involved large numbers of people could be, the more time and energy they would contribute to the cause.*[5]

Further, Brandeis spoke of lawyers as public educators and "as early as 1900 . . . had urged lawyers to voluntarily assist state legislators in reviewing proposed laws, in order that legal principles and social needs be in harmony."[6]

For some, sharing in civic responsibility did not mean buying into the ideals of Progressivism. Vigilante groups operated sporadically but forcefully during these years. Tobacco farmers in Kentucky and Tennessee, for example, had a large and well-organized "night rider" association for "protection." The Ku Klux Klan had officially disbanded in 1870, after white Southerners were restored to political power. But in 1915, a new and much more discriminatory Klan was born. The membership intended "to make it a national, standard, fraternal order composed of American manhood, who believe in preservation of pure Anglo-Saxon institutions, ideals, and principles."[7] The twentieth-century Klan, therefore, set itself up against Catholics, Jews, blacks, and foreigners. World War I intervened in the rebirth of the Klan, but by 1920 the organization was again widespread.

As the Progressive movement aroused the conscience of the middle class to the condition of the poor, changes occurred in social welfare programs. The introduction of large-scale philanthropy, the creation of state and national organizations, and the professionalization of social workers supplanted much of the spontaneous volunteerism that had previously met people's needs. As one contemporary reformer wrote:

> *A worker in a large city charity . . . looks back with no small degree of envy upon the time when the place was simple and village-like. Deeds of charity were then relatively easy and natural, for the best way to help people is to know them before they need help, to know them as employees, neighbors, fellow church members, and fellow citizens who have duties and pleasures in common with ourselves. But the village grew into a town, wealth and poverty grew with it, funds were created to take the place of the old neighborhood help.*[8]

Yet, individuals continued to be concerned with the needs of others, reviving the doctrine of the social gospel.

Religious congregations became involved in the immediate needs of their communities, as exemplified by a Philadelphia congregation around 1900:

> *The city was their workshop, and into it [the Reverend] fed them freely, associating them with every uplifting work that was going forward. Some of his men visited prisons, and became volunteer probation officers in charge of individual boys, others founded an equitable loan company for the poorer sort of borrowers, and many worked hard in municipal campaigns. The women of his church visited families in distress under the best guidance he was able to secure for them, and gave efficient aid on hospital committees and in children's work.*[9]

By 1908, the Federal Council of Churches of Christ in America and the National Methodist Conference had proclaimed it "the duty of all Christian people to concern themselves directly with certain practical industrial problems" and had endorsed a host of welfare proposals. The Salvation Army had developed into a widespread "church for the churchless," utilizing hundreds of volunteers to bring salvation to the slums.

The movement to provide more effective family services continued. By 1911 there were sixty-two societies throughout the country that together had formed the National Association of Societies for Organizing Charity. Soon the name was changed to the Family Service Association of America, paving the way for the creation of voluntary family service agencies and community welfare councils. Volunteers were given an important supplementary role in this movement in 1907 when Mary Richmond reintroduced the idea of "friendly visitors." Although she actively advocated the professionalization of social work, she also believed that the paid worker could never become a "complete and satisfactory substitute" for the volunteer:

> *The volunteers were to her no longer Lady Bountifuls, but a "non-professional group of social servants . . . the real sons and daughters of the community, while the paid worker, though she may be a loving daughter, is often the adopted one." She held it to be a basic responsibility of trained social workers and social agencies to instruct the volunteer and to guide his work so as to enhance the volunteer's personal growth.*[10]

Thus, many agencies recruited volunteers during the early 1900s to provide clients with a measure of neighborly interest; volunteers visited individual families who benefited from such continuous and supportive contact. Friendly visiting exemplified one of the ways in which upper-class women became involved in Progressivism. Suddenly it was not enough simply to be kind to the poor and assume the limited obligations of handouts.

As women had more time for activities outside the home, a collective social conscience emerged. The General Federation of Women's Clubs and the other national women's organizations, which had expanded considerably in the previous period, concentrated their energies on vital social issues. Clubs now grappled with child welfare, public health, the protection of women in industry, pure food legislation, expansion of educational facilities, and civil service reform. By 1912, the federated Clubs had more than a million volunteer members and represented a vast social and civic movement.

> *Their assistance was invited by the Federal government when social discontent among workers on the Panama canal threatened to postpone its completion; a representative was sent to the Isthmus, and organized the wives and daughters of government employees into clubs. The Federal government recognized the power of women's organizations, and approved their interest in public questions.*[11]

The major issue of child welfare attracted many volunteers. Some helped establish baby care clinics and "milk depots." Others founded the Big Brothers Association in 1903 in Cincinnati; although it eventually came to use paid social workers, the Association's primary function was (and is) to pair volunteers with needy boys. The first Big Sisters program was founded in 1908 in New York City and was committed to working with court-referred delinquent girls. Juvenile courts continued to be developed across the country, largely staffed by volunteers. As the era progressed, however, paid court staff gained increasing importance, while volunteers filled supplemental roles.

A group of women interested in the welfare of mothers and infants voluntarily organized the Children's Bureau in 1912. Although placed under the auspices of the Department of Labor, the Bureau encountered a great deal of opposition from the federal government. Nevertheless it grew rapidly with the leadership of women who "possessed the spirit of crusaders."[12] Their cause was greatly bolstered when Jeannette Rankin entered Congress as its first woman member and introduced a bill for federal grants-in-aid for maternal and child care.

Early volunteer efforts to aid poor tenants occurred during this time. A typical example was the Octavia Hill Association in Philadelphia, whose functions were described as follows:

> *Offers its services as agent to owners of property in poor neighborhoods. Also buys dwellings and improves them. Enlists the services of volunteer rent collectors.*[13]

The question of women's suffrage was of continuing concern. The women's clubs and other female groups first concentrated on educating women themselves to understand the need for change and the importance of the vote. The equal suffrage movement gained strength as many restrictions against women were challenged.

> *The movement in America was stimulated between 1909 and 1914 by sensational dispatches from England . . . In America the "suffragette" movement indulged in no violence, except [in a few instances] . . . The women's suffrage movement was part of a broader trend, which in the whole of its manifestations was called "feminism," an emancipation of women from ancient taboos of all kinds.*[14]

The election of Woodrow Wilson became a focal point for women: "Wilson was alleged to have said, when asked why he had not come out for or against women's suffrage, that it had never been brought to his attention. Very well, said [Alice] Paul, we will soon make up for that oversight."[15] Accordingly, a mass demonstration was planned for his inaugural in 1913, bringing five thousand women to Washington from all parts of the country. On March 4 they attempted their suffrage parade but were met by an angry throng of counter-protesters who effectively prevented them from continuing their march. Newspapers recorded the scene, at times approaching riot proportions, with headlines such as:

POLICE WATCH ABUSE OF WOMEN

SHOCKING INSULTS, SEIZED AND SPAT UPON[16]

The failure of the local police and some of the National Guard units to protect the women was loudly condemned, even by the Senate. It should be noted, however, that members of the Thirteenth Regiment, Pennsylvania National Guard, and students from the Maryland Agricultural College did volunteer to try to clear a path for the women.[17] The suffragists made good use of the nationwide publicity given their demonstration, and volunteers collected signatures on new pro-suffrage petitions all over the country. By July 31, 1913, the women had delivered over two hundred thousand names to the Senate. President Wilson could no longer ignore the issue.

Also in 1913, the suffragists formed the National Women's Party, the group that later spearheaded the introduction of the first Equal Rights Amendment in 1923. Between 1913 and 1920, the suffragists sought ways to continue the visibility of their cause. One noteworthy example was the establishment of volunteer pickets at the White House gates. For months, women stood in silent vigil at either side of the entrance. The public never complained, though the women were often taunted, but their presence unnerved President Wilson to the point that he eventually ordered their arrest for obstruction of traffic. This and other unsympathetic actions ultimately served to win begrudging support for the women's cause. But it was to be the monumental effort by American women during the coming World War that finally convinced the skeptics that females deserved an equal voice in society.

Black Americans were becoming increasingly vocal after the turn of the century as they sought to equalize their position as citizens. College-educated blacks joined together in what was to become the Niagara Movement. Their meeting in 1905 called for human brotherhood and an end to discrimination. Because of financial and organizational tensions, the Niagara Movement lasted only five years, but it laid the groundwork for the creation of the National Association for the Advancement of Colored People in 1909. The NAACP had an interracial board of directors, and all but one of the first national officers were well-known whites. The organization had widespread black support in opposing federal Jim Crow policies, an effort furthered by the 1913 convention of the National Negro Press Association.[18] By 1914, some success was visible as federal departments slowly began to end discriminatory practices. The plight of city blacks was specifically addressed by a 1910 conference in New York. Out of this meeting came the National League on Urban Conditions Among Negroes, later known as the National Urban League. The volunteer members of the League and the NAACP, both black and white, managed to bring the issue of racial prejudice to public attention.

The conscience of the times found another voice in articles written by muckrakers. All political and social issues were potential subject for close scrutiny, and newspapers and magazines vied with each other to print the most moving exposés. Though solutions were rarely proposed by the muckraking articles, journalists prided themselves on the detailed research and accurate facts presented.

> *The muckraking crusade was important for at least two reasons. It indicated that the literate middle and upper classes, or those among them who read magazines, were disposed to believe that much was wrong with American civilization; and second, if it assuaged a psychic itch it also created further inflammation and a desire to do something about it.*[19]

Unfortunately, the desire to do something sometimes stopped short of action, leaving the work of reform to later generations.

Change did occur, however, in the way funds for charity were raised. Following the lead of the earlier Charity Organization Societies, there now appeared united funds and "donor associations." One of the first fully organized "community chest" drives took place in Cleveland in 1914 and was described as

> *an intensive city-wide campaign for a two or three week period in which all agencies accepting the plan joined together to raise funds for the coming year. By means of a large volunteer organization, an effort was made to reach each individual donor by calling him in his home or at his office.*[20]

The idea of cooperative fundraising caught on quickly, as those engaged in social welfare work realized its benefits: fostering social unity within a city; reducing competition among agencies; and more effectively utilizing volunteer time and energy.

Educational reform and development were also products of the period prior to World War I, as educational institutions were strengthened. One European observer described American education as a

> *half-built house, or a virgin forest of freely and spontaneously improvised institutions that have cropped up from time to time, without any general plan, to meet requirements as the various states came into being . . . [But] every one of these numerous free institutions operates under the superintendence and the constant and devoted control of the person chiefly interested—fathers, mothers, brothers, former pupils, subscribers and good citizens . . . Individual initiative makes up for what is lacking in general management and experience.*[21]

Though paid personnel now ran the educational facilities, volunteers continued to be involved, especially as policy makers, trustees, and advisers. The General Federation of Women's Clubs was active in this area as well. Beginning in 1908, its volunteers approached Congress requesting that a Department of Education be established as part of the president's Cabinet. In 1914, the Federation began to petition for preschool education and in 1916 cooperated with appropriate agencies to make continuing education classes available for adults.

> *Virtually the entire nation indulged in an educational crusade as high schools were built on the average of one a day. Yearly state after state raised its minimum school-leaving age.*[22]

Universal education was becoming a reality.

Progressive causes tended to attract strange bedfellows. A good example was the demand for industrial education, which for a time rallied a "loose alliance of social workers, the American Federation of Labor, the National Association of Manufacturers, the Chamber of Commerce, and the Grange [who] found common ground in the National Society for the Promotion of Industrial Education."[23] This unusual collaborative effort ended in 1917 when its goal of expanding educational opportunities was achieved through legislation.

The first two decades of the twentieth century brought a myriad of health-related activities, all of which involved volunteers as founders and supporters. Medical science was making great discoveries. Among the many national voluntary health organizations forming in response to this progress were the American Social Hygiene Association (1905), the American Conference for the Prevention of Infant Mortality (1909), the American Child Health Association (1909), the American Society for the Control of Cancer (1913), and the Association for the Prevention and Relief of Heart Disease of New York City (1915). Volunteers participated in a variety of ways. Particularly dramatic was the eradication of yellow fever in Havana after 1900 by a sanitary commission headed by Dr. Walter Reed: "Volunteers came forward; nurses, soldiers, and Cuban natives risked their lives to help the commission."[24]

Many became interested in the inspection of food preparation facilities. Various volunteer service agencies assisted governmental authorities, and the National Consumers League led a campaign to gain passage of the first Pure Food and Drug Law in 1906. The Women's Municipal League of Boston began, in 1908, to advocate the training and regulation of midwives. In 1909, the National Committee for Mental Hygiene was founded by Clifford Beers, an ex-mental patient who sought to use his personal experience to benefit others.[25]

Aid to disabled persons also received attention, largely through Goodwill Industries, which began in 1902. It defined its goals as: "volunteer activity in assisting handicapped persons improve their quality of life."[26] For much the same purpose, the Maryland Association of the Colored Blind was formed in 1913 by Robert Coleman, who "many of his peers have referred to . . . as the first volunteer social worker in the city of Baltimore."[27] Coleman, himself black and visually impaired, led his volunteers in the establishment of the first public vocational school for blind black boys.

One of the most militant propagandists of this period was the feminist Margaret Sanger who, despite legal and religious condemnation, spoke out in favor of birth control measures. In 1914, she published the first issue of the *Woman Rebel* and was immediately charged with violating postal anti-pornography laws. Sanger's efforts did not stop at contraception; she was also one of the first to attempt venereal disease education. Following her lead, a variety of volunteer groups were formed, ultimately uniting in the National Birth Control League.

The individual efforts of Edgar Allen led to the founding of an organization that would later become the National Easter Seal Society.

After his own son was injured in a trolley car accident and subsequently died because of insufficient medical help, Allen resolved that never again in his town of Elyria, Ohio, should anyone die for lack of care. He gave up his business and raised funds to build the Elyria Memorial Hospital in 1908. During the next few years, he became aware of the needs of Ohio youngsters with disabilities and proceeded to raise funds on a statewide basis in order to build the Gates Hospital for Crippled Children. But he soon discovered that few parents brought their children to the hospital to receive help, demonstrating a need for greater public education as well as expanded services. Enlisting the aid of the Rotary Clubs in 1919, he established the Ohio Society for Crippled Children.

The crusade against tuberculosis continued to attract a great deal of attention and volunteer involvement, spurred on by the formation of the National Tuberculosis Association in 1904. One form of activity initiated at this time was the Modern Health Crusade, which invoked the symbols of medieval chivalry to teach American children proper hygiene. Local Tuberculosis Association volunteers established Modern Health Crusade chapters in most schools and staged many social functions, complete with feudal pageantry, to keep the students interested.

> *By 1920 at least 7 million kids were in fealty to hygiene, having pledged to take ten deep breaths a day, sit and stand erect, eschew tobacco, alcohol, and soft drinks "containing injurious drugs," eat three meals a day, chew thoroughly, avoid fried foods and pickles, brush the teeth and use dental floss, cough discreetly, bathe twice a week, polish their shoes, be helpful to others, keep their minds clean and cheerful, sleep ten hours a night with the windows open, get up smiling, omit putting pencils up their noses, and so forth.*[28]

The Modern Health Crusade made a significant contribution to the nation's health and was discontinued only after most pubic schools had absorbed its principles and were teaching cleanliness to their students as part of the regular curriculum.

The National Tuberculosis Association also created and maintained interest in more effective tuberculosis control through its touring exhibits, technical periodicals for physicians, and services to sanatoriums and hospitals. The public paid directly for all these programs by purchasing Christmas Seals. The Christmas Seal idea was originally created by volunteer Emily Bissell in 1907, in an effort to save the struggling Delaware Anti-Tuberculosis Society. The seals became immensely successful and were soon adopted nationally.

Still another form of aid to tuberculosis victims was the City of Hope. In 1912, the National Jewish Consumptive Relief Organization developed the concept of the City of Hope, and in 1913 a small group of men and women from Los Angeles erected two tents in Duarte, California, to treat tuberculosis sufferers. The following year, a wooden cottage was built voluntarily by a local union, thus beginning the long history of union support for tuberculosis care and research.[29] During the next few years, a sanatorium was opened with some paid staff, and the City of Hope became interdenominational. Volunteers continued to play a major role, as stated in the City of Hope "Articles of Faith":

> *Article X: Since* the restoration of health and the saving of life should be the concern of all mankind, and *since* such unique service requires the wholehearted voluntary contributions and voluntary efforts of a great many people, *It is fitting that the work of the City of Hope should be carried on by a people's movement.*[29]

One of the earliest and largest of the privately endowed voluntary organizations grew out of the personal concern of two men—John D. Rockefeller, financier, and Frederick T. Gates, Baptist minister—both of whom possessed a deep feeling for the welfare of humanity. Early benevolent acts focused on providing educational opportunities for blacks through the General Education Board in 1903. A few years later, the idea of a great medical research institution evolved, and both Rockefeller and Gates became committed to the formation of the Rockefeller Foundation (1913). One of the first research projects conducted involved a grant of $1 million to combat hookworm disease in the South. This foundation became a model for well-organized and businesslike philanthropy.

Rural America was not insulated from the Progressive movement that was sweeping the cities. The Farmers' Alliances and Granges of the previous century underwent name and structural changes, but the concept of cooperative economic and social activity remained the same. Perhaps the most important new agricultural organization was the Farmers' Union, formed in Texas in 1902 and active nationally through 1913.

> *Next to the Grange, the Farmers' Union was the longest-lived general farmers' organization in the country . . . As an agricultural counterpart of the progressive movement of the day, this organization was able to capitalize on the work of the earlier organizations.*[30]

The Union maintained all the social activities plus brought a new business sophistication to the marketing of farm products. Membership for farm families offered fraternal fellowship and aid in the regulation of prices. In some areas, Union members developed secret rites and other trappings of fraternities.

Around 1910, county level farm bureaus began to develop, growing strong enough to join together as the American Farm Bureau Federation in 1921. The farm bureaus were based on family membership and stressed the economic self-interest of farmers and ranchers in an increasingly complex marketplace. Lobbying efforts forced government on all levels to listen to such "farmers speaking for farmers."

Youth activities were an important aspect of rural volunteering. Farm children were encouraged to organize agricultural clubs for learning and experimental purposes. Clubs sprang up everywhere, such as Springfield Township, Ohio (1902), Winnebago County, Illinois (1902), the Texas Farmers' Boys and Girls League (1903), and Sigourney, Iowa (1904).[31] There were demonstration clubs, corn clubs, and canning clubs.

> *Work with farm boys in Illinois reached a spectacular climax at the Louisiana Purchase Exposition, St. Louis, Mo., in 1904, when 8,000 Illinois farm boys contributed to the corn exhibit at the Palace of Agriculture.*[32]

Also in 1904 the agricultural clubs in Ohio formed a state federation and received support from the college-level Agricultural Students' Union. Out of these many concurrent beginnings, the 4-H movement was born in 1912 with the help of the Extension Service of the Department of Agriculture. Since that time, countless farm and even city youth have benefited from 4-H activities—all conducted by volunteer leaders.

The twentieth century saw rapid developments in the labor picture as the organizing techniques of the previous era proved ineffective against the changing technological environment. Mass production industries quickly barred unions, and by 1903 the National Association of Manufacturers was able to wage an effective open-shop campaign. Courts enforced the Sherman Anti-Trust Act and ordered injunctions against strikes and boycotts. Yet, despite this strong opposition, the unions survived because of the loyalty of the rank-and-file members:

> *Unions became the workers' instrument precisely because they avoided ideology and offered a sense of community and power that tempered corporate impersonality. They also combined individualism and group action. These responses produced a conservative movement, dedicated to the piecemeal advancement of general interests.*[33]

By and large, the national unions sought only to maintain jurisdiction over their organized industries, not to move into new trades.

The area of child labor drew much attention as part of the general concern for child welfare. In 1904, the National Child Labor Committee began to coordinate state and local volunteer efforts at securing restrictive legislation. The Committee advocated banning children under fourteen from full-time work, limiting day work to a maximum of eight hours for fourteen- to fifteen-year-olds, and eliminating night work for children entirely. By 1907 the Committee was chartered by Congress and contributed to the formation, in 1912, of the United States Children's Bureau.

During the early 1900s mill laborers continued to benefit from volunteer activity, with the endorsement and financial aid of the mill owners. In 1906, in Spray, North Carolina, the employees of nine mills formed a civic association for the purpose of improving their community. Eventually this led to the creation of such benefits as reading rooms, branches of the YMCA, medical services, picnics, girls' clubs, and fraternal clubs and lodges. Most of this community work was begun by volunteers—as individuals or in groups—such as members of the Red Cross, who gave time above and beyond their regular duties to run baby clinics and homemaking classes.[34] As time went on, mill owners became less and less concerned with the welfare of their workers and no longer lived in the mill towns themselves; volunteer activity was increasingly left up to the initiative of individual communities as well as to the workers.

Emphasis on education for mill workers continued as in earlier times, but changed slightly in format when the "moonlight school" enthusiasm struck in 1911. By July 1915, North Carolina had eighty-two evening schools with sixteen hundred illiterate students enrolled—the average age of whom was forty-five.

> *Seven thousand North Carolina teachers volunteered for service the next year . . . There seem to have been seven or eight hundred classes for illiterates with nearly ten thousand enrolled.*[35]

In 1917, the legislature appropriated funds for the moonlight schools. Ultimately the state and federal governments began incorporating these schools into the regular school system, thereby removing the need for large-scale volunteer participation.

Just as laborers were acquiring increased independence and solidarity, businessmen's organizations were also gaining momentum.

> *Two common themes run through the formation of trade associations in the 19th and 20th centuries: that many business problems can be solved by voluntary joint efforts of businessmen; and when a trade association fails to meet the needs of a substantial number of members, a secession group starts a new association.*[36]

At the start of the century there were approximately one hundred national and interstate trade associations. But by 1920, there were more than a thousand, and the number would double again by 1949. Standards and ethics were important areas of concern, and, in many fields, trade and professional associations effectively developed and enforced new professional qualifications. For example, the American Hotel Association was developed in 1910 for the purpose of "apprehension and punishment to the fullest extent of the law, of professional deadbeats, check forgers, dishonest and undesirable employees, crooks of all description."[37] The Association of Iron and Steel Electrical Engineers gave impetus in 1913 to the first Congress of the National Council for Industrial Safety. In 1914 this group changed its name to the National Safety Council and broadened its agenda to include all aspects of industrial, home, and street safety. By 1917, the American Association of Public Accountants had voluntarily established a written exam for accountants in all states.

Associations of businesspeople and increased support of Chambers of Commerce stimulated cooperative activities for economic, civic, and social purposes:

The consideration of organized businessmen is incomplete without pointing out the organizations for social purposes among themselves and for civic betterment and social service in their respective communities . . . The City Club and later the Athletic Club and to a certain extent the YMCA furnished a new type of meeting place.[38]

Groups like the 1900 National Civic Federation attempted to foster good relations between business and labor groups, as well as with the public at large. Volunteer civic improvement projects became a way to achieve healthy public relations, while club members aided one another. Similarly, the National Negro Business League was established in 1900, having some six hundred state and local branches by 1915. The Rotary Clubs (national, 1910), Kiwanis Clubs (national, 1916), and Lions Clubs (1916) led the way in community involvement.

In this respect it was their function to organize businessmen behind such projects. In another respect these organizations illustrate in a most flagrant form the American tendency of seizing upon a popular idea or movement and institutionalizing it.[39]

By 1912, a Chamber of Commerce study concluded that commercial organizations were:

engaged in civic improvement programs, developing local retail trade, sponsoring courses in transportation problems, and advertising the local community's merits as a place to hold conventions.[40]

Volunteer business groups ran youth programs, recruited laborers to meet local business needs, and aided charity efforts. This was a way to meet community responsibilities while gaining new social status through fraternal membership.

With advances in the technology of business and industry came advances in the technology of communications. Radio came on the scene in full force during this period, both commercially and privately.

Amateur operators, especially in the United States, multiplied amazingly . . . As early as 1906, when President Theodore Roosevelt visited the naval Fleet off Cape Cod, the nearby Newport Naval Station was unable to communicate messages

> *to him by wireless because of amateur interference. Destroyers were obligated to carry messages back and forth.*[41]

By 1912, Congress was forced to established legislative controls to prevent the misuse of ham radio communication. There were some practical jokers who sent false messages and found other ways to interfere with important relays, but most ham operators used their hobby in positive ways. In 1914 the American Radio Relay League was formed. Staffed entirely by volunteers and even privately publishing its own magazine, the League had broad purposes. It promoted interest in amateur radio communication and supported technological advancements in the radio art. But it also urged members to relay emergency and other public messages without charge and to find ways to aid rescue and welfare work.[42]

Communication by mail improved, the most important development being the introduction of air service. This giant step was brought about because of the determined efforts of volunteers. Beginning around 1911, sportsmen pilots and off-duty commercial pilots approached the United States Postal Service with plans to test the potential of transporting mail by air. The postal authorities were largely uninterested in such new-fangled nonsense. However, when the pilots refused to be dismissed without at least testing their idea, an experiment was agreed upon. The pilots would have to prove that their planes and their expertise could do the job reliably. So weekend air runs were inaugurated, at first with the volunteers flying blank paper from point to point. Airplane designers were invited to submit modifications and ideas to improve the mail planes. All this activity had to be coordinated and the results submitted. Some postal workers soon became allies, but it took a long time to convince those in authority:

> *Without appropriation for expenses, and through what amounted to contribution of time and individual money both by postal employees and the confident prophets of the "Air Age," experiments continued for the next five years. In state after state, city after city, wherever volunteers in aviation would give time and equipment, the airmail experiments proceeded.*[43]

By 1916, the Postal Service had finally initiated air routes on a limited basis, an example of the successful contribution of volunteers—and of lost history.

Conservation continued to grow as a political issue in this period, largely in response to the waste of natural resources by heavy industry. All types of local and state volunteer groups advocated controls on consumption of resources and the establishment of public parts and forests. During the early years of this century, the Sierra Club and others like it stimulated the development of the National Park Service and Forest Service, the formation of several national parks, and the battle to preserve Yosemite and the Grand Canyon. In 1903 the Public Lands Commission was established, followed in 1908 by the National Conservation Commission. Both commissions studied the recommendations of conservationists and attempted to influence congressional legislation toward protecting the environment.

While the first recreational facilities and playgrounds were established by philanthropic persons and societies, the twentieth century brought new emphasis to the concept of public provision for play. By 1910, many American cities were constructing and administering such facilities through tax money, instead of relying solely on philanthropy. The Playground Association was still an active force in the early 1900s, raising money and recruiting volunteer helpers even where municipal orchestras and bands were concerned:

> *The most notable expression . . . was the organization of the Civic Music Association of Chicago, chartered by the State of Illinois in the spring of 1913 . . . This association arranged artist recitals and orchestral and choral concerts in the recreation centers and school auditoriums of the city through the generosity of philanthropists and musicians alike, the latter donating their talent.*[44]

Gradually, however, city-wide recreational plans decentralized. Independent neighborhood associations were formed, consisting of local residents of a particular area who participated as volunteers. They established community centers that reflected their own needs and desires:

> *The aim of the social center is that public money shall provide simply the basic physical opportunity for recreation, while the people themselves, through the effort of organized voluntary groups, shall make their own recreation, govern it, and pay for it.*[45]

New approaches to rural recreation developed as well. In 1908, the government sanctioned the formation of the Country Life Commission. Commissioners were unpaid, but their work expenses were met by foundation funds. The group studied rural America and recommended more cooperative activities as a way to overcome the isolation of country life.[46] Related to this was the "rural life" movement that emerged in such areas as Wisconsin, North Dakota, and Kansas. Among other things, the movement organized informal recreation. Community houses were acquired as centers for recreation and other collective projects; though usually obtained by purchase, a few such buildings were donated by wealthy members of the community. School personnel were very involved in such efforts: "in West Virginia during 1913-15 . . . one thousand rural teachers volunteered to undertake the organization of social centers of a democratic type in their school buildings."[47]

Along with these developments came a further expansion of group recreation activities. By World War I the Boy Scouts had become the preeminent boys' organization in the United States. By 1913 there were three hundred thousand Scouts and eight thousand volunteer Scoutmasters. Though the movement was largely middle- and upper-class in nature, it also helped to Americanize immigrant youth and spread appreciation of Indian lore.[48] Camp Fire Girls was founded in 1910, and the Girl Scouts of America came on the scene in 1912. Both eventually had some paid staff, but most planning bodies and all local group leaders and officials continued to be volunteers.

The organized camping movement was becoming more unified. Prior to the turn of the century each camp was organized and administered according to the ideals and standards of its owner and founder. But in 1903, the first formal meeting of camp directors was held in Boston for the purpose of discussing mutual problems, interests, and ways of acting cooperatively. This group was eventually to become the American Camping Association in 1935.[49]

The need for a regular army and a strong National Guard became greater as America continued to assume a more and more active role in international affairs. The 1903 Dick Act legislated greater cooperation between the professional army and the volunteer reserve force. It limited National Guard service on behalf of the federal government to nine months but also allowed the Guard to volunteer, in units, for continued federal service beyond this initial tour of duty. In such cases, the unit would become part of the regular army but maintain its own officers.[50] This concept was later broadened by the Volunteer Act of 1914. Controversy continued between those who thought the non-drafted soldier could be effective only with prolonged training and professional leadership, and those who felt that a minimal program of peacetime training was enough. The question became more than academic as the threat of war loomed larger and a decision had to be made about conscription.

Generally, the country preferred to rely on a defense force of volunteers—those who chose to serve but were also given a salary. However, the news of the harsh realities of the war now raging in Europe dampened the willingness of Americans to sign up. A few daring individuals enlisted in the fighting early by joining the Canadian army or by signing up for the advance units of American forces. Although President Wilson personally preferred the volunteer system, the government soon realized that conscription would be a necessity if and when the United States openly declared war. But Wilson knew that there would be strong negative reaction to a conscription law because of the public's memory of the Civil War draft riots. So, the plan to initiate a draft was actually developed clandestinely:

> *Wilson's decision to conscript America was made before he called on Congress to declare war, and more than two months before Congress passed the act that legalized the draft. By agreement, kept secret, . . . the colossal machinery for enforcing the draft was set up and made ready long before the country knew there would be a draft—while, indeed, the country continued to take it for granted that only the volunteer system would be used.*[51]

To avoid public outcry, a system was devised to make conscription look as much like volunteering as possible. No uniformed soldiers would appear at private doors. Instead, local civilian volunteers would first register eligible young men in much the same way as persons registered to vote; in fact, registration was even held at each precinct's voting location. Then the civilian board would choose which men would fight and which would be exempt.

> *The process would be one, not of the army walking into the draftee's home, but of civilian officials, mainly neighbors, delivering the draftee to the army . . . But the draftee would reach the army just as if the army had come and taken him.*[52]

Substitutions, exemptions, and bounties were not allowed. In this way, the government avoided some of the worst mistakes of the Civil War draft attempt, and the Selective Service Act of 1917 created a system that was to last a long time.

When war was declared, young black men responded eagerly. The American Negro Loyal Legion notified Washington that ten thousand black recruits could be raised on short notice. However, army officials were not ready to accept this offer. Only through the draft did blacks begin to be accepted into military service, but throughout the war army discrimination against nonwhite soldiers was rampant. In response to the exclusion of blacks from officer training camps, a protest was lodged by a Central Committee of Negro College Men, whose volunteers met with army officials and members of Congress.[53] Finally, in May 1917, this effort resulted in the establishment of a reserve officers' training camp for "colored men."

Indians were not drafted in World War I, though many volunteered. In fact, the Comanche, with several other tribes, rendered unique service through the use of their unwritten language in telephone communication across German lines.[54]

Beginning in 1914, several civilian volunteer groups led the campaign for national preparedness, which was defined as "the moral organization of the people, an organization which creates in the heart of every citizen a sense of his obligation for service to the nation in time of war."[55] Two groups worked actively toward this end: the American Rights Committee and the National Security League. Among their activities was the organization of summer camps (1914-1915) where college students could receive military training if they paid their own way. Similar camps were opened for business and professional men, paid for by voluntary contributions.

> *The preparedness movement assured there would be volunteers; a few weeks' training . . . assured that influential citizens would go home not only with basic military training, but also with renewed enthusiasm for preparedness.*[56]

The Girls' Division of the United States Junior Naval Reserve trained young female volunteers to be operators of wireless telegraphy as well as to hold more traditional roles. The Reserve subsidized those girls unable to pay for such training.[57]

Even before the country readied itself for war, pacifists increased their efforts to keep the nation at peace. The American Peace Society sponsored national peace congresses in New York (1907), Chicago

(1909), Baltimore (1911), and St. Louis (1913). In 1910 a philanthropic donation of $1 million by Edwin Ginn formed the World Peace Foundation, to which Andrew Carnegie donated $10 million more. Carnegie gave another $2 million in 1914 to develop a Church Peace Union. Women were involved in the Women's Constructive Peace Movement, and the energy of youth was channeled through the 1908 American School Peace League. So popular was the pacifist cause that by 1913 as many as eighty different peace groups flourished across the country.[58]

These peace groups were countered by pro-involvement volunteers such as the Navy League. Made up of retired naval officers and other sympathizers, the Navy League was developed with the backing of armament manufacturers and banks with foreign interests.[59] Such organizations boosted military preparedness.

When war was officially declared, American women again mobilized extensive support systems:

> *A few days after the declaration of war the National Woman's Committee was created by the Council of National Defense . . . and charged with the duty of coordinating the patriotic activities of the women of the nation.*[60]

Quickly, the National Woman's Committee formed state organizations, which in turn developed local committees of volunteers in every county and city. "Under the supervision of these central committees the war work of the women attained a degree of efficiency unrivalled in the history of the world."[61]

Women had to register, or actually enroll, in order to participate in these activities.

> *The Woman's Committee's plans were pushed with all speed. Forms were drafted . . . The Council of National Defense agreed to furnish 500,000 cards . . . In four states . . . the Governors designated special days for the registration. The undertaking was backed by all kinds publicity, and definite registration days had been set aside in 15 states by September, 1917.*[62]

All sorts of approaches were used to obtain signatures, and registration continued even after the initial deadlines. Volunteers went door-to-door, set up booths in public places, and generally tried to reach as many women as possible. The sign-up cards asked women to offer their services in eight categories: agricultural, clerical, domestic, industrial, professional, public service, social service, and Red Cross and Allied Relief. They were to indicate if they could volunteer, would need some help to meet expenses, or would need to be paid. Also, women had to indicate in which areas they already had training or required training:

> *154 items of possible service were listed. The list must have had a tremendous effect on the thousands of women who studied it and who saw that skills they had taken for granted such as sewing, housekeeping, care of children, gardening, poultry raising, reading aloud, and dozens of others, could be used for war service. It is easy to imagine the different outlook that resulted from the personal stocktaking back of each filled out card.*[63]

Among the possible activities were: providing bandages, food, and clothing for the Red Cross; running Liberty Loan and Liberty Bond campaigns; handling necessary civil service jobs; protecting girls near army camps; and raising money for dorms and community houses in which civilian friends and relatives could stay while visiting soldiers. Black women were especially involved in thrift clubs and bond drives. In fact, "a Negro bank, Mutual Savings of Portsmouth, Virginia, was awarded first place among the banks of the country in the Third Liberty Loan Drive, having oversubscribed its quota nineteen times."[64] Another organization, the National League for Women's Service, found that one of its more popular assignments was canteen work, perhaps because women could feel that they were offering direct services to the fighting men. All sorts of canteens were set up, some in permanent locations and others on a more temporary basis at railroad stations and other transit points.

The War Department organized the Woman's War Council in order to mobilize business and professional women on behalf of the war effort. This group continued after the war, evolving into the 1919 National Federation of Business and Professional Women's Clubs.[65]

In this war, women served in new roles. Some actually went abroad with the troops for the first time: "In the maintenance of the morale of the troops perhaps no single factor was of more importance than the unswerving patriotism of the women."[66] Furthermore, since the war came just as the feminist movement was gaining momentum, women at home no longer limited themselves to traditional roles such as nursing:

> *They also did work that women had never done before. They became messenger "boys" for the telegraph companies, operated elevators, acted as street-car conductors, labored as full-time and able-bodied operatives in munition factories, and railroad repair-shops.*[67]

American women would never be the same again.

By 1915, the American Red Cross had become the major disaster-relief agency in the United States and was developing a professional nursing program and a first aid training department. Then, with the outbreak of fighting,

> *the war brought a challenge of organization and service development that turned it in effect into a civilian army. This was an army administered, organized, and trained by a skeleton paid staff and filled in its ranks by volunteers.*[68]

Red Cross war-related activities abroad included the organization of fifty-eight military base hospitals; the operation of forty-seven ambulance companies to transport the wounded from the field to the hospitals; the assignment of twenty thousand nurses; and the assignment of field directors to counsel servicemen and provide better communication between them and their families. In addition, by the end of the war, the Red Cross was operating seven hundred servicemen canteens in the United States, over half of which also included such other extras as first aid stations, showers, and free telephone booths:

> *all of which took an enormous amount of work—cleaning and cooking and dishwashing and carrying out the garbage. Who did this? Some 55,000 women who found time away from their homes and children or their own regular war time jobs to be Red Cross volunteers.*[69]

This period also saw the formation of the Junior Red Cross as more and more youth were eager to serve.

World War I brought unprecedented cooperative action among major service organizations. The YMCA, YWCA, National Catholic War Council (Knights of Columbus), Jewish Welfare Board, Salvation

Army, and American Library Service all coordinated their efforts to assist the soldiers and the public. Though maintaining their autonomy, the groups even raised funds together in 1918.[70] These groups, and government units such as the Food Administration and the Fuel Administration, urged on the noncombatant public with slogans and appeals:

> *A phrase became current . . . "doing your bit"; one patriotic lady who thought the phrase implied too little, suggested "doing your all." The number and variety of such organized and sloganized urgings reached a point where, in an apotheosis of organization, it was proposed that a "What Can* I *Do? League" be organized.*[71]

There were all sorts of ways to help the cause. One of the greatest contributions of women to victory was food conservation. Women regularly scheduled wheatless and meatless days, placed pledge cards in their windows, and planted "war gardens." Female farm laborers even called themselves the Woman's Land Army of America.[72] Such widespread food-growing and conservation efforts were amazingly effective and bolstered public morale.

During 1918, the War Camp Community Service (an outgrowth of the 1906 Playground and Recreation Association of America) organized the social and recreational resources of 604 communities near the temporary quarters of American military and naval forces around the country.

> *A force of 2700 trained workers was employed [plus] a volunteer staff of 60,000 additional leaders of . . . activities . . . besides those who received soldiers and sailors in their homes . . . Among the distinctive types of activities were community singing, pageants, dances, block parties, athletic meets, motion pictures, artist recitals, game rooms and home hospitality.*[73]

In this way, War Camp Community Service was developed as a means of promoting the health and spirit of the nation's fighting forces. After the signing of the armistice, popular demand insisted that such community service be continued during peacetime. So, in 1919, the organization became Community Service, Inc., coordinated nationally but operating locally through the use of trained volunteers.

It was perhaps inevitable that German-Americans would become the objects of some suspicion during World War I. Unfortunately, such suspicion was evidenced in discriminatory ways; the works of German artists were all but banned; aliens who tried to organize support for the allies were misunderstood; those of foreign birth were coerced into buying Liberty Bonds. Most distasteful was self-appointed spying on immigrants and naturalized citizens: "With volunteer spying by Americans on alleged German spies, went volunteer censorship, informal punishment of persons suspected of lack of loyalty."[74]

Despite this suspicion of some foreigners at home, most Americans still responded overwhelmingly to aid those suffering abroad. The Provisional Executive Committee for Zionist Affairs was an emergency organization called into being to alleviate the distress of Jews in the war-torn countries of Europe and the Middle East. From 1917 to 1918, other groups gave food, medicine, and clothing to ten countries, aiding some 157 million people.[75] Even more help was extended after the armistice.

> *The worldwide efforts of the American people to help others through public and private organizations are not generally considered a part of foreign policy. In important ways, however, they have affected the attitudes of foreigners toward the United States.*[76]

America, as a nation, was accepting the obligation to help the needy in other parts of the world. This represented a unique expansion of the volunteer spirit that had been present in individual citizens for so long.

The turn of the century brought activity by many types of volunteers on behalf of a staggering diversity of causes. Pressure stemmed from the Populist farmers of the Midwest and South, the rising labor unions, the threatened middle class, the dissatisfied educated elite, the women's movement, the immigrant urban groups, business people, clergy, and vocal individuals.

> *To satisfy all these bewildering and often conflicting pressures for change the political system imperfectly moved toward a series of compromised written into the statute books of cities, states, and the nation, which in sum was known then, and has been called since, Progressivism.*[77]

The Progressive spirit at home was interrupted by the pull toward involvement in foreign affairs. Despite the efforts of isolationists, American entry into the European war was unavoidable. In line with the tradition established by previous wars, Americans volunteered both militarily and on the homefront. The aid to Europe, with relief as well as fighting forces, cemented the role of the United States as a world power. Though many of the reform crusades were reactivated after the war, World War I effectively marked the end of the Progressive era.

Endnotes for Chapter 5

1. Dewey W. Grantham, Jr., "The Progressive Era and the Reform Tradition," in *Progressivism: The Critical Issues,* ed. David M. Kennedy (Boston: Little, Brown, 1971), 115.
2. Richard Hofstadter, ed., *The Progressive Movement, 1900–1915* (Englewood Cliffs, NJ: Prentice-Hall, 1963), 5.
3. Melvin I. Urofsky, *A Mind of One Piece: Brandeis and American Reform* (New York: Scribner's, 1971), 167.
4. Ibid., 7.
5. Ibid.
6. Ibid., 389.
7. Col. Winfield Jones, *Knights of the Ku Klux Klan* (n.p., n.d.), 81.
8. Mary E. Richmond, *The Good Neighbor in the Modern City,* special ed. (Philadelphia: Lippincott, 1908), 100.
9. Ibid., 147.
10. Max Siporin, *Friendly Visiting Among the Poor* (Montclair, NJ: Patterson Smith, 1899, republished 1969), xxxv.
11. Lloyd Morris, *Postscript to Yesterday* (New York: Random House, 1947), 34.
12. Wilson G. Smillie, *Public Health, Its Promise for the Future* (New York: Macmillan, 1955), 468.
13. Richmond, *Good Neighbor,* 81.
14. Mark Sullivan, *Our Times: The United States, 1900–1925* (New York: Scribner's, 1935), 4: 127.
15. Emily Hahn, *Once Upon a Pedestal* (New York: Crowell, 1974), 228.
16. *The New York Times,* March 15, 1913, quoted in Emily Hahn, *Once Upon a Pedestal* (New York: Crowell, 1974), 229.
17. Ibid., 228.
18. Benjamin Quarles, *The Negro in the Making of America,* rev. ed. (New York: Collier Books, 1969), 177.
19. George E. Mowry, *The Progressive Era, 1900–1920: The Reform Persuasion,* 212, American Historical Association pamphlets (Washington, DC: AHA, 1958, reprinted 1972), 14.
20. Edward L. Ryerson, *A Businessman's Concept of Citizenship, A Series of Lectures Delivered in Australia during the Fall of 1958 under the Auspices of the Fullbright Committee* (privately published, 1960), 39–40.
21. Paul H. B. D'Estournelles de Constant, *America and Her Problems* (New York: Macmillan, 1915), 318.

22. Mowry, *Progressive Era,* 11.
23. Urofsky, *Mind of One Piece,* 165.
24. Harvey Wish, *Contemporary America: The National Scene Since 1900* (New York: Harper and Row, 1966), 48–9.
25. Descriptive material of the National Association for Mental Health, Inc., in response to authors' questionnaire, Spring 1977.
26. Matthew Warren (director of public relations, Goodwill Industries of America, Inc.), in response to authors' questionnaire, July 27, 1976.
27. Dorothy Lymas Coleman, *Robert Coleman and The Association for the Handicapped* (Baltimore, MD: Bay Printing, 1971), 1.
28. Richard Carter, *The Gentle Legions* (Garden City, NY: Doubleday, 1961), 74.
29. Aaron Levenstein, *Testimony for Man: The Story of the City of Hope* (private printing, 1968), 43.
30. Theodore Saloutos, *Farmer Movements in the South, 1865–1933,* vol. 64, *University of California Publications in History,* ed. Theodore Saloutos (Berkeley: University of California Press, 1960), 184.
31. Extension Service, U.S. Department of Agriculture, *Early Development of 4-H* (Washington, D.C.: Government Printing Office, n.d.), 2.
32. Ibid.
33. H. Wayne Morgan, *Unity and Culture: The United States, 1877–1900* (London: Allen Lane, The Penguin Press, 1971), 23.
34. Harriet L. Herring, *Welfare Work in Mill Villages* (Chapel Hill: The University of North Carolina Press, 1929), 116–25.
35. Ibid., 71.
36. Joseph F. Bradley, *The Role of Trade Associations and Professional Business Societies* (University Park: Pennsylvania State University Press, 1965), 23.
37. Ibid., 22.
38. James C. Malin, *An Interpretation of Recent American History* (New York: Century, 1926), 118.
39. Ibid.
40. Bradley, *Role of Trade Associations,* 43.
41. Gleason L. Archer, *History of Radio to 1926* (New York: The American Historical Society, 1938), 104–5.
42. Descriptive materials of the American Radio Relay League, Inc., in response to authors' questionnaire, April 5, 1976.
43. Arthur E. Summerfield, as told to Charles Hurd, *U.S. Mail* (New York: Holt, Rinehart and Winston, 1960), 96–7.
44. Clarence E. Rainwater, *The Play Movement in the United States* (Washington, DC: McGrath, 1922), 120.
45. Ibid., 143.
46. Gifford Pinchot, *Breaking New Ground* (New York: Harcourt, Brace and Company, 1947), 341–2.
47. Rainwater, *Play Movement,* 167.
48. Harold Underwood Faulkner, *The Quest for Social Justice, 1898–1914,* vol. 11, *A History of American Life in Twelve Volumes,* eds. Arthur M. Schlesinger and Dixon Ryan Fox (New York: Macmillan, 1931), 181.
49. *Camping at Mid-Century* (American Camping Association, January 1953), 2–3.
50. Russell F. Weigley, *History of the United States Army* (New York:

Macmillan, 1967), 322.
51. Sullivan, *Our Times,* 5: 290.
52. Ibid., 291.
53. Quarles, *The Negro,* 182.
54. Ruth Murray Underhill, *Red Man's America* (Chicago: University of Chicago Press, 1953), 328.
55. Weigley, *United States Army,* 342.
56. Ibid., 343.
57. "Wireless for Women," *The Literary Digest* 53, no.17 (October 21, 1916): 1029.
58. Faulkner, *Quest for Social Justice,* 326–7.
59. Ibid.
60. Arthur M. Schlesinger, *New Viewpoints in American History* (New York: Macmillan, 1925), 156.
61. Ibid.
62. Margaret Culkin Banning, *Women for Defense* (New York: Duell, Sloan and Pearce, 1942), 39.
63. Ibid., 40.
64. Quarles, *The Negro,* 187.
65. National Commission on the Observance of International Women's Year, *To Form a More Perfect Union...Justice for American Women* (Washington, DC: Government Printing Office, 1976), 6.
66. Schlesinger, *New Viewpoints,* 157.
67. Sullivan, *Our Times,* 4: 458.
68. Charles Hurd, *The Compact History of the American Red Cross* (New York: Hawthorn Books, 1959), 155.
69. Ibid., 157.
70. *Twenty-five Years: Keeping Faith with Our Armed Forces Since 1941, U.S.O.* (New York: United Service Organizations, Inc., 1966), 8.
71. Sullivan, *Our Times,* 5: 457.
72. Schlesinger, *New Viewpoints,* 157.
73. Rainwater, *Play Movement,* 181.
74. Sullivan, *Our Times,* 5: 473.
75. Perry E. Giankos and Albert Karson, *Withdrawal and Engagement, 1919–1941,* vol. 3, *American Diplomacy and the Sense of Destiny* (Belmont, CA: Wadsworth, 1966), 5.
76. Ibid.
77. George E. Mowry, *The Progressive Era, 1900–1920: The Reform Persuasion,* 212, American Historical Association pamphlets (Washington, DC: AHA, 1958, reprinted 1972), 35.

Chapter 6

Volunteering amid Shifts of Fortune

1920-1945

1920	Eighteenth Amendment, prohibiting sale of intoxicating beverages, goes into effect. Nineteenth Amendment, giving women the vote, is ratified.
1924	Congress confers citizenship on Native Americans.
1929	Stock market crash; Great Depression begins.
1933	Franklin Delano Roosevelt inaugurated president. New Deal begins. Prohibition repealed.
1938	Fair Labor Standards (wages and hours) Act.
1941-1945	United States fights in World War II.
1942	Japanese-Americans are interned under the War Relocation Act.
1945	Germany surrenders. Atomic bombs dropped on Hiroshima and Nagasaki; Japan surrenders.

In the wake of World War I, America turned its back on the responsibilities and reform of the earlier Progressive era. The 1920s were indeed "roaring," with frivolous, energetic, and hedonistic fads. There were all sorts of new diversions and pleasures: movies, jazz, Lindbergh, Freud, and of course, the automobile. Values of young and old, urban and rural, became increasingly polarized. As traditions were challenged by the young, the media, and city sophisticates, moral opposition came from fundamentalist religious groups and the advocates of prohibition. The combined effect of the continued suffragist protest and the monumental contribution of women to the war effort ultimately gave the final push to ratification of the Nineteenth Amendment. In 1920, the right to vote was extended to women.

On the international front, the close of World War I brought an end to enthusiastic foreign involvement. Strong isolationist sentiment fostered nativist attitudes, resulting in an increasing intolerance toward foreign-born residents. Prejudice against cultural, ethnic, and political differences gave rise to "pure American" groups, and new quota laws limited immigration. A Red scare swept the country as Bolshevism triumphed in Russia.

The pursuit of wealth was the major preoccupation of a large percentage of Americans. Business was king, and new ventures were launched almost daily. But by the mid-twenties, inflation was eroding newly-made profits, unemployment had become severe, and economic recession took hold. The process culminated in the stock market crash of 1929, after which the nation experienced a devastating depression.

President Hoover was optimistic about the many citizen efforts to rally against the severe economic hardships of the day. He later described the nature of these efforts:

> *These committees had no politics. They were men and women experienced in large affairs, sympathetic, understanding of the needs of their neighbors in distress. And they served without pay. In those days one did not enter into relief of his countrymen through the portals of a payroll. American men and women of such stature cannot be had as a paid bureaucracy, yet they will serve voluntarily all hours of the day and defer their own affairs to night.*[1]

Hoover regarded volunteering as a part of the national character. He stressed the concept of service over and over again, defining it as a mixture of altruism and self-interest. But the country was in a crisis unlike any it had faced before, and while citizen action maintained morale and provided temporary relief, the public looked to the federal government for more lasting help.

With the election of Franklin Roosevelt in 1932, the federal government began to assume unprecedented, broadened responsibilities in order to lift the country out of its immobilized state. The New Deal ushered in such public programs as the Public Works Administration, the Tennessee Valley Authority, the Social Security Administration, and the Civilian Conservation Corps. Before the era ended, the American government was irrevocably entrenched in welfare state programs that brought a measure of relief to millions but also raised new and problematic issues.

News of foreign hostilities grew increasingly ominous. Despite all efforts to remain neutral, the United States was dramatically drawn into the new world war in 1941. Though another war was not welcomed, World War II did serve to end the depression at home.

The wartime prosperity following World War I continued into the early 1920s. Though unemployment was high in certain trades, most industries grew and modernized. Harmony between employers and employees was evidenced by the general decline in labor union membership. However, farmer cooperatives and agricultural youth programs were still popular and rapidly enlarged. By 1923 the thrust for more and better schools of agriculture had also produced student organizations on local and state levels. Volunteer groups such as Young Farmers, Junior Farmers, and Future Farmers of America all provided support to agricultural students.

Business people, too, organized around common concerns. One issue of increasing importance was safety of all kinds: industrial, home, and automobile. At the Eleventh Safety Congress of the National Safety Council in 1922, various approaches to the need for public education on daily safety precautions were discussed. Volunteers attending the Congress noted the correlation between technological advance and the accident rate:

> *Each mechanical device—and these account for 95 percent of public accidents—is virtually a development of the twentieth century. Therefore, something needs to be done to develop capacities in the individual for taking care of himself with reference to hazards that create complex conditions of life on our streets and in our homes.*[2]

Much emphasis was placed on safety education within the public schools. Safety textbooks appeared, meetings of educators on safety topics were common, and the children themselves were organized into safety committees. In a midwestern city, one boy had developed the habit of hopping onto passing trucks; the other children were worried about this unsafe act:

> *After some little debate they decided it would be wise to create a committee of boys, whose duty it would be to keep children from hopping trucks, and they appointed the boy as chairman of the committee.*[3]

Children wrote thousands of letters to the National Safety Council describing their many safety clubs and efforts to promote safety in and around their schools.

The National Safety Council's work was voluntarily supported in large measure by the business community. Studies were run to determine the causes of accidents and to find ways to eliminate mechanical safety hazards as well as to alert citizens. Although the proceedings of the early Safety Congresses seem today to speak about obvious problems, in their day these concerns still had to be brought before a public uneducated as to safety hazards. It is a measure of the success of the Council's efforts that today's public has grown up to be more aware of the need for safety.

Automobile safety increased as a special area of concern through the 1920s. More and more cars jammed the roads, causing accident statistics to soar. The response to the problem began with local traffic control organizations, and by the early 1930s, guides and models were being published to aid communities in developing volunteer safety councils. One such guide prefaced its directions with:

> *Now a thoroughly aroused public is ready for the facts and the period of reconstruction—reconstruction of its attitudes toward driving, its habits and actual driving skills . . . The question they ask today: "what shall we do about it and how shall we do it?"*[4]

Citizen groups were organized across the country, enlisting civic and business leaders, as well as anyone with an interest in promoting auto safety. The widespread campaign resulted in such diverse actions as more standardized traffic regulations, accident-reporting systems, and police-related accident prevention offices; the development of traffic courts; better approaches to street design and traffic routing; and driver education courses for high school students. The positive impact of such citizen and business involvement was immediate.

The advent of the catastrophic Great Depression ended the comparatively peaceful business and labor scene of the 1920s. Though at first labor unions suffered even greater membership loss due to overwhelming unemployment, the depression ultimately served to make unions stronger than ever before. Legislation began granting rights and privileges to labor in an effort to improve the employment situation. Also, the major unions underwent important internal reorganization, bringing new and vocal leaders to the forefront.

One of the critical new concerns of labor unions was to organize in more trade areas. Prior to the 1930s, the unions were almost isolationist toward unorganized industries. But fueled by angry indignation, unions now regained the desire to organize as many workers as possible so as to protect themselves from ever again falling victim to such economic disaster. The first demands concerned shorter hours and higher wages but were coupled with American Federation of Labor (AFL) support for public unemployment insurance. This willingness to accept government programs was a radical departure from the earlier adherence to voluntarism and self-reliance.

The new approaches of labor leaders did not appeal to all unions. For example, the craft unions resented the push to organize more industries at what they felt was the expense of traditional members and jurisdiction. The tension came to a head in 1935, and the outcome was a split between industrial unionists and the craft unions. The split resulted in the formation of the Committee for Industrial Organization (CIO), which pursued its own goals in opposition to the more traditional AFL.

With the development of full-time paid staff, labor unions moved even further from their volunteer roots, though the rank-and-file membership as a mass remained the basic source of power. Membership was open to all concerned laborers, including left-wing leaders. Socialists were welcomed as effective partners because

> *as a voluntary association in a pluralistic society, the labor movement necessarily judged men by performance, not by belief or by other affiliations. Participants had only to adhere to the code of priorities; while in the role of trade unionists, they had to place union objectives first.*[5]

Minority workers, often excluded from mainstream labor union membership, formed their own organizations. One example was the Chinese Workers Mutual Aid Association, begun in San Francisco in 1937 by Chinese-Americans who had learned about unions when leading a successful strike against their Alaskan salmon cannery employers the year before. In 1938, the Chinese Ladies Garment Workers' Union, supported by the International Ladies Garment Workers' Union, gained wage concessions after a highly publicized strike.[6]

While laborers grappled with unionization, American farmers turned to their associations to see them through the hardship. Farmer cooperatives played a key role in organizing rural communities to share meager resources and to advocate for farm relief legislation. Further: "In the countryside farmers organized to prevent, by persuasion if possible and by force if necessary, the loss of their farms through foreclosure or tax sale."[7] One of the more militant protest groups was the Farmer's Holiday Association, which organized strikes to win higher prices for midwestern farmers. Before this, strikes were largely the domain of the urban factory worker.

Business people also coped with the prosperity-depression-prosperity cycle by turning to one another. The business and professional groups that had developed before World War I grew in size, and new volunteer organizations were formed. Their interest in youth, as well, was shown by Kiwanis Key Clubs and Circle K Clubs, initiated during this period to offer vocational guidance and community service programs to high school and college students. By 1943, Key Clubs became an international organization. The diversity of associations was demonstrated by groups such as the Toastmasters Clubs, incorporated in 1932. The original Toastmasters Club was formed in 1924 to help members develop effective speaking abilities while presenting programs of civic value. Through the support of the YMCA, the clubs spread rapidly.

Another example of volunteer involvement late in the era was the Wilkie Clubs organized to support Wendell Wilkie's presidential nomination in 1940. Something of a protest against the Tennessee Valley Authority, these volunteer clubs were at first filled with local power company employees. After Wilkie lost the election, he

> *called on his followers to form "a loyal opposition." There were insistent calls on both sides for "unity." "Good Losers' clubs sprang up. There was a sense of having done a brave thing in a dangerous time.*[8]

The period between the two world wars saw many different types of movements rise and fall.

The same year (1920) that saw passage of women's suffrage also ushered in Prohibition. This "noble experiment" at legislating the drinking habits of Americans owed its existence to the decades of dedicated work by temperance volunteers, known as the "drys." But no sooner had the amendment been ratified than some sober souls recognized that Prohibition would not work and would even be counterproductive. Volunteer protest groups sprang up, such as the Women's Committee for Modification of the Volstead Act (by 1927 this became the Women's Committee for Repeal of the Eighteenth Amendment) and the Women's Organization for National Prohibition Reform. By 1929 such groups were joined by labor unions and others in agitating for the repeal of the amendment. In 1933, despite the counter-protests of the Woman's Christian Temperance Union and the Prohibition Party, the "noble experiment" ended.[9] Concern over alcoholism continued, however, and in 1934 Alcoholics Anonymous began the volunteer self-help tradition of alcoholics supporting each other's battle against the bottle.

During the 1920s the reborn Ku Klux Klan gained momentum, embracing current strong anti-foreign and anti-black sentiment. These white supremacists affected political life in Indiana, Maine, Colorado, Oklahoma, Texas, Oregon, Arkansas, Ohio, and California. Estimated membership was four to four and a half million.[10] While terrorist tactics were used, the Klans also developed charitable and youth programs.

The southern Klans retained the tactic of lynching, but by 1930 southern women organized to abolish this practice, forming the Association of Southern Women for the Prevention of Lynching. These women's groups also took the lead in forming interracial committees. As early as 1919, a Commission on Interracial Cooperation was developed, which included some black women members. This interracial volunteer effort was supported through the Methodist, Baptist, Presbyterian, Episcopal, and Disciples churches, plus the YWCA and the Association of Women's Clubs.[11] By 1933, the National Council of Women (made up of twenty organizations representing a total of 5 million American women members) was able to hold an International Congress of Women. It was convened as part of the Chicago "Century of Progress" and demonstrated the effort of women's groups to reach out across borders of all kinds.

Women led the way in other areas, as well. Educated as to their newly bestowed electoral and civic duties by such organizations as the League of Women Voters and the American Association of University

Women, women found many causes requiring their energy. Once again, consumerism was an issue. This involved comparison shopping, distrust of advertising and certain products, and better public education. Even university courses in consumer education sprang up. One new cause was public control of electricity. Some groups, such as the 1936 Consumers Union, researched products and published private lists of approved items. These lists were mailed to one hundred fifty thousand families and undoubtedly reached many more through loan and word of mouth. Such activity continued for several more years, until the government slowly became involved:

> *Despite apathy by the press and open hostility from many commercial concerns, but under urgent pressure from women's organizations, the food, drug and cosmetic act of June 24, 1938, scrapped obsolete legislation and widened the domain of federal authority.*[12]

One outgrowth of active consumerism was the development of Better Business Bureaus in the early 1930s. Bureau volunteers worked to correct marketing abuses by handling consumer complaints and monitoring local advertising and selling.

Citizen activity was also directed toward the needs of minorities. For several decades, Indians had received little attention from white Americans, and the potential of existing tribal organization and custom was unrecognized:

> *No one considered how the Indian tradition of cooperation could be put to work; how the "potlatch" and "give-away feast" could be turned into mutual benefit societies; how some psychological satisfaction could be found for the warrior deprived of his function.*[13]

After World War I, focus was once more placed on Native Americans, stimulated by the activities of loyal Indians during the War. Yet in 1922 legislation was introduced forcing the Pueblo Indians to prove ownership of the land that had been set aside for them earlier. "The iniquitous legislative proposal drew the fire of private citizens and citizen groups, who entered the controversy to help the Indians organize a common defense."[14] This cause later resulted in a national movement to reform the government's policies toward Indians. It was not until 1926 that the volunteers succeeded in pressuring Washington to authorize a study of Indian conditions. The 1922 protest by outsiders also taught the Indians themselves a new approach:

> *In November 1922, encouraged by the citizens groups, all the Pueblos sent delegates to Santo Domingo . . . It was the first time they had acted together since 1680 . . . In the name of the newly formed All Pueblo Council, an appeal was issued to the American people and a delegation visited a number of American cities to explain the issue and appeal for financial support.*[15]

During the 1930s, federal laws that had barred Native Americans from preserving and practicing their tribal culture were lifted. This enabled the tribes to reinstitute their traditional gatherings, called powwows, at which dances, songs, and ancient customs could once more be celebrated. The success of these events was due largely to the volunteer efforts of individual Indians scattered in separate tribes. As the powwows grew in size and were opened to non-Indian audiences, they became fundraisers to further Native American causes, such as education, health care, and land preservation.

Mexican-Americans also became politically aware after World War I, especially as Chicano veterans returned from military service with the desire to become part of mainstream America. The Order of the Sons of America (Orden Hijos de America), founded in San Antonio in 1921, sought to end prejudice against Mexican-Americans, achieve equality before the law, acquire political representation, and obtain greater educational opportunities. The Order stressed that its members learn English and become United States citizens. In 1929, this and other Latino groups consolidated to form the League of United Latin American Citizens (LULAC).

Asian-Americans also turned to their own voluntary associations as a way to maintain their identity while gaining a collective voice in American society. Chinese-Americans founded their own versions of mainstream organizations. By 1921, there were five Chinese YMCAs, three YWCAs, and numerous scouting and youth groups across the country. The Anti-Opium League in Hawaii raised money and provided support to Chinese addicts seeking to break their habits. The Chinese American Citizens Alliance, formed in the early twentieth century, urged its members to exercise their political clout through the vote. In 1932, the New York Chinese American Voting League successfully turned out the vote for Roosevelt.[16]

In Japan, life was ordered and organized, so it was natural for Japanese immigrants to form structured associations for themselves in the United States. One influential group was the Japanese Association, which reached its prime in the 1920s and 1930s. It provided translators, established graveyards, connected newcomers with necessary services, and served as a police and court system to maintain Japanese values. It was conservative regarding acculturation, taking as its motto, "Don't become too American too quickly."[17] The Japanese formed a large network of service agencies, many offering acculturated programs such as scout troops and basketball. All-Japanese athletic leagues were prevalent in California.

Another mutual aid organization was the Japanese-American Citizen's League (JACL), a consolidation of several local groups. JACL tried to deal with issues of discrimination and prejudice and was the primary Japanese-American organization to deal with the American government during World War II. The evacuation of citizens of Japanese descent into detention camps was the major crisis faced by that community. Because the JACL was seen as cooperating with the government, it lost its influence.[18]

For blacks, the mid 1930s brought Garvey's Back-to-Africa movement and Father Divine's Peace Movement. Black neighborhoods held mass meetings, raised money, and formed solidarity groups. A Negro press grew in importance, and slowly white America developed some consciousness of the problems of black citizens. The depression gave impetus to black-oriented pressure groups, labor organizers, and militant civil rights workers. By the 1940s, tensions exploded in several urban racial riots.

The Brotherhood of Sleeping Car Porters became America's first all-black union. As such, it was instrumental in combating job discrimination in the defense industry. In 1941, the union threatened to stage a national Negro march on Washington. The possibility of a hundred thousand blacks descending on Washington was enough to convince Roosevelt to issue an executive order reaffirming the federal policy of nondiscrimination.[19]

New extremist volunteer groups gained support during the depression, having in common anti-foreign, anti-Semitic, anti-Catholic and anti-anything-modern feelings. Groups sprang up with names like National Gentile League, American Rangers, Militant Christian Patriots of Los Angeles, America Awake, and the Silver Shirt Legion. Many had a religious veneer and stressed fundamentalism. One 1930s movement was led by Father Coughlin, a Roman Catholic priest, whose radio ministry was estimated at 19 million. He agitated against Roosevelt, the New Deal, Jews, banks, welfare, and communism. His audience contributed over $500,000 in 1938 alone, despite the depression.[20]

The number of voluntary health and social welfare agencies continued to grow during the twenties. Many were concerned with educating community policy makers and the public in general and with providing funds for research. Volunteers continued to play an active role as fundraisers, speakers, and organizers.

Cancer was one of the diseases that drew new attention in this period, following the formation of the American Cancer Society in 1913 by a group of gynecologists and lay people. The organization quickly established a strong relationship with the General Federation of Women's Clubs. In 1927, a contest was held in an effort to find a cure for cancer, with a prize of $50,000; there was no winner, proving that there was no easy solution to the problem. The contest also raised public awareness about the dangers of cancer. Further efforts to spread the word were launched by the Women's Field Army in 1936. However, this volunteer army was so large that management proved difficult, and in 1946 the emphasis was changed to that of raising funds for research.[21]Meanwhile, a parallel organization, the National Cancer Foundation, was founded by volunteers who responded to the plight of cancer patients and their families, who needed all types of specialized help

One product of the early 1920s was the Junior League, which began as a way for young society women to become instructed in the philanthropic and civic interests of their cities. Each year, an increasing number of debutantes eagerly joined, and Junior League members soon were in great demand as volunteers in all types of charity work.

Some took up the plight of children. The National Child Labor Committee had been continuously working for legislative reform in individual states, and by 1924 it was prepared to fight for a child labor amendment to the Constitution. Though not immediately successful, it did contribute to the passage of a comprehensive Fair Labor Standards Act in 1938, which contained wage as well as child labor standards for industries that produced goods for interstate commerce. Volunteers also helped with a national school lunch program that was launched in 1935. Federal and local authorities split the cost, while the

Parent Teacher Association, the Junior League, the American Legion, and others provided volunteer labor and equipment; fewer than ten years later, the program was feeding 9 million school children at least one hot meal a day.[22]

Still another example of citizen effort on behalf of children came in the form of a block-mother plan established in 1942 by the PTA as part of the civil defense program. Designed to protect children during air raids, it ended up uncovering tens of thousands of neglected children. Before the war ended, it had become a means for ensuring the general welfare of young children, at a local level and on a voluntary basis. As juvenile delinquency began to increase, citizens experimented with various approaches to the problem. A 1936 survey by the National Probation Association indicated that "60% of larger probation departments in the United States use volunteers."[23] In 1940, in Clark County, California, a unit of volunteer boy sheriffs was formed and trained in self-defense and first aid. This relatively successful effort won the support of many in Hollywood, including actress Joan Crawford.[24]

Women were also active in the continuing fight for birth control. Several volunteer groups merged in 1921 to form the American Birth Control League and renewed their efforts in the areas of public education, lobbying, and the establishment of birth control clinics. Although church groups largely fought the contraception movement, a major step forward occurred in 1931 when Pope Pius XI approved the rhythm method for Catholics. By 1940, birth control clinics had sprung up everywhere, and the Birth Control Federation was making planned parenthood a reality in thirteen states.

In 1921, the earlier Ohio Society for Crippled Children expanded into the National Society for Crippled Children, and within another year reached international status. In 1934, the first national campaign for funds was launched, and by 1941, there were active Societies for Crippled Children in thirty-seven states. After World War II, the organization changed its name and broadened its focus to include adults, spurred by the rehabilitation needs of disabled veterans. It eventually became known as the Easter Seal Society: "The great strength of the Easter Seal Society lies in its volunteers . . . concerned citizens who know the importance of sharing responsibilities in a variety of ways."[25] Those responsibilities included advocate, baby-sitter, tutor, friendly visitor, recreation and therapy aide, receptionist, and file clerk. Furthermore, many specialized volunteers, such as bankers, media experts, printers, and rehabilitation professionals, were involved in public education campaigns, legislation advocacy, information and referral services, and equipment loan programs.

The Maryland Association for the Colored Blind, established in the last era, now broadened its scope to include blacks who were deaf and physically disabled. Between 1922 and 1927, the group evolved into the Association for the Handicapped. These volunteers raised money to erect special schools and conducted "save-a-sight" campaigns to provide eyeglasses for needy black children. The group was instrumental in introducing the word "handicapped" to the Maryland public, replacing the previous label of "subnormal."[26]

Epilepsy continued to attract much public interest, and in 1933 a group of concerned citizens founded the Bowditch School in Maryland. This facility for epileptic children later became the National Children's Rehabilitation Center. As miracle drugs began to be discovered, lay people took new hope and sought to foster more cooperation in the battle against this disease. Their efforts, with the help of Eleanor Roosevelt, culminated in 1939 in Boston with the founding of the Laymen's League Against Epilepsy. It grew into a strong organization, becoming the American Epilepsy League in 1944. At this time, New York volunteers formed their own organization, the National Association to Control Epilepsy, and sponsored the Baird Foundation Clinic in New York City.

During the 1930s, the concept of the "community school" was created, with the first one being established in Flint, Michigan. This involved making public schools a resource for all ages by keeping the facilities open eighteen hours a day and offering a wide range of adult classes. The community schools, which spread rapidly, were managed by local volunteers, who often taught classes as well.

Migrants and transients were also aided by volunteers. As far back as colonial times, communities had been suspicious of those who did not settle down as long-term residents. However, after World War I, groups such as the Salvation Army and Volunteers of America became more actively involved; many social agencies appointed "transient committees" to develop better services.[27] The Interchurch World Movement of North America conducted a survey of migrant farm labor on the east coast:

> *Added to the hardship of irregular work and low pay, the survey found "the very acute problem of housing, sanitation, and morals"; it recommended "trained workers directed by some*

joint agency of the churches" and "itinerant missionaries who would follow the migratory movement itself as counsellors and companions of the transient workers."[28]

Thus began the Migrant Ministry of the National Council of Churches. In 1920 it established day care centers in farm labor camps, with donations from the surrounding communities. By the end of the 1930s, the ministry was working in fifteen states. Its volunteers acted as catalysts in motivating more community participation and were involved in activities such as staffing mothers' clubs and weekend centers, teaching English, building shelters, and providing information on local services.

The Red Cross, too, continued as a major volunteer effort during this period, developing new techniques in disaster relief and expanding its health and welfare services. Relief was provided during the Mississippi and Ohio River floods in 1927 and 1937. Public health nursing was offered in more than half the counties of the nation, and new training programs in first aid, nursing skills, and water safety were begun in urban and rural areas alike. During the depression years of the 1930s the Red Cross was called upon to help distribute food and clothing and also initiated its first attempts at recruiting blood donors. Though such peacetime activities were important and widespread, the Red Cross organization responded to World War II with even more impressive assistance measures.

Because of the Great Depression, enormous changes took place in the social welfare field during this period—perhaps more dramatic than at any other time in American history. The self-sufficient and carefree attitude of the Roaring Twenties suddenly vanished when the stock market crashed, and it became painfully clear that the individual was helpless in the face of widespread unemployment and general insecurity. Equally helpless were the church and local agencies, financially incapable of meeting the needs of the destitute as they had in the past.

Until the summer of 1932, the Hoover administration contended that the relief of unemployment and destitution was a problem to be met by private philanthropy and local and state governments. Modest neighborhood efforts, such as cookies baked by Muncie High School girls for Red Cross relief, were applauded as productive and appropriate.[29] But as the depression worsened, it became increasingly apparent that Hoover's reliance upon traditional charity was inadequate. Some private agencies considered their relief work to be merely a part of their general religious or social reform programs, rather than a full-time responsibility. And in many cases, the job was simply too overwhelming

> *as when Philadelphia was obliged for lack of funds to suspend all relief payments for a period of five weeks in the summer of 1932. The 52,000 destitute families which had previously been receiving modest food orders managed by one means or another to escape starvation during this crisis, largely because neighbors shared with one another in a form of primitive communism.*[30]

With the launching of the New Deal, the emphasis switched to nationwide programs enacted in Washington, and new federal laws offered old-age pensions, maternity and dependency assistance, low-cost housing, loans to home owners, subsidized school and health programs, and other direct benefits resulting from the overall recovery plan. "Before the decade ended, private social service agencies were able to disavow any responsibility for the basic economic needs of the family and to concentrate instead on personal maladjustment."[31] This is not to say, however, that there were not many volunteer efforts during this period. True, in the field of social work per se, the role of the volunteer was diminished, as the "professional" (paid) social worker was now considered more competent. Most volunteers were allowed to participate only as board members and fundraisers. But there were other fields in which volunteers were crucial.

Americans made valiant attempts to fight the economic disaster on their own. In a January 3, 1932 article in the *New York Times,* the efforts of private citizens across the land were characterized:

> *If there is a hero of this hour . . . it is this average American . . . He is the force behind the "drives" which seem funny to the satirist, stupid to the Socialist, and to every clear-eyed observer inadequate, whether the sum collected is $18,000,000 in New York or $10,000 in a county seat in Dakota.*
>
> *But if these campaigns are not the sound method of coping with hunger and unemployment, they are, up to date, the only method. They represent a communal effort unequaled even during the war.*[32]

During the depression, survival depended upon creativity. When money was short for everyone, and when the charity drives and bread lines could no longer meet the growing relief needs, barter returned to the American scene. The same *New York Times* article described the renewal of barter as

> *one of the striking phenomena of the present chaos . . . There is something joyous about these transactions; trading without money is an entirely different temper from ordinary buying and selling. You see multiplied proofs these days of how gladly people turn to the primitive, but none more convincing than the lively zest of this new-old commerce at the crossroads.*[33]

The extent of the bartering system was again highlighted by the *Times* in September 1932:

> *These men and women out of work are establishing a labor exchange . . . in dozens of cities from Portland, Ore. to Rochester, NY . . . like pioneer settlements, where the carpenter builds a porch for a suit of clothes and the cobbler mends shoes for a crate of garden truck.*[34]

The barter communities became cities within cities, augmented by farmer produce exchanges and home preserving and canning of all surplus fruits and vegetables. Volunteer energy was expended in tremendous amounts in such diverse self-help activities as rehabilitating abandoned shacks to use as subsistence farms and converting crossroads stores and street corners into bartering centers. All of which made the *Times* conclude that a new social, economic, and political era was dawning:

> *It waits only for the liquidation of our biggest frozen asset, the active and responsible citizen. Revolution? America has gone through not one but a series since 1900. It's all over but the official and social recognition.*[35]

An important side effect of the self-help process was the revival of the town or neighborhood meeting. Community spirit and local pride ran high in most areas, "partly the effect of the civic drives for relief funds, conducted with a wartime fervor, and partly the welding heat of a common protest."[36] Everywhere, people met to complain about conditions as well as to mobilize local relief efforts. The volunteer protests centered universally on taxes. If the nation's unemployed had fully recognized their potential political clout merely on the basis of numbers, the result might have been violent civil unrest.

As the depression wore on, government intervention was increasingly looked to as the answer. Government officials and private citizens alike favored cash grants as a direct means of regaining economic balance. The height of this thinking was reached in California with the 1939 "Ham and Eggs" or "Thirty Every Thursday" vote. In simplified terms, the Ham and Eggs bill proposed to give $30 in cash each Thursday to every unemployed person in California over fifty years of age. The effort to pass this unusual measure "enrolled some 400,000 dues-paying members, had more than 12,000 trained volunteer workers, and even by California standards it was an impassioned movement."[37]

The many victims of the depression were aided by innumerable soup kitchens and bread lines established by charitable volunteers. There were also free medical dispensaries. Homeless men in particular were helped by various types of missions that provided shelter and temporary care. Most of these missions included evangelistic attempts to save the men's souls. Regardless of their motives there were many well-meaning individuals who volunteered their time and money on behalf of these transients: doctors who gave medical care for free; donors of thousands of books and magazines; and businessmen's service clubs that paid for one meal a day for needy men at a local restaurant.[38]

The Roosevelt administration developed the Civilian Conservation Corps (CCC) to put unemployed men (almost 3 million nationwide) to work doing worthwhile, needed jobs in the country's parks and recreation areas. Many of the log shelters, bridges, fire towers, trails, and walkways built by these men are still used today. Some CCC programs remain active through the present day.

The benefits of the original CCC went beyond the tremendous amount of work completed and the much-needed paychecks provided to the workers. The CCC experience demonstrated that bringing citizens together in a shared experience, especially one that is physically and mentally challenging, develops an esprit de corps and pride in one's community that can lead to substantial results.

During the depression, interest in religion declined sharply among Protestant denominations. This was largely because the churches slackened their efforts to feed and clothe the poor as public agencies assumed this burden. The destitute accordingly became disenchanted with churches and semi-religious bodies such as the YMCA. The Catholic churches fared better during these difficult times, as they were more successful in retaining contact with their unemployed members. The National Catholic Welfare Conference increased the scope of its secular activities by adding such special services as the Interracial Council of New York (1934), the War Relief and Refugee Service (1936), and the Association of Catholic Trade Unionists (1937). It was also during the 1930s that the Catholic Youth Organization was begun in Chicago, comprised of a dedicated Catholic laity of both adult volunteer leaders and youth volunteer members. Another result of the economic and secular pressures on churches of this era was the appearance of new collective action through the ecumenical movement. There was a joining together of all faiths for mutual aid and cooperation, which led to the formation of organizations such as the 1934 Committee on Religion and Welfare Activity.[39]

The arts in America were still viewed either as the domain of a few rich patrons or as something to be popularized for a mass audience. Not until well into the twentieth century did most Americans have the leisure and subsequent need and desire for the arts. But it was recognized that free expression in books, plays, and other art forms was essential to a democracy. Unprecedented private patronage of American artists occurred in the 1920s, but after the depression such voluntary support was largely replaced by New Deal programs such as the Works Progress Administration (WPA).

In this period, an innovation in entertainment was introduced that would radically alter all former concepts of audience size and type: radio. It began with an engineer, Frank Conrad, who was employed by the Westinghouse Company in Pittsburgh. As early as the 1910s, Conrad had set up a radio station in his home as an experiment. In April 1920 he relicensed his station under the call letters 8XK and discovered, almost by accident, that his amateurish radio talks were being picked up by an audience of ham radio operators. These operators had been silenced during the war and were now eager to return to the airwaves.

> *Tired of talking to the group, he finally resorted to phonograph records as a means of entertaining his growing public. By the summer of 1920 his listener response was growing a bit*

> *troublesome. Letters and telephone calls were coming in, many of them making odd requests . . . In sheer self-defense Dr. Conrad finally announced that at 7:30 o clock on Wednesday and Saturday evenings he would broadcast for two hours.*[40]

Conrad's volunteered entertainment took on an added dimension when he negotiated a deal with the town record merchant to borrow expensive records in exchange for mentioning the store's name on the air. When the store's sales increased, media advertising was born. Conrad's two sons loved sharing the job of announcer, and the family soon found other local talent to assist in the venture. Their audience continued to grow. "The Conrad family now occupied the position of public benefactors, yet it was the position of entertainers who receive nothing but glory as their reward."[41] The contributing merchants and even Westinghouse had increased their sales, but no profits came to the Conrads. In late 1920, after Conrad had made several improvements in his experimental station, Westinghouse itself opened station KDKA. It began broadcasting in East Pittsburgh on election night and was a success from the start.

Other firms soon became involved in commercial radio, and its volunteer roots were quickly forgotten. It was some time, however, before much profit could be made from stations. For the Telephone Company's WEAF and WCAP radio stations "revenue was only incidental to . . . broadcasting activities . . . [that] were largely actuated by motives of scientific research and public service."[42]

Radio as an important entertainment medium was here to stay. Though it became a commercial industry, it had access to the public to an unprecedented degree. This led to variations on the theme of citizen cooperation. For example: "When in 1940 the Metropolitan Opera Company in severe financial straits appealed to its invisible [radio] audience, they contributed a third of a million dollars to 'save the Met.'"[43]

Other artistic media prospered during this period, especially the movies. But almost from the beginning some people raised the issue of sex in films, blaming what they considered to be un-Christian movies on supposed Jewish movie moguls. In 1934, the Legion of Decency was formed by Catholic bishops, and Protestant groups threatened to boycott films they considered immoral. Ultimately, these volunteer pressures were effective in altering the types of movies Hollywood produced. While controversial subjects such as prison reform, racism, and the plight of miners were still explored, this was the era of the "pigtails and gingerbread" movies.[44]

Entertainment also included recreation and sports. The trend in the 1920s was toward more active personal involvement rather than spectator sports, especially because the depression made it impossible to stage expensive athletic events. The same problem, however, fostered sports that could cheaply invite mass participation. In addition:

> *In seeking to redress the past neglect the conscience of the thirties considered the needs of low-income groups, particularly the growing generation. With municipal budgets badly slashed, however, the authorities could hardly rise to the occasion. The supervision of many playgrounds would have broken down completely in 1932-1933 save for the volunteering of some citizens as recreation leaders aided by a skeleton staff of paid workers.*[45]

After 1933, the New Deal public works programs were able to supply publicly funded recreation leaders, though volunteers continued to be involved in all aspects of the new activities.

One question confronting the public was how best to use increased leisure time:

> *Various philanthropic agencies have come forward with programs devised to fill the gap in providing motivation and facilities for these more constructive and educational types of activities. The Christian and Hebrew Associations, Knights of Columbus, Scouting and Camp Fire Organizations, social settlements, boy's clubs, and various church organizations have made important contributions to the development of our sense of leisure activity values as well as to the recreational facilities of the nation.*[46]

These voluntary groups assumed leadership of the recreation movement, though they concentrated on youth programs almost to the exclusion of adults. One study made of the American recreation scene during the period predicted that the government's role would be to add and expand local programs on a larger scale, while philanthropic agencies would continue as experimenters and skill developers.

Among the organizations seeking to counteract the increase in juvenile delinquency by providing lawful outlets to youth were the Cub Scouts (1937) and the Little League (1939). The Little League began in Williamsport, Pennsylvania, with fifty volunteers who organized three baseball teams for boys twelve years old and under, and the craze was on.

In 1936 the National Ski Patrol got its start after a series of unfortunate accidents on the newly-popular ski slopes. The New York Amateur Ski Club, motivated by the accidental death of a member, formed a volunteer committee to study skiing safety. In 1938, the club's members went to the National Downhill and Slalom Races, where they scrounged up donations of toboggans, blankets, and bandages. Then they convinced the local hospitals to supply ambulances and enlisted the services of doctors. By race time, equipment and volunteers were placed strategically about the slopes and assisted whenever needed. This display brought the support of the Red Cross and the National Ski Association, after which the ski patrol idea spread rapidly.[47]

As part of the push for better recreation facilities, advocates aligned themselves with the conservationists who were clamoring for the preservation of America's natural resources. The conservation groups focused their activities in a variety of ways. In 1918 the Save-the-Redwoods League was founded in California, dedicated to raising funds for the acquisition and protection of redwood trees in public parks. Over fifty-five thousand volunteer members raised over $20 million in fifty-seven years and helped to create a system of twenty-seven state redwood parks. In 1921, the League began a "memorial grove" program whereby for $10,000 an individual could begin a redwood grove.[48]

In addition, there were many outdoor clubs along the Pacific coast, and in 1932 a group of them formed the Federation of Western Outdoor Clubs, working together to maintain wilderness areas for public use.

In 1928 the volunteers of the American Forestry Association started fire prevention campaigns in Florida, Georgia, Mississippi, and South Carolina. Schools were the primary target for the films and lectures by this dedicated group of "Dixie Crusaders," but presentations were also made to

> *women s clubs, 4-H groups, and the workers in lumber and turpentine camps. They traveled more than 300,000 miles before the drive ended in 1931. By 1933, when the CCC boys came to plant trees and fight fires, local sentiment had already changed in favor of trees and against those who set fires. Much of the later improvement in southern forestry and in wood-using industries is credited to this campaign of the Dixie Crusaders.*[49]

Another conservation effort was represented by the National Wildlife Federation. It evolved in 1936 after a North American Wildlife Conference was held by presidential request in response to the decline in wilderness animal and bird populations. Federation members voluntarily worked toward the preservation and proper use of all natural resources.

Following World War I, there was a general lapse in enthusiasm for military-related activities. Membership in the National Guard declined, and Congress would not appropriate enough funds for ongoing training. So some volunteered for occasional training, some took correspondence courses, and many others simply allowed their skills to fade away. Even when the next war broke out in Europe, Americans were slow to become involved. The peacetime draft of 1941 met with a good deal of hostility from the draftees, who resented training for a war they did not expect to enter. The public in general viewed the draftees as losers of the lottery, and troop morale was extremely low, especially in the small towns near training camps where there were no recreation facilities for the soldiers.

One effort to combat this problem appeared in the form of the United Service Organizations for National Defense, established in 1941. The USO was a cooperative effort by six organizations—YMCA, YWCA, National Catholic Community Services, National Jewish Welfare Board, Salvation Army, and National Travelers Aid Association—aimed at increasing the amount of live entertainment available to servicemen. At first the federal government planned to institute its own program of on-leave recreation and so hesitated about supporting the private USO undertaking. But President Roosevelt emphatically endorsed the volunteer approach, instructing the Federal Security Agency and the War Department to construct appropriate facilities in which the USO could run its program. The USO soon affiliated with other civilian volunteer groups such as the Friends of New York Soldiers and Sailors, and Camp Shows, Inc. The latter was created by Hollywood movie professionals to recruit volunteer performers and coordinate traveling shows to entertain military personnel.[50]

As the Second World War spread through Europe and even touched British shores, the fighting spirit of America revived. Many towns tried, with limited success, to induce state and federal officials to instruct the local citizenry in the art of guerrilla war. When the response was negative, they took matters into their own hands. For example, Hamilton, Ohio, devised a plan by which local businesses would subsidize those of the town's young men who joined the National Guard or participated in any other government-supervised military training. More than fifty other towns and cities copied the Hamilton plan. Many more, however, followed the example of Lexington, Massachusetts, which armed, drilled, and organized its citizens as a militia—much like in the days of the American Revolution. Still another type of activity was found in the Military Training Camps Association, which provided military training to volunteer middle-class professionals and businessmen who would then be available as an officer reserve.

Such mobilization was not limited exclusively to males, for the women of America found their own ways to join the ranks. Virginia Nowell of North Carolina organized the Green Guards, an all-female militia dedicated to the defense of hearth and home; her command included nearly a thousand volunteers.[51] Furthermore, an American Women's Voluntary Service came into existence, patterned after the British WVS. Its two hundred sixty thousand members drove trucks, navigated for military convoys, made maps, chauffeured army and navy officers, taught housewives what to do during an air raid, and staffed information centers for the Air Warning Service. It should be noted that both the War Department and the army consistently refused to encourage any of these local volunteer efforts.

Some women's groups became involved in the continuing pacifist movement. They crusaded against toy soldiers and even against Memorial Day, preferring to stress maimed veterans as the focal point of "peace parades." During the 1930s, pacifism gained small victories in diverse areas, including changing Girl Scout uniforms from military khaki to more neutral green. In 1935, the National Education Association voted down a proposal to put military training into tax-supported schools.[52] As Roosevelt moved closer and closer to United States involvement with the Allied cause in Europe, anti-war sentiments grew stronger.

Although the country was still not officially in the war, sympathetic Americans tried to aid the British and French people. The Red Cross managed to raise about $7 million for relief. Women busied themselves making dresses, socks, and sweaters for refugees and bandages for soldiers. More than three hundred organizations were involved in collecting money and other items—groups such as the Allied Relief Fund, Bundles for Britain, Bingo for Britain, American Friends of France, and Le Paquet au Front. As in World War I, an American Volunteer Ambulance Corps was organized.

> *And London boasted a mobile defense unit of the Home Guard which was composed entirely of Americans with business or property interest in England. Like their British counterparts, they were middle-aged and did not look particularly ferocious. But they roared about the countryside armed with Thompson submachine guns and called themselves the Gangsters.*[53]

Spontaneous volunteer movements sprang up in some areas, especially the South and Pacific Northwest, promoting the purchase of British-made goods. And the actors and actresses of Hollywood and Broadway staged many benefit performances to aid the British cause; Gypsy Rose Lee even "stripped for Britain." One remarkable example of support for England came from a group of factory workers:

> *Workers at Lockheed sent their own Christmas present to the British people: With their own skills, and on their own time, and with their own money, they built, paid for, and dispatched a brand new Hudson bomber as a Christmas gift.*[54]

Even convicts tried to help, such as those in the Washington State Penitentiary at Walla Walla who gave fundraising concerts for the cause.

Another organization aiding Britain was Save Europe's Children, which led a campaign to bring British children to the United States and Canada and place them under the care of willing families. This volunteer effort was hampered by existing immigration laws, but, by stimulating popular demand, congressional passage of a Mercy Ships bill was obtained, authorizing unlimited entry of evacuated British children. Later on, the organization was again stymied by the fact that the Germans had sunk several of the ships carrying children. But American volunteer perseverance found a solution by sponsoring hostelries in the English countryside to which the children could be evacuated from the cities.

Volunteers were also involved in setting up local draft boards during the winter months of 1940-1941; more than twenty thousand individuals enthusiastically gave their leisure time for this purpose. But by the spring of 1941, their high spirits were sagging, and even the most loyal volunteer was beginning to doubt the worth of the draft effort, since it seemed to provide neither universal military training nor mobilization.

Once the United States had formally entered the war, however, Americans rallied again and found many ways in which to support their troops through volunteering. Most families collected newspapers, tin cans and fats, donated blood, and purchased bonds. High school students were eagerly carving, sanding, and gluing together millions of model airplanes for military and civilian use. Students also joined the Victory Corps:

> *To absorb the excess energies of students who wanted to join in the war effort, a High School Victory Corps was created in the summer of 1942 . . . ostensibly they were being prepared for war work or services, but for the most part they were kept busy with parades, scrap drives, bond sales and calisthenics. For these activities the high schools gave academic credit.*[55]

Young and old alike signed up to learn the rudiments of first aid instruction. Further, the Office of Strategic Services requested that all citizens search their attics and photograph albums for any recent pictures taken in Europe and Asia that might provide information on terrain features and new construction.[56] Even the family pet was called to action. Through Dogs for Defense, families volunteered over ten thousand dogs of all breeds, which were then trained for active duty as couriers and other support to the soldiers in Europe and the South Pacific.

In June 1942, President Roosevelt publicly stressed the critical need for rubber. The result was a nationwide campaign:

> *Sally Rand gave fifty balloons . . . When Roosevelt declared that the rubber floor mats from the White House cars had been sacrificed, Boy Scouts staked out service stations to plead with passing motorists to surrender their floor mats. Federal agencies even donated their spittoon mats, including 500 from the Senate and 1200 from the House. For all these drives the slogan was "Give till it hurts."*[57]

At about the same time, another crisis faced America: a massive shortage of farm workers. As more and more men were drafted or lured into the well-paying war industry jobs, the country risked losing millions of tons of food from its untended farms. But thanks to the efforts of hundreds of thousands of volunteers, mainly from the YWCA, the High School Victory Corps, and the American Women's Voluntary Service, nearly all crops were saved.

Another volunteer effort related to agriculture was embodied in the slogan "An Acre for a Soldier." Sponsored by the Farm Security Administration, the movement became a gratifying success in most rural areas, as farmers gave the cash raised from an acre's crop to such things as canteens for servicemen. Even those without an acre to spare participated by donating a pig or a couple of sheep. North Platte, Nebraska, opened a canteen for the trains of soldiers passing through on their way to and from the war. The residents mobilized their entire region, and towns from miles around took turns bringing homemade food to the depot. The spot soon became known for its warm hospitality, and by the end of the war hundreds of thousands of soldiers had been so welcomed.

World War II brought an increase in seamen but no on-shore services to meet their needs. Finally, in 1942, the United Seamen's Service (USS) was established in order to provide housing, medical care, counseling, and recreation. As a private, nonprofit organization, it relied heavily on volunteers and voluntary donations and cooperated with such groups as the YMCA, Travelers' Aid Society, and the Red Cross. Most of the volunteers were women, who provided wholesome female companionship to the sailors. But the seamen themselves also volunteered, willingly giving their free time to fix needed equipment at the clubs and to serve on advisory committees:

> *In many other ways, too, USS was heavily indebted to its volunteer workers, not only because they provided services which the organization could not afford to buy, but even more because their contributions comprised intangibles of personality and atmosphere which could never be stated in pecuniary terms at all.*[58]

The Office of Defense Health and Welfare, which was created before Pearl Harbor, became the Office of Community War Services in 1943. It was comprised of two sections: Social Protection and Recreation. The former recruited doctors, dentists, and teachers for communities lacking health care, obtained extra rations when special needs arose, cleaned up shanty towns and trailer parks, and opened venereal disease clinics. The Recreation section set up adult education centers, sponsored athletic contests, and built hundreds of community centers and more than three thousand teenage recreation centers. "The federal government provided money and often the initiative, and then found hundreds of thousands of local volunteers to take over what it had created."[59]

Youth activities at home were emphasized during World War II.

> *The era of physical fitness programs and scrap drives gave way to a new phase in which the rudiments of an adolescent sub-culture asserted themselves . . . Social centers, glamorized as counterparts to servicemen's "canteens," were established in thousands of American communities in the last two years of the war . . . Public and private money poured into these centers with names like 'The Rec," "Coke Bar," "Club Victory," and "Teentown Night Club."*[60]

While adults started most of these centers and soft drink companies contributed financial support, the day-to-day operation of them was handled mainly by the high school students themselves.

Business associations made many volunteer contributions to the war effort:

> *Associations supplied the federal government with specifications on defense contracts, with information about materials on hand, and they acted as a communication link between the federal government and individual business firms.*[61]

Among the notable efforts was the transporting of six hundred thousand troops by the Association of American Railroads during the first month and a half after the outbreak of war. Further, the Council of Machine Tool and Equipment Services inventoried and cross-indexed two hundred fifty thousand pieces of production equipment and machinery in over four hundred fifty plants, for government use. By 1944, the American Society of Association Executives could identify over fifty types of projects developed by its members, such as selling war bonds, distributing pamphlets on gasoline conservation, and providing technical assistance to Washington agencies.[62]

Another way that business contributed to the war effort was through the War Advertising Council. Sponsored through the USO Public Relations Committee, the businesses in the Council used their combined expertise to deliver public service messages about war bonds, rationing, and supporting the USO. This cooperative, voluntary venture in public service advertising successfully channeled business know-how into public information needs. After World War II, the effective War Advertising Council apparatus continued as the Advertising Council, providing peacetime public service information.

Still another form of citizen involvement during the war was seen in the civil defense movement. Toward the latter part of 1941 cities began to organize large-scale programs, and although the first Office of Civil Defense was somewhat disorganized and confused, the people's enthusiasm remained strong. By February 1942, there were more than 5 million volunteers seeking to assist the war effort in their local communities, and the number continued to grow. Urban volunteer fire brigades came into existence once again. Classes in survival techniques during air raids attracted hundreds of thousands. After several regional experiments, the government began to establish a nationwide network of amateur aircraft spotters to track potentially hostile aircraft; patterned after the British model and known as the Civilian Air Warning System, it soon involved a half million volunteers. In addition, some forty thousand civilian male and female pilots joined the Civil Air Patrol. Their chief duties consisted of carrying high-priority documents from place to place and conducting anti-submarine patrol flights over coastal waters. They were joined in this latter activity by thousands of small boat owners, despite the Navy's disapproval of such amateur involvement.

Upon American entry into World War II, the Red Cross recruited more than seventy-one thousand registered nurses for military duty and provided a wealth of volunteer staff energy for military hospitals. Volunteers were also involved in operating clubs and clubmobiles for servicemen in overseas rest and recreation areas and cooperated with Red Cross societies in war-torn countries to provide relief and rehabilitation for the civilian victims of the war. The American people further supported the Red Cross through contributions of nearly $785 million. One special activity was the prisoner-of-war packaging project. From 1942 to 1945, volunteers in five selected Red Cross centers gave a total of nearly 2 million hours to the preparation, in assembly-line fashion, of more than 27 million packages for American and Allied prisoners in Europe and the Far East.[63]

All in all, the period between the end of World War I and the end of World War II was marked by both economic and social extremes. The intense ups and downs did much to shape the personality of modern America. The major difference between this and the previous era was that

> *Progressivism, which dominated a relatively prosperous and decidedly hopeful age, represented a kind of voluntarism, while the New Deal, unfolding in the midst of the nation's most devastating depression, represented a kind of compulsory program.*[64]

Because of the many New Deal projects, services previously offered by private initiative now grew to rely on government support.

> *And a great change had come over the nation's life that would not be shaken off with the end of the war. Through half a dozen major agencies—Social Security, Internal Revenue, Selective Service, the Office of Price Administration, the Office of Community War Services—Americans were now more closely tied to their government than any other generation in history.*[65]

Despite this dependency on Washington, the need for volunteer time, energy, and creativity remained strong. As individuals and as members of organizations, citizens attempted to improve the quality of life in every facet of society. Once again, war had demonstrated the power of the people to mobilize in times of crisis.

Endnotes for Chapter 6

1. Herbert Hoover, "The New Deal Further Explored; With Special References to the Bank Panic and to Relief," in *American Ideals Versus The New Deal: Ten Addresses Upon Pressing National Problems* (New York: Scribner, 1936), p. 40.

2. National Safety Council, *Proceedings of the Eleventh Annual Safety Congress* (Detroit, MI: August 28-September 1, 1922), 325.

3. Ibid., 324.

4. *Creating Safer Communities* (New York: Governor's Highway Safety Council, Commonwealth of Pennsylvania, 1936), 4.

5. David Brody, "The Expansion of the American Labor Movement," in *Institutions in Modern America,* ed. Stephen E. Ambrose (Baltimore, MD: The Johns Hopkins Press, 1967), 27.

6. Shih-Shan Henry Tsai, *The Chinese Experience in America* (Bloomington: Indiana University Press, 1986), 109-10.

7. E. David Cronon, *Twentieth Century America: Selected Readings,* (Homewood, IL: The Dorsey Press, 1966), 2: 42.

8. Geoffrey Perrett, *Days of Sadness, Years of Triumph: The American People, 1939-1945* (New York: Coward, McCanns and Geoghegan, 1973), 53.
9. Emily Hahn, *Once Upon a Pedestal* (New York: Crowell, 1974), 246-7.
10. John Harold Redekop, *The American Far Right* (Grand Rapids, MI: Erdmans, 1968), 179.
11. Mary R. Beard, ed., *America Through Women's Eyes* (New York: Macmillan, 1933), 250-1.
12. Dixon Wecter, *The Age of the Great Depression, 1929-1941,* vol. 12, *A History of American Life in Twelve Volumes,* eds. Arthur M. Schlesinger and Dixon Ryan Fox (New York: Macmillan, 1948), 279.
13. Ruth Murray Underhill, *Red Man's America* (Chicago: University of Chicago Press, 1953), 328.
14. D'Arcy McNickle, *The Indian Tribes of the United States* (London: Oxford University Press, 1962), 54.
15. Ibid., 54-5.
16. Tsai, *Chinese Experience,* 96-7.
17. Harry H. L. Kitano, *Japanese Americans: The Evolution of a Subculture* (Englewood Cliffs, NJ: Prentice-Hall, 1976), 55-6.
18. Ibid., 57.
19. Benjamin Quarles, *The Negro in the Making of America,* rev. ed. (New York: Collier Books, 1969), 216-7.
20. Redekop, *American Far Right,* 179-80.
21. Richard Carter, *The Gentle Legions* (Garden City, NY: Doubleday, 1961), 143-54.
22. Perrett, *Days of Sadness,* 326.
23. National Information Center on Volunteerism, *Volunteers in Social Justice,* 5, nos. 4 and 5 (November 1972).
24. Marshall Perham, "Boy Sheriffs Help Fight Crime," *Popular Science* 137 (July 1940): 96-8.
25. Descriptive materials of the National Easter Seal Society for Crippled Children and Adults, in response to authors' questionnaire, April 1, 1976.
26. Dorothy Lymas Coleman, *Robert Coleman and The Association for the Handicapped* (Baltimore, MD: Bay Printing, 1971), 2-5.
27. Philip E. Ryan, *Migration and Social Welfare* (New York: Russell Sage Foundation, 1940), 59-96.
28. Louisa R. Shotwell, *The Harvesters* (Garden City, NY: Doubleday, 1961), 176.
29. Harvey Wish, *Contemporary America: The National Scene Since 1900* (New York: Harper and Row, 1966), 492.
30. Cronon, *Twentieth Century,* 42.
31. Wish, *Contemporary America,* 492.
32. *The New York Times,* January 3, 1932, cited in Anne O'Hare McCormick, *The World at Home* (New York: Knopf, 1956), 86-7.
33. Ibid., 92.
34. *The New York Times,* September 4,1932, cited in Anne O'Hare McCormick, *The World at Home* (New York: Knopf, 1956), 124.
35. Ibid., 126-7.
36. *The New York Times,* January 3, 1932, 92.
37. Perrett, *Days of Sadness,* 22.
38. Jesse Walter Dees, Jr., *Flophouse* (Francestown, NH: Marshall Jones, 1948), 10-23.
39. Wecter, *Age of the Great Depression,* 211.
40. Gleason L. Archer, *History of Radio to 1926* (New York: The American Historical Society, 1938), 199.

41. Ibid., 200.
42. Ibid., 321.
43. Wecter, *Age of the Great Depression,* 234.
44. Ibid., 237-23.
45. Ibid., 222.
46. A Group of Social Scientists in the Ohio State University, *Democracy in Transition* (New York: Appleton-Century, 1937), 251.
47. Descriptive materials of the National Ski Patrol System, Inc., in response to authors' questionnaire, March 29, 1976.
48. Descriptive materials of the Save-the-Redwoods League, in response to authors' questionnaire, March 30, 1976.
49. David Cushman Coyle, *Conservation* (New Brunswick, NJ: Rutgers University Press, 1957), 97.
50. *Twenty-five Years: Keeping Faith with Our Armed Forces Since 1941, U.S.O.* (New York: United Service Organizations, Inc., 1966), 8.
51. Perrett, *Days of Sadness,* 38.
52. Wecter, *Age of the Great Depression,* 306.
53. Perrett, *Days of Sadness,* 64.
54. Ibid., 66.
55. Ibid., 368.
56. Ibid., 235.
57. Ibid., 254.
58. Elmo Paul Hohman, *Seamen Ashore* (New Haven, CT: Yale University Press, 1952), 57.
59. Perrett, *Days of Sadness,* 352.
60. Ibid., 349.
61. Joseph F. Bradley, *The Role of Trade Associations and Professional Business Societies* (University Park: Pennsylvania State University Press, 1965), 26.
62. *Ibid.,* 26-7.
63. Charles Hurd, *The Compact History of the American Red Cross* (New York: Hawthorn Books, 1959), 292.
64. Dewey W. Grantham, Jr., "The Progressive Era and the Reform Tradition," in *Progressivism: The Critical Issues,* ed. David M. Kennedy (Boston: Little, Brown, 1971), 120.
65. Perrett, *Days of Sadness,* 356.

Chapter 7

Protest and Change

1946-1969

1948	Marshall Plan implemented.
1950-1953	Korean War.
1954	Supreme Court's desegregation decision, *Brown v. Board of Education of Topeka*, handed down.
1955	Successful boycott of segregated bus system in Montgomery, Alabama.
1960	John F. Kennedy elected president.
1961	First American orbits the earth. United States sends troops to Vietnam.
1962	Cuban Missile Crisis.
1963	Kennedy is assassinated.
1964	Civil Rights Act passed.
1965	Vietnam conflict escalates. Watts riots.
1968	Martin Luther King Jr. is assassinated.
1969	United States lands first person on moon.

After World War II, the country remained irrevocably linked to the international community. This was demonstrated by the American role in the formation of the United Nations (UN) in 1945. The structure of the UN recognized the United States as a world leader on a par with only a few other big powers. This leadership position brought America new responsibilities for the welfare of other peoples as well as diplomatic confrontation with the Soviet Union and other communist countries in an ongoing cold war.

Despite intentions to remain at peace, American military troops were once again mobilized in 1950, this time against the communist invasion of South Korea. The subsequent three years of fighting gave impetus both to pacifist groups and to a growing fear of communism. In the early 1950s this fear became hysteria as loyalty programs were enacted, immigration and foreign visitation were restricted, and Senator Joseph McCarthy led his crusade against suspected traitors.

Economically, the expected depression following the World War II boom never materialized, and the country even experienced some growth. Truman's "Fair Deal" kept workers working and assured benefits for returning GIs. But the mood of the country shifted away from support for the earlier government-sponsored welfare programs. Eisenhower's election in 1952 and reelection in 1956 marked a relatively inactive period for federal involvement in local programming.

One of the few major social issues to receive federal and court attention during the postwar years was civil rights. A series of Supreme Court decisions from 1948 through 1960 dealt with the inequality of racially segregated schools, especially in the South. Resistance to educational integration was growing stronger, as were the activities of black civil rights groups such as the National Association for the Advancement of Colored People (NAACP). The issue came to a head in 1954 when the case of *Brown* v. *Board of Education of Topeka* once and for all determined school segregation by race to be illegal. Although the law was now clear, enforcement would prove to be a long process of local actions by citizen groups, backed by legal clout.

In 1960, John Kennedy was elected president. His "New Frontier"—symbolized by his presence as the nation's first Catholic president, and its youngest—ushered in a new phase of American life. The 1960s were a decade both of idealism and of unrest. The fight for civil rights increasingly won legislative and social successes, though only after boycotts, sit-ins, and other volunteer demonstrations gained public attention. There was irony in a decade that witnessed both the creation of the Peace Corps and the escalation of involvement in the Indochina war. Vietnam aroused the passions of supporters and protesters. Like their civil rights counterparts, war protest activists developed new mass demonstration techniques designed to get media attention, to win public support, and to convince the government that they represented the majority. Although other volunteers were actively participating in less volatile ways in all areas of the nation's progress and welfare, the 1960s were dominated by citizen movements that grew up around a handful of critical issues.

World War II heightened American willingness to aid other countries, especially by providing food to war-torn nations. In 1946, Harry Truman summed up the volunteer nature of such relief efforts:

> *The cooperation of every man, woman and child, the food trades and industries, the transportation industry, and others will be needed to make [relief] measures effective. I know the conscience of the American people will not permit them to withhold or stint their cooperation while their fellow men in other lands suffer and die.*[1]

When negotiations were underway for the formation of the United Nations, the federal government also sought the involvement of citizen groups, notably the General Federation of Women's Clubs. The Federation's recommendations resulted in the Commission on Human Rights being included in the UN charter.[2] The spirit of international cooperation was further exemplified by the formation of International Voluntary Services. It was founded in 1953 by concerned individuals who felt the need for a nonprofit development assistance agency controlled neither by government nor by a religious group. Once established, this organization provided volunteer technicians to underdeveloped countries.[3]

When the war ended, demobilization affected others besides the soldiers. The Civil Air Patrol was reorganized and chartered by Congress in 1946 as a nonprofit, volunteer organization for humanitarian purposes. Two years later, it also became the civilian auxiliary of the United States Air Force, thus continuing to provide a significant way to involve thousands of citizens. Agreements were made to work together with the Red Cross, the Salvation Army, and the Veterans of Foreign Wars and to provide disaster relief, air and ground searches, and aerospace education.

The USO, on the other hand, had its services curtailed, and its volunteers limited themselves to providing services to homeward-bound GIs and entertaining the wounded in hospitals. By the end of 1947, the USO was officially terminated, with commendations. Its dormancy was short-lived, however, for in 1951 it was reactivated to help in the Korean conflict. From then on, its existence continued to be justified by the presence of thousands of American service people stationed abroad. Another group serving veterans was founded in 1948, the Veterans Bedside Network. Volunteers came into veterans' hospitals and organized the patients to produce radio plays and sing-alongs to be broadcast within the hospital. This therapeutic activity later evolved into closed-circuit television shows and continues today.

The Korean War sparked numerous peace crusades, both by organized groups and by individuals. The unprecedented status of this undeclared war added to the indignation of peace advocates. Nationally, spokespeople were calling for special United Nations peace programs and American commitment of huge sums of money toward maintaining peace. On a far smaller scale, one graduate student in Chicago demonstrated what an individual citizen could do:

> *He decided to act for peace. He . . . flooded Congress with letters on the subject. He [wrote] to various representatives in the United Nations and to the Ambassadors of foreign powers. He [made] popular analyses of our military policy and publishe[d] them on postals . . . He placed an advertisement in the Chicago Sunday Tribune reading "you can help to stop the needless slaughter of Americans in Korea now by writing your Congressman immediately. For complete information, phone Albert."*[4]

Albert received one hundred phone calls in response to his terse ad and convinced many to write Washington and also to attend a peace meeting. Later he published several books, peace directories, and a work entitled *You Can Change the Course of History.*

Peace groups were not solely concerned with the Korean crisis. For many, the priority was pressuring for a nuclear test treaty. This was the first goal of SANE (A Citizens' Organization for a Sane World), established in 1957 as a national organization of many local chapters. By 1959, SANE had broadened its interests to include world disarmament, strengthening the United Nations, and transforming the American economy into one based on peacetime needs. SANE introduced the strategy of large peace demonstrations in key cities.

The fear of communism underlying the Korean War pervaded the American psyche in the late 1940s. By 1947 Truman had initiated the federal loyalty program and, though not one undercover communist was found, set the tone for the intense investigations to come. Fears of foreign infiltration converged in the 1948-1949 trial of Alger Hiss and the hearings of the House Un-American Activities Committee. But anti-communist feelings were whipped into a frenzy by the actions of Wisconsin Senator Joseph McCarthy. When McCarthy made his first accusations in 1950 he was practically ridiculed, yet by 1953 he was one of the most powerful men in America. McCarthyism became a highly emotional movement as pro-McCarthy volunteer groups threw themselves into the task of ferreting out suspected communists, identifying disloyal literature and art, and generally pointing a finger at anything deemed liberal or internationalist. Blacklisting became commonplace.

McCarthyism also galvanized volunteers in protest of such blatant infringement of basic citizen rights. Many resented the implication that membership in any forward-looking or international organization automatically brought a person's patriotism under question. They pointed out that volunteer involvement in the right could be just as undemocratic as volunteer involvement in the left. Groups mobilized to counteract the loyalist investigations with a united front. The entertainment industry, especially hard hit by blacklisting, was the focus of much anti-McCarthy activity—though fear of reprisal effectively limited the extent to which protesters would go. Ultimately it was television that brought about the fall of McCarthy. In 1954, the nation was mesmerized by the Army-McCarthy hearings; thirty-five days of watching McCarthy rant and rave irrationally was enough to turn the tide against him. Edward R. Murrow exposed the senator on his "See It Now" broadcasts.

The end of McCarthy's power did not automatically end the feelings he had engendered. Extreme conservative and radical right groups continued, but without the political clout they had derived from McCarthy. The most influential of the rightist volunteer groups was the John Birch Society, founded in 1958:

> *[This] large and monolithic organization of self-proclaimed patriots operating through some 4,000 semisecret chapters at the grass-roots level in communities from coast to coast and boasting some 75,000 to 85,000 members spread throughout every state of the Union.*[5]

Through such activities as radio broadcasts, rallies, tent shows, and political schools and publications, the radical right disseminated its propaganda and recruited new supporters.

Agricultural, labor, and business volunteerism resumed after World War II. The only changes were in terms of numbers and scope rather than in types of organizations or projects. Farmers retained the concept of the cooperative as the best approach to issues of housing, farm marketing and supply, insurance, credit, rural electrification, group health, education, and even travel. Labor unions continued to press for wage and condition changes that would make the American capitalist system more equitable for all concerned. One new dimension was the need to organize the vastly increased number of women workers. They had joined the labor force during the crisis of the war years, but many had remained on the job to demonstrate their new out-of-the-home freedom. The late 1940s and early 1950s also saw the rise of the full-time, paid union organizer—a development that changed the voluntary nature of the unions.

The business community expanded the interests of local and state Chambers of Commerce. After World War II, Chambers of Commerce opposed business tax increases, developed standards for business ethics, helped with public welfare activities such as the distribution of polio vaccine, worked to eliminate slums, and began to act as tourist and convention centers on behalf of their region. Chambers of Commerce consciously saw themselves as channeling the voluntary efforts of their members into community projects. Business executives, as individuals, continued to serve on citizen policy-making boards as they had in the past, with business leaders calling for creative participation in community affairs.

Corporate giving increased in importance. The organization that actually developed the legal grounds for corporate giving was the Council for Financial Aid to Education. It began officially in 1952 to promote voluntary support of higher education, especially from the business community. In the twenty years after its founding, the Council raised over $22.3 billion and became unique as "perhaps the only organization involved with higher education that was inspired, founded, and led by businessmen throughout its entire career."[6]

The Council for Financial Aid to Education wanted to test the legality of a business contribution to a college, a gift without relation to the product or activities of the company. In 1952, the A. P. Smith Company's $1,500 gift to Princeton University was declared legal by the New Jersey Superior and Supreme Courts. The most interesting aspect of the legal decision was that: "corporate contributions were valid, even in the absence of benefit and statutory authority, because of the responsibility of business toward the community."[7] The lower court went even further, stating that corporate contribution was a "major, though unwritten, corporate power" to preserve American society and therefore amounted to "solemn duty." Thereafter, this legal sanction of business donations stimulated the voluntary involvement of many corporations.

Historically, sponsorship of the arts by private individuals was the accepted way of financing cultural projects. But after the war, arts patronage became systemized through foundations and relied heavily on corporate support; individual patrons diminished in importance. The role of the dedicated patron was kept alive largely by the "lady bountifuls" who supported struggling artists:

> *Miss Horniman backed a whole theater, as Rebekah Harkness backs a whole ballet company. Institutional benevolence on this scale is more often bestowed by the men, and they like to work in a big way, with corporations and foundations, which have screening procedures, questionnaires, rules, and regulations. With the women it is just a year-round Christmas spirit. They are not organized; it's a hit-or-miss proposition; they meet someone who wants a meal, they invite him in, and behold, a masterpiece.*[8]

The War Advertising Council of the 1940s, formed to "marshal the forces of advertising so they would be of maximum help to the national interest,"[9] found an active peacetime role as the Advertising Council. The Red Cross and fire prevention campaigns launched during the war were retained, and new public interest causes were sought. The Advertising Council promoted "voluntary citizen actions to help solve national problems." The whole communications industry became involved in the Council's public service campaigns, donating free advertising expertise and free time and space in all media. The "Smokey the Bear" forest fire prevention campaign emerged as one of the Council's greatest successes.

In general, citizen groups grew in clout and scope in the postwar years. They became involved in everything from approving or fighting television and radio franchise license applications to advising on the design of postage stamps through the Citizen's Stamp Advisory Committee (1957). Safety Councils, popular before the war, continued in the 1950s to be the forerunners in accident prevention education and in advocating for better traffic control.

> *A safety council provides services no other official or private agency provides. No public or private agency other than a citizen's safety council is capable of objectively assembling the*

> *data . . . and then developing . . . corrective programs and educating the public to their necessity . . . Other agencies are subjected to political pressures or . . . special interests . . . Only a citizen organization dedicated to accident prevention, and to that alone, can perform the service every city in this nation needs and deserves.*[10]

In the 1950s the School Safety Patrol was established on a wide scale with guidelines from the American Automobile Association, National Committee on Safety, National Safety Council, and others.

Another interesting type of volunteering developed during this period. The Aerial Phenomena Research Organization was created in 1952 by three volunteers because they felt the United States Air Force was not taking the UFO question seriously. It was the first group to interest the scientific community in UFOs and continues to be the only UFO research organization conducting legitimate scientific studies of such phenomena. Volunteers have served and continue to serve as consultants, administrators, foreign representatives, and field investigators.[11]

The Red Cross continued as a symbol of America's volunteer spirit. Immediately after the armistice in 1945, the American Red Cross joined with the International Committee to search for the missing and to help families who sought to be reunited with relatives across political barriers. In the years that followed, changes occurred in both the organizational structure and the program of the Red Cross. Emphasis was placed on involving the entire community, and volunteer opportunities for young people and senior citizens were expanded. Beginning in the 1950s, the Red Cross began to field large-scale relief operations following major natural disasters. The victims of the severe floods in Kansas, Missouri, Oklahoma, and Illinois in 1951 and the devastating eastern and western floods of 1955 required the aid of thousands of volunteers. Without the self-sacrifice and immediate response of these citizens, such disasters would have taken higher tolls. The Red Cross constantly proved its worth, and as one author stated: "When disaster strikes the problem is not that of getting volunteers to work but is that of getting volunteers to stop working."[12]

Voluntary health agencies and organizations continued to proliferate, providing needed services and developing new methods and knowledge. By 1946, the National Heart Association had changed from a group comprised of medical professionals to a voluntary health organization with a lay membership, although volunteers were still restricted to certain specific roles. The search for greater understanding in the field of mental health continued as the National Association for Mental Health was organized in 1950. Neuromuscular diseases were fought by such groups as the National Multiple Sclerosis Society (1946) and the Muscular Dystrophy Association of America (1950). By 1947, the American Association of Blood Banks had enlisted the help of approximately 4,800 volunteers.[13] While these health foundations and organizations were frequently criticized for oversoliciting, competition, and overemphasis on lesser diseases, it is important to remember that they nevertheless enjoyed "the active loyalty of not less than 15 million volunteers— more Americans than were in uniform at the height of World War II."[14]

One of the most well-known health efforts during this period involved the massive public trials of the Salk vaccine against polio— an almost totally volunteer undertaking.

> *The original plans called for the employment of 10,000 clerks to maintain the millions of forms required in logging the tests. But O'Connor put his foot down. "What makes you think our volunteers can't do it better?" he asked. "You can't hire ten thousand clerks with that kind of ability. But our people will do it free and do it better."*[15]

In the years 1953 to 1955, more than two hundred thousand lay volunteers enabled the vaccine tests to proceed smoothly and accurately. Their duties included learning the complex procedures, herding youngsters through the lines, dispensing lollipops and "Polio Pioneer" buttons, staffing recovery rooms, transporting children to and from the inoculation centers, keeping all records in order, checking supplies, and preparing press releases to keep rumors to a minimum. They all took their jobs seriously, as can be seen from the fact that in one city volunteers were so upset at being disqualified from the final evaluation because of inaccurate forms that they worked all summer to correct their mistakes. That city's tests were finally included in the total results.[16]

The voluntary agency became a primary dispenser of service and aid, maintaining a visible and substantial role for volunteers. The postwar years brought a new search for ways in which volunteers of all types could be utilized:

In this movement, the volunteer and the "indigenous worker" have regained their valued status in social work and in the helping professions generally. Drawn not only from the ranks of the well-to-do and the middle-class, but also and especially from the poor, the individual and personal services given . . . are an essential force in the current war against poverty.[17]

One outcome of this trend was the formation of several self-help groups, such as Parents Without Partners. It began in 1957, when two individuals ran an ad in a New York newspaper that brought twenty-five people to the first meeting. The group provided many types of help to divorcees, widows, widowers, and others and grew steadily through volunteer effort. Another self-help organization formed in the late 1950s was Little People of America, providing programs for dwarfs and midgets. These and many other organizations demonstrated the success of the self-help concept, filling gaps in community services and creating a common fellowship. "Your actual community may turn its back on you, ignore your problem, or turn you out, but there is a separate community of those alike who welcome you in."[18]

Social welfare volunteer activities spanned a broad range during this time. In 1945, the Braille Club of New York formed a clearinghouse that eventually became the National Braille Club. The Braille Book Bank was also begun as a totally volunteer effort, transcribing texts into Braille in cooperation with the Library of Congress. The National Child Labor Committee participated actively in the Mid-Century White House Conference on Children and Youth and prepared the Conference's fact-finding report on child labor and youth employment. In 1959, the Committee created the National Committee on Employment of Youth, and began concentrating more heavily on the problems confronting migrant children.

Migrants were receiving help from other voluntary groups as well in the 1950s. In Pennsylvania, the Department of Public Welfare established a demonstration day care center for migrants in Potter County (1954); though financed by government funds, citizen assistance was still crucial:

Voluntary organizations contributed toys and equipment and collected clothes for thrift sales. The [American Friends Service Committee] helped to staff the center . . . Neighbors frequently brought vegetables and ice cream for the children. It was a real community project.[19]

In Colorado as well, many communities demonstrated concern for the health problems of migrants. More than twenty state and local groups, including growers' associations, church groups, welfare organizations, physicians, schools, and others cooperated in migrant programs. And in other areas, homemaking courses were established in which migrant women were taught by volunteer teachers trained by the United States Extension Service.

The middle to late 1950s saw the resurgence of organized volunteering in court programs. It was becoming increasingly evident that crime was a growing problem, too big to be handled solely by paid justice personnel. Adults in Eugene, Oregon, and college students in Lawrence, Kansas, sought new ways to involve volunteers on behalf of offenders. Following this lead, programs in Boulder, Colorado, and Royal Oak, Michigan, expanded the role of volunteers in juvenile and adult courts.[20] In some ways, justice had come full circle. Probation and parole had begun with volunteer pressure and work, then paid professionals had edged out the untrained citizens, and now volunteers were invited back, but this time with appropriate training and assignments. The idea spread quickly across the country.

Another old idea was given a new twist. Posses, still a necessity in rural and desert areas, exchanged horses for modern jeeps. In 1952 a squad of forty-five jeeps and volunteer drivers was organized in Nevada. It began in readiness for a possible war-connected bombing of the west coast but was mobilized to comb the desert for outlaws and to rescue people in trouble.[21]

Members of long-standing fraternal orders continued to show an interest in volunteering to meet social welfare needs. The Order of the Mystic Shrine built and maintained a series of hospitals in which disabled children of the poor were treated for free. The Modern Woodmen of America maintained a tuberculosis sanatorium and hospital. The Odd Fellows operated homes for the aged and orphans, while the Elks equipped children's playgrounds and donated coal, clothing, and food to the needy. Volunteers continued to provide much-needed assistance in the field of recreation by supervising playgrounds, making camping possible for inner city children, and running programs for retarded and disabled children.

As described in previous chapters, management of American schools had passed since the Revolution into the hands of special boards created solely for the purpose of school administration. School board members now had a well-defined role for which most received no salary:

> *It is fortunate that some able men and women do seek positions on local school boards, despite the fact that they must serve without pay and will frequently find themselves in nasty community fights.*[22]

The American educational system developed additional citizen roles in the 1950s as some two hundred thousand men and women began to volunteer in public and parochial school classrooms. The time was ripe for such involvement, as the postwar baby boom caused a tremendous increase in school enrollment: almost 34 million children in 1957 as compared with 25 million in 1950. Crowded classrooms made it virtually impossible for teachers to provide any type of extra help to children with special needs. In 1954, as educators began to realize the size of the problem, the Public Education Association sent a representative to England to observe a program that utilized volunteer teacher aides and to adapt the idea to the American system. Before long, volunteers were involved in many aspects of the American school day: organizing and running school libraries; escorting children on field trips; and visiting sick and disturbed children in their homes or in hospitals. The influence of these volunteers on the improvement of the quality of education in the United States cannot be overstated.

Education was one important aspect of the conservation movement during the late 1940s and 1950s. Youth programs for conservation and beautification were popular, such as the annual Conservation Camp for New Hampshire Young Leaders, begun in 1947.[23] Roadside improvement contests and successful campaigns to obtain gifts of forest land were among the activities of numerous forest protection societies. The American Forestry Association held national congresses in 1946, 1953, and 1963. These influenced the establishment of Departments of Forestry in New York and Pennsylvania and the development of schools of forestry. Volunteer activities ranged from fighting fires to locating, measuring, and indexing trees in the national forests; "such activities require[d] supervision by technical and professional staff, but most of the input [was] by volunteers."[24] The United States Forest Service and the network of national forests owe their existence entirely to the hard work of volunteer advocates.

By the 1950s visits to the country's parks and forests were so numerous they reached uncontrollable proportions. Conservationists feared that tourists would overrun and destroy the recreational areas. Money and legislation were sorely needed, and citizens made themselves heard through the "tourist vote . . . By 1956 there was a strong movement toward more generous appropriations in support of 'Project 66,' an Interior Department program of park improvement."[25] Also in the 1950s, volunteer groups with formerly local emphases, such as California's Sierra Club, developed national programs for conservation advocacy and for wilderness outings.

Spanning the period from the late 1940s to the early 1970s was the black civil rights movement, the collective effort of countless volunteers that permanently changed relations among all Americans. Perhaps no issue struck as deep as the debate over segregation. Legislative gains, particularly in the areas of school and public facility integration, were negated by the refusal of local communities to implement recent laws. By the 1950s, however, a new and visible militancy developed. One of the first actions was the Montgomery, Alabama, bus boycott:

> *On December 5, 1955, the 50,000 Negro residents of Montgomery . . . began a boycott of the local busses in protest against segregation and discrimination by the bus company. The boycott, organized and led by southern Negroes, continued for months, with as many as 95% of the Negro population of Montgomery participating, often at great personal sacrifice.*[26]

This boycott was sustained by the Montgomery Improvement Association, with Rev. Martin Luther King as its president. The organization raised money, organized car pools, provided instruction in nonviolent resistance, and generally kept morale high. Its success and the successes of many similar activities in the following years were possible only through the determined efforts of thousands of volunteers.

Other organizations stimulated the new black activism. One such group was the Southern Christian Leadership Conference (SCLC), founded in 1957 by one hundred clergy. Dedicated to the belief that the church should be a dominant force in the battle for civil rights, SCLC grew to be a loose union of eighty-five religious affiliates throughout the South. At the same time, the Congress of Racial Equality (CORE) became an interracial urban volunteer movement. Its origin lay in the Chicago Committee on Racial Equality, established by James Farmer in 1942. By the mid-1950s CORE was recruiting students throughout the South and training them in new techniques to combat discrimination.

One popular technique was the sit-in, which quickly enlisted the involvement of enthusiastic southern blacks. After the 1960 incident in Greensboro, North Carolina, when four black students sat down at a segregated Woolworth lunch counter, the sit-in movement assumed massive proportions. Within eighteen months, seventy thousand blacks and whites had participated in sit-ins. More than 3,600 demonstrators were jailed during the first six months, many refusing bail and conducting hunger strikes; some even volunteered for solitary confinement.[27] Although the sit-in movement received much support from CORE and other civil rights groups, its primary organizing body was the Student Non-Violent Coordinating Committee (SNCC, pronounced "Snick"). Aided by volunteers from the Northern Student Movement, SNCC focused on ending segregation in public places.

Meanwhile, other citizens became "freedom riders," challenging Jim Crow practices in transportation. The first such action was initiated by CORE in 1961, and the ordeal encountered by the riders in Alabama evoked much sympathy from church groups and the press. Undeterred by threats of violence and the likelihood of being jailed, others volunteered to follow this example and eventually eliminated discrimination in mass transit.

Numerous organizations sought various ways to improve the employment situation among blacks. One approach used in many of the larger cities was that of selective patronage campaigns. Black clergy urged their congregations to boycott businesses that did not hire or upgrade blacks. Such action was similar to "don't buy where you can't work" campaigns of the 1930s but was much more successful because of the increased purchasing power of and cooperation among black consumers. The struggle for equal employment opportunities also included mass picketing and roadblocks at construction sites.

In advocating fair housing practices, it was necessary for Negro organizations to dispel the belief that property values would decline when a black moved into the neighborhood. Many volunteers came forward to support open occupancy, often at the risk of evoking panic selling or even physical violence. This included religious groups that

> *[had] taken a stand for fair housing practices, and in many communities voluntary groups of "citizens for integrated living" [had] been at work. And the successful operation of more than 100 interracial community developments in the early sixties was a measurable step toward an open market in housing.*[28]

By February 1963, eighteen states had passed open occupancy laws, and fifty-five cities had done the same.

Despite the 1957 Civil Rights Act, white supremacy advocates in the South had succeeded in maintaining discrimination at the polls. In order to deal with this situation, and to overcome the widespread political apathy among blacks, Negro organizations and community leaders conducted get-out-the-vote campaigns. One example was the Mississippi Summer Project of 1964, aimed at bringing a large number of white and black volunteers into the state to inform, support, and register local black voters. Several of these activists were killed by those in opposition.

Typifying the intensity and commitment of all those engaged in the civil rights struggle was the March on Washington for Freedom and Jobs in August 1963. Sponsored by more than four hundred national organizations, it brought over two hundred thousand black and white Americans to the capital in a reaffirmation of the nation's democratic principles.

> *An effort that brought together all the major civil rights organizations, plus many church groups, the March was a climax and beginning. It served notice that America's Negroes were no longer willing to wait generation after generation for rights that other citizens took for granted. And it brought America face to face with her full responsibilities as a nation.*[29]

From that point on, events moved rapidly. Legislative gains, King's march from Selma to Montgomery, the abolition of literacy tests for voter registration, outbreaks of racial violence, the formation of black student unions and heritage-awareness groups such as the American Society of African Culture—all contributed to a growing sense of black power and black pride.

Self-help projects became more numerous, harnessing the creativity and energy of black volunteers. Operation Bootstrap in Los Angeles, Opportunities Industrialization Center (OIC) in Philadelphia, and the National Economic Growth and Reconstruction Organization (NEGRO) focused on employment and business development. Black churches sponsored commercial enterprises, ran day care centers, and opened job placement centers. Many large corporations contributed money and equipment to Negro self-help groups. Public education about the nature and effects of all types of prejudice was the concern of several volunteer organizations, notably the

National Conference of Christians and Jews. NCCJ inaugurated National Brotherhood Week in an attempt to draw attention to the need for racial and ethnic understanding.

Civil rights and the rights of poor people were intertwined. The National Welfare Rights Organization (NWRO) was the most visible grassroots effort reflecting this connection. Formed in 1966 by an interracial coalition of middle-class organizers, church workers, and members of CORE, the backbone of NWRO was poor, black women. During the next few years, NWRO organized demonstrations in welfare offices and lobbied legislators in an effort to reshape public policy relating to poor families.

> *As an assertion of the strength and competence of poor women; as a demonstration of the potential power in the fusion of race, class, and gender; as a channel for helping poor women transform their ideas of welfare into entitlement . . . NWRO remains a remarkable and significant episode in American social history.*[30]

Black Americans were not the only group seeking equality. In the mid 1960s, the Chicano movement gained strength. Student activist groups in the Southwest demanded attention from the educational system. La Raza Unida was formed as a political party to achieve Mexican-American self-determination. It gained enough votes in Texas to begin winning local elections. Mexican-American women, or Chicana, broke tradition and organized themselves into groups such as the National Chicana Businesswomen's Association.

As is true with any large-scale movement, the civil rights issue engendered extremist groups at both ends of the spectrum. The Black Muslims represented one such group, asking that a portion of the United States be set aside exclusively for Negroes. Militant groups, such as the Black Panther Party and the Revolutionary Action Movement, advocated armed rebellion as the only way to achieve equality. On the other hand, "citizens councils" led the resistance movement of white supremacy groups. Consisting mostly of business and professional people, the councils organized political and economic strategies in order to defy the changes dictated by law.

Increasing American military involvement in Vietnam in the mid-1960s evoked strong emotion in most citizens. As the undeclared war continued year after year and as the death toll rose higher by the month, opposition to the fighting and the draft increased as well. The number and type of protest groups proliferated all over the country. The American Friends Service Committee remained true to its historical pacifist stance and organized thousands of volunteers into draft resistance counseling centers and other projects. Additional volunteer groups such as SANE, Women's Strike for Peace, the Writers and Artists Protest Committee, and the Veterans and Reservists to End the War in Vietnam mobilized diverse citizens to demonstrate actively against the war. Celebrities volunteered their time and effort to endorse these groups' activities. While the peace movement and its close ally, the anti-draft movement, had precedents in every war fought since colonial times, some political observers noted that the anti-Vietnam factions were predominantly white, middle-class, and well-educated. However, because of the inequitable structure of the Selective Service System, minorities were actually the hardest hit by the Vietnam draft call and subsequently resented the peace protesters, who seemed to be rejecting those who were actually forced to fight.[31] Minority citizens did not necessarily favor the war, but they were disproportionately absent from most resistance demonstrations.

Since students were intimately involved with the draft issue, much of the volunteer anti-war effort was understandably focused on college campuses, where there was already vocal concern for a greater say by youth in their education. At the University of Chicago's "We Won't Go" Conference in December 1966, when

> *the Chairman was asked, "Is this an antiwar conference or an antidraft conference?" he answered: "It's both—we wouldn't be here today if it weren't for the Vietnam war, and it's antidraft because it is through the draft that the war meets the citizen."*[32]

The nationwide resistance movement gathered volunteers in increasing numbers between 1965 and 1970. Activities included draft counseling hotlines, letters and petitions to Congress, the burning of draft cards, and constant efforts to win public support through media coverage. There were also those who refused induction, choosing instead to go to prison or to flee the country:

> *The exodus of young men from America . . . constitutes one of the saddest ironies of the recent past. A nation which had once welcomed men fleeing from conscription now found*

herself losing some of her finest young men for the same reason. Support groups in Canada have estimated that there are about 80,000 draft-age Americans there.[33]

A highly organized minority of anti-war dissidents began engaging in what became known as the "ultra" resistance. These extremists, typified in the public's mind by the Students for a Democratic Society (SDS) and by such individuals as the Berrigan brothers, attacked the Selective Service in a series of dramatic raids.

The episodes ranged from minor harassments such as sit-ins and bricks thrown through windows to attacks on draft files. In May 1969, fifteen persons invaded the central draft depository in Chicago and destroyed all the records of twelve local boards, and some files of eight others. It required four months of work plus forty additional workers to reconstruct the files.[34]

Volunteer protest was also directed at banks and corporations involved with the war. The Dow Chemical Company, major manufacturer of napalm, was the target of boycotts, numerous demonstrations, and even some violent incidents. The televised clash between demonstrators and authorities at the 1968 Democratic Convention in Chicago epitomized the temper of the times.

Those who supported the war vehemently opposed the supposedly un-American, longhaired, hippie protesters. Pro-war volunteers held loyalist parades, vigils, and religious services across the country, often sponsored by the National Committee for Responsible Patriotism. In 1967, for example, two thousand people held a two-day vigil in New York's Battery Park to show support for the fighting troops.[35] When a coalition of resistance supporters—forty thousand strong—marched on Washington in 1967, they were met by loyalist groups and a virtual army of National Guardsmen, police, and Marines. Ironically, because the response of the authorities was so blatantly disproportionate to the civil disobedience of the demonstrators, marches on Washington became a favored tactic of the anti-war movement. The ensuing publicity shocked many Americans, and each succeeding march gathered thousands of new volunteer participants.

At the same time that national attention was focused critically on the military, key commanders recognized the need for expanded support of soldiers and their families. In 1965, the Army Community Service (ACS) program was officially established to offer assistance in the resolution of personal and family problems. Three factors contributed to the formation of ACS:

> *(1) A large increase in the number of married soldiers, (2) the inability of the existing system to handle the resulting flood of family problems, and (3) a realization by the Army that family problems were having a negative impact on soldier performance overseas (e.g., the Dominican Republic and Vietnam).*[36]

From the beginning it was expected that volunteers would be integral to the delivery of ACS services. This was actually written into the regulations and signified "the first credentialing of the 'community volunteer' as a member of the Army team."[37] Regulation AR608-1, 1965, states:

> *Major personnel support will be provided by organized volunteer groups of dependents . . . The organizational concept of Army Community Service assumes a foundation of a volunteer corps comprised primarily of Army wives or other adult dependents.*[38]

The other branches of the military eventually formed their own similar self-help agencies. In addition, the National Military Family Association was founded in 1969.

When President Kennedy called for a corps of dedicated and skilled Americans to volunteer on behalf of the world's developing nations, he ushered in a new national emphasis on volunteer service. The Peace Corps, begun in 1961, channeled the idealism of young Americans into productive activities abroad. Five years later, President Johnson initiated VISTA (Volunteers in Service to America) to work on problems here at home.

> *There was initial skepticism, and predictions were that Americans would not volunteer for domestic service which lacked the glamour and adventure that many felt was an incentive to Peace Corps service. But the skeptics were mistaken, thousands of Americans applied to work in unglamorous and difficult conditions to help the poor of their own country.*[39]

VISTA and the Peace Corps were experiments by the federal government to test the viability of large-scale, government-supported volunteer programs.

There was, however, some controversy about these programs. First, Peace Corps and VISTA volunteers received a basic subsistence allowance and a modest monthly compensatory stipend. Some purists objected to this payment of volunteers, even though the allowances simply enabled citizens to spend one to three years in service without personal hardship. In another vein, some conservative groups viewed the Peace Corps as too liberal and communal:

> *The prospects for international idealism [were] considered grim to nonexistent, and the young conservative's reaction to the Peace Corps [was] illustrative. First Young Americans for Freedom (YAF) tried to hamstring it by demanding anti-Communist affidavits from the conscience-sensitive applicants. Then they labeled it the Kiddie Korps . . . These countries need[ed] businessmen, not students.*[40]

VISTA, on the other hand, was criticized for placing volunteers into highly political situations, such as voter registration drives in the South. Despite such adverse reactions that affected the number of applicants, the Peace Corps and VISTA continued to provide service.

While VISTA and the Peace Corps tended to attract mainly young people, there was a vast untapped reservoir of volunteer power in the growing number of retired persons. As early as 1967, the Community Service Society in New York began an older volunteer program called Serve and Enrich Retirement by Volunteer Experience. SERVE had government support from the beginning through a grant from the Administration on Aging. By 1969 there were forty-two pilot SERVE programs operating throughout New York State, placing senior volunteers in a vast range of agencies and institutions.[41] SERVE was an unqualified success and became the model for the federal Retired Senior Volunteer Program (RSVP).

In 1965, the United States Department of Education launched the Adult Basic Education (ABE) program to teach basic skills to adults. It grew to fourteen thousand local ABE programs, one-third of which utilized volunteers extensively as tutor aides.

The government's new interest in the volunteer approach to problem solving was also evident when President Johnson suggested to Henry Ford II that businesspeople tackle the challenge of unemployment. In 1968, Ford initiated the National Alliance of Businessmen (NAB): "Ford took the task seriously; under his prodding 12,500 firms were organized in eight regions, pledged to seek out and hire large numbers of the hard-core."[42] By July 1969, the original goal of hiring one hundred thousand had been exceeded by close to 50 percent, while almost 60 percent of those hired were still on the job. Despite the offer of federal cash assistance for hiring a hard-core unemployed person, "companies that employed two-thirds of the hard-core had chosen to forego [the] assistance . . . , keeping the program wholly on a private enterprise basis."[43] NAB was kept operational by business executives loaned to NAB for a specific interval, demonstrating volunteerism on the corporate level.

At the same time that business was increasing its social role, corporations were being challenged on other fronts. In 1965, a Connecticut lawyer wrote *Unsafe at Any Speed,* a critique of the American auto industry based on his work in litigating car accident cases. This publication catapulted its author, Ralph Nader, and its cause, consumerism, into the limelight. Nader recruited student volunteers, soon dubbed "Nader's Raiders," to do independent research on the effectiveness of government regulation of a wide variety of health and safety issues.

> *Students have long come to Washington to work in Federal agencies for the summer. My idea is to have them come down and work on the agencies: to come and study relentlessly on a daily basis what an agency is doing—this has never been done before.*[44]

In time, Nader and his "public interest research groups" brought consumerism into the political vocabulary. They examined everything from the ingredients in hot dogs to issues of industrial safety. The consumer movement eventually affected the purchasing decisions of most Americans and the production decisions of a large number of industries.

In the late 1960s, John Gardner invited citizens to join Common Cause, a "new, independent, non-partisan organization for those Americans who want to help in the rebuilding of this nation."[45] Common Cause sought to counteract the distrust of government and the alienation of the Vietnam era by addressing government obstacles to citizen representation. Over the years, it advocated many causes, including sunshine laws and ethics reform, and generally acted as a watchdog on legislators. Through a system of state and local chapters, individual members could volunteer to monitor local government activities.

Volunteering during the 1950s and 1960s was often vocal and passionately political in nature. Causes such as civil rights, McCarthyism, and the Vietnam War were supported and opposed by innumerable groups, with tactics ranging from research to violence. It was a period of movements, in actuality the collective impact of countless volunteers.

Not all volunteer involvement, however, was concerned with large-scale social change. The many forms of community action developed in earlier years continued to bring results in a wide range of social and civic projects. Though this chapter concentrates on political activism, it would be unjust to overlook the contribution of those volunteers who served in the fields of health, welfare, education, recreation, and the arts during this period. Their day-to-day efforts continued uninterrupted as a supportive base for meeting many social needs.

Endnotes for Chapter 7

1. Perry E. Giankos and Albert Karson, *War and Challenge, 1942-1966,* vol. 4, *American Diplomacy and the Sense of Destiny* (Belmont, CA: Wadsworth, 1966), 20.

2. Anne David, *Help Yourself by Helping Others: A Guide to Volunteer Services* (New York: Simon and Schuster, Cornerstone Library, 1970), 119.

3. Descriptive materials of International Voluntary Services, in response to authors' questionnaire, April 21, 1976.

4. Jerome Davis, *Peace, War and You* (New York: Henry Schuman, 1952), 249.

5. Benjamin R. Epstein and Arnold Forster, *The Radical Right: Report on the John Birch Society and Its Allies* (New York: Random House, 1960), 3-4.

6. *The Twenty-Year Old Idea That's Still Producing* (New York: Council for Financial Aid to Education, n.d.), 5.

7. Ibid., 11.

8. William Garland Rogers, *Ladies Bountiful* (New York: Harcourt, Brace and World, 1968), 13.

9. "The Advertising Council: An American Phenomenon," *Advertising Age,* November 21, 1973.

10. American Public Health Association, Technical Development Board, Program Area Committee on Accident Prevention, *Accident Prevention* (New York: McGraw-Hill, 1961), 15.

11. Descriptive materials of the Aerial Phenomena Research Organization, Inc., in response to authors' questionnaire, March 28, 1976.

12. Charles Hurd, *The Compact History of the American Red Cross* (New York: Hawthorn Books, 1959), 292.

13. Elizabeth Thompson (secretary to the executive director, American Association of Blood Banks), in response to authors' questionnaire, March 29, 1976.

14. Richard Carter, *The Gentle Legions* (Garden City, NY: Doubleday, 1961), 18.

15. Ibid., 133.

16. Ibid., 133-4.

17. Max Siporin, *Friendly Visiting Among the Poor* (Montclair, NJ: Patterson Smith, 1899, republished 1969), xxvi.

18. Ralph Keyes, *We, The Lonely People: Searching for Community* (New York: Harper and Row, 1973), 127.

19. *The Community Meets the Migrant Worker,* U.S. Department of Labor, Bulletin 221 (Washington, DC: Government Printing Office, 1960), 12.

20. National Information Center on Volunteerism, *Volunteers in Social Justice,* 5, nos. 4 and 5 (November 1972).

21. "Desert Posse Mounts 45 Jeeps," *Popular Science* 115 (February 1952): 172.

22. Carroll Atkinson and Eugene T. Maleska, *The Story of Education* (Philadelphia: Chilton, 1962), 211-2.

23. William Robinson Brown, *Our Forest Heritage* (Concord: New Hampshire Historical Society, 1958), 163.

24. Henry Clepper (special projects director, The American Forestry Association), in response to authors' questionnaire, April 2, 1976.

25. David Cushman Coyle, *Conservation* (New Brunswick, NJ: Rutgers University Press, 1957), 241.

26. Carl N. Degler, *Affluence and Anxiety* (Glenview, IL: Scott, Foresman, 1968), 97.

27. Benjamin Quarles, *The Negro in the Making of America,* rev. ed. (New York: Collier Books, 1969), 253.

28. Ibid., 259.

29. Ibid., 265.

30. Michael B. Katz, *In the Shadow of the Poorhouse* (New York: Basic Books, 1986), 254.

31. James R. Flynn, *American Politics: A Radical View* (Auckland: Blackwood and Janet Paul, 1967), 110-3.

32. American Friends Service Committee, *The Draft?* (New York: Hill and Wang, 1968), 42.

33. John O'Sullivan and Alan M. Meckler, *The Draft and Its Enemies* (n.p.: University of Illinois Press, 1974), 224.

34. Ibid., 227.

35. "March on the Pentagon," *Newsweek,* October 30, 1967, 20.

36. D. Bruce Bell and Robert T. Iadeluca, *The Origins of Volunteer Support for Army Family Programs,* research report for U.S. Army Research Institute for Behavioral and Social Sciences, September, 1980, 11.

37. Joanne H. Patton, "Army Community Service: Another Kind of Volunteer Army," *Volunteer Administration,* 13, no. 2 (Summer, 1980): 3.

38. Ibid.

39. Joseph H. Blatchford, "Federal Volunteer Programs," in *Volunteerism: An Emerging Profession,* eds. John G. Cull and Richard E. Hardy (Springfield, IL: Charles C. Thomas, 1974), 18.

40. Edward R. Cain, *They'd Rather Be Right: Youth and the Conservative Movement* (New York: Macmillan, 1963), 251.

41. "National RSVP Training Started by SERVE Sponsors," *Aging,* 212 (June 1972): 13.

42. Blatchford, "Federal Volunteer Programs," 16.

43. Ibid., 19.

44. Ralph Nader, quoted in *The Politics of the Powerless,* eds. Robert H. Binstock and Katherine Ely (Cambridge, MA:Winthrop, 1971), 172.

45. Quoted in Fred Wertheimer, "Window of Opportunity," *Common Cause Magazine* (July/August 1989): 44.

Chapter 8

Volunteers Move into the Spotlight

1970-1989

1970	Campus anti-war protests continue; Kent State killings.
1972	Watergate scandal begins.
1973	Vietnam War ends.
1974	President Nixon resigns.
1976	Nation's Bicentennial.
1979	Three Mile Island nuclear power plant accident occurs.
1980	Mount St. Helen's erupts.
1981	First space shuttle *(Columbia)* launched.
1989	*Exxon Valdez* Alaskan oil spill.

The turbulence of the 1960s continued into the early 1970s. Many major incidents of the decade became national symbols of unrest: Kent State, Attica, the Chicago Seven, Watergate. By 1973, when the Vietnam War officially ended, the nation was more than ready for a respite. A period of introspection set in, with the desire to refocus on one's own life. This turning inward led many to conclude that Americans had become apathetic and unwilling to become involved in causes and movements. The phrase coined by social critic Tom Wolfe—"the me decade"—was repeated endlessly by the media and became synonymous with the 1970s. The quest for self-improvement led many to explore new religions and eastern philosophies—any group that led to a sense of belonging. Emphasis was placed on personal growth and self-awareness, as Americans made decisions based on the all-consuming question: "What's in it for me?" A best seller was

Robert Ringer's *Looking Out for Number One.* Some observers interpreted this selfish preoccupation as malaise and predicted the demise of community involvement:

> *Some will mourn the passing of the Sixties-style politics, others will rejoice. Both will miss the point. For Americans in the Seventies did not turn away from the politics of direct action. They merely domesticated it, institutionalized it, and embraced it in the bosom of the middle class.*[1]

Citizens discovered their power to create legislation directly through the electoral "initiative," which was a way of circumventing legislatures that voters felt could not be trusted. Proposed laws affecting a wide variety of issues from drinking ages to educational vouchers were placed on local and state ballots by petition to permit the electorate to express immediate approval or disapproval. This trend accelerated throughout the decade, culminating in the passage of California's Proposition 13 in 1978. Proposition 13 marked a turning point, as voters opted for less government services in exchange for less taxes. In terms of effect on taxes and government priorities, the strategy of political initiatives may have had more lasting impact than the preceding civil unrest. This period saw a backlash against the liberalism of the 1960s; for example, thirty-seven states restored the death penalty.

The political realities and election reform legislation of the period spurred the growth of political action committees (PACs) as a way to limit the inordinate influence of wealthy individuals in the election process. PACs began as a legitimate vehicle for citizen input and for volunteer associations concerned with influencing legislation. By 1988, however, there were more than four thousand PACs registered with the Federal Election Commission, and political reformers were asserting that PACs themselves were having a disproportionate effect on the outcome of elections.[2]

Volunteerism faced a number of direct challenges in the 1970s. There was some vocal opposition, especially from the growing feminist movement. This raised controversy about the value and role of volunteer work.

One of the major social changes of the 1970s was the redefinition of the role of women. As part of their advocacy for equality, feminists attacked volunteering as low-status work that exploited the time and talents of women. Most women's rights organizations drew a distinction between service volunteering, of which they disapproved, and change-oriented or political volunteering, which was acceptable. In 1971, the National Organization for Women (NOW) passed a resolution cautioning its members to distinguish between these two types:

> *Why has NOW taken a position against service-oriented volunteering? NOW believes:*
>
> - *That such volunteering is an extension of unpaid housework and of women's traditional roles in the home (such as helper, buffer and supporter) which have been extended to encompass the community.*
> - *That such volunteering reinforces a woman's low self-image by offering work which, because it is unpaid, confers little status.*
> - *That volunteerism has been society's solution for those, including but not limited to women, for which there is little real employment choice.*
>
> *Essentially, however, NOW believes that service-oriented volunteerism is providing a hit-or-miss, band-aid, and patchwork approach to solving massive and severe social ills which are a reflection of a social and economic system in need of an overhaul. More than this, NOW believes that such volunteering actually prevents needed social changes from occurring because with service-oriented volunteering, political energy is being used and will increasingly be used, to meet society's administrative needs. Women (as well as some men) have been and are being used to perform tasks for which society would otherwise pay if the priorities of the country were more socially oriented.*[3]

These arguments stemmed from the basic assumption that volunteers were mostly women who were not part of the paid work force. For feminists, this was an economic issue, inseparable from women's second-class status in the world of work.

During the 1970s, many debated this question. The feminist position had the effect of making individuals and organizations think seriously about why and how volunteers were utilized. It was true that some organizations abused the time and talents of their volunteers and that volunteers deserved greater input to the decision-making processes of the organizations to which they gave their time. Also, just as in the paid work world, volunteer programs had perpetuated certain stereotypes about which roles were appropriate for men and women. These criticisms were valid and stimulated needed changes.

The problem was that the feminist position was too severe. It negated the positive personal benefits of volunteering that many women experienced. These included career exploration, development of job skills, and the opportunity to contribute significantly to causes about which they cared. By flatly opposing service volunteering, the women's groups failed to recognize that many volunteer positions had clout, impact, and status, and were worth doing. "The impulse to volunteer is a simply human one—that's been sexualized by our culture . . . The problem is not volunteering; the problem is femininity and the demands that have been made on women by the nuclear family."[4] The argument was made that "consciousness-raising is crucial—but not at the cost of a lowered conscience."[5]

Women were seeing progress in many areas as more opportunities in employment and education opened to them. This change was also mirrored in the volunteer world as women began to be recruited for new leadership roles such as serving on policy-making boards. By the end of the decade, NOW had changed its bylaws to remove the prohibition against service volunteering. Volunteering was acknowledged as a valid option for both women and men seeking to make a difference in their communities.

> *Feminist women can use the volunteer structure for their own ends, experimenting with its training and mind-expanding "opportunities" to nourish a more conscious identity. Voluntarism in new dress—with mini, midi, or maxi innovations and benefits to the women serving in it—must be judiciously altered to fit woman's growing need for real work in a real life.*[6]

In 1971, the Nixon administration launched the first peacetime effort to stimulate a major American volunteer force. Over 24,000 full- and part-time volunteers in six existing programs were brought together to form ACTION: the Peace Corps, VISTA, the Foster Grandparent Program, RSVP, the Service Corps of Retired Executives (SCORE), and the Active Corps of Executives (ACE). Also included were the Office of Voluntary Action Liaison and the National Student Volunteer Program. ACTION programs had the potential to involve thousands of Americans in solving community problems. After a time, ACE and SCORE moved out of ACTION and into the Small Business Administration, while ACTION added the Senior Companion Program, University Year for Action, and the Youth Challenge Program. ACTION also fostered the concept of state offices of volunteerism by offering seed money to governors to establish state-level resource centers promoting volunteering.

Further, by 1971, several major federal departments had inaugurated some form of volunteer program. Policy statements favoring volunteers had been issued by the Departments of Agriculture; Commerce; Housing and Urban Development; Justice; Labor; Health, Education and Welfare; and the Office of Economic Opportunity. Some, such as the Law Enforcement Assistance Administration, began requiring the inclusion of a volunteer component in grant applications for federal money.

At the same time that ACTION was created as the federal umbrella for volunteerism, Congress mandated an independent private-sector agency, the National Center for Voluntary Action. NCVA was designed to educate the public about the potentials of volunteerism and to assist in program development. It began operating an information bank, known as the Clearinghouse, providing materials and technical assistance upon request.

In 1974, the U.S. Census Bureau conducted a survey for ACTION, "Americans Volunteer," concluding that a total of nearly 37 million Americans volunteered.[7] This meant that 24 percent of the population, or one out of every four citizens over the age of thirteen, did organized volunteer work annually. This was greater than the figure determined by a Department of Labor study in 1965. However, both surveys admitted to touching only the tip of the volunteer iceberg—a slippery entity difficult to measure regardless of technique. Since these studies did not include informal or unaffiliated volunteering, there was general agreement that the total number of people who did some form of volunteer work was undoubtedly much higher. The 1974 study was quoted widely for over a decade but was not repeated.

The composition of the volunteer work force was expanding as well. To the protester of the 1960s, the label "businessman" connoted a profit-hungry person without social conscience. While this accusation had little visible effect at the time, the 1970s saw the development of "corporate social responsibility" efforts. Businesses created new community roles for themselves as companies and for their employees as individuals. In 1971, the Committee for Economic Development issued a policy statement that declared:

> *Business is being asked to assume broader responsibilities to society than ever before and to serve a wider range of human values ... to contribute more to the quality of American life than just supplying quantities of goods and services.*[8]

Corporate financial and in-kind donations were made to a greater diversity of groups and agencies. Employees were increasingly encouraged to volunteer with local organizations and to participate in company-sponsored community projects. Some of the largest corporations offered time-release plans and other incentives, the most generous of which loaned company executives to nonprofit organizations for up to a full year. This meant that the individual still received his or her company salary but, from the perspective of the nonprofit organization, this executive was a volunteer. Early pioneers of such corporate citizenship were Levi-Strauss (with a program formed in 1968), Exxon (1969), IBM (1971), Allstate Insurance (1972), Bank of America (1973), Phillip Morris, Xerox, and Honeywell (1974).

The rationale for launching such corporate community programs included enlightened self-interest and social investment.

> *Some of this concern among ... executives has been the result of the crisis confrontation of the sixties; much of it is the result of sober, sophisticated reflection on what the future holds for business in this country—unless it becomes more active in helping to heal some of the sores afflicting our system ... Business must be accepted as one of the vital elements in the social problem-solving matrix, and business must show, by its own actions, the capacity to contribute to these solutions.*[9]

By the late 1970s, some companies had designated a staff position for the purpose of coordinating employee volunteering. This position was frequently part of the company's public relations efforts. As local organizations learned that some companies were willing to offer volunteer help, the number of requests for assistance increased. Public relations departments had to develop ways to respond to such requests, often expanding to become community relations or community affairs departments. Though corporate volunteer efforts sometimes fell short of the mark in terms of measurable community service, the goal was to project a positive, caring image for business.

Labor unions expressed contradictory views on volunteering. Some perceived volunteers in unionized work sites as threatening to job security and strike actions and tried to limit the roles volunteers were allowed to fill. On the other hand, most unions supported volunteering by their own union members. In 1971, the AFL-CIO voted to support "labor community service agencies" or "united labor agencies" to coordinate and stimulate community service by its members. Such service involvement was recorded as early as the 1940s, but now the unions were attempting to formalize their outreach efforts. Just as corporate management sought the positive public relations value of visible community work, unions also wanted to garner favorable public opinion.

Volunteering in the workplace itself received much attention through the development of "quality circles." American businesses studied the management strategies of the Japanese and discovered that assembly line workers in Japan had direct input into how goods were manufactured. In an effort to boost American productivity along with quality, plant managers were trained in formal ways to elicit practical suggestions from employees. The quality circle was a small group of employees in the same production area who met regularly to discuss how the work could be streamlined or otherwise improved. While the circles met on company time, involvement was meant to be voluntary.

Another population segment joining the volunteer ranks in the 1970s was students. In the past, children and teenagers had well-defined responsibilities in the family and in the community. Youth was no barrier to participation where survival was concerned. As American society became more advanced, young people were freed from the burdens of early employment and required instead to attend school until they reached the age when their contribution would be valued. At the same time, the world of work was becoming more complex and career choices more dependent on one's level of education. By the 1960s, there was an increasing gap between what was taught in the classroom and what was perceived to go on outside it, as portrayed by television and other sources; the campus anti-war demonstrations were as much a demand for relevant curricula as a cry for peace. Relevance was achieved through volunteerism, which allowed the youth of the 1970s to explore careers and to become contributing members of the community once again.

Through their involvement as volunteers in a wide range of projects, youth gained new skills, developed leadership potential, got to know their communities better, and acquired social awareness. An outgrowth of the desire to mesh classroom theory with real-life experience was the development of "service-learning" programs. The principle of learning by doing was formalized into a variety of school-community arrangements, enabling the student to earn academic credit for volunteer service given. Such programs proliferated dramatically in the early 1970s, with great variation: spanning elementary school through graduate school; ranging from schedules of three hours a week to forty hours a week; accommodating almost every major from technical subjects to liberal arts.

Businesses became involved in the career education of students by agreeing to create positions for student interns. Whether or not the students were paid a salary (work co-op plans) or were volunteers, the company had to free staff time for training, supervising, and evaluating the student on the job. This constituted a volunteer act on the part of the company. Student organizations formed to promote community service projects, such as the National Affiliation of Concerned Business Students. In 1977, a project was launched by the National Information Center on Volunteerism (NICOV) to introduce the concept of a high school curriculum on volunteerism, based on the assumption that those who volunteer early in life tend to continue volunteering in their adult years.

Older students, notably women seeking degrees after years as homemakers, were given the opportunity to receive academic credit for their lifelong learning experience, which included volunteering. Community volunteer work was thereby acknowledged as relevant to academic and vocational education. The next step was to convince employers to consider volunteering as a valid form of work experience (both for older students and for younger ones who had participated in service-learning programs). By the mid-1970s, the United States Civil Service Commission had revised its basic employment application form to permit job seekers to include volunteer experience as part of their employment history. A number of states and municipalities followed suit. However, the challenge remained of convincing private employers to do the same.

Concurrently, volunteer programs were encouraging volunteers to translate the skills, knowledge, and abilities honed through volunteering into the vocabulary used by employers. Special materials and workshops became available on career development for volunteers, such as the "I Can" program first developed in 1977 by the Council of National Organizations for Adult Education. In 1981, the material was revised and piloted by a coalition of seven national volunteer associations: the Association of Junior Leagues, the Association for Volunteer Administration, the Girl Scouts of the USA, the YWCA, the National Center for Citizen Involvement, the National Council of Jewish Women, and the YMCA. Though the "I Can" program proved too cumbersome for wide use, it stimulated many efforts to assist volunteers in developing skill portfolios.

By the early 1980s, the term *transitional volunteer* was being used to describe those individuals utilizing volunteer service as a bridge between life changes: after divorce or death of a spouse; after institutionalization of any sort; as part of a career change; or in preparation for re-entry into the work force. In times of high unemployment, some organizations enabled job seekers to volunteer as a way to learn new skills and add to their resumes.

The recruiting of families to volunteer together began to be explored. Some activities tackled by family units were campground monitoring, neighborhood cleanup, and group visiting of institutionalized people. The intergenerational spirit added to the community service, and the families themselves benefited from the time spent together. Another segment of American society targeted for involvement during the 1970s was senior citizens. People over sixty years of age became the fastest-growing portion of the population, living longer and in better health than in the past. Seniors were retiring with many years of productivity ahead of them, yet society had only begun to utilize their potential. Volunteer work could channel older people's time and expertise into meaningful community roles. The desire to remain both physically and mentally active, and to be needed, motivated more retired people to volunteer. Because of new academic knowledge about gerontology, programs began to design assignments suitable to the needs of the elderly. The federal government was a forerunner in supporting older American volunteer efforts through ACTION's RSVP, Foster Grandparent, and Senior Companion programs. The latter two focused on low-income seniors, giving a stipend to encourage service.

Senior citizens became more aware of their legal and social rights and of the discrimination often practiced against them. Such consciousness-raising resulted in "gray power" activist groups whose volunteer members agitated for improved services and did much to dispel the myths about the elderly. The Gray Panthers, formed in 1971, were the most vocal. The American Association of Retired People (AARP), founded in the previous decade, gained momentum throughout the 1970s. By 1986, AARP reported a membership of 24 million members over the age of fifty and was coordinating a wide variety of service projects staffed in large measure by local members, including Volunteer Tax Aid, 55-Alive driving program, and the Volunteer Talent Bank.

In 1975, the Second Careers program began in Los Angeles, recruiting retired professionals to put their skills to new use in volunteer assignments. Replicated in New York two years later and in other cities throughout the decade, the program promoted the concept of volunteering as a lateral move for those facing retirement.

All of these activities marked an expanded awareness of older Americans as a volunteer resource, but there was still some resistance to the concept from both agencies and the seniors themselves. The desire to increase the number of retired volunteers continued through the 1980s. One approach was the development of intergenerational programs, teaming children and seniors in mutually beneficial activities. It was often hard to distinguish who was the giver and who the receiver of services when the "latchkey" elementary school student with nowhere to go after school and the older adult lonely without visitors in a nursing home both enjoyed the contact of visiting together and helping with homework.

The continuing education interests of seniors became the focus of volunteer activity through the establishment of college-affiliated, noncredit courses and workshops for retired people—frequently taught by senior volunteers themselves. Two prime examples were the Temple Association of Retired Professionals (Temple University, Philadelphia) and the Institute of New Dimensions (Palm Beach Junior College, Florida). By 1982, the latter had nearly one thousand retirees taking courses taught entirely by volunteers.

New social services for older people were being funded by federal and state dollars. Most states created local distribution systems for allocating resources to senior centers, nutrition programs, services to homebound elderly, and transportation. These "area agencies on aging" were mandated to create advisory councils composed of seniors themselves. The goal was to ensure that older citizens had a say in what would affect them. On the other hand, volunteers of all ages were recruited to help in the delivery of services. In response to the needs of the 1970s, volunteers served as nursing home ombudsmen, surrogate decision makers (including *Guardian ad litem),* and assistants to seniors completing complex Medicare and tax forms.

In the search for innovative responses to the problems confronting senior citizens, some local governments showed creativity. One example was the Senior Citizens Property Tax Workoff program of Larimer County and the city of Fort Collins, Colorado. This allowed any person over the age of sixty-five to work off property taxes by volunteering a certain number of hours of service in various government departments.

The concept of involving volunteers in local government became more formalized during the 1970s and 1980s, as evidenced by the establishment of interdepartmental municipal volunteer programs in communities as diverse as New York City, Virginia Beach, and Marin County, California. These programs coordinated the recruitment of citizens to work as volunteers in all aspects of local government, from libraries to the streets department. While volunteers may have been active in such roles before, the new city and county volunteer program staff helped to support volunteers and make their involvement more effective.

Ironically, concurrent with such projects to recruit volunteers to help government, the number of local officials serving without salary declined rapidly. Municipal officeholders traditionally maintained full-time employment while accepting the additional responsibilities of volunteer public service. For instance, in 1966, twenty-nine out of the seventy municipal governing bodies in Bergen County, New Jersey, were unpaid. But by 1976, the number had dropped to eighteen.[10] This nationwide trend was largely attributed to the increased amount of time needed to handle the complexities of government work, even in the smallest towns.

In line with the mistrust of bureaucracy and the desire to return power to ordinary citizens, the 1970s saw the growth of various efforts to involve people in self-government. Independence, Missouri, formed neighborhood councils in 1971 to "facilitate meaningful communication of, by and among neighbors, neighborhoods and the various institutions of the community."[11] Within ten years, these councils were active in sixty-four neighborhoods, involving nineteen hundred members in 350 projects a year. Their motto was, "you don't have to move to live in a better neighborhood."

The much-publicized national war on crime provided the impetus for a multitude of volunteer activities: town watch programs, neighborhood safety campaigns, and "safe house" projects to protect children on their way home from school. By 1979, concern for crime in New York City led to the formation of the Guardian Angels. Seen by some as a vigilante-type group, these young volunteers patrolled subways and public housing projects in an effort to make life safer for innocent citizens. In the 1980s, television became a crime-fighting tool as viewers were shown details of unsolved crimes and urged to come forward with information helpful to the police. Real estate agents and postal letter carriers formed special projects to monitor neighborhoods for signs of crime. The letter carriers also volunteered to pay attention to homebound elderly residents on their routes and to report any indications of need for help.

A large number of court systems formed structured volunteer programs to provide supportive services to adult and juvenile probationers and parolees. This was stimulated by the availability of federal grants for such citizen involvement, largely through the Law Enforcement Assistance Administration (1968-1982). Volunteers provided tutoring, job finding and counseling, and one-to-one mentoring. Prisons, jails, and police departments also created new roles for interested volunteers. Nonprofit organizations such as Partners (Denver) and Offender Aid and Restoration were established to match community volunteers with offenders needing individualized attention.

Offenders were not simply recipients of services. Inmates of prisons developed surprisingly creative projects in which they themselves volunteered. In 1979, inmates in Pennsylvania organized a "prison runathon" in which prisoners would run in their exercise yards to raise money against pledges obtained through community volunteers. The funds raised were distributed to youth-serving agencies selected by the incarcerated runners. The runathon became an annual event, raising over $56,000 during the next decade.[12] Prisoners in New Jersey developed the controversial Scared Straight program to bring teenagers at risk of delinquency to the prison to hear harsh lectures by inmates about the consequences of crime. Across the country, prisoners found other ways to serve the community: making Christmas toys; baking bread for food banks; recording books for the blind. The Little Rock, Arkansas, school system created the Partners Project, in which inmates produced learning aids and teaching materials for use in the classroom. Over a hundred inmates were involved in the first year, eleven of whom were imprisoned for murder.

A special category of lawbreakers was those who avoided the draft or went AWOL in protest against the war in Vietnam. In September 1974, President Ford signed a limited amnesty under which these fugitives could return home without fear of incarceration. However, they were each to fulfill a sentence of two years of community service, the specifics varying with each case. Nonprofit agencies and local government units were asked to create assignments for these amnesty workers.

Victims of crime were also a focus of attention. Lobbying efforts were directed at compensating for violent crime through legislation requiring restitution. Rape victims in particular were supported by new volunteer projects that encouraged prosecution, offered counseling, and accompanied the women through the painful and confusing legal process. Through the activities of outspoken victims themselves, domestic violence (both spouse abuse and child abuse) became more visible as a national concern. Volunteers led the way in creating counseling programs, shelters, and hot lines designed to help both the victims and the perpetrators.

Another group that emerged from the shadows in the 1970s was the physically disabled.

> *In 1972, Congress began considering major revisions to the rehabilitation legislation then on the books. Four social and political currents shaped those deliberations: the legacy of the sixties, consumerism, the federal government's experience with citizen participation efforts, and the new assertiveness of minority group politics.*[13]

Building on the spirit of the black civil rights and women's movements, disabled citizens sought greater participation in mainstream America. They wanted jobs, accessibility to public places, and a voice in the policies and services affecting them. People with disabilities became volunteers as board members, lobbyists, and fundraisers for disabled rights organizations—and as a new resource for volunteer programs unrelated to disabilities. In 1981, the International Year of Disabled Persons provided a banner under which activists could rally.

The physically disabled were not the only client group seeking self-determination. Welfare recipients, hospital patients, and mental health patients all sought to make institutions more responsive to their needs. Client rights became an important issue during this time, mobilizing many volunteers.

As already mentioned, the quest for social equality was of growing concern to the majority of Americans—the 51 percent who were women. In 1972, the Equal Rights Amendment (ERA) passed Congress and was sent to the states for ratification. Women's groups of all sizes and views mobilized to urge the speedy acceptance of what they saw as a long-overdue recognition of women's legal rights. They faced an uphill battle and were opposed by equally vocal volunteers who feared that the ERA would somehow negate all differences between men and women. Though thirty-five states ratified the amendment and an extension of three years beyond the original seven was granted, the ERA was defeated in 1982, falling just short of the thirty-eight states needed. Fourteen states passed Equal Rights Amendments to their own state constitutions during this period.

In 1973, the Supreme Court ruled in *Roe* v. *Wade,* extending the legality of abortion upon a woman's request. While abortion had been an issue for some time, this decision launched a new level of volunteer activity. Anti-abortion forces began campaigns at the local level to pass state laws restricting abortion and to harass local contraception and abortion clinics. These activities, in turn, galvanized pro-choice volunteers, who attempted to counter the protests and to retain the rights to abortion. For many, choice in this personal matter was undeniably connected to women's rights, and therefore the feminist movement adopted reproductive freedom as a cornerstone of its position. By the late 1980s, the abortion question had become one of the most divisive political issues, as it remains to this day.

Conservative politics garnered most of the publicity during the 1980s. Organizations such as Moral Majority and Religious Roundtable claimed to represent the views of fundamentalist Christians concerned about the decay of values they perceived in American society. They worked hard to defeat liberal candidates in all elections, often with the support of televangelists who raised funds and motivated their audiences of believers to become activists. Though never truly indicative of the majority of the population, such conservative and even reactionary groups in what was called "the New Religious Right" influenced the legislative and electoral process in a variety of ways. By the 1987 presidential campaign, the word *liberal* had been transformed into a label of questionable integrity.

Despite the swing of public opinion, various social changes were still being advocated that challenged the status quo. The gay rights movement encouraged many homosexuals and lesbians in the 1970s to "come out of the closet" to acknowledge their alternative life-style. Beginning in major cities such as New York and San Francisco, volunteers fought discriminatory legislation and worked to gain more acceptance of gay people as part of mainstream America. Because the ostracism was so pervasive, gays were forced to create alternative associations for themselves in business, health care, and religion. A network of Metropolitan Community Churches ministered to gay and lesbian Protestants, while Dignity met the religious needs of Catholic homosexuals. The emergency of the AIDS crisis in the late 1980s brought fresh resistance against the gay community and required new types of volunteer self-help.

Volunteers had long supported museums, especially as docents and guides, fundraisers, and curatorial assistants. The desire for more training and information exchange led to the formation of museum volunteer networks. In 1975, the World Federation of Friends of Museums was founded as an international association for supporters of museums around the world, while the U.S. Association of Museum Volunteers was formed in 1979 to focus on American museums. The latter eventually affiliated with the American Association of Museums, changing its name in 1986 to the American Association for Museum Volunteers.

An innovative form of volunteering on behalf of art was pioneered in the 1970s by artist Judy Chicago. Her "Dinner Party" project involved the creation of a room-sized depiction of a dinner table representing lost women of history. She carefully selected over four hundred volunteers to assist in the production of handcrafted materials to be incorporated into the final design. Taking five years to complete, this project was the first communal art work of its kind and represented an expanded way for volunteers to participate in the artistic process. Chicago's second effort, the "Birth Project," was accomplished from 1980 to 1988 and consisted of supervising a similar national group of volunteers who embroidered and appliquéd a multitude of wall hangings depicting the experience of childbirth.

Artists and entertainers continued to reach out as volunteers in order to bring high-quality entertainment to social service institutions. One group, Bread and Roses, began in Marin County, California, in 1974 and became a model for similar programs across the country. By 1988, members were producing four hundred shows a year to a combined audience of over sixteen thousand five hundred institutionalized persons, with five hundred performers donating their time.

An important event of 1970 was Earth Day. On April 22, 1970, thousands of Americans in hundreds of cities staged demonstrations designed to raise awareness of the danger to the planet from pollution and abuse of natural resources. Environmentalism became a movement, mobilizing activists on several fronts—clean air and water preservation, conservation of resources, and toxic cleanup efforts. Volunteer activities ranged from the scientific to the dramatic. Some tested water samples; others blocked bulldozers. Some developed recycling centers; others planted inner-city community gardens. In 1973, a group of New York City architects, botanists, and horticulturists, calling themselves the Green Guerrillas, formed to give advice to urban gardeners. The Soil Conservation Service of the U.S. Department of Agriculture established the Earth Team, galvanizing volunteers on behalf of soil and water conservation.

In 1971, Educational Expeditions International recruited thirty-two amateur volunteers to work with four scientists on field research projects. Renamed Earth Watch, by 1982 the group was sending 1,500 volunteers (who paid their own expenses) to assist seventy-five scientists on worldwide testing and observation expeditions. Conservationists quickly recognized the interdependency of all countries and the need to think globally about natural resources. The Arab oil embargo of 1973 drove this point home dramatically. It also gave impetus to energy conservation efforts here at home.

More environmental issues surfaced. In 1979, the accident at the Three Mile Island nuclear power plant in Pennsylvania added impetus to the debate about the benefits and safety of nuclear energy, as did the nuclear accident at Chernobyl in the USSR a decade later. The growth of the nuclear industry eventually was seriously limited by the actions of numerous volunteer protesters. Groups advocated alternative sources of energy such as solar and wind power and the effective conversion of waste. Concern for dumping of toxic substances led to campaigns against landfills and transportation of hazardous material.

Throughout the 1970s and 1980s, pollution crises kept appearing. For every clean-up initiative, another problem site was identified. In the summer of 1988, hospital waste, including vials of blood and used syringes, washed ashore along several miles of the New Jersey coast. This generated volunteer and legislative reaction to regulate medical waste disposal. Despite universal agreement that the environment was in jeopardy, lasting solutions remained elusive as the 1980s ended.

The effects of Vietnam continued even after the hostilities ended formally. Americans were faced with an influx of immigrants from Southeast Asia. The first group of refugees came in 1975 and was comprised mainly of young, urban, educated people of relatively high economic status. They were sheltered temporarily in four refugee camps to await job offers and resettlement. Run primarily by the federal government and the military, the camps received social, educational, and recreational services from a variety of voluntary agencies. Volunteers were recruited to translate, teach English, and generally help the families to learn about the United States.

The voluntary agencies were charged with locating individual and group sponsors to assume financial and personal responsibility for a refugee family for up to two years. Sponsorship involved major obligations, particularly in providing shelter, food, and clothing until the Vietnamese became self-sufficient. The sponsors only received a resettlement stipend of a few hundred dollars, while the actual cost was estimated at a minimum of $5,500. The sponsorship program effectively scattered the Vietnamese across the country, wherever willing volunteers were found.[14]

A second wave of Vietnamese refugees left their country after the fall of Saigon in April 1975. Most ended up in Malaysia, to which they could flee in small boats. By 1978, it was estimated that one hundred thousand of these "boat people" were living in squalid, makeshift camps in Laos, Thailand, and Malaysia. As it had done in previous conflicts, the United States (and other western countries) government only permitted a percentage of these refugees to enter the country. When displaced Cambodians also needed aid, the situation worsened. Volunteers responded by going to Southeast Asia to offer medical aid, food, and other survival help. At home, others lobbied for a more humane response by the American government to these new victims of the prolonged military conflict.

Worldwide hunger became visible as an international concern. The famines in Biafra and Bangladesh generated a huge outpouring of volunteer relief and fundraising effort. World Hunger Year was declared in 1975, spawning the Hunger Project and other large-scale organizations. Entertainers such as Harry Chapin and George Harrison organized benefit concerts to attract public attention and support. This was especially effective in reaching young Americans.

One example of international activism was boycotts. Grapes, lettuce, and coffee from certain producers were all targets of boycotting at various times. One of the most extensive efforts was the Nestlé boycott, which was in effect from 1977 through 1984. Volunteers alleged that Nestlé was marketing infant formula in Third World countries in ways that increased infant malnutrition and disease. The boycotters generated public awareness of this problem and succeeded in forcing the company to agree to conform with a new international code on breast milk substitutes. In 1989, those monitoring compliance called for a resumption of the boycott because of continued abuse.

What volunteerism was in the 1970s depended on the eye of the beholder. One point of view was that malaise and self-involvement dominated everything: "If the emblem of the '60s was the angry banner of a protest marcher, the spirit of '79 was the jogger, absorbed in the sound of his own breathing—and wearing a smile button."[15] But another point of view perceived a new form of citizen activism in the public interest movement: "It has created a nationwide network of informed, articulate citizens, dedicated to giving real meaning to the ideal of participatory democracy."[16]

Somewhere in the middle lay the truth. What was clear by the end of the decade was that people who volunteered expected to see tangible results from targeted efforts. Self-interest was an acceptable motive for joining a cause. Articles appeared in popular magazines with titles such as "The New Volunteer: Getting Ahead While You Give to Others" *(Ladies Home Journal,* April 1979); "Volunteers are Getting Choosier" (*New York Times,* April 16, 1978); and "Volunteering: Its New Status" *(Town and Country,* December 1979).

The opening of the 1980s was dominated by the political stance of President Ronald Reagan, who promoted voluntarism and volunteering as a major theme of his eight years in office. He saw voluntary effort as the cornerstone of his plan to "give government back to the people."

> *The truth is, we've let government take away many things we once considered were really ours to do voluntarily, out of the goodness of our hearts and a sense of neighborliness. I believe many of you want to do those things again.*[17]

He took every opportunity to praise individuals who demonstrated compassion or heroism, exhorting all citizens to take part in solving community problems.

Reagan also called on churches to become more active in addressing needs, especially those of the poorest citizens. His view of America was of a former time in which mutual aid and self-sufficiency, rather than government programs, provided adequate help. This vision allowed individuals to take pride in themselves and be reassured that the nation was moving forward. But it also minimized concern for serious social problems that remained unaddressed by not acknowledging how many Americans were falling through the "safety net."

In seizing on the President's calls for citizen action, the media coined the phrase "the *we* decade" to contrast the 1980s with the supposedly selfish decade just ended.

The Reagan administration moved quickly to add substance to rhetoric. All eight presidential budgets contained massive cuts in social spending, with the rationale that the private sector would step in to fill resulting gaps. The budgets also proposed tax cuts whose benefits were meant to trickle down to the root causes of social problems by stimulating new jobs and a general economic upturn.

Though the public stance of the Reagan administration was to favor the volunteer role in accomplishing social good, the political reality was that support for volunteer effort was systematically eroded. When social program budgets were cut, no provision was made to fund even the basic expenses of the volunteers who were supposedly to pick up the slack. The Internal Revenue Service waged its campaign to limit the ability of 501(c)(3) tax-exempt organizations to conduct any lobbying activities, which the IRS defined in increasingly broad terms. Congress studied the "unrelated business income tax" (UBIT) under pressure from small businesses, which claimed unfair competition from nonprofit and volunteer groups conducting fundraising through gift shops, group travel tours, and other such commercial activities. The Tax Reform Act of 1986 eliminated the ability of non-itemizers to deduct charitable contributions from their income tax and limited deductions available to itemizers, as well.

A Presidential Task Force on Private Sector Initiatives was formed to identify and publicize successful examples of "public/private partnerships," a new phrase coined to describe collaboration to solve community problems. A number of states created their own governor's task forces with state-level goals. The idea was that when business, government, and voluntary agencies joined forces, any need could be met—especially if government played the minor role. While no one argued against the benefits of collaboration, many nonprofits objected to the expectation that they "do more with less" government financial assistance. Typical of the projects favored by the task forces was one in Ohio that responded to a cut in state unemployment services by finding a way to decrease the rent of a local unemployment office—a vacant building was located, and high school vocational students did renovations using materials donated by local businesses.

National awards programs for individual volunteers and for socially involved corporations were established and promoted. In 1982, the President's Volunteer Action Awards were inaugurated to recognize the accomplishments of outstanding individual, group, and business volunteers. The awards were co-sponsored by ACTION and by VOLUNTEER: The National Center on Citizen Involvement (formed in 1979 by a merger of the National Center for Voluntary Action and the National Information Center on Volunteerism; a few years later, the organization shortened its name to VOLUNTEER: The National Center; see the chart on pages 344-345).

The business community responded to the president's challenge with varying degrees of commitment. There were, of course, those companies that had already developed a track record of corporate social responsibility and now received some public recognition for their activities. But many remained unconvinced that it was appropriate for business to expend resources on community issues. Endorsement of corporate philanthropy came from a number of influential sources, including the United States Chamber of Commerce and the National Association of Manufacturers, who issued a position paper in 1981 that referred to such philanthropy as both "good business" and "an obligation." In 1983, a Gallup Poll survey indicated that 91 percent of corporate leaders acknowledged the obligation to meet community needs. Not all acted on their beliefs.

Those business leaders and social observers who questioned the government budget cuts and the role of business said:

> *There is something a bit confused about cutting social welfare in order to give business more money to invest, then expecting business to divert money back into social welfare. And there is something very confused indeed about supposing that philanthropy by large business corporations is "voluntary" on the part of those who are really paying.*[18]

Businesses were in demand for money, material goods, expertise, and volunteers. Corporate financial giving rose in the first half of the decade from $2.3 billion in 1980 to $4.2 billion in 1985, but then leveled off and even declined as the business economy shifted and tax incentives changed toward the end of the decade. Employee volunteer programs varied from encouragement of individuals to become involved in community agencies to corporate sponsorship of group projects. Volunteer activity ranged from park cleanups to picnics for disabled children to tutoring illiterate adults. Programs such as Adopt-a-School took off, and corporations as varied as CBS and Hunt Manufacturing Company committed themselves to supporting a specific public school, especially with employee volunteers. Business Volunteers for the Arts formed a dozen chapters in major cities.

In metropolitan areas, representatives of companies with employee volunteer programs formed associations, often called corporate volunteer councils, to exchange information and collaborate on service projects. The National Corporate Volunteer Council linked the groups.

A new approach to corporate philanthropy was "cause-related marketing," invented by American Express to describe its campaign to increase use of its credit card by promising users to donate a small percentage of any transaction to selected charities. By the end of the 1980s, this concept had many variations, from new product lines to special advertising promotions. This connection between profit and corporate giving raised ethical considerations and concern about its impact on more traditional forms of philanthropy.

It was difficult to assess the net number of viable corporate volunteer programs, the degree to which corporate social responsibility was entrenched in the business ethic, or the commitment to continue partnership with either government or voluntary agencies. Corporate mergers, tax reform, and international competition served to diminish the initial enthusiasm for Reagan's calls for community service.

A number of professions also responded to the call for business community involvement during this period. *Pro bono publico* work was always a tenet of professionalism, particularly in law and medicine. Professional societies and professional firms became involved in more structured efforts to recruit their members as community volunteers. In Philadelphia, Community Accountants and Architects Workshop, both founded in the early 1970s, were two examples of organized public service offering free professional assistance to small nonprofit organizations. In recognizing the work of the Currie Free Architectural Clinic in helping Appalachian residents out of Blacksburg, Virginia, one professional journal noted: "Most architects enter the profession in a spirit of idealism that is not easy to sustain in practice. To work on some project, however small, for the good of society, keeps this spirit alive."[19] Similarly, in 1987 *JAMA* (the Journal of the American Medical Association) and the *ABA Journal* (of the American Bar Association) both extolled the importance of volunteer work. For the first time in history, the two journals jointly published the same editorial, entitled "Fifty Hours for the Poor." It included the statement:

> *We believe that all doctors and all lawyers, as a matter of ethics and good faith, should contribute a significant percentage of their total professional efforts without expectation of financial remuneration . . . There is a great tradition behind the giving of this gift. In the church, it is called* stewardship. *In law, it is called* pro bono publico. *In medicine, it is called* charity. *In everyday society, it is called* fairness.[20]

Each publication included additional articles describing the community service work of its members.

In conjunction with the general endorsement of donated professional services, however, the legal community also raised concerns about the growing trend of mandating pro bono legal work to handle the poor's increased need for legal services. The opponents' arguments involved mainly the impracticality of arbitrarily assigning lawyers to cases for which they had no expertise. Through the 1980s and after, the debate continued as to whether it was necessary or advisable to legally mandate formal pro bono services.

Community involvement by the professions was not limited to services in the United States, especially in medicine. Surgical Eye Expeditions (SEE) International focused on curing operable blindness both here and in Third World countries. In 1985 alone, SEE volunteer doctors treated forty-four hundred individuals, performed four hundred sight-saving operations, and donated over $2 million in surgical services and medical supplies in the United States and six foreign countries.

In 1986, the Chivas Regal Company established an awards program for entrepreneurs under forty years of age whose business creativity fueled the American economy. In 1989, recognizing a shift in the attitudes of business people toward community involvement, the company renamed its award by coining a new term, *extrapreneur*, which it defined as "the founder or owner of a business who applies entrepreneurial techniques to perform exceptional public service work of direct benefit to the community—the entrepreneur of the 1990s."[21]

The entertainment community responded to the call for involvement in a variety of ways. The record "We Are the World" was produced by volunteers of United Support of Artists for Africa (USA for Africa) to raise millions of dollars for famine relief. It was followed by a series of fundraising concerts by musicians of every type, comedy telethons, and other show business personality endorsements of charitable causes. In 1987, *Sports Illustrated* broke tradition and designated "Athletes Who Care" as its Sportsman/Woman of the Year, highlighting the volunteer activities of eight community-involved athletes.

Ronald Reagan's interest in volunteer efforts led to a new degree of visibility for projects recruiting volunteers. Much of the publicity simply promoted the work already underway of organizations established much earlier. In other cases, media attention to a growing cause helped to mobilize new volunteer projects. In 1983, volunteerism won the "triple crown" of publicity: it was the theme of the Rose Bowl Parade; it was adopted as an Ad Council cause, generating the slogan "Volunteer—Lend a Hand"; and a commemorative stamp was issued using the Ad Council slogan. The big news of the 1980s was that volunteering had become news.

Capitalizing on the receptivity of the media to the subject of volunteering, several campaigns were launched to use television and radio to raise public awareness of charitable giving of both time and money. The "Volunteer Connection" used public service spots to get listeners to call their local volunteer center and offer their time. It began in Dallas and was replicated across the nation by VOLUNTEER: The National Center and Aid Association for Lutherans (AAL). The "Give Five" campaign, organized by INDEPENDENT SECTOR, urged Americans (via print, billboard, radio, and television ads) to donate 5 percent of their income to charity and to give five hours a week as a volunteer. Group W Westinghouse sponsored the "Time to Care" television promotion that highlighted involved individuals in local communities in order to motivate viewers to volunteer themselves. "Local Heroes" and the Giraffe Project sought to identify and publicly recognize the work of individual volunteers. The Coors Brewing Company launched its "Volunteers under 30" media project encouraging young adults to add community service to their quest for success. Ads appeared in popular magazines with slogans such as "If You Want to Earn More, Try Working for Free." All of these marketing activities continued as the decade ended, though it was difficult to measure the actual dollars and hours donated as a direct result of the publicity.

Media coverage of volunteerism produced contradictions and inconsistencies. Consider the following article titles and sources:

- "Is Charity Obsolete?" (*Forbes*, February 5, 1979)
- "The Reservoir of Voluntarism Dries Up a Bit" (*Philadelphia Inquirer*, May 31, 1981)
- "A Vision of Voluntarism: Calling for a Return to a Self-Help Society" (*Time*, October 19, 1981)
- "Voluntarism, So Far, Fails to Compensate for U.S. Budget Cuts" (*Wall Street Journal*, June 22, 1982
- "Had It with Pride, Covetousness, Lust, Anger, Gluttony, Envy and Sloth? It's Time to Start Doing Good" (*New York*, October 13, 1986)
- "The New Volunteerism: High-paid Yuppies Are Pencilling Compassion into their Calendars" (*Newsweek*, February 8, 1988)
- "Volunteering to Help Your Career" (*Nation's Business*, April 1988)

These articles reflected various perspectives. Some responded to the optimism of the Reagan philosophy, while others reacted to the negative effect of budget cuts. Some saw volunteers as a dying breed due to the demands on working women and the profit-motivated younger generation. Others acknowledged the appeal of new motivations for volunteering. By 1988, there were even medical revelations: "The researchers found that doing regular volunteer work, more than any other activity, dramatically increased life expectancy."[22]

For the first time in history, volunteerism—and voluntarism—had become legitimate subjects for research of all kinds. Academics and pollsters discovered the lack of data about the size, scope, and nature of voluntary activity. Under the sponsorship of INDEPENDENT SECTOR in 1981, the Gallup Poll organization conducted an update of the 1974 study "Americans Volunteer." This time it revised the questions to gather information on a much broader range of volunteer activity, including informal efforts previously undocumented. The results were impressive: 52 percent of adults indicated they volunteered. The Gallup Poll was repeated several times during the decade and established a baseline of statistics around which other research could be conducted. State and local surveys of giving patterns also added to the available documentation of the extent of volunteer involvement.

Throughout the 1980s, the voluntary sector became the subject of books, periodicals, dissertations, research grants, and university curricula. Most of the attention was focused on topics other than volunteers, as nonprofit management became a discipline encompassing many skills and issues. By the end of the decade, some attention was redirected specifically to nonprofit boards of directors, in a desire to increase the effectiveness of these decision-making volunteers. Leading business management authority Peter Drucker observed:

> *Twenty years ago nonprofit institutions tended to believe that they did not have to "manage" because they did not have a "bottom line." More and more of them have since learned that they have to manage especially well precisely because they lack the discipline of the "bottom line" . . . In general there has been a shift from emphasis on the "good cause" to emphasis on accountability and results. The greatest and most important change has been with respect to volunteers, their role, their treatment, their numbers.*[23]

The attention being paid to volunteers was also evident in the action of legislators. During the 1980s, a large number of bills were introduced in both Houses of Congress designed to encourage volunteer effort in some way, such as raising permitted tax deductions for mileage or limiting volunteer liability in lawsuits. Most failed to pass. A Volunteer Protection Act (always numbered H.R. 911) was introduced in various forms in 1987, 1988, and 1989. All died in committee. Several states did enact laws providing some immunity to volunteers from prosecution for negligence, though this was often limited to firefighters and emergency corps. In 1988, a federal resolution did pass both Houses that promoted volunteer involvement as legitimate work experience and urged local governments and private employers to take a job candidate's volunteering into account when offering employment.

Several social needs received national attention during the 1980s. One was education and illiteracy. In 1983, the National Commission on Excellence in Education released its report, "A Nation at Risk," warning of the inadequacies of America's public schools. This also provided a platform for literacy programs to publicize the challenges they faced in the numbers of adult illiterates.

School volunteer programs and literacy projects dramatically increased, as did community awareness and funding sources. Projects to teach reading and writing skills were adopted by high school and college groups, corporate employees, church clubs, and civic associations. The Federal Employment Literacy Training Program recruited federal workers as volunteers for literacy efforts. Literacy Volunteers of America and Laubach Literacy Action, both well-established volunteer tutoring organizations, expanded into new communities. Project Literacy U.S. (PLUS) was a major national media outreach project undertaken as a public service by the American Broadcasting Company (ABC) and the Public Broadcasting Service (PBS). It sought to educate the public about illiteracy, encourage illiterate adults to seek help, and motivate readers to become volunteers.

Prevention of illiteracy was the focus of a variety of in-school volunteer efforts. By 1983, the National School Volunteer Program (NSVP) reported that 79 percent of all public schools had some form of volunteer program. As the Adopt-a-School concept caught the interest of business, more volunteer resources became available. To reflect the increased cooperation of business, NSVP changed its name in 1988 to the National Association of Partners in Education (NAPE). *Time* magazine formed its Time to Read project in which staffers tutored elementary school students, prison inmates, and adults in every community where *Time* subsidiaries were located.

Cable television emerged as a major national commercial enterprise, and along with it came volunteers. In most major cities groups formed to advocate the insertion of public access clauses into the license requirements and contracts of cable stations. This movement was successful and resulted in certain channels being designated for community programming. Stations provided free video equipment and instruction to local residents and nonprofit agencies and then aired the volunteer-produced programs free of charge.

Computers proliferated in the home, in schools, and in the workplace. Personal computer owners quickly discovered the complexities of operating their hardware and understanding the maze of available software. A solution was to form "user groups," generally associations of people all owning the same brand of computer. User groups met regularly to exchange information and to help one another. They also started electronic bulletin boards and periodically held conferences with colleagues from other geographic areas.

Computers were seen as a new tool for grassroots community organizing. Electronic community bulletin boards were introduced as experiments in some towns to demonstrate the future applications of this new medium as a public service. The bulletin boards allowed for notice of special events, bartering opportunities, and other neighbor-to-neighbor exchanges.

There were some who voiced concern about the threat to personal privacy from mass computerization. They tried to make the public aware of the dangers of potential "big brotherism." To the work of these volunteers was added the efforts of volunteer computer experts who sought to protect computer networks from tampering and viruses.

Three major problems of the 1980s were hunger, homelessness, and drug abuse. The existence of poverty was not new, but the novelty now was the numbers and types of people who fell from marginal survival to having nothing. The exact causes of mass homelessness were hotly debated, but contributing factors certainly included rising housing costs, almost-nonexistent federal housing subsidies, inflation versus fixed incomes, and regional unemployment patterns. Also, the success of mental health advocacy limiting institutionalization increased the number of mentally ill people attempting to function in the community, without the promised social service support networks. Finally, drug and alcohol abuse diverted addicts' cash from meeting food and lodging needs.

Volunteers addressed this problem from many directions. Food kitchens and emergency shelters for street people opened, frequently housed in local churches. Food banks were formed to accept donations of groceries and cash to purchase food from businesses, farmers, and restaurants. A myriad of food drives took place. Food banks often worked closely with "gleaning" projects in which volunteers gathered the remaining fresh produce from fields after mechanized equipment passed through.

In 1984, the National Student Campaign Against Hunger initiated its annual Hunger Cleanup event, which combined community work with fundraising activities to benefit the hungry and homeless. In 1988, this effort included 8,000 volunteers working in 109 cities, where they raised $100,000 for local, national, and international projects.

Government surplus supplies of cheese, butter, and other commodities were released for distribution to seniors and low-income families, necessitating the development of a system to do this efficiently. Volunteers were recruited in large numbers by county government agencies to receive and give away tons of food to thousands of individuals.

Some tackled the need for permanent shelter. Founded in 1976, by 1988 Habitat for Humanity had organized home-building programs in 277 American communities. Habitat recruited volunteers to work side by side with homeless individuals to construct or renovate their own homes. This "sweat equity" concept, based on the philosophy of self-help, was used by similar housing programs around the country. Volunteers also worked on the legislative front to demand government funding of low-income housing.

One galvanizing activity was the Hands Across America project staged on May 25, 1986. For months before, Hands Across America staff, funded by major corporations, recruited people to participate. The concept was to create a human chain 4,000 miles long, reaching all the way across the United States. Each person in the chain would pay for a place in the line so that the project could be a fundraiser. The goal was to raise $50-100 million to be distributed to agencies serving the homeless and the hungry in America. The event had mixed results. Though there were gaps in the chain and the actual amount of money raised was never clear (several million dollars were later distributed), the effort did demonstrate that many citizens were looking for a tangible way to show their concern.

A similar outpouring of volunteer assistance occurred in 1987 when drought threatened the crops and livestock in several mid-Atlantic and midwestern states. Farmers in New England rallied to help by arranging for hay lifts to these areas. Communities joined together and volunteered trucks, hay, and drivers to make many trips to their stricken neighbors—an effort that undoubtedly averted a more severe agricultural disaster. The country-and-western music industry responded to the need of bankrupt farmers with benefit concerts and relief programs, such as Farm Aid.

Drug abuse was not a new issue, but it evolved in type and magnitude from the 1960s to the end of the 1980s. During the sixties, there were two distinct drug cultures: the urban ghetto underworld dominated by heroin addiction and the hippie, college-centered fascination with marijuana and LSD. During the seventies, LSD and other hallucinogenic drugs declined in popularity, to be replaced by cocaine as the glamour drug of both the upper and lower classes. Drugs became big business for organized crime, creating international operations of drug producers, smugglers, and dealers. By the eighties, the incidence of violent crime could be directly traced to drug traffic and the wars between competing drug rings. The introduction of new and relatively inexpensive substances such as PCP and the crack form of cocaine added another dimension by making drugs more accessible and also more dangerous—and by involving younger and younger children as users and dealers.

Volunteers tackled drug abuse in a variety of ways. Some gave their attention to addicts by offering counseling. Crisis hot lines were established, often staffed by former addicts themselves, such as Drugline 9 in Denver (1982). Self-help support groups, modeled on Alcoholics Anonymous, were formed for addicts and their families. Infants born addicted to drugs because of their mothers' dependency received special attention and care from volunteer projects.

Other volunteers focused on prevention of drug abuse, particularly among schoolchildren. Nancy Reagan adopted this cause and chaired the national "Just Say No" campaign to encourage youngsters to reject offers of drugs from their friends or adults. This project gained much publicity, and a variety of entertainers spoke out in public service ads to make it socially acceptable to refuse drugs. While many felt that the "Just Say No" project was too superficial—especially because the Reagan administration was simultaneously cutting funds from drug enforcement and rehabilitation—a variety of related prevention activities were spawned by the national publicity. Curriculum modules were introduced into schools at all grade levels, such as the Drug Abuse Resistance Effort (DARE), which was sponsored by local police departments. Projects such as the Commonwealth Alliance for Drug Rehabilitation and Education (CADRE) in Virginia trained volunteers to speak in classrooms. One of CADRE's slogans was "It's About Time Parents Became the Pushers."

Several new types of volunteer activity sprang up during this period in response to other specific health needs. For example, specialized services for victims of brain and head injuries were created, led by volunteers from the families involved. Many hospitals also welcomed volunteers into their neonatal care units to provide comfort to high-risk infants, as typified by the "cuddlers" at the Hershey (Pennsylvania) Medical Center and the "godmothers" at Beth Israel Medical Center in New York. The 1976 swine flu epidemic mobilized volunteers in a nationwide vaccination effort.

The prevalence of single-parent and two-income households led to a generation of "latchkey children." These were youngsters left alone before and after school while their parent(s) were at work, a situation that created a set of unique physical, educational, and emotional needs. Volunteers were quick to develop a variety of support programs to assist with homework, provide after-school activities, respond in the case of emergencies, and offer companionship. An example was the Phone Friend project sponsored by members of the American Association of University Women in State College, Pennsylvania.

Missing children received much publicity during the 1980s. There was a perceived increase in the number of kidnapped or abducted children, including those who were taken by one estranged parent as retaliation against the other. Volunteer organizations sprang up across the country to generate publicity for this problem and to find new ways of using modern technology in the search for the children. One innovation was the enlistment of dairies in printing the photographs of selected children on milk cartons. This public service placed the issue directly into the homes of the general public. Police departments and parent groups offered voluntary programs to fingerprint children, giving parents a vital tool that could be used to locate their youngsters if later abducted.

One-to-one friendship programs matched volunteers with mentally retarded, emotionally disturbed, and developmentally disabled individuals. The Compeer program began in Rochester, New York, in 1974 as a way of supporting mentally ill people of all ages who had no family or friends; by 1986, it had spread to twenty-two states and involved over a thousand volunteers.

As a result of technological advances, new services were made possible for those with physical disabilities. Telecommunications Exchange for the Deaf was established in the greater Washington, D.C., area to provide round-the-clock telephone relay service for hearing- and speech-impaired residents. The program was maintained by a staff of three hundred volunteers. The Independence Factory, an all-volunteer organization in Middletown, Ohio, designed and manufactured self-help devices for disabled people throughout the country.

Although organized self-help was certainly not new, the 1970s and 1980s saw a dramatic proliferation of such all-volunteer groups. Their activities were aimed at a wide range of mutual-help, self-care, and self-reform issues as shown by this list: Heart-to-Heart (for those with coronary problems); Overeaters Anonymous (for those with weight concerns); Mensa (for persons with high IQs); Better Breathers Club (for those with chronic lung disease); Boonfellows (for agoraphobics); Added Care (for women with breast cancer); and Urban Survival (for single parents). In 1981, the first computerized clearinghouse on mutual aid self-help programs was established in New Jersey by St. Clares-Riverside Medical Center, soon followed by similar services in other states and the creation of the National Self-Help Clearinghouse. This type of volunteering received additional recognition in 1987 when the U.S. Surgeon General endorsed self-help as an effective method for dealing with stress, personal hardship, and pain.

When the decade began, driving under the influence of alcohol was perceived as more of a social than a criminal problem. Then came Mothers Against Drunk Driving (MADD). Founded in 1980, MADD grew to 111 chapters in thirty-six states by 1983. Because the original members were mothers whose own children had been killed by drunk drivers, the movement had a fervor and sincerity that could not be denied. It captured the attention of judges and public officials, who began to enforce existing and new legislation punishing intoxicated drivers. By the end of the decade public opinion had been permanently changed. Students organized programs to help teenage drinkers with alternate forms of transportation, especially after parties and proms. "Designated driver" campaigns, often supported by radio personalities and bartenders, encouraged one member of any group to refrain from drinking in order to drive the rest of the group home safely.

Another shift in public opinion involved attitudes toward smoking or, more accurately, toward the rights of nonsmokers. The Surgeon General's Office issued a series of definitive studies identifying smoking as a major health hazard. It was also acknowledged that nonsmokers were at risk from inhaling the second-hand cigarette smoke of nearby smokers. This prompted a wave of volunteer protest actions that resulted in local ordinances restricting smoking in the workplace and public areas, especially restaurants. Several states adopted restrictive laws, and the Federal Aviation Authority responded to citizen and flight attendant pressure to ban all smoking on domestic flights of less than two hours (which during the 1990s became a prohibition of any smoking on any flight).

One area that had always been heavily dependent on volunteers was emergency services—local firefighting and ambulance corps. Several trends combined to strain the existing system and create a crisis by the end of the 1980s. Volunteer emergency services began on the premise of neighbor helping neighbor in a mutual-protection plan. It was presumed that most people (men) worked in or near their homes and so could respond quickly when needed. Modern American suburbs changed this as residents commuted further and further to their jobs. The result was that most volunteer fire companies and ambulance corps began having trouble recruiting daytime help. They also found that commuters felt less affiliation with their home communities and therefore less interest in volunteering evenings and weekends. Some localities responded by offering a salary to their day shift, while retaining volunteers at other hours. Others saw the opportunity to recruit new types of volunteers: women, active retirees, students, and minorities.

Adding to the recruitment problems of emergency service providers was the concern for legal liability affecting every aspect of American life in the 1980s. Fear of lawsuits made recruitment of volunteers in all settings more difficult, and rising insurance premiums added to the cost of volunteer programs. Various types of volunteer immunity legislation were proposed at the national and state levels; by 1989, over forty states had passed some form of protection, particularly for boards of directors and emergency services. Some municipalities assumed insurance costs for government volunteers. As the decade ended, legal liability remained an unanswered question for a variety of organizations.

A major volunteer effort affecting the health care field during this time was the hospice movement. Believing in the benefits of caring support for terminally ill patients and their families, a group of volunteers in New Haven, Connecticut, established the first hospice program in 1974. They provided a compassionate environment to help families cope with stress and grief, often enabling the dying to spend their last days or weeks at home rather than in the hospital. Despite resistance from the medical establishment, the hospice concept quickly spread across the country, increasing in number to over six hundred programs by 1983. In December of that year, the federal Medicare system officially accepted hospices as legitimate health care providers. Many hospice projects eventually hired paid coordinators and affiliated with hospitals or nursing services, but the movement continued to be dominated by volunteers.

By far the biggest medical crisis of the 1980s came in the form of Acquired Immune Deficiency Syndrome, or AIDS. The potential enormity of the situation was first recognized by volunteers. In 1981, a few dozen homosexual men were struck with a rare cancer and a disease that had no name. In alarmed response, some New York men banded together to form the Gay Men's Health Crisis. Beginning as a support group for disease victims and their lovers, the group added services as the number of diagnosed cases grew. The disease was soon known as

AIDS, and associated terms such as HIV-positive and ARC (AIDS-related complex) became commonly recognized. By the mid-eighties, it was clear that AIDS was an epidemic and not at all limited to the big cities, nor to the gay community.

Volunteer organizations formed all across the country: Nashville CARES, ActionAIDS (Philadelphia), Idaho AIDS Project, Minority AIDS Project (Los Angeles), and the Aliveness Project (Minneapolis). They all sought to do several things: provide "buddies" and one-to-one assistance to persons with AIDS (referred to as "PWAs"); organize support groups for all the affected subgroups, including family and friends of those with the disease; and conduct public education campaigns to prevent further transmittal, separate fact from fiction about AIDS, and limit discrimination against sufferers.

> *City officials say they shudder to think of what would have happened in New York if the homosexual community had not formed the Gay Men's Health Crisis and other spin-off organizations to care for the sick, educate the healthy, and lobby for attention and funds. "When the story of New York's AIDS epidemic is written, that self-help effort will be the bright part of it," said Dr. Joseph, the City Health Commissioner. Added Dr. Sencer, his predecessor: "There is no way to put a dollar value on it."*[24]

From 1981 to 1989, the AIDS issue evolved rapidly. First, the number of newly diagnosed AIDS and HIV-positive cases rose dramatically. This overloaded existing resources, causing rapid expansion of services and volunteer networks. Second, new treatment modalities lengthened the amount of time someone could expect to live after diagnosis. While this was good news, it meant that support services were needed for longer periods, again straining the service system. Third, government and private funding sources began pouring money into both medical research and patient services. Previously all-volunteer organizations were transformed overnight into million dollar operations, often with no time to consider what management structures would be most effective. Despite new paid staff, every major AIDS organization continued to rely heavily on the work of volunteers, particularly as buddies or client visitors.

Fourth, the reliance on the gay community to provide support to PWAs changed. At first, the need to recruit volunteers from outside homosexual circles was based on burnout: there was only a finite number of healthy gay people to handle the service demands and level of stress. Later, as more and more heterosexuals were diagnosed, it became evident that helping PWAs was everyone's concern. Because a large percentage of the new PWAs were intravenous drug users, the volunteers already working in substance abuse programs found themselves addressing AIDS-related needs as well. Two special areas of activity were help to those acquiring AIDS through blood transfusions and help to infants and children with AIDS (many abandoned at birth).

Those who were mourning the death of AIDS victims sought ways to express their grief. One outlet was the Names Project quilt. Created as part of the Lesbian and Gay Rights March on Washington in October 1987, the quilt consisted of hundreds—and then thousands—of three-foot by six-foot panels sewn in memory of specific friends, family members, and lovers. Taking on a life of its own, the project office over the next two years received panels from all across the country and soon the quilt, when completely displayed, covered the area of several football fields. It traveled to dozens of American cities in sections, allowing visitors to see the newest panels from their local area and to experience a sense of shared grief. The quilt personalized the AIDS crisis and gave many new insights about its magnitude. Volunteers hosted the quilt displays and used the opportunity to raise funds and distribute educational literature.

Several unique events occurred during the decade that were in large measure dependent on volunteers. The 1984 Summer Olympics held in Los Angeles involved 30,000 volunteers in roles ranging from entrance monitoring to officiating. This number was even higher than the number of volunteers who also worked to make the 1980 Winter Olympics in Lake Placid, New York, possible.

From August 1985 through the end of 1986, a cadre of volunteers kept "Halley Watch"—an organized effort by NASA to keep Halley's Comet under constant surveillance. An application fee of $9 registered each volunteer, who then received a government manual with instructions on how to do the job.

The United States reached its Bicentennial in 1976, but the celebration was actually extended over more than ten years to include various anniversaries such as the 200th birthday of the Constitution in 1987. State and local festivities proliferated and involved thousands of volunteers in everything from major restoration projects to historic event reenactments to festivals and parades. Concurrently, the 1984–1986 campaign to renovate the Statue of Liberty attracted the financial support of both corporations and elementary school children. The organizers took pride in reaching their goal of restoring this national treasure by July 4, 1986—without any government funds—and of raising enough excess money to also renovate the immigrant arrival area on nearby Ellis Island.

By the 1980s, there was enough distance from the Vietnam War to permit consideration of memorializing those who died in the conflict even if controversy still surrounded the war itself. A Vietnam Veterans Memorial Fund was established and, despite debates over the design selected, $7 million was raised to complete the monument in 1986. A black granite wall inscribed with the names of those who died in the war, it became the most visited memorial in Washington, D.C. Along with the efforts of many veterans to get the monument built, volunteers from the Veterans Vigil Society began a round-the-clock vigil at the wall to help visitors locate specific names and keep alive the drive to locate those individuals still missing in action (MIAs). The concern for MIAs and prisoners of war (POWs) in Southeast Asia and for victims of Agent Orange also became causes for other veterans groups and associations of family members. Since the building of the national Vietnam War Memorial, numerous states and municipalities have responded to volunteer efforts to construct similar local monuments.

Another controversial debate revolved around United States involvement in Latin America. While the federal government accepted refugees from certain countries, it did not recognize the pleas for asylum from residents of others. By mid-decade it was clear that many families were fleeing Central America for their lives, coming to the United States illegally and facing deportation. This problem led to a sanctuary movement, largely involving church congregations. Taking advantage of their historical right to provide protection from arrest through physical sanctuary within their property, religious congregations across the country made the commitment to house Latin Americans seeking protection from deportation. By 1986, at least 330 congregations were actively involved, providing shelter, food, legal assistance, and other volunteer support to such refugees.

Other refugees also received services from volunteers, including help in finding shelter and jobs, tutoring in English, and a general orientation to American life. Depending on the part of the country and its source of immigrants, such services were offered to Indochinese, Mexicans, Russian Jews, and Cubans. Illegal aliens, particularly in the Southwest, found both advocates and protesters.

Americans responded with a great outpouring of concern and tangible aid after several major natural disasters at home and overseas. The devastation of earthquakes in Italy (1980), Mexico (1985), and Armenia (1988) elicited massive airlifts of donated clothing, food, and medicine as well as the fielding of volunteer rescue and medical teams. Mud slides and forest fires threatened California residents a number of times during the 1980s, also bringing volunteer help. The 1988 Yellowstone National Park fire required the efforts of paid and volunteer firefighting units from all over the country who, in turn, received the attention of volunteers who cooked meals and established on-site rest points.

One of the heated political issues of the 1980s centered on South Africa and its apartheid practices. Many Americans lost patience with the slow pace of change in the fight for racial equality in that country and with corporations that seemed to be providing the economic base for the whites-only regime. Protest actions were first aimed at the companies themselves but then shifted focus to pressure major stockholders to divest their portfolios of stocks in corporations trading in South Africa. College students were especially vocal in this effort as it became evident that a number of universities were themselves such stockholders.

The resulting publicity prompted some individual stockholders to consider the social conscience of their own portfolios and to sell stocks in companies whose practices did not match the investor's personal values. Socially responsible investing concerns included: South African involvement, pollution control, the number of women and minority board members, defense contracts, and animal experimentation. There were two schools of thought on how to express one's corporate philosophy: not to own any stock in an offending company; or to buy a minimum number of shares in order to attend and express opposition at annual stockholder meetings.

In the three decades since 1960, community service by young people experienced a pendulum swing. The youth of the Kennedy, hippie, and Vietnam era idealized activism; those in the seventies largely rejected it; by the late eighties it was popular again. Many school-based service-learning programs waned in the seventies as the concern for social relevance gave way to an emphasis on career preparation. The "young urban professional" population of the eighties was schooled in the late seventies—the "Yuppie" curriculum had no place for activities that diverted attention from the best ways to earn more money.

Perhaps because of negative reaction to the outright greed and conspicuous consumption of the mid-eighties, young people themselves led a major turnaround in attitudes toward volunteering. By 1989, the Campus Outreach Opportunity League (COOL) enlisted the support of student leaders in over 450 colleges and universities to stimulate and expand community service projects. COOL's founder, Wayne Meisel, had begun the organization in 1984 as a student by walking across New England to talk to other campus activists.

> *At the time of the walk there was little talk about student involvement in community service. A few schools had strong community service initiatives. Most, however, had deteriorated or disappeared during the past 20 years. There had been a steady decline in the prestige, presence and participation of service programs at colleges over the years.*
>
> *Five years later there is a national movement of student involvement in the community that continues to gain momentum . . . Student community service is now on the forefront of higher education and at every political level. I knew we had arrived when during half time of the Fiesta Bowl, the biggest college football game of the year, students at Notre Dame were highlighted for their work in the community.*[25]

In 1985, 121 college presidents signed on to the Campus Compact, pledging to create opportunities for their students to learn about and practice volunteering. Brown and Harvard established million-dollar endowments for scholarships to students active in community projects. The National Association of Independent Schools reported that 277 of their 448 private school members offered compulsory or voluntary service components; one-quarter required some form of volunteer work prior to graduation.

By the close of the 1980s, the movement to include community service in public school curricula became vocal. The Atlanta school system pioneered a plan requiring all high school students to perform a set number of hours of service each year. California and Pennsylvania were considering legislation mandating a similar requirement for all students, including those in public universities.

During the 1970s, full-time service programs such as VISTA, Peace Corps, Experiment in International Living, and projects of the American Friends Service Committee continued to attract new recruits. The Carter administration actively supported such activities and increased VISTA to field over 4,000 volunteers a year. Volunteers were encouraged to do community organizing and voter registration as well as economic development projects. In 1981, Ronald Reagan drastically reduced funding because of these very activities. By 1982, VISTA had been cut to half its size and its new director went public with the Reagan wish to eliminate the program altogether. The debate over VISTA demonstrated a fundamental disagreement about the nature of volunteerism.

> *The more conservative view has been that volunteers should provide direct social services to those in need; the liberal inclination has been to argue that volunteers should encourage social action by and for those in need. This "case versus cause" debate reflects broader differences in social outlook.*[26]

The Peace Corps was moved out of ACTION entirely and aligned with State Department initiatives instead.

During the 1988 presidential campaign, the subject of national youth service became a public issue. Proponents of some sort of community service program for young adults had been proposing such projects since the Vietnam War. Originally seen as a civilian alternative to military service under the draft, interest in the concept lessened when the war ended. In 1979, the National Committee for the Study of National Service issued its report, "Youth and the Needs of the Nation," in which a possible large-scale volunteer system was outlined. The National Service Secretariat and others kept the idea alive and, by the mid-eighties, had gained the support of such diverse groups as Youth Service America and the Democratic Leadership Council, which hailed national service as a way to "foster a new spirit of citizenship and patriotism."[27]

By the end of 1988, there were already forty state and local programs spending over $124 million annually in stipends for young people doing community service. The programs varied widely. Some involved as few as twelve and others as many as 12,500 participants. Ages ranged from nine to twenty-six. Some kept the old name of Conservation Corps, others called themselves Volunteer Corps (New York) or Ranger Corps (Philadelphia). Almost no federal money was involved.

In 1988 and 1989, more than a dozen bills were introduced in Congress to create some form of national service initiative. The proposed plans were diverse, ranging from full-time service to weekend projects, from completely volunteer to significant hourly wages, from no-strings-attached to tied-to-student-loan programs. The first President Bush unveiled his own strategy of a federally funded private foundation to be called "YES to America"—with "YES" standing for "Youth Engaged in Service." His strategy was to recruit young people from teenagers to college graduates in a wide range of service options. He also proposed a Points of Light Initiative to encourage Americans of all ages to do more voluntary community service and declared: "From now on, any definition of a successful life must include serving others."

Whereas all of the proposed government-sponsored community service corps had the potential to be of genuine benefit to both individual participants and recipient agencies, the major concern of many was that the assignments offered would be make-work. There was lack of agreement about what was community service and what was simply undercompensated jobs, about what was coerced and what was voluntary, and about the difference between such corps members and more traditional volunteers working in the same setting.

National youth service was only one idea related to what some observers considered mandatory volunteer efforts. Other ideas were court-referred community service, workfare, service credit banks, and volunteering connected to workers compensation.

The idea of community service as a sentencing option began in Great Britain in the late 1960s as the British penal system was investigating ways to alleviate prison overcrowding. The tasks offenders typically performed included answering the phones in a community center, constructing adventure playgrounds, planting trees, tutoring, reading to blind persons, and working on reclamation projects.

Acceptance of this concept in the United States proceeded rather slowly at first. Only a few judges utilized community service as more than an occasional sentencing alternative and most of these sentences were imposed on middle- or upper-income offenders who had special skills (such as doctors or lawyers) that the judge believed could be put to use for the good of the community. By the mid-1980s, however, more and more courts began to impose such sentences on a broader basis. In 1984, for example, more than 15,000 New Jersey court clients performed over one million hours of community service, ranging from picking up litter to computer programming. Although no precise figures are available on the number of people performing community service on a nationwide basis, the popularity of these programs increased sharply.

> *Whatever the reasons, experts say it is changing sentencing patterns throughout the criminal justice system. Locally and elsewhere, a greater proportion of first-time offenders are working off their sentences by stuffing envelopes for the American Cancer Society, caring for children in Head Start centers, becoming Big Brothers, sorting clothes for charities, and maintaining public roads and parks . . . It is a part of life unknown to the public. For the most part, few realize that some of the people shelving books at the public library or working at Special Olympics track meets are fulfilling obligations to a court.*[28]

Some projects were seen as restitution, others as companions to probation or parole. Some were designed to teach the offender new skills, while others were meant to instill values of community affiliation. While the trend grew steadily, there was great variation in how and when it was applied. Some states, such as California, developed a statewide community service system with fairly consistent guidelines and sentencing policies. Other states, such as North Carolina, established sentences for specific offenses (for example, driving under the influence of alcohol) and created a statewide network to implement them.[29]

Some observers raised legitimate concerns over four issues: involuntary service, discrimination, disparity, and expansion of social control. Because of the many variations in the application of the community service option, there was no uniformity in who was offered this alternative and how. This led to similar offenses being treated very differently from one jurisdiction to another. Also, there was a definite bias toward using community service when the crimes were white-collar or the offenders well known. This was especially controversial when entertainment celebrities were able to work off their drug convictions in the community while unknown offenders went to prison.

Regardless of these criticisms, alternative sentencing ideas were often creative. In Quincy, Massachusetts, the "Earn It" program placed juvenile offenders into volunteer jobs provided by local businesses or community groups. The National Community Service Sentencing Association was formed in 1985 to link program leaders and share expertise. One of the important trends documented by many of these projects was that a meaningful percentage of the people who began their community service under court order remained active as volunteers in their assignments long after their mandatory time had elapsed.

Another government-mandated form of community service came to be known as "workfare." The basic principle of workfare was that it is unproductive to give able-bodied people welfare checks without expecting something in return. In theory, making community service a condition for public assistance allowed work-fare participants to retain self-respect, contribute to their communities, gain needed work experience, and develop new, marketable skills. A few scattered pilot programs operated during the early 1980s. The Family Support Act of 1988, which was the most comprehensive revision of the nation's welfare system since its inception in the 1930s, required that welfare families with children over the age of three had to enroll in various training and job search programs. The Act also created a mandatory community work experience component to begin in 1990.

With the increase in the number of people over sixty years of age, public policy makers faced new challenges in providing long-term care for the elderly. Because many older people did not require a nursing home or other institutionalization, the major need was for assistance with home chores, transportation, and other limited daily support that allowed the elderly to remain self-sufficient. One innovative response was the service credit bank or time bank, which combined elements of volunteering and barter. The concept was simple: in exchange for helping one's older neighbor today, a volunteer could receive "credit" toward similar help later in life. The idea was similar to the incentive system of blood banks. Some of the proposals also allowed volunteers to designate their service credits to be used on behalf of someone else.

In 1985, Florida passed State Bill 301-1652-85, directing its Department of Health and Rehabilitative Services to "initiate a statewide, computer-based volunteer service credit program." In 1987, the Robert Wood Johnson Foundation gave grants to St. Louis, Missouri, the District of Columbia, and Dorchester, Massachusetts, to start service credit programs. Several other states were studying the concept. While elegant in its apparent simplicity, the project posed a variety of serious problems in application. For example, there were questions about which types of volunteer work would qualify, who would keep the necessary records for how many years, and other practical considerations. Some proponents also wanted to expand the concept to include a variety of service recipients beyond the elderly.

Toward the end of the 1980s, the corporate community involvement concept developed a new twist. Corporate mergers and the decline in domestic manufacturing resulted in increased plant closings. Companies provided severance pay but included a new idea: since the company was, in effect, still paying the laid-off workers a salary, the company could deploy such individuals to work as "volunteers" (at least from the recipients' perspective) in community agencies.

This practice was also applied to employees receiving workers compensation. Again, though these workers were still receiving a salary from a corporate employer, from the point of view of the organizations benefiting from their services, these people were volunteers.

The impact of these two decades on the evolution of volunteering remains undeniable, but not because of the quantity of activity. Despite the fact that volunteering was statistically measured for the first time in this period, there is no reason to believe that the data uncovered either more or less volunteer activity than occurred before such studies were done. Rather, what happened was that volunteerism became conscious of itself. A growing number of organizations became concerned with the support of volunteers and of their leaders. Scholars, reporters, and presidents discovered that volunteering deserved recognition. The answer to the question "Who is a volunteer?" expanded to include a wider spectrum of community resources than ever imagined. Volunteering had become visible.

Endnotes for Chapter 8

1. Michael Nelson, "Power to the People: The Crusade for Direct Democracy," *Saturday Review* 6, no.22 (November 24, 1979): 12.
2. Gary Lipton, "The ABCs of PACs," *Elected Leader* 7, no. 1 (Winter 1988): 17.
3. Report of the National Organization of Women Task Force on Volunteerism (November 1973).
4. Wendy Kaminer, *Women Volunteering* (Garden City, NY: Anchor Press, 1984), 211.
5. Ellen Sulzberger Straus, "In Defense of Unpaid Labor," *Ms.* 3, no. 8 (February 1975): 75.
6. Doris B. Gold, "Women and Voluntarism," in *Woman in Sexist Society,* eds. Vivian Gornick and Barbara K. Moran (New York: Basic Books, 1971; Signet, 1972), 551–2.
7. *Americans Volunteer, 1974,* ACTION, Pamphlet 4000–17 (Washington, DC: Government Printing Office, February 1975), 1–3.

8. Quoted in Milton Moskowitz, "Corporate Social Responsibility 1967–1977: An Overview," *Social Responsibility* (n.p.: LeviStrauss, 1978), 4.

9. Stanley G. Karson, "The Social Responsibility of Management," *Nation's Business* (July 1975).

10. John H. Kuhn and Jane McGuire, "Fewer Officials Work Unpaid," *The Record* (Bergen County, NJ), June 8, 1976.

11. *Independence Neighbors* (April/May 1981), 2.

12. Letter dated May 1989, Volunteers in Prison project of the Voluntary Action Center of Centre County, PA.

13. Rita A. Varela, *Self-Help Groups in Rehabilitation* (Washington, DC: The American Coalition of Citizens with Disabilities, Inc., 1979), 1–2.

14. Darrel Montero, *Vietnamese Americans: Patterns of Resettlement and Socioeconomic Adaptation in the United States* (Boulder, CO: Westview, 1979), 24–9.

15. "The Limits of Power," *Newsweek* (November 19, 1979): 87.

16. Edward M. Kennedy, "Citizen Involvement: Present Realities and Future Prospects," in *Citizen Participation Perspectives,* ed. Stuart Langton (Boston: Lincoln Filene Center for Citizenship and Public Affairs, 1979).

17. Ronald Reagan, as quoted from a televised budget message, *Time* (October 19, 1981).

18. Michael Kinsley, "Waiting for Lenny: Stinginess Masquerading as Charity," *Harpers* (March 1982): 11.

19. Mildred F. Schmertz, editorial in *Architectural Record* (May 1982).

20. George D. Lundberg and Laurence Bodine, "Fifty Hours for the Poor," *JAMA* 258, no. 21: 3157 and *ABA Journal,* 73: 55. Jointly published December 1987.

21. Chivas Regal Company borchure, *Are You an Extrapreneur?* (New York: 1989).

22. Allan Luks, "Helper's High," *Psychology Today* (October 1988).

23. Peter Drucker, "The Quiet Revolution," *The Wall Street Journal* (September 8, 1988).

24. *The New York Times* (March 16, 1987).

25. Wayne Meisel, "Farewell Letter" to COOL, 1989.

26. Ann Hulbert, "VISTA's Lost Horizons," *The New Republic* (August 30, 1982): 19.

27. "Enlisting with Uncle Sam," *Time* (February 23, 1987): 30.

28. *The Washington Post* (November 6, 1983).

29. Katherine H. Noyes, *Opportunity or Dilemma: Court-Referred Community Service Workers* (Richmond: Virginia Department of Volunteerism, 1985).

Chapter 9

A Millennium Ends and a New One Begins

1990	Americans with Disabilities Act passes.
1991	First site opened on the World Wide Web.
	U.S. goes to war in the Persian Gulf.
1993	Standoff between the FBI, ATF agents and Branch Davidians in Waco, Texas ends in a tragic fire.
	Intel pentium processor introduced.
1994	The Hubble telescope proves Einstein's theory of black holes.
1995	Federal building in Oklahoma City bombed.
	O.J. Simpson, after the most watched trial in the century, is acquitted.
1996	Welfare Reform Bill signed into law.
1998	President Clinton impeached on perjury and obstruction of justice after sex scandal.
1999	Columbine High School shootings in Littleton, Colorado.
	Fear of the Y2K "bug" grips New Year's Eve.
2000	Presidential election (G.W. Bush vs. Gore) undecided for weeks.
2001	International Year of Volunteers.
	Hijacked airplanes crash into the World Trade Center and the Pentagon on September 11.
2003	The U.S. invades Iraq to depose Sadam Hussein.

The second edition of this book was published in 1990. The subsequent dozen years were quite remarkable in just about every way, including events of direct impact on volunteerism. So much occurred, in fact, that the 1990s and early 2000s deserve this chapter on their own, though we offer the usual caveat that any recount of recent events should be read more as observation than as history.

Consider just a few world news items since 1990:

- The breakup of the Soviet Union, the reunification of Germany, and all of the subsequent optimism and unrest of what we are calling the "emerging democracies" of post-communist eastern Europe. The violent end to Yugoslavia as one nation.
- The ending of apartheid in South Africa, Nelson Mandela freed after twenty-seven years in prison, and the return to majority rule.
- Two Persian Gulf wars, highs and lows of the Israel/Palestine conflict, Islamic jihad actions. Terrorism of all sorts culminating in the September 11, 2001, attacks on the World Trade Center and the Pentagon.
- The opening of the "Chunnel" linking England and France by train. The European Union introduces the euro, replacing twelve national currencies.
- The invention of the World Wide Web.
- Cloned sheep, mad cow disease, and the Ebola virus scare.
- The impeachment of a U.S. President and the untimely death of a British princess.
- The start of a new millennium, along with panic about a possible "Y2K bug."

This was also the decade that introduced 24-hour news media, eliminating much of the sense of distance between events across the globe and our own homes. Even a partial list of buzz words highlight the trends affecting the United States internally in the last dozen years: Generation X, Anita Hill, hanging chads, Megan's Law, don't ask/don't tell, Viagra, text messaging. Life has been fast and certainly not dull.

Without question, the single most important occurrence of the 1990s was the introduction of the World Wide Web and the explosion of Internet-access and e-mail. By the end of the century it was apparent that e-mail would have as profound an effect on human communication as did the telephone a century before. Ironically, we now find the world both connected and divided.

The proliferation of computers and e-mail accounts opened fascinating new opportunities for volunteers. Cyberspace even gave birth to the first truly new form of volunteering in decades: virtual volunteering, or online service. Further, concepts such as "online community" opened new ways for people with similar interests or concerns to find and support one another. Political activism gained an exceptional new tool and determined volunteers are still discovering all the ways they can affect public opinion, mobilize protests to government officials and even direct real-world demonstrations, raise money, and otherwise rally like-minded citizens.

The Web itself had its roots in volunteer efforts, starting with the man credited with inventing Linux, the groundbreaking open-source computer operating system that makes it all possible. Linus Torvalds was a twenty-one-year-old Finnish student in 1991:

> *After developing the system, he did something revolutionary. He posted Linux on the Internet for free, inviting users to download, share, and modify the code—even sell it as their own . . . Today, the open-source community hails Torvalds as a hero.*[1]

Torvalds, who moved to Silicon Valley soon after going public, titled his 2001 autobiography, *Just for Fun: The Story of an Accidental Revolutionary* (Harper Information). In a television interview publicizing the book, Charlie Rose asked him: "Did anybody come to you and say, look, you can be as rich as Bill Gates?" To which Torvalds replied:

> *. . . [S]ure, people did later on—especially when Linux started taking off. And people really hadn't gotten the idea of open source. People said, "Why did you do that?" Especially in the United States, but also in Finland. People just did not understand the concept of creating a program because you like programming, and they did not understand the concept of Hey, sure, I like money, but on the other hand I'm a programmer, I will get paid.*
>
> *It's not as if programmers go hungry in this world. So, I wasn't worried about money and making money. At the same time, I'd done this project for myself. I didn't want to commercialize it because I didn't want to go through the headaches. And I had no incentive to.*[2]

From the beginning, Web sites, online discussion groups, electronic newsletters and other types of resources were developed by people who wanted to use the medium to communicate their opinions or share their passions. Commercial interest came later and, even after the for-profit world seemed to dominate the Internet, volunteers continued to play a critical role in facilitating information sharing and discussion.

The true power of the Web was evidenced by its ability to make the phrase "global village" real. Online, it did not matter where or when someone accessed or sent a message. Activists concerned with issues of international import, from global warming to AIDS, could now find one another and join forces virtually. Although at the present time English has become the default language of the Web, translation programs are continually being improved to help cross language boundaries.

The military conflicts of the decade were transformed by the Internet, too. Whether in Bosnia, Iraq, Afghanistan, or anywhere else, both sides of a conflict used e-mail and the Web to communicate with each other and with the outside world (even if transmission was only possible for a few hours a day). This made news of the situation immediately accessible without the media as "middleman." American soldiers deployed in these actions were also able to use e-mail continuously to keep in touch with loved ones at home.

The new technology had its down side, too, of course. First was the continuing problem of the "digital divide," separating once again those with the resources to buy and run computers from those either too poor to pay for the service or living in an area without the available communications structure to support it. Advocates worked hard to keep this issue in the public eye and they had an impact. Throughout the decade in the U.S., both the government and private funders initiated projects designed to "connect" populations in danger of being marginalized by the Internet explosion. One of the most successful was NetDay, first held in California in 1995. It inspired a grassroots volunteer effort to wire the nation's K-12 classrooms for Internet access. Over five hundred thousand volunteers wired more than seventy-five thousand classrooms in forty states from 1996 to 2001.[3]

Another successful organization was CompuMentor, whose purpose is expressed on their Web site as: "We help nonprofit organizations and schools use technology more effectively to achieve their missions. Ultimately, our behind-the-scenes work benefits low-income and underserved populations."[4] Volunteers have always been instrumental to CompuMentor's outreach and provide coaching and technical assistance on everything from computer and software purchasing to designing Web sites. In its July 25, 2001 edition, the *San Francisco Bay Guardian* named CompuMentor "The Best Place to

Volunteer After You've Been Laid Off"—quite a compliment as Silicon Valley "dot-coms" were in turmoil. American volunteers also worked to bring Internet technology to developing countries, using everything from cell phones to laptops to increase the flow of communication and technical assistance.

Three controversies related to the Internet received attention in the period: information privacy, copyright protection, and pornography aimed at children. It soon became clear that going online could lead to all sorts of benign and malicious observation. New computer crimes were rapidly invented as hackers, virus developers, and outright thieves found ways to grab credit card information, personal identification materials, and business data from Web sites and e-mail. In response, law enforcement, software developer professional associations, and concerned Web users worked to catch and stop such criminals and to frame appropriate laws against such activity.

The ease of sharing information electronically, sound as well as text, led to copyright violations that could hardly have been imagined when copyright laws were first written. Some of the dissemination was indeed an attempt to bypass purchasing of the source material, but in other cases the copying was unintentional. Writers, recording artists, and other content providers organized to limit the financial damage of electronic transmissions, while consumer groups fought to keep the Web as open an environment as possible.

Everyone who was concerned about the availability of pornographic images to children in printed form immediately recognized the ease with which the Internet could broadcast sexual material to minors. The anti-pornography lobby therefore moved its focus to cyberspace, advocating for tools to allow parents to block certain kinds of sites and e-mail and urging worldwide prosecution of anyone using children in their sexual materials. When the outrage spilled into wider demands, other volunteers protested censorship. The tension between the two sides continues.

One of the key books published in the 1990s was by Harvard political scientist Robert D. Putnam titled *Bowling Alone: The Collapse and Revival of American Community* (Simon and Schuster, 1995). Putnam crystallized what many people already felt: Americans had become more fragmented, tended to engage in individual activities with little social interaction, and no longer wanted to "join" associations. He used the metaphor of the demise of bowling leagues to highlight his observations, but backed up the theory with data, including the serious decline in the membership rosters of long-established civic groups such as Rotary, Lions, and Women's Clubs. For such all-volunteer organizations struggling to understand their lack of popularity, Putnam's work put voluntary membership into the context of disaffected neighborhoods, hours of sedentary television viewing, and incessant Web surfing.

Other scholars were also concerned with the changes in American society. They pointed to indicators such as consistently declining voter turnout, road rage and other discourteous public behavior, and the continuing social segregation of different races and cultures as calls to action to rebuild "civil society." Civil society proponents focused on everything from improving basic civility between individuals to rediscovering the value of public discourse, town meetings, neighborhood organizing, and other political action. A popular new term introduced as the century turned was community or civic "engagement." This encompassed many activities, from voting to volunteering.

Despite the hand wringing about the demise of community, some social analysts looked at the same data and reached the opposite conclusion. They noted that perhaps bowling leagues and civic clubs had run their course and were no longer relevant in today's world. Instead, people gravitated to new forms of social interaction. This position held that the Internet had, in fact, created a completely new form of "community"—online, independent of geography or even nationality, and extremely flexible. Rather than joining together with people simply because they live or work nearby (still a factor for some sorts of activities), an individual was free to find others who shared a common interest, no matter how arcane. For the first time in human history, distance was no longer a detriment nor a cost factor. Online communities, with chat rooms, listservs, and other exchange forums, created true relationships among people, relationships that often blossomed into real-world contact.

The Internet has facilitated "virtual volunteering," whereby people can be of service using their computer, Internet connection and e-mail. Not only has this added to the pool of talent available to existing volunteer programs, but it has spawned completely new kinds of outreach as well. All sorts of new self-help and support groups have formed, such as connecting women forced to stay at home with problem pregnancies or people suffering from rare "orphan" diseases without formal institutional representation. Cyberspace has also transformed the deaf community. Since the deaf had already used a keyboard in their telecommunications for decades, they were especially prepared to adopt e-mail and grab the new level playing field offered by the Internet. For people with many kinds of physical disabilities, the Web provided entry to previously-inaccessible activities, including new job opportunities.

The business world was naturally affected greatly by the commercial opportunities of the Web. We gained a new term to describe companies whose existence was mainly virtual and too often unreal: "dotcoms." It became a modern version of the Gold Rush to launch a Web site and try to make money online.

Another trend for the decade was the merging of big and small corporations into increasingly huge ones, usually resulting in work force reductions and customer confusion. Mergers became common in the nonprofit arena as well, especially transforming hospitals into "health systems." Volunteers were often caught in the middle of these changes, affected by the reorganizing yet rarely included in the planning for it.

Although the official unemployment figures hit all-time lows in the 1990s, workers soon got the message not to be complacent about their jobs. The expectation of getting that retirement gift at the end of twenty-five years with one company all but ended, both because employees considered their career prospects to require mobility and because businesses treated their human resources without loyalty. Not surprisingly, the worker of the 1990s became reluctant to make long-term commitments to volunteer assignments, too. The old-fashioned approach of offering to serve an organization for x hours a week, for however long as necessary, quickly changed to new volunteers wanting projects with a clear beginning, middle and end. While many agencies struggled to accommodate this desire, new short-term volunteering approaches blossomed, most notably the CityCares concept, in which young businesspeople were given a monthly calendar of community service opportunities from which to pick and choose. CityCares was formed in 1992 to serve as the umbrella organization for local affiliated organizations (it changed its name in 2004 to Hands On Network):

> *Across the country, millions of concerned Americans face the challenge of finding a way to reconcile a busy lifestyle with an interest in volunteering. Local CityCares organizations were formed in response to this challenge, with the goal to make*

> *volunteering possible for everyone. CityCares affiliates, known as "Cares" or "Hands On" organizations, engage over 250,000 volunteers in direct service to their communities each year. In cities large and small, 30 Cares affiliates have been established in the U.S., one affiliate in the Philippines, and an additional 13 partner organizations in the U.K.*[5]

Management gurus stressed the need for "flattened" organizational structures, eliminating layers of middle management in favor of project-oriented teams, internal consultants, and contract workers. The downside of this trend was part-time workers without benefits or security. As always, volunteering was affected, too. Corporate volunteer programs were stressed as morale boosters, community service was recommended as career (or retirement) exploration, and more emphasis was placed by some agencies on volunteers as consultants providing technical assistance, rather than as interchangeable helpers.

Finally, a major issue became the privatization of government services or the transition of formerly nonprofit organizations into for-profit businesses. This blurring of previous distinctions carried practical and ethical considerations of all sorts for service recipients, managers, employees, and volunteers.

No other field has been as radically affected by the changing business environment as health care. In one short decade, almost every community in the country watched its long-established hospitals merge into "health systems," often with institutions formerly considered rivals. The supposed economy-of-scale derived from such mergers made health care of interest to profit-making companies. Almost overnight major companies began to buy and operate huge swaths of medical facilities across large geographic areas. Nursing homes, outpatient services, and other health facilities were also targets of for-profit takeovers. The advent of "managed care," driven entirely by pressure to hold down the soaring costs of providing medical services, gave disproportionate power to insurance companies and those paying the bills. Outpatient procedures multiplied and someone had to be seriously ill to warrant an overnight hospital stay.

From a volunteer perspective, these developments posed many challenges. Too often, mergers and buy-outs happened without concern for the local volunteers who had supported the hospitals involved since their founding. The attitude of new management was to expect a transfer of volunteer loyalty from the original institution to the new, larger system. Sometimes this happened and sometimes not. For-profit owners had to re-think exactly what it was they expected volunteers to do, just as volunteers had to decide if they wanted to do it. In-service hospital volunteer programs, for decades focused on serving patients in beds, needed to redesign the ways volunteers could support patients and their families, including pre- and post-procedure contact outside of the facility.

The public was often outraged at the systematic dismantling of their established health care system, yet felt powerless. In the decade, therefore, new advocacy groups sprang up to protest the more egregious actions of the businesses involved, to urge better government regulation, and to fight for patients' rights. Physicians and other health care professionals, not always known for their public policy stance, became more vocal in the protest efforts. As this is being written, the newest crisis concerns the cost of malpractice insurance, which in some areas of the country has risen so high, so fast that doctors are actually closing their practices or moving to other states.

AIDS continued to dominate the health care scene for most of the decade, though treatment breakthroughs changed the issue from helping someone die to helping someone "live with AIDS." Volunteers remained vital to this cause, giving their time to food preparation and delivery services, "buddy" programs, and support groups of all sorts. HIV prevention campaigns widened to target new vulnerable populations, way beyond the original focus on gay men. The deadly reality of the enormous impact of AIDS in Africa and some Asian countries also generated public education campaigns and groups working to provide the necessary medicines at affordable prices.

By the end of the century, the hospice movement had evolved into a fully-recognized service, often run by the very hospitals earlier opposed to the concept. Even tight-fisted medical insurance companies and federal Medicare/Medicaid plans approved hospice care for reimbursement, assuring financial viability. Volunteers continue to play a vital role in hospices, both residential and in-home programs, offering supportive visits, respite service, and grief counseling. In fact, it became a federal requirement that 5 percent of patient care hours must be provided by volunteers.[6]

The theme of social services in the 1990s was "welfare reform," culminating in the Welfare Reform Law of 1996. This legislation, "ending welfare as we know it," was designed to "to break rising welfare dependency and return more young people, especially parents, to lives of self-reliance and dignity"[7]—meaning off the public assistance rolls and into paid employment. Many anticipated a crisis as the cut-off deadlines approached. Though the worst-case predictions seem to have been avoided, the ultimate impact is still unclear. Social service agencies geared up, often with volunteers, to provide world-of-work preparation programs (including such projects as recycling women's business clothes to allow former welfare recipients to dress appropriately for job interviews and office work) and other mentoring of welfare-to-work hires. Particularly under the G.W. Bush Administration, expectations were expressed for the role faith communities might play in supporting community development efforts.

One component of welfare-to-work programs had direct relevance to volunteerism. It was understood that not everyone on welfare is capable of getting full-time employment and so states provided alternative ways that someone can continue to receive public assistance. Public opinion also holds that people receiving government benefits ought to give something back to the community in exchange for the money they get from taxpayers. In most states, a person wishing to continue receiving public money needs to document some combination of employment, vocational training or education, which can include a certain number of community service hours each week. Welfare-to-work participants have therefore provided a new talent pool of unpaid help to nonprofit agencies, although the concept has been challenged as discriminatory and possibly unethical. The potential of introducing previously unemployed people to volunteer involvement through such programs is still experimental.

A similar rationale was behind other time-use requirements such as large companies expecting employees on disability benefits to use their time productively in volunteer work that was not as physically strenuous as their original jobs. The Quality Housing and Work Responsibility Act of 1998 required that a certain number of hours of community service be made an obligation of renting an apartment in a public housing project. However, in late 2003 when this rule was finally enforced after five years of dormancy, it caused an outcry. By mid-2004, new legislation had been proposed to limit the requirement to special situations.

Homelessness reached crisis proportions in the late 1980s and continued to affect every urban area throughout the next decade. The increase in homelessness was often the result of earlier deinstitutionalization efforts to move people with mental illness into community homes (which never materialized in the number or quantity necessary); other times it was due to alcoholism or drug abuse. The major precipitating problem was the removal or absence of decent low-income housing. It was apparent that homelessness affected everything from work performance to school attendance, not to mention street crime and public health. Emergency shelters sprang up, often with volunteer staffing, but these put a bandaid on the symptom without a cure for the problem.

Public housing construction slowed to a crawl during the 1990s, leaving the issue of affordable homes to new, nonprofit community development agencies, such as "reinvestment funds." Using private money lent by socially-conscious investors, these funds offered no- or low-interest loans for the building of houses by local nonprofits. Habitat for Humanity also expanded dramatically, to 1500 affiliates in the United States by 2002. Applying their principle of "sweat equity," Habitat builds or restores homes one at a time, utilizing volunteer labor and the participation of the family designated to live in the new house.

Education, or at least school reform, received much attention during the 1990s. While the common theme was dismay about the underachievement of public schools, the solutions proposed tended to divert resources from universal public education. The crusade for school "vouchers" was a good example. Proponents questioned the fairness of taxing everyone for public schools when a growing number of families were choosing to send their children to private (often religious) schools. Why not give all parents "vouchers" to direct public funds to the school of their choice? This might stimulate healthy competition to improve the public schools while allowing for freedom of choice. Opponents of school vouchers resisted this effort as a backdoor approach to funding religion, thereby violating the separation of church and state. Opponents also preferred concentrating attention—and money—on improving the public school system. Activists on both sides of this debate were taxpaying volunteers.

The desire for school reform also led to the concept of "charter schools." These were small, locally-developed projects that had to meet minimum curriculum standards and have qualified teachers, but then could approach education in any creative way they wished. Charter schools applied for official recognition from their school districts and access to district funds and services. In many cases, charter schools started with the dreams of individuals or a few families, who gathered like-minded parents together to develop the new school, seek contributions for it, and help staff it. By 1999, twenty-seven states permitted charter schools, with an estimated enrollment of 252,009 students.[8]

One of the issues that continued to concern school reformers was the number of high school children unable to read at grade level. Whether one blamed video games, illiterate parents, or "social promotion" policies, it was clear that something needed to be done. During the 1990s, a wide number of literacy tutoring programs sprang up with names like "Read by 3" and "Success by Six." These deployed volunteer tutors to work with pre-school and elementary school children in an attempt to teach the basics of reading early in life. Adult literacy programs also initiated "family literacy" projects, in which adults were taught to read better by encouraging them to read to their children, help with homework, and generally work together to make reading a skill all family members shared.

Service-learning proponents successfully convinced an ever-growing number of school districts to offer curriculum-based community service options to students of all ages. While most such programs were voluntary, much attention was paid to the case made for mandating every student to complete a set number of hours of service as a graduation requirement. In 1993, Maryland became the first state to require this as a condition of high school graduation, to be fully implemented by 1997.[9]

Naturally debate raged about whether it was contradictory to coerce students into doing something inherently voluntary. In 1990, a lawsuit filed in Bethlehem, Pennsylvania, became the first in a series of litigation challenging the constitutionality of mandatory community service, calling it "involuntary servitude" under the Thirteenth Amendment. While the Third Circuit Court "virtually admitted that the program constituted a textbook definition of servitude,"[10] it nevertheless upheld the program on the grounds that schools routinely require students to take specific subjects. All subsequent court cases also lost.

> *The number of school systems that now mandate some form of service has mushroomed. According to the National*

Service-Learning Clearinghouse based in St. Paul, Minn., the number of high school students performing service increased nearly seven-fold from 1984 to 1997. In 1997, 96 percent of school districts offered some form of community service, up from 27 percent in 1984. Between 16 and 18 percent of school districts required service for graduation . . .[11]

The ripple effect of service-learning was visible. By 2000, *U.S. News and World Report* was able to write:

In 1998, 30 percent of college undergraduates reported taking a "service-learning" course, according to a study published last January by the Higher Education Research Institute at the University of California-Los Angeles. In part, the boom can be explained by the surge of volunteerism in high schools. In 1999, a record 75 percent of college freshmen arrived on campus as experienced volunteers; from 1984 to 1997, the number of high schoolers involved in service-learning leapt an astonishing 3,663 percent. Today, prospective applicants making the rounds are weighing volunteer opportunities along with academics and the party scene. And many are shopping for a faculty that teaches through service work.[12]

As the new century began, student community service no longer seemed novel, with diverse programs in all states, spanning elementary school through college. According to the U.S. Department of Education, by 2003 more than half of American high schools required community service as a condition for graduation.

Crime continued to be a great concern as the century ended, both street-level attacks on people and property, and also boardroom-level corporate corruption. Both prevention and punishment received attention. Alternative sentencing programs, counseling of all sorts, neighborhood watches, anti-drug campaigns, gun buy-back projects, and other approaches often centered on volunteer involvement. At the same time, mandatory sentences, "three strikes" laws, and other get-tough measures were lobbied for by those who preferred such strategies. For the first time, researchers attempted to evaluate the success of all such programs. In 1998, the National Institute of Justice issued a study, *Preventing Crime: What Works, What Doesn't, What's*

Promising, which found it difficult to prove the success of most approaches. However, one-to-one mentoring and life skills/decision-making training was seen to have a positive effect. Programs such as DARE (Drug Abuse Resistance Education), in which police officers spoke to 5th and 6th graders about drugs, were judged ineffective.[13]

One everything-old-is-new-again approach gaining support in the 1990s was community policing.

> *The community-oriented policing movement is actually a return to roots, as the father of public policing, Sir Robert Peel, established the basic philosophy and principles for the new profession in setting up the first agency in London in 1829. The duty of the police is to prevent crime, Peel declared, adding that the best indicator of success is the absence of crime. Thus, he called his police peace officers.*
>
> *Community policing requires partnerships that include all public and private agencies in the jurisdiction as well as active participation by community residents. Under ideal conditions, citizens lead the effort to analyze neighborhood needs and set priorities for dealing with crime-breeding situations. COP is a philosophy, rather than specific tactics, as each community must determine its agenda to create its own plans and programs.*[14]

Community policing led in some places to the formation of community courts, in which local residents (often tenants of public housing projects) formed a jury of peers to hear stories of harassment, domestic abuse, and even criminal acts, and then to resolve these disputes through mediation, fines, or other punishments. In middle-class communities, such community courts and also youth courts (teens judging other teens) were seen as a diversion from the formal justice system. But in poorer neighborhoods, such courts substituted for absent law enforcement. "In a world of limited governmental services, where police are a rare sight and the city no longer seems to care for tenants' needs,"[15] self-help may be the only viable alternative.

Ironically, some even observed a new activity, "gangland philanthropy." During the 1990s in Chicago, violent and drug-abusing gangs:

> *. . . added a twist to their otherwise not-very-attractive behavior: they became community philanthropists, giving money to needy households, sponsoring large dances with free food and drink, and hosting "back-to-school" parties for local chil-*

> *dren, where they gave away clothing and sneakers. J.T., a high-ranking gang leader, explained his motives: "We ain't angels or nothing, that's true, but we can do something for folks 'round here who got no one else for them. We give them food, we watch over them, protect the community, we try to give something back, try to better the community."*
>
> *For families living near or below the poverty line, these outward gestures to "better the community" aren't easy to turn down.*[16]

Yet another crime reduction concept rediscovered in this period was restorative justice, a proactive approach to dealing with crime after it occurs.

> *Here again, the new approach is in fact a "return to the future" idea, since nonadversarial, consensus-based tribunals and penalties were used in tribes and small communities around the world before "civilization" brought structured legal systems . . .*
>
> *The philosophical principles underlying restorative justice hold that crime is an offense against human relationships—and against individuals and the community–not governments. Thus, first priority is to assist victims, and second priority is to restore community to the degree possible. To do this, the offender must accept his or her responsibilities to the victim and the community, while the community has the responsibility to reclaim and reconcile with the offender as the debt is paid.*[17]

Environmentalism continued as a focus of volunteer efforts. There were successes as some previously endangered species were "de-listed," including the Atlantic and Arctic peregrine falcons, the Aleutian Canadian goose, three species of kangaroo, and the grey whale (in some areas).[18] But concern for the effects of industrial activities on threatened wetlands, rain forests, and ice fields grew rather than lessened. Protecting the Arctic National Wildlife Refuge in Alaska from oil drilling became a major political issue in the early 2000s.

Consumers sent contradictory messages as sales of SUVs and ever-larger family vans soared while calls increased for finding alternatives to fossil fuels. Solar power advocates made small gains and "hybrid" cars appeared on the market, merging electrical and gas powered technologies. The number and frequency of long-distance railroad lines continued to diminish while train enthusiasts attempted to save as many routes as possible.

Global warming and climate change made the news in various ways. Despite the efforts of countless activists to frame international air pollution standards, in 2001 the G.W. Bush Administration withdrew the United States from the Kyoto Climate Accords, questioning global warming predictions. Yet during Earth Week 2000, the Federal Emergency Management Agency (FEMA) reported that "damage from more frequent and severe weather calamities and other natural phenomena during the [1990s] required 460 major disasters to be declared, nearly double the 237 declarations for the previous ten-year period and more than any other decade on record."[19] FEMA acknowledged that global warming had to be considered a contributing factor in this increase in disasters. Internationally, "the 1990s saw 86 great disasters (major natural catastrophes requiring outside assistance due to extensive deaths or losses). In contrast, the 1950s saw 20, the 1970s 47."[20]

Volunteers, as always, responded in droves whenever Mother Nature unleashed her worst. Enormous relief efforts were organized in response to Hurricane Andrew in 1992, the costliest storm in U.S. history with $60 billion in damage and forty-one killed.[21] In 1993, torrential floods covered the entire Midwest all along the Mississippi River. As one example of volunteer effort, the St. Charles (Missouri) Emergency Communications Association was vital during what came to be called the Great Midwest Flood of 1993, both in using ham radio communication and in managing an additional 16,000 walk-in volunteers at sandbagging staging areas.[22]

Unfortunately, the shining moments for spontaneous volunteer disaster response came on some of the worst days in American history. On April 19, 1995, the unthinkable occurred in Oklahoma City, Oklahoma. The Murrah Federal Building was bombed, blowing away half of the nine-story building in the downtown area and leaving 168 people dead in the worst terrorist attack on U.S. soil to that point. For days the nation watched search and rescue efforts at the site, as well as every variety of support to the survivors.

The potential magnitude of terrorist acts became clear on September 11, 2001. When the hijacked airplanes crashed into the World Trade Center in New York City, the Pentagon outside of Washington, D.C., and a field in western Pennsylvania, life in the United States altered dramatically. Sadly, it rapidly became clear that there would be few survivors that day, and hundreds of spontaneous volunteers were turned away at area hospitals. But volunteer fire companies and search and rescue teams flew to New York from all over the country at their own expense to assist in the painstaking effort to examine the rubble at "Ground Zero." Other organizations deployed volunteers to look for pet animals suddenly homeless, cook meals for the rescue workers, and channel grief in countless ways. Outside of the directly-affected areas, Americans unified behind blood drives and gave money to victim support funds.

As time passed, September 11th evolved into only the second commemoration day known by its date (joining July 4th). Some started the event, One Day's Pay, as a "voluntarily-observed national day of service, charity, and compassion"[23] to honor the victims of the terrorist attacks on America. The families of the victims themselves formed their own association and became an influential lobbying group instrumental in getting Congress to form the "9/11 Commission," studying the causes of the attacks and formulating plans to prevent future disasters.

The group most praised for its efforts on September 11th were the New York City Fire Department, whose members selflessly charged into the collapsing buildings as others rushed out—and paid the ultimate price. The acclaim for these firefighters did not encourage new volunteers around the country to join their local fire departments. Ironically, volunteer fire companies suffered their worst losses and questioned the viability of maintaining community safety in this way. In the 1990s, the number of volunteer firefighters declined nationally between 5 and 10 percent; in New York State it declined by 25 percent.[24] Many factors were identified, including changing demographics, the fact that people no longer work and live in the same community, and the long-term commitment necessary to be trained as well as to serve.

While Americans dealt with the rarity of violence brought to our shores, the rest of the world was filled with political upheaval and wars large and small. Yugoslavia disintegrated during the 1990s, coups hit Nigeria, the Israeli-Palestinian conflict continued, the Chechen uprising occurred, and civil wars erupted in Haiti and Sierra Leone, to name only a few places people waged war. Television and the Internet brought these and other conflicts directly to Americans, eliciting predictable responses from humanitarian relief assistance to political lobbying.

For those preferring to focus on peaceful places, the United States began to export a new sort of technical assistance: helping other countries to develop (or restart) non-governmental organizations. Seminars and consultations on nonprofit management proliferated through government programs, universities such as Johns Hopkins, and private efforts, most notably the Open Society Institute, funded by the foundation of billionaire capitalist, George Soros.[25] American nonprofit leaders were recruited largely as volunteers to provide much of the consultation, on the premise that citizen-to-citizen education would be most effective and welcome. Such technical assistance was especially extended to countries formerly under the communist regime, first in eastern Europe and then in China and the Pacific rim. Whether or not our voluntary sector system, including the formal involvement of volunteers, can be adapted to so many different cultures is still being tested.

Volunteers did not necessarily have to travel to assist colleagues in other parts of the world. Virtual volunteering options evolved in which someone could be of genuine help to developing countries via the Internet. Two of the most successful of these online service programs were NetAid and UNITeS (United Nations Information Technology Service).[26]

Political activists of all persuasions galvanized around continuing and new causes, including abortion, gay marriage, and gun control. In October 1995, the "Million Man March" brought to Washington, D.C. the largest gathering of African-Americans in the history of the United States:

> *. . . all Black men telling the nation that they will take responsibility for the social despair in their communities—each of them telling the nation that he will help reduce Black-on-Black crime, respect Black women, and seek spiritual support and guidance.*[27]

Almost 2.2 million people watched the event on television, "more people than watched the Pope's address or any of President Clinton's speeches in 1995."[28] It was hoped that the March would have a lasting impact through ongoing political mobilization (a "national black agenda") and changed individual behavior.

Capitalizing on the publicity surrounding the name of the Million Man March, the "Million Mom March" brought thousands to

Washington on Mother's Day 2000. But these moms were focused on urging federal gun control laws, especially bans on assault weapons. Debate still rages over the number of protesters on the Mall that day, with estimates ranging from 200,000 to 750,000, and counter-protesters such as the "Second Amendment Sisters" organized their own events decrying gun control.

In 1999 the World Trade Organization met in Seattle, Washington. The meeting became a gathering point for activists concerned with everything from worker exploitation, globalization of business, free trade zones, and industrial destruction of the environment. The size and vehemence of the protests caught local police off guard, as did the effect of new tools such as wireless computers and cell phones that enabled the demonstrators to organize the movement of large numbers of people quickly.

The last dozen years have continued the rapid acceleration of changes to volunteerism as a field, which will be examined in more depth in chapters eleven and twelve. The federal government was a major player in a number of ways. The National and Community Service Act of 1990, signed into law by President George H.W. Bush, created both a private, nonprofit organization, the Points of Light Foundation, and a new independent federal agency, the Commission on National and Community Service. Further:

> *In 1992, a bipartisan group of Senators . . . drafted legislation to create NCCC (National Civilian Community Corps) as a demonstration program to explore the possibility of using post-Cold War military resources to help solve problems here at home. The NCCC, enacted as part of the 1993 Defense Authorization Act, is a residential service program modeled on the Depression-era Civilian Conservation Corps and the United States military. The NCCC became a part of a network of national service programs when the National and Community Service Trust Act of 1993 was signed into law.*[29]

By 1993, it was President Bill Clinton who signed this legislation creating the Corporation for National and Community Service, through which "more than 2 million Americans serve their fellow citizens each year through the Corporation's three main programs: AmeriCorps, Senior Corps, and Learn and Serve America."[30] The

Corporation merged the work and staff of two predecessor agencies, ACTION and the Commission on National and Community Service, and transferred such programs as VISTA and RSVP to the new entity. An amazing opportunity for visibility occurred on April 27-28, 1997, when all the living Presidents of the United States came together for a weekend in Philadelphia to hold what was first billed as "The Presidents' Summit for Volunteering," but evolved instead into the "Presidents' Summit for America's Future."

> *Presidents Clinton, Bush, Carter, and Ford with First Lady Nancy Reagan representing her husband, challenged the nation to make youth a national priority. Their call to action included a commitment on the part of the nation to fulfill the Five Promises. Also attending were nearly 30 governors, 100 mayors, 145 community delegations, dozens of prominent business leaders and several thousand concerned citizens. The Summit was co-sponsored by the Points of Light Foundation, the Corporation for National Service and The United Way of America.*[31]

Under the unexpected leadership of ex-General Colin Powell, the event mixed messages but did serve to focus national media attention on both the needs of children and on volunteering. The Summit, in turn, gave impetus to the creation of the organization "America's Promise: The Alliance for Youth," headed by Powell, that attempted to galvanize action on the local community level to fulfill the following "Five Promises":

1. Ongoing relationships with caring adults—parents, mentors, tutors or coaches;
2. Safe places with structured activities during non-school hours;
3. Healthy start and future;
4. Marketable skills through effective education; and
5. Opportunities to give back through community service.[32]

America's Promise at first insisted that it would close its doors after three years, but it remains active, though with critics who question its effectiveness. Powell moved on to become Secretary of State under the new Bush administration, but volunteer efforts continue in many local "Communities of Promise" around the country to improve life for children.

The same year as the Summit, and after a long period of lobbying by diverse supporters, President Clinton signed the Volunteer

Protection Act of 1997, which limited liability under certain circumstances for the actions of volunteers. The goal was to encourage volunteering, which many felt was discouraged by the fear of lawsuits.

> *The purpose of this Act is to promote the interests of social service program beneficiaries and taxpayers and to sustain the availability of programs, nonprofit organizations, and governmental entities that depend on volunteer contributions by reforming the laws to provide certain protections from liability abuses related to volunteers serving nonprofit organizations and governmental entities.*[33]

Critics of the legislation noted, however, that the law missed the opportunity to require nonprofit organizations to obtain general liability insurance or to require insurance companies to cover volunteers under existing policies. Further:

> *However, we believe that the Act has a downside. Providing immunity to a volunteer who has injured someone as a consequence of his carelessness would seem to clash with the charitable goal of helping others. Many might believe, for instance, that those who volunteer for a nonprofit should be held to the same standard of care as the rest of us. In cases where a nonprofit has no assets to speak of, a party injured as a result of the carelessness of a volunteer may well have no recourse against anyone and will not be compensated for her injuries. Because it lacks assets, the nonprofit will not be worth suing and because of the Act's protection, the volunteer will be immune from suit. One may fairly wonder whether it is in the long-term interest of a nonprofit's reputation to let someone go uncompensated in these circumstances.*[34]

The jury is still out on this legislation and its effects.

In 1991, the National VOLUNTEER Center was merged into the fledgling Points of Light Foundation, largely through the urging of George Romney, who led both boards of directors. At first the merger caused consternation in the field, as it put into question the future of many volunteer program support activities. Over time, however, the Foundation proved able to continue key services and even to enlarge its annual conference by co-locating with large national partners. In 2003, the Foundation expanded its name to the Points of Light

Foundation & Volunteer Center National Network, highlighting the vital role of local volunteer centers in its work.

In his State of the Union Address on January 29, 2002, President George W. Bush responded to the attacks of September 11 with two initiatives aimed at fighting the "war on terrorism." The first was the formation of a new Cabinet-level Department of Homeland Security. The President then called on all Americans to dedicate at least two years over the course of their lives to the service of others and created the USA Freedom Corps by executive order to provide more opportunities for Americans to contribute their talents through community, national, and international service programs. The Freedom Corps proposed to make the largest public investment in national service programs since FDR's Civilian Conservation Corps, proposing more than $1 billion a year to support new and existing national and community service programs.

The day after the Address, the USA Freedom Corps unveiled a Web site with information on a variety of existing volunteer efforts in several government departments—combined in one spot for the first time, itself a unique contribution. To assist citizens in finding volunteer opportunities, the Freedom Corps Web site provided direct access to the VolunteerMatch national online database. The site also served as a vehicle to direct people wanting to give money in response to major disasters, such as the 2005 tsunami relief effort headed by Presidents Clinton and Bush.

As a White House office and coordinating council for the entire government on community and national service issues, the Freedom Corps was instrumental in developing new service initiatives and directing increased government funding to them. All were under the direct administration of specific departments, particularly Homeland Security and its newly-created Citizen Corps Councils, intended to increase the preparedness of local communities to react effectively to crises. By 2005, Citizen Corps Councils had been formed in more than seventeen hundred communities, more than three hundred Medical Reserve Corps units had been established to deploy health care professionals in times of disaster, and a new Fire Corps had been created to enlist volunteers to assist fire departments in more than three hundred communities.

Also by 2005, AmeriCorps had grown from 50,000 to 75,000 members, Peace Corps was at its highest levels in thirty years, and Senior Corps had grown from 500,000 to 540,000 members. Because there were more than two hundred thousand requests for applications for the 7,500 Peace Corps slots, the Freedom Corps created a new international service initiative called Volunteers for Prosperity, which operated as a clearinghouse to connect highly-skilled American professionals to programs and organizations serving developing countries with urgent needs.[35]

The faster speed of life and the stress of multi-tasking (a twenty-first century term) drove volunteers to seek opportunities doable in short time slots. Many local United Ways began to hold "Days of Caring," in which donors—usually employees of large corporations—were given the chance to volunteer in teams during one day at agencies receiving United Way funds throughout the year. This, in turn, gave rise to multiple "days of service," each a specific date commemorating a person or event, or celebrating a theme. Sponsors then arranged for all sorts of volunteer activity on that date, locally organized but nationally coordinated and publicized. The popularity of this sort of service day was evident in the diversity and quantity of projects:

- In 1994, the Martin Luther King Jr. Federal Holiday and Service Act expanded the mission of the holiday as "a day of community service, interracial cooperation and youth anti-violence activities."[36] Sponsors developed the slogan: "Make it a day ON... Not a day off!"

- Created by *USA WEEKEND Magazine* in 1997, Make A Difference Day was scheduled for the fourth Saturday of every October. It was designed as a "national day of helping others—a celebration of neighbors helping neighbors."[37]

- An annual service day in honor of one of the world's greatest humanitarians, the National Gandhi Day of Service (October 2) was started in 1997 by the Indian American Student Association at the University of Michigan and then became a national day under sponsorship of South Asian American Leaders of Tomorrow (SAALT). In 2005, the name of the event became *Be the Change,* "to appeal to all South Asians."[38]

- National Youth Service Day, celebrated in the United States since 1988, became Global Youth Service Day in late 1999, through a partnership between Youth Service America, the Global Youth Action Network, and dozens of other international agencies.[39]

- To round out its growing "Seasons of Service" calendar with a summer day of service, the Points of Light Foundation approached the National Fraternal Congress of America and the annual Join Hands Day was inaugurated on June 17, 2000, specifically targeted at developing relationships between young people and adults through neighborhood volunteering.[40]

- The Cesar Chavez Day of Service and Learning (May 31), honoring the life, work, and values of activist Cesar E. Chavez, became an official holiday in six states and dozens of cities and counties throughout the nation. [41]

Points of Light Foundation began to refer to this growing calendar of service events as "seasons of service." The popularity of such one-day projects is what led to the September 11th commemoration, One Day's Pay (originally called United Day of Service).

The world volunteer community received a huge boost when the United Nations declared 2001 as the International Year of Volunteers(IYV)—a remarkable way to start the new millennium. Throughout the world, new projects, research and publicity provided clear proof that volunteering was not a uniquely American phenomenon. Although the United States government and the many American organizations concerned with volunteerism did not participate in IYV to the extent that other countries did, the international recognition was truly a coming of age for the field.

The USA Freedom Corps also served as a catalyst to develop new research and statistical data gathering about volunteer service. One of its most important accomplishments in this area was to work with the U.S. Bureau of Labor Statistics and the U.S. Bureau of the Census to create the annual Volunteer Survey as a part of the Current Population Survey—the first time the federal government returned to such research since the 1970s. With a baseline of September 2001, this Volunteer Survey showed that the number of Americans who regularly volunteered through a school, house of worship or other organization grew from 59.8 million in the year after September 2001 to 63.8 million in the following year, growing further to 64.5 million Americans by December 2004, or 28.8 percent of the population.[42]

Various social scientists believed this was significant because not only did volunteerism grow in the year after September 11, 2001, which was to be expected, but levels of volunteerism increased in subsequent years, showing hopeful signs that these civic trends were continuing.

ENDNOTES FOR CHAPTER 9

1. Charlie Rose interview summary description, Nov/Dec 2001, http://business.cisco.com/app/tree.taf?asset_id=75234 (accessed June 2003).
2. Ibid.
3. "About NetDay," NetDay, http://www.netday.org/about_netday.htm (accessed June 2004).
4. "About Us," CompuMentor, http://www.compumentor.org/about/default.html (accessed June 2004).
5. "History," City Cares, http://www.citycares.org/about.htm (accessed June 2004); site changed to reflect new name, Hands On Network, http://www.handsonnetwork.org (accessed September 2005).
6. Hospice Foundation of America, http://www.hospicefoundation.org/what_is/volunteer.htm (accessed June 2003).
7. "Achievements of the Welfare Reform Law of 1996," The White House, http://www.whitehouse.gov/news/releases/2002/02/welfare-book-02.html (accessed July 2005).
8. RPP International, *The State of Charter Schools 2000*, Office of Educational Research and Improvement (2001), 18.
9. *Education Week on the Web*, April 4, 2000, http://www.edweek.org/context/topics/civics.htm (accessed June 2003).
10. Institute for Justice, "'Compulsory Volunteering': Constitutional Challenges to Mandatory Community Service," *Litigation Backgrounder*, http://www.ij.org/cases/welfare/mandatorybk.shtml (accessed June 2003).
11. Diane Loupe, "Community Service: Mandatory or Voluntary?" *School Administrator*, August 2000.
12. Joellen Perry, "Doing Well by Doing Good–for Credit," *U.S. News and World Report*, 129, no. 10 (September 11, 2000): 96.
13. Lawrence W. Sherman, Denise C. Gottfredson, Doris L. MacKenzie, John Eck, Peter Reuter, and Shawn D. Bushway, *Preventing Crime: What Works, What Doesn't, What's Promising*, http://www.ojp.usdoj.gov/nij/pubs-sum/171676.htm (accessed June 2003).
14. Gene Stephens, "Proactive Policing: The Key to Successful Crime, Prevention and Control," *USA Today Magazine* (May 1, 2001): 32-4.
15. Sudhir Venkatesh and Michael Pyatok, *Midst the Handguns' Red Glare: Philanthropic Gangs and Police-Tenant-Gang Justice* (San Rafael, CA: Whole Earth, 1999), 41-5.
16. Ibid.
17. Stephens, "Proactive Policing."
18. Threatened and Endangered Species System (TESS), US Fish & Wildlife Service, http://ecos.fws.gov/tess_public/TESSWebpageDelisted?listings=0 (accessed June 2003).
19. "USA's Warming Continues Record Pace," *USA Today*, April 21, 2000, http://www.usatoday.com/weather/news/2000/warmex.htm (accessed August 2005).
20. Earth Crash/Earth Spirit, http://eces.org/archive/ec/population/naturaldisasters.shtml (accessed June 2003).

21. 'Time Line," Red Cross Austin, http://www.redcrossaustin.org/historyhtml1/chaptera.html (accessed June 2003).

22. St. Charles County Emergency Management Agency, http://www.win.org/county/depts./ema.vol.htm (accessed June 2003).

23. One Day's Pay, http://www.onedayspay.org/.

24. *New York Times*, June 22, 2000.

25. Soros Foundation, http://www.soros.org/ (accessed October 2004).

26. NetAid, http://www.netaid.org; United Nations Information Technology Service (UNITeS), http://www.unites.org.

27. Michael H. Cottman, *Million Man March* (New York: Crown Trade Paperbacks, 1995), 9.

28. Ibid.

29. "History," Corporation for National and Community Service, http://www.cns.gov/about/lhistory.html (accessed June 2004).

30. Ibid.

31. America's Promise: The Alliance for Youth, http://www.americaspromise.org/about/index.cfm (accessed June 2004).

32. "Five Promises," America's Promise, http://www.americaspromise.org/about/factsheets/fivepromises.cfm (accessed June 2004).

33. *Volunteer Protection Act of 1997,* Public Law 105-19, http://www.explorium.org/PL_105-19.htm (accessed July 2005).

34. Nonprofit Coordinating Committee of New York, commentary on the Volunteer Protection Act of 1997, 1998-90, http://www.npccny.org/info/gti2.htm (accessed April 2005).

35. Information obtained from the USA Freedom Corps (http://www.usafreedomcorps.gov), AmeriCorps (http://www.americorps.org/), and Volunteers for Prosperity (http://www.volunteersforprosperity.gov/), the Citizen Corps Office at the U.S. Department of Homeland Security, and e-mail from John Bridgeland (former director of the USA Freedom Corps), September 2005.

36. "Chronology," The King Center , http://www.thekingcenter.org/rca/kho_chronology.html (accessed June 2004).

37. "Frequently Asked Questions," Make a Difference Day, http://usaweekend.com/diffday/aboutmadd.html (accessed July 2005) .

38. "Be the Change Day," South Asian American Leaders of Tomorrow (SAALT), http://www.saalt.org/bethechange.php (accessed September 2005).

39. E-mail from Benjamin Quinto (director, Global Youth Action Network), January 11, 2002.

40. Press release, Join Hands Day, http://www.joinhandsday.org/scripts/media_jhd.cfm(accessed June 2003).

41. "Cesar Chavez Day of Service and Learning," The Cesar E. Chavez Foundation, http://www.chavezfoundation.org/Default.aspx?pi=45 (accessed June 2005).

42. Bureau of Labor Statistics press release summary, *Volunteering in the United States 2004* (December 16, 2004), http://www.bls.gov/news.release/volun.nr0.htm (accessed September 2005), and Bridgeland, e-mail.

Chapter 10

A Nation of Volunteers
The 21st Century

It is simple to identify present-day volunteering, but overwhelming. Examples are everywhere, and one needs only to pick up a newspaper, watch television, or listen to friends to learn about the diversity of volunteer work being done. But this very diversity and quantity make it impossible to discuss absolutely everything happening in the field. The complexity of modern society evokes a complexity of volunteering. Therefore, this chapter presents an overview that categorizes volunteer efforts in every area of American life. Included are examples of voluntary citizen involvement that either are modern continuations of historical volunteering or are unique to this period. Some will be familiar to the reader, while others may come as a surprise, but it is almost certain that the reader will discover his or her own volunteer identity somewhere within the following pages.

While reading the list about to be presented, certain points should be kept in mind:

- Some of the types of volunteering mentioned overlap more than one field but are listed only once (for example, child abuse prevention is listed under social welfare but could also be categorized as medicine or justice).
- Although it is not always specifically stated, many of the kinds of volunteer activities listed can be part of both national (general) and local (specific) efforts.
- The list includes some activities that might be done both by volunteers and by paid workers, depending on the situation or location (for example, ambulance and rescue corps).

- Though the list is comprehensive, it is not all-inclusive; when specific organizations are named they are meant to be taken as examples only.

The following catalogue of volunteer efforts at the start of the twenty-first century concentrates on what is being done. It does not give details as to the diversity of people doing each activity, nor does it account for the accomplishments resulting from each activity.

This chapter cannot be considered history, as the distance provided by time is needed to evaluate the true impact of what is happening today. Therefore, the reader is free to draw personal conclusions as to the ramifications of the incredible amount of volunteering outlined here.

It is revealing to begin looking at modern volunteerism through the cluster of fields most associated with the economic base of our society. For despite the profit-making factor integral to labor, agriculture, business, communications, and transportation, all these areas also include activities clearly fitting the definition of volunteer work. Such volunteering is frequently forgotten or unrecognized.

Labor and Employment

- *Labor unions*: while most union officials today are salaried, volunteers still serve as local shop stewards and union representatives, handling their union liaison tasks in addition to their regular, paid work; unions also sponsor community service projects.
- *Employee/employer relations*: employees volunteer to provide feedback to management on work policies and procedures, assist with employee grievances, and ensure standard and safe working conditions; quality circles.
- *Mutual benefit*: employees plan parties and group travel, and offer aid in times of family illness or crisis (as in "sunshine" clubs).
- *Advocacy and reform*: volunteers lobby for a variety of industrial legislation issues.
- *Optional work plans*: volunteers advocate the adoption of split shifts, job sharing, flex time, telecommuting, and other innovations.
- *Credit unions*: volunteers establish and help to manage these alternative banking systems.

Agriculture and Food

- *Farmers' and ranchers' cooperatives*: operated locally (and affiliated nationally) by farm-owning volunteers to share information, support and strike for farm legislation, coordinate marketing and pricing, and offer social activities.
- *Specialized associations*: formed by farmers with mutual concerns. Can sponsor special community service projects, such as the holiday delivery of 4,000 boxes of sweet red grapefruit sent by the Texas Citrus Growers in December 2001 to the New York City police officers.[1]
- *Associations of farm workers*: patterned after labor unions. A subcategory is migrant labor, in which a variety of volunteer efforts aid transient workers; includes self-help activities by migrants themselves.
- *Hardship assistance*: mutual aid among farmers battling drought or facing foreclosure.
- *Youth groups*: designed to foster the agricultural education of rural young people and to provide recreational outlets for them. Adult volunteers serve as group leaders, program developers, and fundraisers; the youth themselves volunteer to be club officers and to participate in a range of community service projects.
- *Gleaning projects*: volunteers go into the fields after mechanized harvesting to gather remaining crops for distribution to food banks.

Business and Industry

- *Social and civic associations of businesspeople:* volunteers form local chapters of nationwide organizations to foster communication, promote local commerce, advise local government, and provide social outlets. Members represent all areas of business: Jaycees, Kiwanis, Soroptimists, Rotary Clubs, Business and Professional Women's Clubs, Lions Clubs, Chambers of Commerce. Such groups are involved in a vast variety of civic projects, including eyeglasses for the needy, scholarships and camperships, holiday parties in hospitals and nursing homes, and local athletic events.
- *Trade associations:* cooperative, voluntarily-joined organizations of people in the same industry dealing with mutual problems.

Includes such bodies as the National Association of Manufacturers; National Automobile Dealers Association; American Association of Advertising Agencies.

- *Professional associations:* volunteers in the same profession seeking to develop and maintain standards, increase communication, and share expertise. Fields range from banking to public relations. Members may also participate in community "pro bono" projects, such as those run by Accountants for the Public Interest.
- *In-kind services and donations:* assistance extended by corporations or individual businesspeople to a nonprofit organization . Takes the form of free products or labor related to the donor's business, such as a donation of food from a processor or canner, or a fundraising brochure designed at no cost by a commercial artist.
- *Corporate volunteer programs:* encourage employees to volunteer; this may include release time and can range from a few hours a week to a year's sabbatical. Examples: Xerox Corporation Social Service Leave Program; projects by the Advertising Council. Also company-sponsored volunteer programs for retirees, such as Telephone Pioneers.
- *Social responsibility:* groups of stockholders mobilize to resist unpopular decisions by corporate leaders; closely connected to volunteer consumer protest groups pressuring the corporation; socially conscious investing; watchdog groups concerned about ethical bioengineering.
- *Anyone who agrees to answer market research survey questions.*

COMMUNICATIONS

- *The Internet:* anyone who creates and maintains a Web site without commercial interest; volunteers who program public domain software available for free; those who moderate online discussions (listservs) and newsgroups; virtual community organizers; groups to safeguard online privacy; computer virus monitoring; volunteers who work to close the "digital divide" by installing computer systems or training people who would otherwise not have access to use the Internet.

- *Ham radio and citizen band (CB) radio operators:* individually and collectively provide emergency communication and warning services, especially during disasters. Examples: Radio Emergency Associated Communication Teams (REACT); American Radio Relay League.
- *Public broadcasting:* volunteers serve on public television and radio station boards and on advisory programming committees; participate in fundraising projects and membership drives.
- *Public access television:* citizens produce their own cable television shows on a wide range of public service topics; the cable stations make video equipment and air time available at no charge.
- *License review:* citizens review and approve broadcasting license applications both on the local level and for the Federal Communications Commission.
- *In-kind services:* commercial broadcasters and technicians volunteer to share their skills with grassroots cable television efforts; commercial stations donate facilities for fundraising telethons.
- *Professional associations:* volunteer organizations of people involved in communications for mutual benefit, professional development, and community service. Examples: National Rural Letter Carriers Association; Toastmasters International. Also trade associations such as the National Academy of Television Arts and Sciences.
- *Corporate support:* the underwriting of Public Broadcasting Service (PBS) and National Public Radio (NPR) programs; staffing of on-air auctions and telethons to raise money for local PBS/NPR affiliates.
- *Monitoring and protest:* individual and collective volunteer efforts to curb violence on television, censor pornography, ensure proper representation of ethnic and minority groups, and improve programming for children. Example: Action for Children's Television. Also, counter-groups against censorship and for freedom of speech.
- *Computer user groups:* self-help associations of personal computer owners, generally organized by brand of computer owned, to share skills and software.

- *Postal advisers:* volunteers serve on the U.S. Postal Service Citizens' Stamp Advisory Committee, selecting the nation's commemorative stamp designs; the over four thousand citizens each year who submit designs for consideration.
- *Anyone who writes a letter to the editor or who presents an editorial reply on the air.*

Transportation

- *Trade and professional associations:* related to railroads, trucking, airlines, bus companies, commercial shipping, and so on. Members occasionally provide transportation services at reduced or no cost for worthwhile causes.
- *Railroad advocacy:* individuals and groups support the continuation of railroad services, for energy conservation and out of nostalgia.
- *Commuters:* volunteers lobby independently and in coalitions for improved transportation services; car and van pools.
- *Travelers' assistance:* volunteers provide reassurance, information, shelter, and service referrals to stranded travelers.
- *Traffic safety:* concerned citizens advocate necessary stop signs, traffic lights, pedestrian crosswalks, bike and bus lanes, play streets; public education campaigns for automobile safety awareness.
- *Adopt-a-highway programs:* volunteer groups or individuals select a two-mile stretch of highway to keep free of litter; similar adopt-a-pothole programs; monitoring street repair progress.
- *Bicycle enthusiasts*: advocate for more bicycle paths, including the conversion of old railroad track beds into recreational areas, as the Rails to Trails Conservancy.

While the categories of business and industry may not immediately come to mind in relation to volunteering, these next categories almost certainly do. Volunteers have always been integral to human services, medicine, education, and religion, and today their role has expanded and diversified.

Human Services

- *Policy making:* volunteers serve as board members or trustees, determining policy and raising funds.
- *Professional associations:* such as the National Association of Social Workers.
- *Child welfare:* volunteers run and assist in day care centers; become long-term and emergency foster parents; financially sponsor individual children in need on a one-to-one basis, often internationally; counsel runaways; search for missing children; provide after-school programs for latchkey children; work for child abuse prevention; visit institutionalized children; sponsor holiday activities. Examples range from Big Brothers/Big Sisters of America to the annual "Toy Runs" by motorcycle clubs and street biker associations, bringing thousands of dollars worth of toys to holiday distribution centers.
- *Senior citizens well-being:* volunteers deliver meals and visit frail elderly in their homes; provide chore services; assist in senior centers and nursing homes to supplement paid staff services. Older adults help themselves and each other by lobbying for legislation in their favor; soliciting discounts for merchandise and recreation; providing transportation; offering companionship and telephone reassurance; and running resident councils in retirement communities and home-sharing projects.
- *Guardians:* volunteers serve as surrogate decision makers, often with court sanction through *Guardian ad litem* programs.
- *Family services:* assistance to families in crisis or victims of spouse abuse through volunteer counseling and legal advice; supportive contact during the divorce process; parenting and single-parent support groups.
- *Shelters:* volunteers establish and help staff temporary emergency housing for homeless and street people, runaways, and abuse victims; provide hot meals.
- *Information and referral:* volunteers locate and catalogue community resources, staff telephone hot lines, and make appropriate referrals. One example is Call for Action, affiliated with local broadcasters.

- *Crisis intervention:* volunteers provide emergency response counseling and referral such as suicide prevention, aid to runaways, intervention to prevent gang warfare, and rumor control; staff telephone hotlines.
- *Food and clothing distribution:* volunteers donate items, raise funds, coordinate and handle distribution. Examples: Meals on Wheels; Needlework Guild of America; Salvation Army and Goodwill Industries thrift shops.
- *Food banks:* centralized repositories of surplus food for redistribution to the hungry; volunteers conduct food drives and collect cooked leftovers from restaurants, hotels, and corporations; government surplus food distribution.
- *Self-help:* people with mutual needs and concerns aid each other through groups such as Alcoholics Anonymous, Gamblers Anonymous, Adoptees' Liberty Movement Association, Parents Without Partners, Welfare Rights Association, tenant organizations; volunteers who start and contribute to Internet sites forming online communities among people with a mutual need, illness, or issue.
- *Disaster relief:* at home and abroad, volunteers provide emergency shelter, clothing, food, medical aid, clean-up materials and labor; aid in sending messages and locating missing persons; staff search and rescue teams.
- *Immigrant welfare:* volunteers assist the adjustment of new Americans with interpreting, English language classes, housing, and employment counseling; established immigrants assist new arrivals.

Health Care

- *Professional associations:* voluntary groups of medical and mental health personnel; members serve as officers, deliver research papers, convene conferences, and generally maintain the standards of the health care profession. Examples: American Nurses Association; American Medical Association; American Psychiatric Association.
- *National voluntary health organizations:* volunteer members support research and public education on a particular health problem, disease, or condition; volunteers also serve on boards and advisory committees, handle fundraising at all levels (including

organizing and staffing telethons), and sometimes serve as experimental subjects. Examples: Easter Seal Society; Muscular Dystrophy Association of America; American Diabetes Association; National Association for Mental Health. Volunteers in such organizations can also be involved in direct service to patients and their families. For example, volunteers with local chapters of the American Cancer Society and the National Cancer Foundation wage anti-smoking campaigns, counsel mastectomy and laryngectomy patients, and run early-detection workshops.

- *Hospices:* support terminally-ill patients and their families through visits and respite care.

- *Hospitals, clinics, and long-term care centers:* volunteers serve as trustees; supplement patient services by raising funds (often through auxiliaries), staffing gift shops, assisting the nursing staff, providing special services to patients and residents (friendly visiting, letter writing), organizing holiday and entertainment events, and assisting with occupational and physical therapy programs; staff ombudsmen and patient relations programs; volunteering with their pets or infants for patient therapy; contribute their professional care services such as hairdressing or massage.

- *Family planning and related services:* volunteers provide birth control information and sex education in schools and clinics and staff venereal disease and AIDS information hot lines. The abortion issue has mobilized volunteers both to support and protest abortion legislation.

- *Services to those with special needs:* volunteers assist blind individuals as readers, braille transcribers, guides, and drivers; assist individuals with speech or hearing problems as sign language translators, adjustment counselors, speech therapy aides, and supporters of the National Theater of the Deaf; do patterning for children with mental retardation; assist physically disabled persons with transportation, physical therapy, and recreational activities; provide massage therapy; provide respite care; assist mentally and emotionally challenged individuals as tutors, therapy and recreation aides, one-to-one companions, and vocational training instructors; construct adaptive tools; and make houses physically accessible. Volunteers in all these fields also promote legislation favorable to citizens with special needs and advocate appropriate architectural designs to accommodate physical disabilities; and run Special Olympics and competitive games for the disabled.

- *Services to people with AIDS:* volunteers provide assistance and support to AIDS patients, especially through buddy programs and chore services; provide support for friends and relatives and for HIV-positive and ARC-diagnosed people; work in public education campaigns to promote safe sex and reduce AIDS discrimination.
- *Patient rights and self-help:* people with mutual needs organize to obtain improved services and treatment, educate the public, and lobby for legislation. Especially active are patient rights associations (in medical hospitals and psychiatric institutions) and organizations of paraplegics, amputees, and others in wheelchairs.
- *Thanatological issues:* campaigns for and against legalizing euthanasia; volunteers advocating living wills and the right to die with dignity; individuals who donate their body organs either while still alive or upon their death.
- *Childbirth services:* volunteers instruct and counsel expectant parents in teaching of childbirth, pre- and postnatal care, and breast-feeding.
- *Public health:* volunteers assist in coordinating and conducting immunization campaigns; serve on poison prevention teams and hotlines; ensure the provision of free medical services to the needy, from organizations ranging from local storefront clinics to the national City of Hope.
- *Anti-addiction projects:* group and individual efforts to prevent drug and alcohol abuse; volunteers work in addiction treatment and rehabilitation programs and support addicts with housing and job counseling.

Education

- *School, college, and library management:* volunteers serve as school board members and trustees; members of curriculum review committees and scholarship organizations.
- *Alumni associations:* alumni raise money and recruit new students; plan reunions and special group tours; help new graduates with job seeking.
- *Professional associations:* mutual organizations of administrators and of faculty—both generically (American Association of

University Professors) and in specific subject areas (associations of math or English teachers).

- *Groups fostering special fields of knowledge:* expert and lay volunteer members further specific areas of study with research, funds, and conferences. Examples: American Anthropological Association; National Geographic Society; Soil and Water Conservation Society.
- *Classroom and library support:* adults and students serve as teachers' aides, hall monitors, playground and lunchroom supervisors; assist with school and community libraries and bookmobiles; conduct story hours and computer classes.
- *Parent-teacher organizations:* volunteer work to improve the quality of education in a specific school and to maintain good relations between the school and the community; raise funds for special projects. Additionally, teachers of a particular school may form volunteer committees to deal with issues such as school discipline.
- *Computers in schools and libraries*: volunteers install donated computer systems; coach teachers in learning online; assist library visitors in using the Internet.
- *Organized and informal tutoring, on all levels.*
- *Literacy groups:* those involved develop reading motivation programs, design and disseminate special books, and teach illiterate children and adults.
- *Programs for students with special needs:* volunteers work to motivate and teach truants and dropouts, gifted and creative children, mentally and emotionally challenged students, and the physically disabled.
- *Alternative and community schools:* parents and students assume responsibility for many functions of program development, maintenance, and administration of experimental learning projects and charter schools; teachers often volunteer or work at reduced pay; citizen pressure groups advocate "back to basics" in education. Examples include noncredit, college-level programs for senior citizens in which the teachers are volunteers, often seniors themselves; adult continuing education workshops in which volunteers plan curricula and coordinate the program.

- *Service-learning programs*: Students of all ages and from all sorts of courses volunteer in community agencies to apply classroom theory to the real world; may be optional or required by the instructor, school, or state board of education.
- *Career education:* community members in a variety of jobs agree to describe their work and skills to students, allow students to observe them on site, and arrange for students to experience the job firsthand; run programs in which students replace local government officials for a day.
- *Student exchange programs:* volunteer host families and group leaders enable students to experience living in a new environment, both within the United States and internationally.
- *Student government and service clubs:* students volunteer to participate in school decision making, curriculum development, and student grievance procedures; club members initiate community service projects of every description. Teachers and parents often assist such projects on their own time. Example: Dwight Hall, the Center for Public Service and Social Justice at Yale University.
- *Issue-oriented activities:* volunteers work for or against sex education, textbook censorship, religion in the schools, bilingual teaching, and other issues.
- *Historical societies:* members work to identify and preserve local and national historic sites; collect, catalogue, store, and display historic documents and artifacts; gather and contribute to oral history projects; create time capsules.
- *Research projects*: "volunteer vacations" in which individuals pay their way to spend several weeks assisting on archeological digs, in ocean exploration, and other scientific projects around the world; people allow their computer "down" time to be used for mammoth calculations or international discovery attempts such as SETI (Search for Extraterrestrial Intelligence).

Religion

- *Missions:* volunteers serve as missionaries at home and abroad and provide financial and material support to missions.
- *Inter-church and interdenominational activities:* run by volunteer clergy and laity to foster unity and to meet mutual goals; can be

local as in joint holiday services, or nationwide as through the National Council of Churches, National Board of Rabbis, Friends Yearly Meeting, and the National Conference of Christians and Jews; includes campus-based centers for social and intellectual exchange such as U.S. Student YMCAs; Hillel Foundation.

- *Congregation activities:* sisterhoods, brotherhoods, and a variety of committees within individual churches, synagogues, mosques, and temples that run fundraising and membership drives; provide deacons, ushers, officers, altar boys and girls, choir members, and child care workers; plan holiday programs; prepare post-service refreshments; donate memorial ornaments and pews.
- *Religious education:* church members volunteer to teach Sunday or other religious school; citizens advocate public funds for parochial schools; adults and youth join in religiously-based recreational programs such as Catholic Youth Organization, Methodist Youth Fellowship, B'nai B'rith Girls.
- *Issue-oriented activities:* congregation members work for or against current concerns such as abortion, religious discrimination, homosexuality, world hunger; efforts at reform, including female clergy; giving sanctuary to political refugees.
- *Community outreach:* volunteer-run work camps providing short-term aid to Americans in need; the contribution and distribution of food and clothing, especially at holiday time; donations toward foreign relief.

Volunteer time and energy are especially critical to recreation, cultural arts, and environmental quality. Citizen leadership and action in these fields have impact, with or without a formal organizational structure. Much of the volunteer work accomplished is of direct benefit to the volunteers themselves, increasing personal pleasure and adding to the quality of life for all.

Recreation and Leisure

- *Parks and forest services:* volunteers blaze and maintain trails; repair buildings and shelters; conduct classes and interpretation walks; form "friends" groups to raise funds and lobby for government support; provide special programs for schoolchildren and the disabled; patrol campgrounds; staff visitor centers; help fight forest fires. Examples: Appalachian Mountain Club; Touch America Project.

- *Sports enthusiasts:* volunteers seek to improve facilities and standardize methods and rules by forming biking clubs, hiking and backpacking groups, boating groups, and hunting clubs. Can also address themselves to issues such as gun control.
- *Amateur athletics:* volunteer team players and individual competitors, coaches, and fundraisers; supportive activities for American participation in the Olympics.
- *Recreational safety:* individuals and groups provide public education; voluntary emergency aid to accident victims. Example: National Ski Patrol.
- *Nationwide coordinating groups:* members promote and organize public recreational opportunities. Examples: Outdoor Recreation Resources Review Commission; National Recreation Association.
- *Youth programs:* adults provide leadership for recreational and service activities. Examples: Boy Scouts and Girl Scouts; Camp Fire; Boys and Girls Clubs; Little League; clubs of all sorts at YMCAs, YWCAs, and neighborhood centers. The young members of such groups often conduct volunteer community service projects.
- *Hobby organizations:* volunteer networks of people with similar leisure-time interests, such as stamp and coin clubs, antique car owner groups, associations of hot air balloonists, contract bridge leagues, travel clubs. Also organizations of pet owners and breeders.
- *Holiday observances:* citizens organize and carry out public events such as parades, historical reenactments, festivals, memorial services, displays.
- *Fraternal organizations:* male and female associations whose purpose is primarily one of social enjoyment, ethnic fellowship, or financial services and insurance, but that sponsor an impressive array of service projects for which members can volunteer. Such projects extend into all areas of community life. Examples: Loyal Order of Moose; Thrivent Financial for Lutherans; Sons of Italy; Daughters of the American Revolution; Free and Accepted Masons.

Cultural Arts

- *Museum and performing arts group management:* volunteers serve as trustees, advisers, and board members; have input regarding new acquisitions, tour schedules, and fundraising campaigns.
- *Public commissions and trusts:* citizens serve as commissioners and trustees, making policy and allocating funds. Examples: National Endowment for the Arts; Public Committee on the Humanities; Historical Museum Commission.
- *Arts support:* businesses and individuals assist performing arts groups with financial and technical advice, legal expertise, publicity, and other skills. Example: Volunteer Lawyers for the Arts.
- *Professional associations:* artists and performers form voluntary networks to increase communication, share resources, and achieve recognition. Examples: American Academy of Arts and Sciences; Asian American Women Artists Association. At the local level, this can take the form of self-help groups of artists for support, cooperative studio rental and sales.
- *Visitor and audience services:* volunteers act as guides and docents, give tours of collections, interpret historical sites, demonstrate traditional crafts and skills; also develop appropriate programs for people with special needs, such as hands-on galleries for the blind.
- *Charitable contributions:* volunteered services by artists and performers to support a charitable cause, such as performing at benefits, donating art objects for auction, chairing national fundraising campaigns. Example: Jerry Lewis Muscular Dystrophy Telethon.
- *Community drama groups, bands, and orchestras:* citizens perform free of charge or are paid through audience donations.

Environmental Quality

- *Conservation:* citizens advocate the protection of wilderness areas and endangered wildlife through public information, lobbying, and research; protest against the fashion use of fur, leather, and skins. Examples: Sierra Club; American Forestry Association; National Wildlife Federation.
- *Animal/bird protection:* efforts to protect animals from abuse and scientific experimentation; rescue of injured wild animals, healing

them and releasing them again into natural habitats; finding homes for unwanted pets; running animal shelters. Examples: Animal Defense League; American Anti-Vivisection Society; People for the Ethical Treatment of Animals (PETA); Raptor Rehabilitation of Kentucky, Inc.

- *Zoo and aquarium support services:* volunteers serve as trustees, assist the animal keepers, guide interpretive tours, and work on special projects.
- *Energy issues:* everything from anti-nuclear power to pro-solar energy lobbyists; protests about nuclear waste transportation and dump sites.
- *Anti-pollution efforts:* aimed at clean air, clean land, clean water, and freedom from noise; environmentalists utilize mass meetings, letter-writing campaigns, and public education to obtain necessary legislation and identify and prosecute offenders; nonsmokers' rights groups; anti-litter and anti-billboard campaigns; issues such as proper disposal of hospital waste and other hazardous materials (such as mercury).
- *Recycling:* individual citizens collect and deliver glass, aluminum, paper, and other substances for recycling; groups lobby and inform the public about biodegradable substances, aerosol can dangers, over-packaging.
- *Voluntary simplicity:* individuals who choose to live a more simple, environmentally aware, and self-sufficient lifestyle.
- *Population control:* volunteers advocate planned parenthood on a global basis in order to solve the problems of overpopulation. Example: Population Connection (formerly Zero Population Growth).
- *Horticultural and garden clubs:* members sponsor exhibits and workshops, local cleanup and beautification efforts, the planting of community and historic gardens.
- *Weather observation:* unpaid weather watchers, recruited by the National Weather Service, give spot-check reports on weather conditions around the country.
- *City planning:* volunteers serve on area planning councils and zoning committees, ensuring appropriate civic growth and development.

The fourth cluster of areas of volunteering includes justice, public safety, the military, international involvement, and political and social action. The volunteers who participate in these areas do so, in part, out of a sense of citizenship and democratic duty. They believe they have a role to play in forming and contributing to responsive government, to the benefit of themselves as well as others.

Justice

- *Court-related programs:* volunteers serve in numerous supplemental capacities to assist court staff and fill gaps in client services; assignments such as court watchers, probation and parole aides, one-to-one sponsors, tutors, clerical aides, temporary foster parents, counselors, recreation aides; teen juries of youthful volunteers participate in disposition making for juvenile offenders; adult volunteers staff arbitration boards; individual lawyers donate time and legal advice to low-income clients.
- *Delinquency prevention:* volunteers work to prevent juvenile crime by providing constructive alternative programs; offer recreational and athletic activities in neighborhoods needing such positive outlets; sponsor leadership development and youth employment projects; parental volunteers intervene in gang warfare; adult offenders counsel youth against crime. Includes special volunteer involvement by police officers, such as the Police Athletic League.
- *Victim and witness support:* volunteer assistance to victims of crime as they go through the legal process; similar aid to crime witnesses who agree to testify.
- *Prisons and institutions:* prisoners' rights groups; reform efforts to improve institutional conditions; volunteers from the community who act as visitors, activity leaders, instructors, and counselors; inmates' own community service projects.
- *Community-based rehabilitation:* volunteers assist with a variety of re-entry and service projects for ex-offenders, ranging from locating housing and jobs to supportive counseling. Also, ex-offenders help each other through self-help organizations.
- *Alternative sentencing plans:* offenders, both adult and juvenile, provide court-referred community service in lieu of a fine or incarceration, or in addition to probation or parole.

- *Professional organizations:* groups of police, lawyers, probation officers, judges, and so on that address mutual concerns.
- *Issue-related activities:* citizens advocate changes in laws and legal procedures by lobbying, public education, and community organizing; work toward decriminalization of drug use and prostitution and modernization of statutes pertaining to rape, marriage, divorce, and domestic violence; take part in the death penalty debate.

Public Safety

- *Volunteer fire companies:* volunteers still account for 75 percent of the national firefighting work force (according to the National Fire Protection Association, of the 1,064,150 firefighters in the United States in 2000, 286,800 were career [full-time] and 777,350 were volunteer[2]); both men and women are involved in all aspects of firefighting, running the companies, and fundraising to purchase equipment.
- *Community emergency services:* citizen first aid specialists serve industry and the community; staff volunteer ambulance corps and paramedical groups. Also, anyone who donates blood.
- *Crime and terrorism prevention:* citizens police their own neighborhoods for mutual protection; provide volunteer safe houses for children along school routes; cruise streets in car patrols to alert police to potential trouble; prepare terrorist attack response systems. Examples: Youth Crime Watch of America; Citizen Corps Councils.
- *Police support:* citizen volunteers handle non-emergency police functions such as switchboard duty, assisting at parades and public ceremonies, and traffic control; staff police reserve units and auxiliaries; gather and analyze statistics. Crime solver projects encourage witnesses to provide clues to apprehend criminals.
- *Civilian review boards:* monitor police department practices to ensure compliance with legal standards.
- *Disaster aid:* volunteers mobilize to assist officials in time of flood, fire, earthquakes, tornadoes, and hurricanes; build barricades and dikes; provide emergency shelter and care; clear debris; rebuild property. Example: VOAD (Voluntary Organizations Assisting in Disaster) at the national and state level.

The Military

As discussed earlier in this book, the word "volunteer" as applied to American military service (the All-Volunteer Army) indicates that enlistment is *voluntary*—as opposed to a draft or conscription—not that the service is *unpaid.* The following military-related activities are, however, examples of uncompensated volunteer work.

- *Assistance to members of the military:* each branch of the service maintains a social service delivery system that utilizes volunteers in counseling service people and their families, particularly for marital problems and spouse employment. Examples: Army Community Service; National Guard Family Support Program.
- *MIA, POW, and hostage concerns:* efforts by families and supporters to obtain information about and speed the return of captured Americans; supplies and messages of hope sent to identified prisoners.
- *Support services to military personnel:* civilian volunteer projects designed to provide recreation, entertainment, and counseling to those in service. Examples: USO; local hospitality centers; United Seamen's Service.
- *Veterans projects:* volunteer services to and by veterans; jobs, counseling, scholarships, hospital support; Memorial Day programs. Examples: Veterans of Foreign Wars; Vietnam Veterans of America.
- *Paramilitary groups:* military preparedness by volunteers, such as the Civil Air Patrol, whose members also teach youth and adults how to fly airplanes.
- *Community service:* assistance given to communities at home and abroad by volunteers in the armed services stationed nearby; special holiday programs, building projects, support of orphanages and schools. Example: the Navy's Project Handclasp.
- *Exploration:* volunteers support and participate in efforts to reclaim lost cargoes, raise sunken ships, and add to the knowledge about little-known geographic areas; support the continuation of the space program.
- *Peace organizations:* work to end war and international conflict, limit nuclear weapons, and influence American military aid abroad.

International Involvement

- *Relief efforts:* organized activities to raise goods and money for peoples overseas, either in response to a crisis or to meet ongoing needs; can take the form of benefits, door-to-door collections, church appeals, group donations.
- *Technical aid:* American volunteers share their technical expertise with underdeveloped nations through such groups as Peace Corps and Volunteers in Technical Assistance (VITA).
- *Aid to foreign children:* sponsorship of needy children; volunteers coordinate programs, raise money, and become individual sponsors; adoption by Americans of foreign orphans. Also, UNICEF fundraising drives by adults and children, especially at Halloween.
- *International cooperation:* citizen support for United Nations programs; advocacy for an international language, primarily Esperanto; world peace efforts such as International Voluntary Service.
- *Services to refugees:* American volunteers providing shelter, food, employment, financial aid, language classes, and adjustment counseling to refugees settling in the United States.

Political and Social Action

- *Town government:* volunteers are active in local political party organizations on an ongoing basis; watch over local government to ensure accountability and efficiency; serve on committees; organize block associations. In small communities, citizens hold public office without salary.
- *Public interest activism:* citizens work on behalf of state and federal government reform, political ethics, and quality-of-life priorities; launch letter-writing campaigns, lobby, collect petitions, raise funds, and propose alternative legislation or procedures. Examples: Common Cause; Electronic Frontier Association.
- *Political campaigns:* volunteers are critical to the entire election process, beginning with the primaries and continuing through the nominating conventions, elections, and inaugural celebrations; citizens gather signatures for candidates' petitions, distribute leaflets and posters, raise money, work in campaign headquarters, register and inform voters, act as poll watchers, assist voters in get-

ting to the polls, organize victory parties. "Politics is people in action and among the more vital factors in any campaign is the number, the dedication, and the productive utilization of volunteers."[3]

- *Protesters:* people who protest government actions or who urge reform; volunteers picket, organize and participate in marches, write letters, engage in civil disobedience and tax resistance.
- *Human rights:* all the volunteer activities supporting a particular human rights cause; consciousness raising, public education, efforts fostering group solidarity, lobbying, demonstrating; volunteers committed to a cause create a movement to ensure the civil rights of blacks, women, Native Americans, Hispanics, Asians, sexual minorities, religious minorities, and any other group considering itself oppressed or exploited. Frequently goals are self-help and self-determination, but groups may also seek involvement of other concerned citizens, as with the American Civil Liberties Union.
- *Consumerism:* volunteers engage in efforts to protect and benefit the consumer; organize boycotts, public information campaigns, and cooperatives for purchasing foods and goods; and participate in research on product ingredients and manufacturing processes.
- *Financial management counseling:* volunteers counsel individuals and families in budgeting, use of credit cards, dealing with debt and bankruptcy; provide income tax form preparation assistance for senior citizens, artists, and new small businesses.
- *Extremist groups:* citizens involved in advocating revolutionary societal change or in fighting to uphold historical tradition; membership requires strong commitment to group goals. Examples: the John Birch Society; American Communist Party.
- *Citizens who voluntarily participate in public opinion polls and surveys.*
- *Individual lobbyists:* citizens advocating a range of causes and making their personal opinions known to Congress or their state legislatures. Range from a group of Washington teenagers persuading Congress to vote more money for their dilapidated schools to a woman urging the adoption of the corn tassel as the national floral emblem.

Though this litany of organized volunteer activities is impressive, let it not be forgotten that *individuals* are the heart of all organizations and sometimes choose to act in more independent ways. They may be called radicals, crusaders, curmudgeons, or eccentrics. They may also be called good neighbors.

It is possible to envision future roles for volunteers, based on the principle that volunteers are experimenters and so are often to be found on the cutting edge of new issues. By extrapolating trends today, here is a list of just a few ideas for tomorrow's volunteers:

- Traveler's aid on the moon
- Trips for active seniors over the age of 100
- Work weekends to rebuild deteriorating bridges, tunnels, and roads
- Test-tube baby alumni associations
- Historic restoration of drive-in movie theaters
- Support groups for video game addicts

The options are limited only by one's imagination and may not be as unrealistic as they may seem when first expressed.

Part Two will examine some of the emerging trends and issues in volunteerism as the twenty-first century begins. Some are continuations of historical threads already introduced, while others are unique to this era. Facing us are questions of the local and global impact of Internet technology; mandated service in various forms; blurring boundaries between the nonprofit, government, and business settings that involve volunteers; and other critical political and social issues. But it is all connected to what has gone before. Just as yesterday's volunteers brought us to the present, today's volunteers will shape tomorrow.

Endnotes for Chapter 10

1. "Texas Citrus Growers Thank NYC Police," Texas Sweet (December 2001), http://www.texasweet.com/news/arc11-2001.html (accessed June 2004).

2. "Fact Sheet," National Fire Protection Association, http://www.nfpa.org/Research/NFPAFactSheets/Fire_Service/fire_service.asp (accessed June 2004).

3. Herbert M. Baus and William B. Ross, *Politics Battle Plan* (New York: Macmillan, 1968), 237.

PART 2

Implications for Our Future

Chapter 11

Volunteer Leadership as a Profession

Although leadership of volunteers has been present throughout history, the latter part of the twentieth century saw the emergence of volunteer administration as a professional field. Groups of volunteers have always looked to key individuals for direction in accomplishing goals, but the title "director of volunteer services" or "volunteer program manager" is relatively new, as is the concept of paying someone a salary to perform this role.

Competent leadership has always been necessary to effective volunteer effort. It is possible to trace the evolution of this leadership along three parallel paths that presently comprise the profession of volunteer administration. All three types of leaders can be found throughout the past and still serve today:

- Selected members of any all-volunteer group, often elected officers;
- Salaried staff who recruit and/or supervise volunteers as a secondary or part-time responsibility; and
- Staff paid for the primary purpose of mobilizing and coordinating volunteers.

In early America, the majority of volunteer efforts were self-led. Sometimes individuals developed a plan of action and rallied others around them, while in other cases a loosely organized group of concerned citizens would choose a few of their number to be in charge. The criteria for selection as leader varied from availability to status in the community to specific expertise. This selection process is evident in many of the volunteer activities described in this book: the heads of the Committees of Correspondence and Safety; the organizers of subscription libraries; the leaders of the temperance and abolition movements; the women who started the Cooper Shop Union Refreshment Saloon; the organizers of the Underground Railroad; early labor leaders; the presidents of women's clubs; the founders of settlement houses; the organizers of community cultural activities; and the leaders of the conservation movement. Almost by definition, self-help organizations are run by the members themselves.

Today's volunteer leaders of volunteers are most often called "president" or "chairperson" and head such diverse groups as Alcoholics Anonymous, local Lions Clubs, hospital auxiliaries, many fire and rescue companies, school parent-teacher groups, and tenant councils. Boards of directors of nonprofit organizations are comprised of volunteers, and therefore their officers are leaders of volunteers as well as trustees of their agencies.

The second type of leadership is provided by individuals who hold well-defined, paid positions in fields to which volunteers are integral. Historically, for example, doctors directed citizens in the provision of community medical care. Epidemic control, free clinics and dispensaries, vaccination campaigns, care of wounded soldiers, community ambulance corps—all required the supervision of physicians. Although the doctors earned their livelihood by caring for patients, they also functioned as directors of volunteers when they became involved in such community projects. The nursing profession actually began with volunteers assigned to assist doctors in providing patient care. As time went on and nurses became salaried, they in turn accepted responsibility for the supervision of patient support services by volunteers.

By the very nature of their job, teachers were in a position to mobilize their students and often to influence the community at large. Therefore, there are countless examples of teachers who spearheaded community service projects as a way to teach active citizenship. Along with the contributions of creative individual teachers and their classes are the examples of volunteer efforts carried on by entire schools, sometimes nationwide: neighborhood beautification campaigns; safety patrols; packages for CARE; and innumerable war-support drives. The expanding number of student service-learning programs and curriculum modules about volunteering at all levels of education demonstrate the current role of teachers in supporting community service.

Ministers and other clergy were expected to recruit and direct the volunteer energies of their congregations. Since the church's influence extended into most areas of early American life, the clergy's leadership was equally far-reaching. Charity was often left to the church, to be coordinated by the clergy. Later, institutions such as the Sunday school societies and the YMCA were developed with significant involvement of ministers and other clergy. The Christian Commission in the Civil War was the mechanism by which Northern church volunteers provided services to soldiers. During Reconstruction, parishes contributed money, supplies, and volunteers to provide education for freed slaves. Religious leaders also began the first fresh air funds, connecting rural congregations with needy urban children. In the twentieth century and still today, clergy have guided their faith community members to participate in foreign relief efforts, the civil rights movement, and other political advocacy for social issues.

Military history also provides examples of volunteer leadership when career military officers directed civilian volunteers, especially in times of crisis. In every war, beginning with the Revolution, spy and smuggling networks consisting of loyal citizens required the sanction and expertise of the military commanders. During wars fought on American soil, civilian support efforts to provide food, clothing, nursing, and some comforts were often coordinated by military personnel. Civil defense, homeland security, and anti-terrorism programs are a more recent example of volunteer energies guided by the military. Each branch of the armed forces also has a program of community service wherever American men and women are stationed.

Today, as before, doctors, nurses, teachers, clergy, and military officers hold salaried positions with primary responsibilities largely unrelated to volunteers. However, their leadership is still critical to the success of related volunteer efforts, and they therefore assume the role of director of volunteers in addition to their primary job. There are other examples. Social workers today are in charge of a whole spectrum of supplementary client services performed by volunteers. Justice system staff also supervise diverse volunteer efforts, from probation and parole aides to prison tutors; this tradition goes all the way back to sheriffs organizing volunteer posses. Park and forest rangers provide necessary liaison and assistance to recreation, conservation, and ecology groups. For many paid staff in many fields, working with citizen advisory committees, commissions, student interns, and various advocacy groups puts them in the position of director of volunteers as part of their job.

The third type of leadership of volunteers, namely people paid specifically for this role, is actually not a totally modern phenomenon.

Though frequently volunteers themselves, there were militia captains who drew a salary solely to recruit and lead volunteer soldiers. The first paid fire chiefs were usually the only firefighters to receive a salary and were expected to keep the volunteer company organized. One role rarely thought of as directing volunteers is that of a wagon train's master. Yet such leaders were hired by groups of inexperienced but willing families who needed the wagon master's knowledge and ability to help the group work together during the hard journey ahead. The personnel of the Freedman's Bureau were paid specifically to coordinate public and private relief programs after the Civil War, especially those run by volunteers. It also should be noted that every political campaign manager is actually a salaried director of volunteers.

Since the 1960s, an increasing number of institutions and agencies have added a staff position for volunteer management to their organizational chart. Hospitals were among the first. Today, volunteer administrators work in courts, parks, counseling services, museums—anywhere a large corps of volunteers is needed. Even churches have begun to hire someone to coordinate their community service projects, though the position may carry a title such as "director of lay ministry."

It is important to recognize that one can be a director of volunteer services regardless of whether the position is salaried or full-time. The position is defined instead by its function: managing volunteers. While salaries are increasingly being paid to directors of volunteers, this trend should not imply that paid directors are necessarily better or more qualified than unpaid directors. If the magnitude of the volunteer effort requires substantial, daily coordination, then a salary is legitimate compensation for the demands of the job. But volunteers who continue to provide leadership to other volunteers are managers in their own right and belong to the profession of volunteer administration as well.

There is an ever-growing body of knowledge and expertise about volunteer management that is being developed and transmitted by books, journals, university curricula, professional associations, and now the Internet. While people enter the field from many different academic backgrounds, there is more and more training available in the generic principles and practical skills of the field.

Research into the nature and scope of volunteering has become more sophisticated and continues to stimulate professional development. While as recently as the 1970s there were only a handful of books on the subject of volunteerism, today there are shelves of them. Further, as the Internet makes resources from any country available around the world, American volunteer administrators now have access to writing from all English-speaking countries. The World Wide Web is perhaps the most important new resource to the field, with volunteer-related Web sites opening continuously. Archives of journals and private collections, long considered "dead," are now being scanned and made available electronically, often for free. New research and practitioner advice is being produced and posted on Web sites sponsored by national resource organizations, consultants and publishers, and even interested individuals (volunteers!). There is no question that, in the future, no newcomer to the field will ever be able to complain that it is hard to find how-to information.

Among the signs that the leadership of volunteers is evolving into a recognized profession is that the title "director of volunteer services" (or some variation thereof) is being applied to those with primary responsibility for volunteer management, no matter what the setting. By the late 1970s, the *Dictionary of Occupational Titles* included "supervisor of volunteers," "coordinator of volunteers," and "director of volunteers" as a three-tier career ladder. By the late 1990's, titles for this role also included "director of community resources," "manager of volunteer resources," and "community outreach coordinator," in order to reflect the broader definitions and terminology of the nonprofit sector. The Association for Volunteer Administration is now using and advocating for including the term "volunteer resources" rather than simply "volunteers" in titles, as the Canadians have been doing for years, on the premise that this helps draw the connection to "human resources management" and so conveys a more valuable concept. On the other hand, in the United Kingdom, the title currently in favor is "volunteers manager."

Regardless of their formal titles, leaders of volunteers have formed a variety of professional associations in recognition of their common purpose and needs. Such groups are either generic to the profession or specific to a type of setting, and they have been organized on the local, state, and national levels. Generic associations bring together directors of volunteers from a wide range of institutions, agencies, and programs. On the local level, these groups often call themselves "DOVIAs," meaning "directors of volunteers in agencies." These professional networks meet regularly to exchange information and share experiences. They may also sponsor community-wide projects such as volunteer recognition events, recruitment fairs, and training workshops. In many states there are similar associations of volunteer administrators with a state-wide membership and scope.

The Association for Volunteer Administration (AVA) is the generic professional network of leaders of volunteers at the national level that holds an annual conference, publishes a journal, establishes the ethics for the profession and connects members with their counterparts across the country. (*Note: Web sites for all organizations mentioned here can be found at the end of this chapter.*) AVA has always had Canadian members, too, and is increasing its scope to be more international. AVA also sponsors a professional credentialing program, under which practitioners can earn the designation "CVA"—"certified in volunteer administration"—by sitting for an exam and submitting a portfolio of materials for peer review.

Professional associations that bring together directors of volunteers in the same field or setting are most numerous on the national level. Some examples are: American Society for Directors of Volunteer Services (ASDVS, formerly part of the American Hospital Association and now independent); National Association of Volunteer Programs in Local Government (NAVPLG), National Association of Partners in Education (NAPE); American Association for Museum Volunteers (AAMV). Several of these have state chapters or affiliate groups, which in turn may have local equivalents. The purpose of these groups is the same as for the all-inclusive associations mentioned above: to exchange information and provide mutual support in order to make the involvement of volunteers more effective. The special interest associations, however, are able to focus in more depth on issues unique to their area of work.

A similar professional network is the corporate volunteer council, whose members are employees of large corporations with the responsibility for developing and managing their company's community service initiatives and employee volunteer projects. These councils tend to form in major metropolitan areas and are informally linked nationally through the National Council on Workplace Volunteerism (NCWV), under the Points of Light Foundation.

In addition to professional membership associations, there are a number of support organizations contributing to the growth of volunteering and to the profession of volunteer administration. On the local and regional level there are volunteer centers, previously known as voluntary action centers or volunteer bureaus. Volunteer centers can be independent nonprofit agencies, units of local government, divisions of a local United Way, or projects of a community organization such the Junior League. They act as clearinghouses of information about volunteer opportunities in their area, referring interested citizens to volunteer projects. Volunteer centers work to make volunteering more visible through annual awards programs, media campaigns, and training workshops.

Volunteer centers were connected for many years on the national level through an organization known as the Association of Volunteer Bureaus. In 1984, that association merged into what was then called VOLUNTEER: The National Center, but maintained an advisory council to represent the volunteer center perspective. The National Corporate Volunteer Council (later known as National Council on Workplace Volunteerism) became a division of VOLUNTEER in 1986. By 1988, the merged organization had changed its name to The National VOLUNTEER Center. In 1991, this entity in turn merged into the Points of Light Foundation, initiated during the first Bush Administration. In 2003, the importance of volunteer centers was made more visible by expanding the organization's name to the Points of Light Foundation & Volunteer Center National Network.

The Points of Light Foundation is a national organization promoting volunteerism, funded both by the federal government and by corporate and foundation grants. Its activities include sponsorship of National Volunteer Week each April (including the President's Volunteer Action Awards); publication of a magazine and several newsletters; sales of books and recognition items; and an annual national conference. In 1989, the "Daily Points of Light" Awards were started by the Bush White House, recognizing an individual or group of volunteers for their local service efforts; 1,020 designations were made by 1993. In 1998 the award was reinstated and administered by the Foundation and the Corporation for National and Community Service.[1]

Nationally, a number of private and government organizations consider volunteerism as one of their major emphases. INDEPENDENT SECTOR, the Corporation for National and Community Service, and the United Way of America all advocate the value of volunteering, work to stimulate the climate for citizen involvement, and attempt to remove barriers to participation. The Association for Research in Nonprofit Organizations and Voluntary Action (ARNOVA), formerly the Association of Voluntary Action Scholars, is composed of academics and researchers in the field.

Finally, in the 1970s ACTION provided funding for the creation of state offices on volunteerism, frequently with a close link to their governor's office. Over the past thirty years, the number of state offices has fluctuated and support for their work has been dependent on the politics of the day in each state. State offices were mandated to promote and strengthen volunteerism, acting as clearinghouses of information on volunteer activities in their state and as a communication link among programs and practitioners, often brokering public/private collaborations. For a time, the state offices formed their own national umbrella organization called the Assembly of State Offices on Volunteerism.

When the Corporation for National and Community Service was initiated in 1993, every state wishing to obtain federal funding from the Corporation was required to form a state Commission on National Service. Every state except North and South Dakota did so. Over time, most states merged their existing state office of volunteerism into the new Commission. This combination tends to provide less attention to community volunteering while focusing on stipended, full-time service programs. There is now a national association of state commissions that meets periodically.

Figure 1(pages 344-345) traces the evolution and various name changes and mergers of some of the largest organizations in the field of volunteer administration in the United States. This is offered in an attempt to preserve some of the historical benchmarks.

The development of the profession of volunteer administration has not taken place only in the United States. Similar evolution has occurred in other countries. For example, there are national volunteer centers throughout Europe, and in countries as diverse as Brazil, Japan, and Australia. In 1996, our Canadian neighbors formed the Canadian Association for Volunteer Resources to go along with thriving provincial associations of volunteer program managers, and by the turn of the century similar national professional groups were developing in the United Kingdom, Australia, Japan and Korea. Conferences to convene volunteer leaders with mutual concerns have taken place all over the world.

International exchanges of site visits, publications, and general information are steadily increasing, driven rapidly by the Internet and e-mail. The International Association for Volunteer Effort (IAVE) is one forum for such communication. Study trips are being sponsored by universities, federal and state governments, and larger nonprofit organizations. It is becoming increasingly clear that a global perspective contributes significantly to the profession of volunteer administration. The field saw its biggest boost in 2001, which the United Nations declared the International Year of Volunteers (IYV). Although the relative lack of celebration was disappointing in the United States, other countries seized the opportunity of IYV to initiate research, hold conferences, and make volunteering visible. AVA used 2001 to focus on the value and role of competent leaders in volunteerism by convening an international working group with representatives from twelve countries. This led to AVA's development of a "Universal Declaration on the Profession of Leading and Managing Volunteers" as a first effort to identify common elements of this role as it appears throughout the world.

Uncertainty continues over the kind of educational preparation appropriate for those in the position of directing volunteers and over the issues of salary and career ladders. There is agreement that a core of general knowledge and skills is necessary to being effective as a leader of volunteers and that these should be based on a philosophy that affirms the importance of volunteering. However, there is currently no academic degree program in volunteer administration, nor is there much interest in creating this option. There are some schools that allow specialization in volunteer management within traditional majors. A few universities have developed certificate programs, some of which offer academic credit; others are offered on a noncredit, continuing education basis. Thanks to the Internet, such courses are beginning to be available online as distance learning, making them accessible to many more people. Therefore, people continue to enter the field of volunteer administration with a wide array of credentials and educational backgrounds.

As research in volunteerism continues and further codification of the knowledge base for volunteer administration occurs, indications are that educational institutions will keep pace with the field. There will undoubtedly be variations as to which academic departments will house volunteer management courses. Some possibilities include public administration, social work, business administration (as part of the trend to offer business degrees in nonprofit management), adult education, and community development. Because volunteer administration cuts across all disciplines, a valid case can be made for each of these options.

Another educational dilemma is that directors of volunteers must be doubly skilled to do their jobs: they must know the general techniques of working with volunteers, and they must have expertise in the

Figure 1. Time Line of National Organizations with a Mission to Promote Volunteerism and/or Support Volunteer Program Leaders

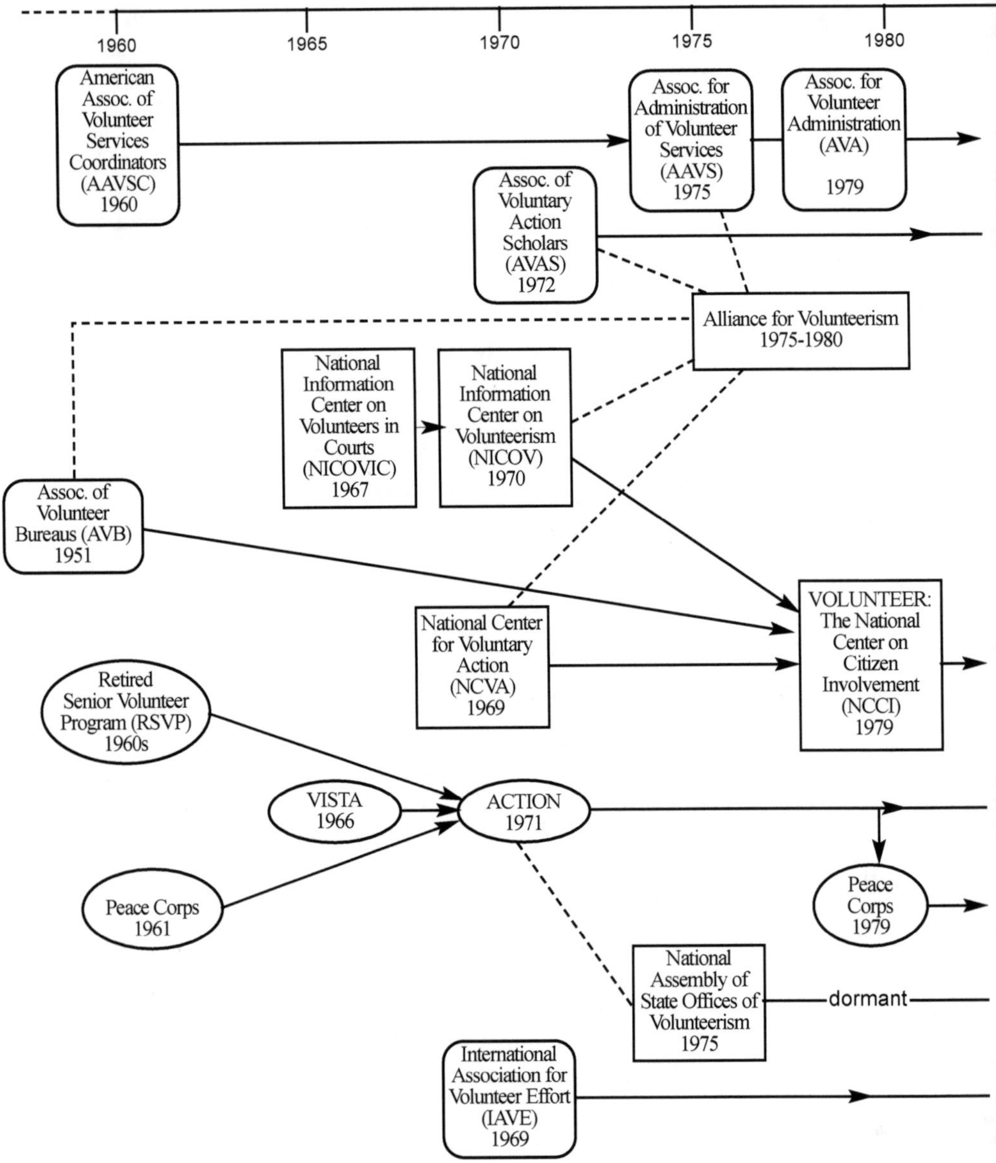

Key:

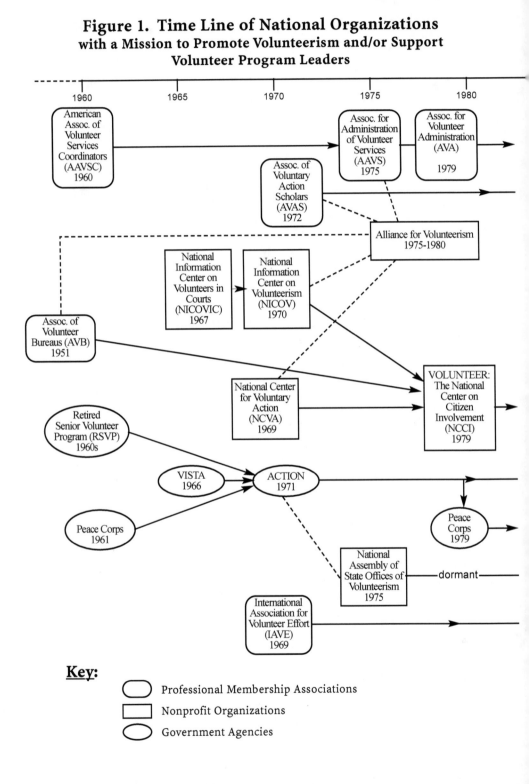

- Professional Membership Associations (rounded box)
- Nonprofit Organizations (rectangle)
- Government Agencies (oval)

Figure 1. Time Line of National Organizations (cont.'d)

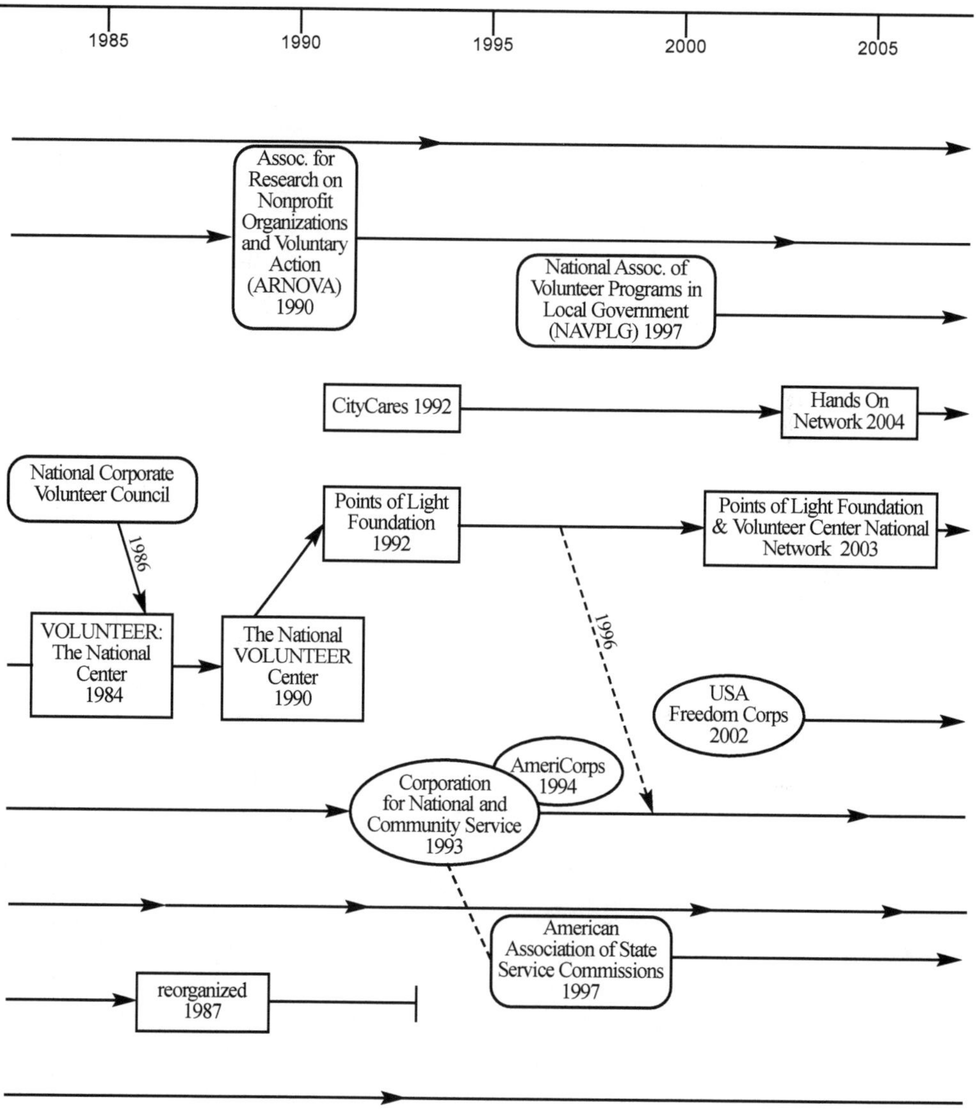

Key (cont.'d):

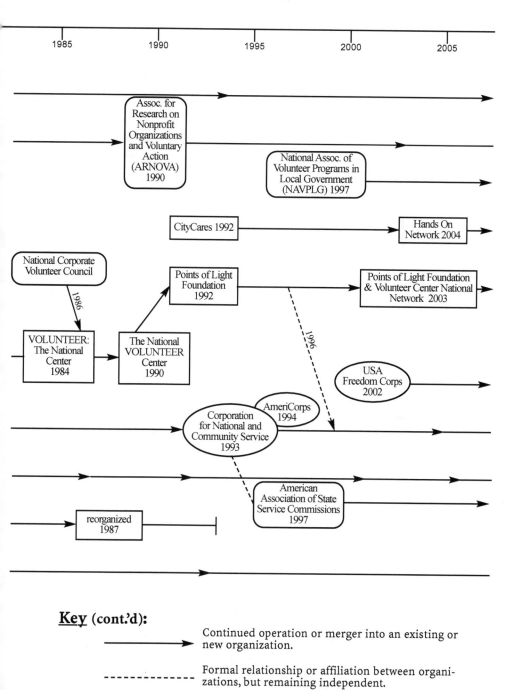

Solid arrow: Continued operation or merger into an existing or new organization.

Dashed line: Formal relationship or affiliation between organizations, but remaining independent.

specific discipline for which they coordinate volunteers. So the challenge of coursework in volunteerism is to reflect its interdisciplinary nature to some degree. For example, a director of volunteer services in a hospital should be able to take both general volunteer management courses and courses pertaining to the health field. Likewise, a director of volunteers for the National Park Service may need to take courses in forestry or recreation to supplement a generic volunteerism program. Such mixing and matching poses difficulty for many university systems.

Conversely, it is increasingly evident that courses in volunteer management are valuable to students majoring in a number of disciplines. Problems of staff resistance to volunteers and lack of commitment to training and supervision responsibilities could be prevented at the source if nursing students, recreation majors, prospective social workers, seminarians, and others learned the value of volunteer participation to their fields as part of their early professional training.

The responsibilities of the role of director of volunteers have expanded as volunteerism itself has evolved. While a large number of organizations still expect the leader of volunteers simply to "find 'em and use 'em," the more forward-looking ones have a broader vision. The most advanced view of the director of volunteers is as a community resource developer—the person who finds a variety of ways to meet needs. This might include (in addition to the most traditional type of volunteer) barter, in-kind donations, court-ordered community service workers, and other resources.

Along with this expanded role have come a number of operational issues affecting how volunteers are managed in an agency setting. As society demands better screening of employees for such things as a past history of abusing children or a criminal record, the screening of prospective volunteers has followed suit. This is particularly true in settings serving children or providing services to clients in their own homes. In fact, most states have passed laws requiring police checks for any worker, paid or volunteer, who will be assigned to work with vulnerable populations.

The concern for screening has been fueled by the fears of legal liability. Directors of volunteers are expected to practice risk management, and screening is one element of a risk management strategy. The challenge has become how to manage risk, not avoid it altogether. The unavailability of insurance for certain types of services is a problem equal to the rising costs of coverage.

There is a new questioning of the traditional separation of *financial* resource development and *human* resource development. Money has been more highly valued than people, and donors have been more respected than volunteers. (Not surprisingly, fundraising has been dominated by men, volunteer administration by women.) But studies show that people who give their time also give their money. Much fundraising activity relies heavily on volunteer staffing. Therefore these two types of resource development are actually intertwined. In an age of competition for philanthropic support, those organizations that understand this interrelationship and avoid stereotypical hierarchies will have the greatest success in obtaining the most resources. Development officers need to be concerned about volunteers, and directors of volunteers need to be concerned about fundraising.

Extended applications of the Fair Labor Standards Act have posed new dilemmas for some volunteer programs, specifically when employees of an organization also want to volunteer in the same setting. Examples would be the kitchen staff of a mental health institution who volunteer to play basketball with young patients who rarely have visitors, or the clerical pool that offers to run the arts and crafts booth at the annual fundraising bazaar. The narrowest legal interpretation of the Fair Labor Standards Act would stipulate that no employee could do such volunteer work because any time given to an employer over forty hours a week should be compensated with overtime pay. However, the intent of the Act was not to prevent genuine volunteer service; it was meant to avoid abuse and coercion by employers. It is up to the director of volunteers to make sure that interested employees are made official participants in the volunteer program and are assigned to roles substantially different from those they are paid to do.

Another management issue is staff relations. Labor unions in some fields have taken strong stands against what they view as volunteer encroachment on their territory. Some unions fear that volunteers can be used as strikebreakers, thereby undermining the workers' bargaining clout. They believe volunteers often handle jobs that someone could be paid to do, thus contributing to unemployment. Further, if volunteers, perceived as amateurs, can perform tasks also done by an employee, then many paid workers feel they cannot demand skilled wages. Because unions view volunteering as a middle- and upper-class phenomenon, the natural assumption is that those who volunteer are basically anti-working class.

The historical section of this book has already recounted the volunteer beginnings of organized labor—beginnings that are all too often forgotten by the salaried union officials of today. Because of closed-shop practices, it is sometimes hard to distinguish whether union membership is still voluntary or is coerced. But unions continue to rely on volunteer shop stewards and committee members to accomplish their goals. Also, unions endorse their own brand of volunteering in the form of mutual aid and selected community service projects.

The unions are correct in pointing out that volunteers are recruited by some agencies to fill personnel gaps resulting from inadequate budgets. This is as much exploitation of the volunteer as it is unfair to the unemployed worker. But the fact that this occurs occasionally is insufficient cause to denounce all volunteers. One important factor in the relationship between unions and volunteers is the quality of the management of the organization in which they both meet. Arrangements can be made in advance to prevent the misuse of volunteers in times of strikes and other work actions, thereby eliminating the allegations that volunteers interfere with the rights of labor. The director of volunteers has an important role in this process.

The relationship between volunteers and "professionals" can also be problematic, especially when such "professionals" place their contributions as employed specialists above those of unpaid workers. Employees may expect volunteers to be undependable, overcritical, naive, or uncontrollable. Objections to volunteer participation are therefore raised on such grounds as safety, insurance, and confidentiality. The challenge to the director of volunteers is to differentiate between legitimate issues (the amount of time it takes to train and supervise volunteers) and underlying sources of resistance such as the professionals' unwillingness to share work, spend time training volunteers, or recognize the value of services that only members of the community can provide.

This problem of nonacceptance by professionals is especially common in agency-related volunteer programs. This has led to some volunteers having a sense of inferiority and to their reluctance to identify themselves with the label volunteer ("I am just a volunteer"). Others defend their value to the organization and take pride in their cost-effective approach to problem solving.

Most organizations in which volunteers participate have never considered their budgets adequate to meet the needs they address. As government funding priorities shift and philanthropic giving fluctuates, organizational budgets also expand and contract. Volunteers become a factor when agency administrators consider them free labor to fill funding gaps. Directors of volunteers are in a position to define the most appropriate roles for volunteers in such a way as to avoid any exploitation.

After all, volunteers are not just stopgaps to hold together services in times of a budget crunch. There are types of volunteering for which no money can compensate and whose effectiveness would be undermined by a salary: board members must be free from financial ties in order to make policy objectively; the friendship offered by a Big Sister on call twenty-four hours a day not only could never be adequately reimbursed but also is of value to her Little Sister because it is freely offered. Inherent in all types of volunteer work is the potential for effecting change for the very reason that the volunteer is not compromised by a salary—if the volunteer makes the most of the opportunity.

In the last analysis, volunteering does involve cost. To volunteers, expenses can range from transportation to day care to the actual value of their time contributed. For the organization, volunteers need coordination, training, recognition—all the types of support any other personnel would require. In the simplest of terms, volunteers are a resource to be managed and applied to help the organization achieve its mission.

In 2004, our field saw the publication of a remarkable new study conducted by the Urban Institute under funding from the UPS Foundation, the Corporation for National and Community Service, and the USA Freedom Corps. Titled *Volunteer Management Capacity in America's Charities and Congregations: A Briefing Report,*[2] the document confirmed the very things practitioners already knew. But now the facts were stated with the authority of research and by people with influence. Here are a few of the major findings:

> *The greatest challenges that charities and congregations face is an inability to dedicate staff resources to and adopt best practices in volunteer management. (p. 2)*

> *Three out of five charities and only one out of three congregations with social service outreach activities reported having a paid staff person who worked on volunteer coordination. However, among these paid volunteer coordinators, one in three have not received any training in volunteer management, and half spend less than 30 percent of their time on volunteer coordination. (p. 3)*

Less than half of charities and congregations that manage volunteers have adopted most volunteer management practices advocated by the field. (p. 3)

Of charities with a paid staff volunteer manager, only one in eight have someone who devotes 100 percent of his or her time to volunteer management. Only one congregation in our study said it has a full-time volunteer coordinator . . . (p. 8)

Taken together, the findings regarding paid staff support for management of volunteers point to low professionalization and capitalization of volunteer administration in the United States. The fact that many coordinators are getting some training suggests that many are interested in learning about how to manage volunteers. However, the small amount of time spent on volunteer administration suggests that charities and congregations do not have the resources to allocate to volunteer management or that they devote their organizational resources primarily to other efforts. (p. 10)

Following the initial briefing report, a Web site was established to permit input from the field. In June 2004 a set of eight proposed national strategies was introduced, incorporating many of the suggestions received. Among the strategies are plans to expand opportunities to receive formal training in volunteer management, establish a research agenda, and advocate for greater support from the executives of organizations. This is a potentially exciting development that will be closely watched. A key statement in the *Briefing Report* affirms the importance of strong volunteer leadership:

We conclude that the belief that volunteers are beneficial leads charities to invest in their management of volunteers, and that investing in the management of volunteers leads them to value the benefits of their volunteers more. (p. 20)

Many refer to volunteer administration as an emerging profession because it is still evolving. The position of director of volunteer resources is more visible today than ever before and has taken on added dimension. The enlarged responsibilities of leading volunteers reflect the diversity and complexity of modern society. The final chapter of this book describes some of the trends and issues facing volunteerism—and the director of volunteers—as the new century begins.

Endnotes for Chapter 11

1. "Awards," Points of Light Foundation, http://pointsoflight.org/awards/ (accessed August 2005).

2. Urban Institute, *Volunteer Management Capacity in America's Charities and Congregations: A Briefing Report* (Washington, DC: 2004), http://www.urban.org/UploadedPDF/410963_VolunteerManagment.pdf (accessed August 2005).

Web Sites of Organizations
Mentioned in Chapter 11

American Association for Museum Volunteers (AAMV)
www.aamv.org

American Society for Directors of Volunteer Services (ASDVS)
www.asdvs.org

Association for Research in Nonprofit Organizations and Voluntary Action (ARNOVA)
www.arnova.org

Association for Volunteer Administration (AVA)
www.avaintl.org

Canadian Association for Volunteer Resources (CAVR)
www.cavr.org

Corporation for National and Community Service
www.nationalservice.gov

Independent Sector (IS)
www.independentsector.org

International Association for Volunteer Effort (IAVE)
www.iave.org

National Association of Partners in Education (NAPE)
www.napehq.org

National Association of Volunteer Programs in Local Government (NAVPLG)
www.navplg.org

National Council on Workplace Volunteerism (NCWV)
www.pointsoflight.org/networks/business/ncwv/

Points of Light Foundation & Volunteer Center National Network
www.pointsoflight.org

United Way of America (UWA)
national.unitedway.or

Chapter 12

The Past Is Prologue

The journey from barn raising to virtual volunteering spans three and a half centuries of American volunteering. These pages have catalogued the remarkable achievements of citizens, individually or in groups, whose voluntary decisions to participate made social progress possible. What is important is not the number of volunteers engaged in each activity noted, but the cumulative effect of all their accomplishments large and small.

It is not the intent of this book to convey the impression that every member of every organization was or is equally active in achieving goals. In fact, the opposite is true. It is common for organizations to benefit from the active commitment of a core of doers while the majority of members are content simply to be joiners. Even so, it is the clout derived from sheer numbers of people willing to lend their name, pay dues, and otherwise show support for a cause that has influence in creating social change. This is why the history of volunteering will always be connected to the history of associations and voluntary organizations.

Volunteerism is both reactive and proactive. It is a response to current events, social problems, and community needs that volunteers are often the first to identify. Volunteers can take action before institutions and government are willing to offer services. As such, volunteers are pioneers and experimenters, unlimited by the restrictions of tradition, public statutes, need to make a profit, or availability of initial funds. By creating or urging others to create programs, volunteering challenges the status quo. This is the inherent political side of volunteer work. The irony is that pressure in one direction elicits pressure in the other; whenever one group of volunteers works toward change, another group often reacts to preserve tradition or advocate yet another alternative. This is why volunteers will continue to be found on both sides of an issue—and at all points along the political spectrum.

Another irony is that, as voluntary agencies mature, they lose the ability to react quickly and take risks—the very hallmarks of their founding volunteers. So society will always need volunteers: to be on the cutting edge challenging the causes of a problem as well as providing services to those experiencing its symptoms.

A cyclical pattern can be discerned in the influence of volunteers on the formation of institutions and professions. First an individual or small group becomes involved in a cause. Soon other volunteers are brought in, and strategies are developed to take specific actions. Once the activity gains momentum, the group seeks funding to support both the cost of materials and other expenses. Employees become necessary as the group evolves into an organization, agency, or unit of government—not because volunteers could not do the job, but because the magnitude of the work grows beyond what part-time volunteers can handle. Employees provide continuity and coordination, and so, at some stage of growth, volunteers are displaced as primary service providers. This is also the stage at which professionalization occurs. In the most mature organizations, volunteers continue to be utilized mainly as fundraisers and policy makers (boards) and in limited support roles. Frequently, by this point, the founding volunteers have moved on to other causes, to initiate the process anew.

This cycle, traceable through history, can be interpreted in several ways. One interpretation is that the ultimate measure of the success of a volunteer effort is the creation of paid positions to institutionalize that response to a need. This contradicts the convenient belief that volunteers can be used as a substitute for adequate budgeting; history proves that the greater the number of volunteers who become involved in services, the greater the chance that stable financial resources will be developed.

Another interpretation of the cycle is that volunteers move from being founders to being assistants—and that this is somehow denigrating. It is important to realize, however, that it is rare for individuals to change from one role to the other. Those whose talents make them reformers and innovators move on to other causes once they have seen the cycle pass its initial phases. At that point, new people come in to volunteer in support roles because they are more comfortable in maintaining services than in initiating them. Part of the decision to become a volunteer rests on choosing which part of the cycle best suits one's personal preference.

One of the values of understanding this cycle is that it explains the various types of volunteering evident at any given time: agitators, founders, fundraisers, maintainers, revitalizers. Each volunteer group evolves at its own pace—some become institutions or professions in just a few years, others remain as small clusters of devoted volunteers for decades, while still others shine for a brief period and then fade away. Most of the societal institutions we take for granted—hospitals, colleges, town government—had their roots in a small group of volunteers even if today volunteers have only a minimal role.

While this book is unapologetically pro-volunteer, it is important to be objective about the limitations of volunteering.

First, though it is always possible to record much volunteer activity, it would be mistaken to conclude that all volunteering is effective, appropriate, or successful. As with any human endeavor, there have been some regrettable incidents, examples of poor judgement, and outright failures. Not all volunteers have been equally skilled, and some well-intentioned efforts may have backfired. From the perspective of this book, however, the point is not necessarily the success of all volunteering but the *attempt* to accomplish something.

Another characteristic of volunteerism past and present is that it is often exclusionary. Self-help and religiously-affiliated groups, in particular, are inherently limited in membership and in whom they serve. This is an argument in favor of government involvement in the provision of basic services. Only the government is mandated to be nondiscriminatory and all-inclusive; it is the right of volunteer groups to focus on a narrower constituency.

Competition and duplication are also part of volunteerism. The freedom to create any type of project leads to many variations. Only time can weed out the less effective or less popular ideas and methods. There are periods in which people's energies are diffused and resources are wasted. But this is the price to be paid for social innovation. Democracy implies choice. In socialist countries, volunteering is perceived as anti-state; the government knows best and provides all that is needed. While it can be argued that the very proliferation of volunteer activities in the United States causes fragmentation that can be counterproductive, it is this very variety that incubates progress. "American values have set much store on process, rather than on the finished product: the assumption has been that America is creative, not merely traditional and imitative."[1]

In the early years of the new century, there are many issues with the potential to affect volunteerism in profound ways. These issues are already shaping the very nature of who volunteers, what volunteers do, and how they are managed. Many experts are predicting a host of possibilities as to what American life will be like in the future.[2] Since all such theories are basically educated guesswork, preference for one over another largely depends upon whether a person is an optimist or a pessimist. Volunteerism is inherently optimistic, since people only give their time and energy to causes they believe can succeed.

Volunteering does not happen in a vacuum; everything that has an impact on individuals in our society will, by definition, impact those individuals as volunteers. The following are some of the trends already being felt by the volunteer world.

Demographics

Our population is aging. The fastest-growing age segment in the United States is ninety to one hundred. This implies enormous changes to come in housing, medical care, social services—and volunteering. One danger is falling into the trap of categorizing all senior citizens as having a single set of characteristics. As life spans lengthen, it becomes important to distinguish between the abilities and interests of "young" older people (in their sixties) and those of "old" older people (in their nineties). In addition, there are the factors of health and mobility, which further affect the types of volunteer work seniors can do.

As often happens, we see contradictory responses to the lengthening of life expectancy. Eligibility for Social Security benefits has been pushed back to age sixty-seven, with further changes to come. Yet senior volunteer programs such as RSVP have actually *lowered* their age requirements in the past decade, in order to attract younger participants. Given the number of aging baby boomers facing retirement, is it anything special to engage an active fifty-five-year-old as a volunteer? What about finding ways to tap into seniors over age ninety?

For those in their twenties and thirties, there has been some attitudinal shift from a preoccupation with personal gain to concern for the future of the planet. While no one predicts the end of the profit motive, there are strong indications that today's young adults are also concerned with the future quality of life. This age group seems once again willing to participate as volunteers in projects helping their neighborhoods, the environment, and international cooperation.

We are rapidly advancing to the point at which the majority of Americans will no longer have a European background. Latino and Asian citizens already have extensive self-help systems in place, including their own nonprofit agencies. But mainstream volunteer programs have not reached out sufficiently to include as diverse a volunteer pool as possible. The challenge facing volunteer leaders is to accommodate cultural differences in attitudes toward helping, charity, the role of government, and family obligations. The need to be bilingual (in a number of languages) in recruitment and management of volunteers may become a priority in some geographic areas. It should be noted, as well, that African-Americans have not yet been fully integrated into many volunteer organizations, and this continues as a goal.

How we define "family" continues to undergo change. The statistics that began to emerge in the 1960s have continued unabated: high divorce rates (even higher for second marriages), single parenting, same-sex partnerships, older children moving back home with parents, multi-generational homes in which grandparents raise grandchildren, couples delaying having children until well into their thirties. All these trends affect volunteering in that we need to change our assumptions about who is available, when, and to do what. Two responses receiving much attention have been efforts to promote family volunteering—a way to allow parents and children quality time together—and service by singles—in recognition of the desire of divorced people to find safe ways to meet new friends. Both forms of service clearly recognize the modern stress of time management by allowing participants to do two things at once: volunteer while meeting personal needs.

Community Life

Bedroom communities are escalating in number, as more people become willing to commute further to work. Not working in the area where one lives influences the degree of commitment and sense of belonging to either location. On the other hand, the Internet is making telecommuting a reality, with the prospect of rekindling a sense of connection to where one lives. Rural America is disappearing as the "megatropolis" spreads, and family farms have almost vanished in the wake of mega-agribusiness. Once again, the Internet is a new factor, reducing previous isolation and giving small towns accessibility to a wide range of resources. Rural areas are fighting to preserve the traditional ties of community.

Public education is facing severe challenges, both in costs and public support. The push to redirect tax dollars to private and parochial schools is popular with many voters, while school reform alternatives such as "charter schools" gain momentum. What will the long-term effect on volunteering be if students are scattered in so many different locations?

The debate over the responsibilities of government at all levels will continue. Volunteers are directly affected as they respond to the degree to which public funds provide for the basic human needs of food, shelter, and health care. When government does not meet minimum needs, volunteers are faced with choosing to remedy the symptoms or the cause of social problems:

> *On the one hand, there is the danger that continuing to provide services when a program is inadequate will perpetuate the problem. But on the other hand, not to provide services in order to devote all of one's efforts toward changing the system while people are hungry or in need of medication is unconscionable.*[3]

Employment Patterns

Very few people stay at a job long enough these days to earn that gold watch—and very few jobs stay around long enough for the employee to earn one. High-profile mergers, technological unemployment, economic downturns, and the departure of jobs to lower-paid workers overseas have all made job insecurity a constant worry. How can we expect volunteers to make long-term commitments to volunteering when they can't make them to their livelihoods?

Varied work schedules, such as the four-day work week and flex-time options are still largely an unfulfilled promise, though the Internet has opened both telecommuting and virtual volunteering opportunities. The implications of such altered work patterns may include more time to volunteer—but at more diverse hours.

The rate of change in the workplace is accelerating. Workers will be needing new skills constantly, and retraining will be a continuous, lifelong process. Volunteering can play a role in this ongoing education if assignments provide the chance to learn and practice new skills.

A universal issue is the reluctance of new volunteers to make long-term commitments to a single volunteer activity. This is partially due to the increased pace of people's lives, the disposability of jobs and marriages, frequent relocations, and the juggling of career/relationships/parenting/adult care. The availability of creative and meaningful short-term or "episodic" volunteer opportunities will be critical to the successful involvement of future volunteers. "Days of service" will remain important.

Increasing specialization within professional fields has a double meaning for volunteerism. On the one hand, volunteers are recruited and utilized to handle specialized tasks for which they are already qualified. On the other hand, they also serve as generalists and as links between specialists and the public at large. Volunteers provide the increasingly rare personal touch of individualized attention to those with special needs—a luxury that paid staff can never totally provide.

For-profit businesses are moving into areas of human services that were previously the domain only of government or nonprofit agencies—particularly management of hospitals, retirement communities, nursing homes, prisons, and group homes. At first glance, there may be some who react suspiciously to the idea that volunteers can be involved in a business enterprise. Indeed, certain types of volunteer assignments may no longer be appropriate. However, the support needs of patients, residents, inmates, or clients do not change with the ownership of the service. Volunteers will still be the best way to provide individualized attention and the intangible elements of care that are completely separate from the issue of money. Friendship, freely offered, will continue to be a uniquely volunteer service.

It is clear that the concept of the volunteer is still evolving and will likely continue to do so. The trend toward mandated forms of service, such as court-ordered community work or requiring employees to volunteer while receiving workers compensation, is becoming generally accepted. In the most positive scenario, such programs offer communities additional people to accomplish necessary work. They also introduce a new audience to the satisfactions of volunteering. But in the worst scenario, the element of coercion can dominate the activity to the extent that community service acquires a negative connotation. The other danger is to confuse inadequate hourly wages with stipended volunteering.

The converse of required volunteering is the prohibition of volunteer involvement. Some people believe that it is wrong for volunteers to provide services when there is no money for paid staff, the demands are too high, or the risks are too great. While some of the arguments against volunteers may be valid in specific cases, it cannot be forgotten that it is the democratic right of all citizens to offer their services to causes in which they believe. This does not mean that an organization cannot refuse the donated services of a particular individual. But no one has the right to question anyone's *desire* to volunteer. For example, if a taxpayer wants to limit government expenses by lowering labor costs through his or her volunteer efforts, it may justifiably offend the union or a laid-off employee, but it is still a valid motivation for volunteering that cannot be arbitrarily dismissed. The field of volunteerism will need to articulate its position on this question in the years ahead.

Connected to all of this is the American ambivalence about the relationship of money and status. On the surface, it would appear that making money is the most valued goal. But there are some things for which being offered money becomes an insult; servants are paid, free agents act because they want to and not because of any financial reward. Benjamin Franklin declared: "He that is of the opinion money will do everything may well be suspected of doing everything for money." The struggle is to find the balance between being successful financially and also being socially responsible and generous. Volunteering will always be the way in which people can demonstrate that they are truly concerned for others.

> *We are a people obsessed with the values of individual freedom and achievement, yet at the same time we are strongly committed to the welfare of our fellow citizens and the quality of community life. The enduring challenge of America is to preserve both these values, not an easy task . . . It requires that the balance between government, business, and the independent sector be continuously adjusted so that community needs are served and protected against the excesses of individualism. This in turn requires an active citizenry that can help shape public policy and carry out business and non-profit initiatives in the community interest.*[4]

This is the meaning of "participatory democracy."

One of the effects of the International Year of Volunteers 2001 was a new global interest in statistics about volunteering—who, what, why. More studies have been produced attempting to count and define citizen participation in the past five years than in all the years before combined. Unfortunately, the findings are hard to interpret, since most of it is really just baseline data. We have no statistics for volunteering in 1776, or 1865, or even 1950. Comparing the rise or fall of percentages within less than ten years may say more about the methodology of collecting the data than about the state of volunteering today.

In general, researchers feel that recently the number of people volunteering has gone up, but the number of hours served by individual volunteers has gone down. Does this reflect a decline in contributed effort or greater productivity in less time? Almost all of the studies survey citizens themselves in self-reporting their volunteering, none of which can be correlated with what organizations might report as volunteer participation levels, since the Federal 990 report form still makes it optional to include information on donated services. And should we count formal agency-related volunteer service, membership in all-volunteer associations, and informal neighborliness all together? We are far from good answers or consensus.

Nevertheless, as this book goes to press in the aftermath of the tsunamis and hurricanes of 2005, volunteering is experiencing the popularity of the limelight, and there is a visible pride growing among volunteers. This climate may prove fleeting, but it is a positive thing while it lasts. It is enabling community service to take new forms and reach out to those who have only participated minimally before. There is a sense of energy, particularly in volunteering that initiates collaborations to make the most of available resources. The potential exists to blur the lines between "givers" and "receivers" as diverse people and groups work together to improve their communities.

History teaches that Americans get involved. Maybe not everyone, all the time. And maybe it is not always called "volunteering." But it is one of the few ways to stand up and be counted.

> *We who volunteer are saying that there is something important enough for me to do, no matter if I'm getting paid or not, because life gets down to ideas, as well as guns and butter, . . . when you volunteer, you are doing something that means enough to you to do it for no money—and you are doing something that is really life oriented.*[5]

Volunteers will always explore, experiment, sustain, and comfort. All will contribute to our collective future in the belief that they do make a difference.

ENDNOTES FOR CHAPTER 12

1. Brian O'Connell, *America's Voluntary Spirit* (New York: The Foundation Center, 1983), 163.

2. For excellent summaries of the demographic and social changes facing volunteerism, see American Red Cross, *Volunteer 2000 Study*, vols. 1 and 2 (1988), and Robert H. Bellah, ed., *Habits of the Heart: Individualism and Commitment in American Life* (New York: Harper and Row, 1985).

3. Mildred M. Reynolds, "Volunteerism: Appropriate or Inappropriate?" *Kyriokos* (May 15, 1982).

4. "Letter from the League and the Filene Center: Toward National Civic Renewal," *National Civic Review* 76, no. 3 (May-June, 1987): 187.

5. Harry Chapin, speech at the Nassau-Suffolk Volunteer Conference, 1977, reprinted as his obituary in *Newsday* (Long Island, NY), July 17, 1981.

The Authors

Susan J. Ellis is president of Energize, Inc., an international training, consulting, and publishing firm that specializes in volunteerism. She founded the Philadelphia-based company in 1977 and since that time has assisted clients throughout North America, Europe, Asia, Latin America and Australia to create or strengthen their volunteer corps.

Susan is the author or co-author of eleven books, including *From The Top Down: The Executive Role in Volunteer Program Success* and *The Volunteer Recruitment Book.* She has written more than ninety articles on volunteer management for dozens of publications and writes the national bi-monthly column, "On Volunteers," for *The NonProfit Times* (since 1990). From 1981 to 1987 she was editor-in-chief of *The Journal of Volunteer Administration.*

Susan's interest in new technology has taken Energize into cyberspace, where its innovative Web site has won international recognition as a premier resource for volunteer program leaders: http://www.energizeinc.com. She co-authored *The Virtual Volunteering Guidebook*, which is available for free in electronic form on the Energize Web site. In 2000, she and Steve McCurley launched the field's first online journal, *e-Volunteerism: The Electronic Journal of the Volunteer Community* (http://www.e-volunteerism.com), for which she serves as editor.

Susan is an active volunteer in a variety of volunteerism associations and community groups, including Books Through Bars and Spark the Wave: Igniting Teen Volunteers.

Katherine H. Campbell (formerly Noyes)) is a consultant in non-profit and volunteer development. She has worked in the field of volunteer resources management for over thirty years as practitioner, author, trainer, and leader. From 1997 to 2003 she served as executive director of the Association for Volunteer Administration (AVA), the international professional association for leaders and managers of volunteer programs. Prior to this position she was director of the Virginia Office of Volunteerism where she worked for fourteen years.

Katie's career began in 1973 at the Philadelphia Family Court where she helped develop an extensive volunteer program to provide support services to the probation officers and their young clients. Since then she has provided training and technical assistance to volunteer program coordinators throughout North America, becoming well-known in the field. She has authored and co-authored several articles and publications on the subject of volunteerism and volunteer management, including *The (Help!) I-Don't-Have-Enough-Time Guide to Volunteer Management, Children as Volunteers, Opportunity or Dilemma: Court-Referred Community Service Workers,* and *Powerful Connections: A Toolkit for Maximizing Your Organization's Volunteer Resources.*

Katie has served on the board of directors of several local, state and national organizations, and is a past president of AVA. She volunteers with the local professional association for volunteer program managers and as a mentor to at-risk teenage girls.

Name Index

A
Adams, Abigail, 34
Adams, "Girlie," 151
Addams, Jane, 136
Allen, Edgar, 166-7
Allen, Richard, 70
Anthony, Susan B., 131
Augustus, John, 49

B
Barton, Clara, 133, 151
Beers, Clifford, 166
Bergh, Henry, 139
Berrigan, Daniel, 236
Berrigan, Patrick, 236
Berry, Wilford, 12
Bissell, Emily, 168
Blackwell, Elizabeth, 100
Bloomer, Amelia, 88
Booth, Ballington and Maud, 138
Bragg, Gen., 108
Brandeis, Louis, 158-9
Brown, John, 88
Bryce, James, 132
Bush, George, H. W., 306, 308
Bush, George W., 287, 296, 302, 305, 306, 308

C
Carnegie, Andrew, 178
Carter, Jimmy, 280, 306
Chapin, Harry, 259
Chavez, Cesar, 310
Chicago, Judy, 257
Clinton, William, 287, 304, 305, 306, 308
Coleman, Robert, 166
Conrad, Frank, 212-3
Cooper, Mr., 99
Coughlin, Father C. E., 196-7
Crawford, Joan, 198

D
Divine, Father, 196
Dix, Dorothea Lynde, 68, 100, 101
Drucker, Peter, 267

E
Eddy, Thomas, 93
Eisenhower, Dwight D., 220
Emerson, Ralph Waldo, 74

F
Farmer, James, 231
Flick, Lawrence, 133
Flint, Timothy, 47
Ford, Gerald R., 255, 308
Ford II, Henry, 238-9
Franklin, Benjamin, 23, 29, 30, 360
Freud, Sigmund, 187

G
Gardner, John, 239
Garrison, William Lloyd, 80-1
Garvey, M. M., 196
Gates, Frederick T., 168
Ginn, Edwin, 178
Girard, Stephen, 60
Godfrey, Matthew, 19
Gompers, Samuel, 121
Gore, Al, 287
Griscom, John, 93

H
Hale, Nathan, 39
Harkness, Rebecca, 225
Harrison, George, 259
Hart, Nancy, 38
Harvard, John, 23
Hill, Anita, 288
Hiss, Alger, 222
Hoover, Herbert, 188, 200-1
Horniman, Miss, 225
Howe, Samuel Gridley, 68

I

J
Jacobs, Frances Wisebar, 138
Johnson, Lyndon B., 237, 238
Jones, Absalom, 70
Joseph, Dr., 275

K
Kelley, Florence, 136
Kennedy, John F., 220, 237
Kennicott, Robert, 95
King Jr., Rev. Martin Luther, 219, 231, 233

L
Lancaster, Joseph, 57
Lee, Gypsy Rose, 210
Lee, Robert E., 107
Lincoln, Abraham, 87, 96, 104
Lindbergh, Charles A., 187
Logan, James, 23
Lynch, Col. Charles, 29

M
McCarthy, Joseph, 222-3
McKinley, William, 157
Manning, W. T., Bishop, 138
Marquette, Pere Jacques, 15
Mather, Cotton, 16
Meisel, Wayne, 279
Mink, Mr., 7
Morse, Samuel, 44
Muir, John, 147
Murrow, Edward R., 223

N
Nader, Ralph, 239
Nixon, Richard M., 243, 246
Nowell, Virginia, 209

O
O'Connor, Mr., 227

P
Paul, Alice, 162-3
Pearce, Mr., 99
Peel, Robert, 300
Penn, William, 15
Pintard, John, 61
Pitcher, Molly, 37
Pius XI, Pope, 198
Powell, Colin, 306
Pratt, Lt., 140
Putnam, Robert D., 291

Q

R
Rand, Sally, 211
Rankin, Jeanette, 162
Reagan, Nancy, 271, 306
Reagan, Ronald, 260-1, 263, 265, 266, 271, 280
Reed, Walter, 166
Richmond, Mary E., 160-1
Ringer, Robert, 244
Rockefeller, John D., 168
Romney, George, 307
Roosevelt, Eleanor, viii, 199
Roosevelt, Franklin D., 187, 188, 195, 196, 197, 203, 208, 209, 211,
Roosevelt, Theodore, 138, 157, 172

S
Sampson, Deborah, 37
Sanger, Margaret, 166
Scott, Dred, 87
Sencer, Dr., 275
Shattuck, Lemuel, 61
Shute, Mrs., 151
Simpson, Mr., 99
Soros, George, 304
Stanton, Edwin, 97
Stanton, Elizabeth Cady, 130-1
Stevens, Thaddeus, 91
Sullivan, Thomas V., 92

T
Thayer, Eli, 93-4
Thompson, Samuel, 62-3
Thoreau, Henry David, 74
Torvalds, Linus, 289
Truman, Harry, 221, 222
Truth, Sojourner, 130
Turner, Nat, 79-80

U

V
Vrabel, Stephen, 12

W
Wald, Lillian, 136
Wanamaker, John, 138
Washington, George, 36, 37, 43
Webster, Noah, 56
Wilkie, Wendell, 192
Wilson, Woodrow, 162-3, 176
Wise, Rabbi Stephen, 138
Wolfe, Tom, 243

Y
Young, Brigham, 94

Organization Index

A
Abington Horse Association, 51
Accountants for the Public Interest, 316
ACTION, 7, 246-7, 262, 280, 306, 341, 344
Action for Children's Television, 317
Active Corps of Executives (ACE), 246-7
ActionAIDS, 275
Added Care, 272
Adirondack Cottage Sanatorium, 134
Adopt-a-School, 263, 268
Adoptees Liberty Movement Association, 320
Advertising Council, 214, 225, 265, 316
Aerial Phenomena Research Organization, 226
AFL-CIO, 249
African Society, 70
Agricultural Students' Union, 169
Agricultural Wheel, 127
Aid Association for Lutherans (AAL), 265
Alcoholics Anonymous, 193, 320, 336
Alianza Hispano Americana, 141
Aliveness Project, 275
All Pueblo Council, 195
Alliance for Volunteerism, 344
Allied Relief (WW I), 179
Allied Relief Fund (WW II), 209
Allstate Insurance, 248
America Awake, 196
American Academy of Arts and Sciences, 327
American and Foreign Emigrant Protective and Employment Society, 92
American Anthropological Association, 323
American Anti-Slavery Society, 77
American Anti-Vivisection Society, 328
American Association for Museum Volunteers, 257, 340, 352
American Association of Advertising Agencies, 316
American Association of Blood Banks, 227
American Association of Museums, 257
American Association of Public Accountants, 124, 171
American Association of Retired People (AARP), 252
American Association of State Service Commissions, 345
American Association of University Professors, 322-3
American Association of University Women, 145, 193-4, 272
American Association of Volunteer Services Coordinators, 344
American Automobile Association, 226
American Bankers Association, 123, 132
American Bar Association, 264
American Bible Society, 69
American Birth Control League, 198
American Brass Association, 123
American Broadcasting Company (ABC), 268
American Camping Association, 175
American Cancer Society, 197, 282, 321
American Catholic Historical Association, 145
American Charity Organization Society, 136-7
American Chemical Society, 144
American Child Health Association, 166
American Civil Liberties Union, 333

American Climatological Society, 145
American Communist Party, 333
American Conference for the Prevention of Infant Mortality, 166
American Diabetes Association, 321
American Epilepsy League, 199
American Express, 263
American Farm Bureau Federation, 169
American Federation of Labor (AFL), 121, 165, 191, 249
American Forestry Association, 147, 207, 230, 327
American Freedmen's Aid Commission, 115
American Friends of France, 209-10
American Friends Service Committee, 228, 235, 280
American Home Missionary Society, 122
American Hospital Association, 340
American Hotel Association, 171
American International Relief Committee for Suffering Operatives of Great Britain, 142
American Iron and Steel Institute, 123
American Legion, 198
American Library Association, 144
American Library Service, 181
American Medical Association, 63, 264, 320
American Medical Society, 21
American Missionary Association, 115
American National Red Cross. *See* American Red Cross.
American Negro Loyal Legion, 177-8
American Nurses' Association, 320
American Ornithologists' Union, 144-5
American Party, 88
American Peace Society, 73, 151, 177
American Protective Association, 142
American Psychiatric Association, 320
American Psychological Association, 145
American Public Health Association, 133
American Radio Relay League, 173, 317
American Rangers, 196
American Red Cross, 133, 150-1, 170, 179, 180, 200, 209, 212, 214, 221, 225, 226
American Rights Committee, 177
American Sabbath Union, 121
American School Peace League, 178
American Social Hygiene Association, 166
American Society for Directors of Volunteer Services (ASDVS), 340, 352
American Society for the Control of Cancer, 166
American Society of African Culture, 233
American Society of Association Executives, 213
American Temperance Union, 66
American Union Commission, 103
American Volunteer Ambulance Corps, 210
American Woman Suffrage Association, 131
American Women's Equal Rights Association, 130
American Women's Voluntary Service, 209, 212
America's Promise, 306
AmeriCorps, 7, 305, 308, 345
Ancient and Honorable Artillery Company of Boston, 36
Ancient Order of United Workmen, 129
Animal Defense League, 328
Anti-Merger League, 158
Anti-Opium League, 195
A.P. Smith Company, 224
Appalachian Mountain Club, 326
Architects Workshop, 263
Army Community Services, 236-7, 331
Asian American Women Artists Association, 327
Assembly of State Offices on Volunteerism, 342
Assistance Society, 64
Association for Administration of Volunteer Services, 344

Association for Improving the Condition of the Poor (AICP), 64, 92, 133
Association for the Handicapped, 199
Association for the Prevention and Relief of Heart Disease of New York City, 166
Association for Research in Nonprofit Organizations and Voluntary Action (ARNOVA), 341, 345, 352
Association for Volunteer Administration (AVA), 251, 340, 343, 344, 352
Association of American Railroads, 213
Association of Catholic Trade Unionists, 204
Association of Economic Entomologists, 145
Association of Iron and Steel Electrical Engineers, 171
Association of Junior Leagues, 251. *See also* Junior League.
Association of Southern Women for the Prevention of Lynching, 193
Association of Voluntary Action Scholars, 341, 344
Association of Volunteer Bureaus, 341, 344
Association of Women's Clubs. *See* General Federation of Women's Clubs.
Asylum for the Deaf and Dumb, 63
Athletic Club, 172
Audubon Society, 147

B

Baird Foundation Clinic, 199
Bank of America, 248
Bank of North America, 54
Bascom Home Guards, 106
Better Breathers Club, 272
Better Business Bureaus, 194
Big Brothers Association, 161-2, 282
Big Brothers/Big Sisters of America, 319
Big Sisters, 162, 349
Bingo for Britain, 209
Birth Control Federation, 198
Black Muslims, 234
Black Panther Party, 234
Bloomingdale Asylum for the Insane, 93
Blue Lodge, 88
B'nai B'rith, Independent Order of, 93; B'nai B'rith Girls, 325
Board of Indian Commissioners, 141
Boonfellows, 272
Boston Dispensary, 62
Boston Juvenile Anti-Slavery Society, 81
Boston Mechanics Institute, 58
Boston Society for the Care of Girls, 67
Bowditch School, 199
Boy Scouts of America, 175, 211, 326
Boys' (and Girls') Clubs (of America), 145-6, 326
Braille Book Bank, 228
Braille Club of New York, 228
Bread and Roses, 257
Brotherhood of Locomotive Engineers, 119
Brotherhood of Locomotive Firemen, 119
Brotherhood of Sleeping Car Porters, 196
Brotherhood of the Footboard, 119
Brown Fellowship Society, 70
Bucks of America, 37
Bundles for Britain, 209
Business and Professional Women's Clubs, 315
Business Volunteers for the Arts, 263

C

Call for Action, 319
Camp Fire (Girls), 175, 206, 326
Camp Shows, Inc., 208
Campus Compact, 279
Campus Outreach Opportunity League (COOL), 279
Canadian Association for Volunteer Resources, 342, 352
Canadian Geological Survey, 95
Canteen Corps, 151
CARE, 336
Catholic Youth Organization, 204, 325
CBS-TV, 263
Central Committee of Negro College Men, 177

Chambers of Commerce, 123, 165, 171, 172, 224, 315
Charity Organization Society, 134, 138, 164
Charleston Museum, 23
Chicago Committee on Racial Equality, 231
Children's Aid Society, 139
Children's Bureau, 162
Children's Leagues, 148
Chinese American Citizens Alliance, 195
Chinese American Voting League, 195
Chinese Consolidated Benevolent Association, 141
Chinese Ladies Garment Workers' Union, 192
Chinese Workers Mutual Aid Association, 191-2
Chivas Regal Company, 264
Christian Arbitration and Peace Society, 151
Christian Commission, 102-3, 337
Church Organization for the Advancement of the Interests of Labor, 121
Church Peace Union, 178
Citizen Corps Councils, 308, 330
Citizens' Organization for a Sane World (SANE), 222
Citizen's Stamp Advisory Committee, 225, 318
CityCares, 293-4, 345
City Club, 172
City Mission School, 136
City of Hope, 168, 322
Civic Music Association, 174
Civil Air Patrol, 1, 214, 221, 331
Civil Service Reform Association, 132
Civilian Conservation Corps (CCC), 189, 203, 207, 305, 308
Civilian Air Warning System, 214
Colored Alliance, 127
Colored Women's League, 130
Commission on Interracial Cooperation, 193
Commission on National and Community Service, 305, 306
Committee for Economic Development, 248
Committee for Industrial Organization (CIO), 191
Committee of Vigilance of 1851, 51
Committee on Religion and Welfare Activity, 204
Committees of Correspondence, 32-3, 336
Committees of Safety, 33, 336
Common Cause, 239, 332
Community Accountants, 263
Community Service, Inc., 181
Community Service Society, 238
Commonwealth Alliance for Drug Rehabilitation and Education (CADRE), 271
Compeer, 272
CompuMentor, 290-1
Congress of Racial Equality (CORE), 231-2, 234
Connecticut Moral Society, 68
Conservation Camp for New Hampshire Young Leaders, 230
Conservation Corps, 280
Constitutional Union Guards, 117
Consumers Union, 194
Cook County Woman's Club, 140
Cooper Shop Soldiers' Home, 100
Cooper Shop Volunteer Hospital, 100
Cooper Shop Volunteer Refreshment Saloon, 99-100, 336
Coors Brewing Company, 265
Copyright League, 45
Corporation for National and Community Service, 7, 305-6, 341, 342, 345, 349, 352
Council for Financial Aid to Education, 224-5
Council of Laborers, 125-6
Council of Machine Tool and Equipment Services, 213
Council of National Defense, 178
Council of National Organizations for Adult Education, 251
Council of Safety, 117
Country Life Commission, 175
Cowboy Volunteers, 150
Cub Scouts, 206
Culper Ring, 37
Currie Free Architectural Clinic, 263

D

Daughters of Liberty, 37
Daughters of the American Revolution, 326

Delaware Anti-Tuberculosis Society, 168
Democratic Leadership Council, 280
Dignity, 257
Dixie Crusaders, 207
Dogs for Defense, 211
Dow Chemical Company, 236
Drug Abuse Resistance Effort (DARE), 271, 300
Drugline 9, 271
Dwight Hall (Yale University), 324

E
"Earn It" program, 282
Earth Team, 258
Earth Watch, 258
Easter Seal Society, 198-9, 321. *See also* National Easter Seal Society.
Educational Expeditions International, 258
Electronic Frontier Association, 332
Elks, 229
Elyria Memorial Hospital, 167
Ephrata Cloisters, 38
Experiment in International Living, 280
Exxon, 243, 248

F
Faculty of Physic, 20
Family Service Association of America, 160
Farm Bureaus, 169
Farmers' Alliance and Industrial Union, 126, 168
Farmers' and Laborers' Union of America, 127
Farmer's Holiday Association, 192
Farmers' Institutes, 128
Farmers' Union, 169
Federal Council of Churches of Christ in America, 160
Federal Employment Literacy Training Program, 268
Federation of Western Outdoor Clubs, 207
Female Benevolent Society, 222
Fire Corps, 308
First Rhode Island Regiment, 37
Foster Grandparent Program, 246, 251
4-H Club, viii, 127, 169, 207
Free African Society, 60, 70
Free and Accepted Masons, 25, 70, 129, 326
Free Enquirers, 56
Freedmen's Aid Society of the Methodist Episcopal Church, 115
Freedmen's Bureau, 115-6, 118, 338
Fresh-Air Fund, 146
Friendly Societies, 62
Friends of New York Soldiers and Sailors, 208
Friends of Universal Reform, 74
Friends Yearly Meeting, 74
Future Farmers of America, 189

G
Gamblers Anonymous, 320
Gangsters, 210
Gates Hospital for Crippled Children, 167
Gay Men's Health Crisis, 274-5
General Education Board, 168
General Federation of Women's Clubs, 130, 161, 165, 193, 197, 221, 292
German Turnverein, 146
Giraffe Project, 265
Girl Scouts of America (the USA), 175, 209, 251, 326
Global Youth Action Network, 310
Gold Hill Union, 121
Good Losers Clubs, 192
Goodwill Industries of America, 166, 320
Grange, 124-6, 165, 168
Gray Ladies, 151
Gray Panthers, 252
Green Guards, 209
Green Guerrillas, 258
Group W Westinghouse, 265
Guardian Angels, 234

H
Habitat for Humanity, 270, 297
"Halley Watch" (NASA), 276
Hands Across America, 270
Hands On Network, 293-4, 345
Harvard College (University), 15, 23, 279
Health Committee, 60-1
Heart-to-Heart, 272
Hebrew Benevolent Ladies Aid Societies, 130

Hillel Foundation, 325
Hint Club, 54-5
Historical Museum Commission, 327
Honeywell, 248
Hunger Project, 259
Hunt Manufacturing Company, 263
Hygiological Society, 95

I

IBM, 248
Idaho AIDS Project, 275
Independence Factory, 272
INDEPENDENT SECTOR, 265, 341, 352
Indian American Student Association, 309
Indian Rights Association, 140
Industrial Brotherhood, 120
Institute of New Dimensions, 252
Interchurch World Movement of North America, 199-200
International Association for Volunteer Effort, 342, 344, 352
International Ladies Garment Workers' Union, 192
International Sabbath Association, 121
International Voluntary Services, 332
Interracial Council of New York, 212

J

Japanese-American Citizen's League (JACL), 196
Japanese Association, 2196
Jaycees, 315
Jewish Federation, 138
Jewish Welfare Board, 180
John Birch Society, 223, 322
Junior Farmers, 189
Junior League, 197, 198, 341; *See also* Association of Junior Leagues.
Junior Red Cross, 180
"Just Say No," 271

K

Kentish Guards of Rhode Island, 36
Kiwanis Clubs, 172; Circle K Clubs, 192; Key Clubs, 192, 315
Knickerbocker Club, 72
Knights of Columbus, 180, 206
Knights of Labor, 120
Knights of Pythias, 129
Knights of the White Camelia, 117
Know Nothing Party, 88-9
Ku Klux Klan, 6, 117-8, 126, 148, 159, 193

L

La Raza Unida, 234
Ladies' Aid Societies, 98-9, 101
Ladies' Benevolent Society, 62
Ladies' Gunboat Societies, 105-6
Ladies' Library Association of Kalamazoo, 91
Lake Mohonk Conference of Friends of the Indians, 140
Laubach Literacy Action, 268
Laymen's League Against Epilepsy, 199
Le Paquet au Front, 210
League of American Wheelmen, 146
League of United Latin American Citizens (LULAC), 195
League of Women Voters, 193
Learn and Serve America, 305
Legion of Decency, 205
Levi-Strauss, 248
Liberal Republicans, 131
Library Company of Philadelphia, 23
Library Society of Charles-Town, 23
Lions Clubs, 172, 292, 315, 336
Literacy Volunteers of America, 268
Literary and Scientific Circle, 143
Little League, 206, 326
Little People of America, 228
Lockheed, 210
Lowell Institute, 59
Loyal League, 104, 116
Loyal Order of Moose, 326

M

Manumission Society, 56
Maryland Association for the Colored Blind, 166, 199
Masons. *See* Free and Accepted Masons.
Massachusetts Emigrant Aid Company, 93
Master Hatters of Baltimore, 55
Meals on Wheels, 320
Medical Reserve Corps, 308
Medical Society of the State of New York, 20

Mensa, 272
Methodist Youth Fellowship, 325
Metropolitan Board of Health, 133
Metropolitan Community Churches, 257
Metropolitan Opera Company, 205
Militant Christian Patriots of Los Angeles, 196
Military Training Camps Association, 209
Million Man March, 304
Million Mom March, 304-5
Minerva Club, 91
Minority AIDS Project, 275
Modern Health Crusade, 167
Modern Woodmen of America, 229
Montgomery Improvement Association, 231
Moral Majority, 256
Mothers Against Drunk Driving (MADD), 273
Mutual Savings of Portsmouth, 179
Muscular Dystrophy Association of America, 227, 321, 327

N

"Nader's Raiders," 239
Names Project, 276
Nashville CARES, 275
National Academy of Television Arts and Sciences, 317
National Affiliation of Concerned Business Students, 250
National Alliance of Businessmen (NAB), 239
National American Woman Suffrage Association, 131
National Arbitration League, 151
National Assembly of State Offices of Volunteerism, 344
National Association for Mental Health, 227, 321
National Association for the Advancement of Colored People (NAACP), 164, 220
National Association for the Study of Epilepsy and the Care and Treatment of the Epileptic, 134
National Association of Base Ball Players, 72
National Association of Colored Women, 130
National Association of Independent Schools, 279
National Association of Life Underwriters, 124
National Association of Manufacturers, 165, 170, 262, 316
National Association of Partners in Education, 268, 340, 352
National Association of Social Workers, 319
National Association of Societies for Organizing Charity, 160
National Association of the Deaf, 138
National Association of Volunteer Programs in Local Government (NAVPLG), 340, 345, 352
National Association to Control Epilepsy, 199
National Automobile Dealers Association, 316
National Birth Control League, 166
National Board of Rabbis, 325
National Board of Trade, 123
National Braille Club, 228
National Cancer Foundation, 197, 321
National Catholic Community Services, 208
National Catholic War Council, 180
National Catholic Welfare Conference, 204
National Center for Citizen Involvement, 251
National Center for Voluntary Action (NCVA), 247, 262, 344, 350
National Chicana Businesswomen's Association, 234
National Child Labor Committee, 170, 197, 228
National Children's Rehabilitation Center, 199
National Civic Federation, 172
National Civilian Community Corps (NCCC), 305
National Commission on Excellence in Education, 267
National Committee for Mental Hygiene, 166
National Committee for Responsible Patriotism, 236
National Committee on Employment of Youth, 228
National Committee on Safety, 226

National Community Service Sentencing Association, 282
National Conference of Charities and Correction, 139
National Conference of Christians and Jews (NCCJ), 234, 325
National Congress of Mothers, 144
National Conservation Commission, 174
National Consumers League, 123-4, 166
National Corporate Volunteer Council, 263, 341, 344
National Council for Industrial Safety, 171
National Council of Churches, 325; Migrant Ministry of, 200
National Council of Jewish Women, 130, 251
National Council of Women in the United States, 129-30, 193
National Council on Workplace Volunteerism (NCWV), 340, 352
National Easter Seal Society for Crippled Children and Adults, 166-7, 388. *See also* Easter Seal Society.
National Economic Growth and Reconstruction Organization (NEGRO), 233
National Education Association, 209
National Endowment for the Arts, 327
National Farmers' Alliance, 126
National Farmers' Alliance and Cooperative Union of America, 127
National Federation of Afro-American Women, 130
National Federation of Business and Professional Women's Clubs, 179
National Fire Protection Association, 124, 330
National Forest Commission, 147
National Fraternal Congress of America, 310
National Gentile League, 196
National Guard Association, 149
National Geographic Society, 323
National Guard Family Support Program, 331
National Heart Association, 226-7
National Information Center on Volunteerism (NICOV), 250, 262, 344
National Information Center on Volunteers in Courts, 344
National Institute of Justice, 299
National Jewish Consumptive Relief Organization, 168
National Jewish Welfare Board, 208
National Labor Union, 121
National League for Women's Service, 179
National League on Urban Conditions Among Negroes, 164
National Methodist Conference, 160
National Military Family Association, 237
National Multiple Sclerosis Society, 227
National Negro Business League, 172
National Negro Press Association, 164
National Organization for Women (NOW), 245-6
National Probation Association, 198
National Recreation Association, 326
National Rural Letter Carriers Association, 317
National Safety Council, 171, 189-90, 226
National School Volunteer Program (NSVP), 268
National Security League, 177
National Self-Help Clearinghouse, 273
National Service-Learning Clearinghouse, 298-9
National Service Secretariat, 280
National Ski Association, 207
National Ski Patrol, 207, 326
National Society for Crippled Children, 198
National Society for the Promotion of Industrial Education, 165
National Student Campaign Against Hunger, 269
National Student Volunteer Program, 247
National Theater of the Deaf, 321

National Travelers Aid Association, 208
National Tuberculosis Association, 167
National Urban League, 164
National VOLUNTEER Center, 307, 345, 357
National Welfare Rights Organization (NWRO), 234
National Wildlife Federation, 208, 327
National Woman Suffrage Association, 130-1
National Woman's Committee, 178-9
National Women's Party, 163
National Women's Trade Union League, 131
Native American Party, 70
Navy League, 178
Needlework Guild, 138, 320
Nestlé, 259-60
NetAid, 304
NetDay, 290
New England Anti-Imperialist League, 151-2
New England Woman's Club, 129
New Jersey Medical Society, 21
New York Amateur Ski Club, 207
New York Chamber of Commerce, 54
New York Charity Organization Society, 137
New York Children's Aid Society, 92
New York City Cooper Union, 59
New York Hospital Board, 93
New York City Humane Society, 49
New York Institution for the Blind, 63
New York Ophthalmic Hospital, 63
New York Peace Society, 73
New York Stock Exchange, 54
Niagara Movement, 163, 176
Northern Alliance, 127
Northern Student Movement, 232
Nurses Society of Philadelphia, 62

O

Octavia Hill Association, 162
Odd Fellows, 119, 129, 229
Offender Aid and Restoration, 254
Office of Voluntary Action Liaison, 247
Ohio Society for Crippled Children, 167, 198
Old School House, Mt. Holly, NJ, 22
Old Swedes' Church, 18
One Day's Pay, 303, 310
Oneida Group, 74
Open Society Institute, 304
Operation Bootstrap, 233
Opportunities Industrialization Center (OIC), 233
Orden Hijos de America, 195
Order of the Mystic Shrine, 224
Order of the Sons of America, 195
Order of the Star Spangled Banner, 88
Orphan Asylum Society of New York, 67
Out-Door Lying-In Charity, 63
Outdoor Recreation Resources Review Commission, 326
Overeaters Anonymous, 272

P

Pale Faces, 117
Parent-Teacher Association (PTA), viii, 140, 144, 198, 336
Parents Without Partners, 228, 320
Partners (Colorado), 254
Partners Project (Arkansas), 254
Patriotic Society, 54
Patrons of Husbandry, 124-6
Peabody Education Fund, 115
Peace Association of the Friends, 151
Peace Corps, 3, 220, 237-8, 246, 280, 308-9, 332, 344
Peace Democrats, 90
Pennsylvania Prison Society, 49
Pennsylvania Society for the Prevention of Tuberculosis, 133
Pennsylvanian Society for the Promotion of Public Economy, *65*
Pennsylvania Society of Friends, 75
People for the Ethical Treatment of Animals (PETA), 328
People's Party, 127
Perkins Institute for the Blind, 68
Philadelphia Academy of Natural Sciences, 59
Philadelphia African Methodist Church, 50
Philadelphia Free African Society, 60

Philadelphia Hospital, 21
Philadelphia Medical Society, 21
Philadelphia Society for Alleviating the Miseries of Public Prisons, 49
Phillip Morris, 248
Playground and Recreation Association of America, 181
Playground Association, 174
Points of Light Foundation (& Volunteer Center National Network), 281, 305, 306, 307-8, 310, 340, 345, 352
Police Athletic League, 329
Populist Party, 127, 182
Poydras Female Orphan Asylum, 67
Prohibition Party, 193
Project Handclasp (U.S. Navy), 331
Protective Association for Women, 131
Provisional Executive Committee for Zionist Affairs, 182
Public Committee on the Humanities, 327
Public Education Association, 230
Public Lands Commission, 174

R

Radio Emergency Associated Citizens Teams (REACT), 317
Rails to Trails Conservancy, 318
Ranger Corps, 280
Raptor Rehabilitation of Kentucky, Inc., 328
"Read by 3," 298
Recreation Services, 151
Red Cross, 143. *See also* American National Red Cross.
Religious Roundtable, 256
Republican Party, 124
Retired Senior Volunteer Program (RSVP), 246, 251, 306, 344
Revolutionary Action Movement, 234
Rifle Clubs, 118
Rockefeller Foundation, 168
Rotary Clubs, 167, 172, 292, 315
Rough Riders, 150

S

Safety Councils, 189-90, 225-6
St. Andrew's Society of Charleston, 19
Saint Cecilia Club, 134
St. Charles (Missouri) Emergency Communications Association, 302
Salvation Army, 138, 160, 180-1, 199, 208, 221, 320
San Diego Mission, 69
SANE, 222, 235
Save Europe's Children, 210
Save-the-Redwoods League, 207
Savings Bank Insurance League, 158
School Safety Patrol, 226
Scot's Charitable Society of Boston, 19
Search for Extraterrestrial Intelligence (SETI), 324
"Second Amendment Sisters," 305
Second Careers, 252
Senior Companion Program, 247, 251
Senior Corps, 305, 308
Serve and Enrich Retirement by Volunteer Experience (SERVE), 238
Service Corps of Retired Executives (SCORE), 246-7
'76 Association, 117
Sierra Club, 147, 174, 231, 327
Silver Shirt Legion, 196
Six Companies, 141
Smithsonian Institution, 95
Social Band, 88
Societies for Crippled Children, 198
Society for the Diffusion of Useful Knowledge, 58
Society for the Encouragement of Faithful Domestic Servants, 66
Society for the Prevention of Cruelty to Animals (SPCA), 139
Society for the Prevention of Cruelty to Children, 139
Society for the Prevention of Pauperism in the City of New York, 65
Society for the Promotion of Agriculture, 54
Society for the Promotion of Arts, Agriculture, and Economy, 34
Society for the Relief of Distressed Debtors, 49
Society For The Relief Of Free Negroes Unlawfully Held in Bondage, 75-6

Society for the Relief of Poor Widows with Small Children, 64
Society of Associated Teachers, 56
Society of Christian Socialists, 121
Society of Saint Vincent de Paul, 93
Soil and Water Conservation Society, 323
Soldiers Aid Societies, 108
Sons of Italy, 326
Sons of Liberty, 37
Sons of the South, 89
Soroptimists, 315
Sorosis, 129
South Asian American Leaders of Tomorrow (SAALT), 309
Southern Alliance, 127
Southern Christian Leadership Conference (SCLC), 231
Sovereigns of Industry, 120
Special Olympics, 321
State Horticultural Society (Colorado), 151
Street Biker Associations, 319
Student Non-Violent Coordinating Committee (SNCC), 232
Students for a Democratic Society (SDS), 236
"Success by Six," 298
Sunday League of America, 121
Sunday School Society, 57
Surgical Eye Expeditions (SEE), 264

T

Tammany Society, 132
Telecommunications Exchange for the Deaf, 272
Telephone Pioneers, 316
Temple Association of Retired Professionals, 252
Texas Citrus Growers, 315
Texas Farmers' Boys and Girls League, 169
Texas Farmers' State Alliance, 127
Thrivent Financial for Lutherans, 326
Toastmasters Club, 192
Toastmasters International, 317
Touch America Project, 326
Travelers Aid Society, 46, 212
Tuberculosis Associations, 167

U

Union League, 116, 117
Union Temperance Society of Moreau and Northumberland, 65
Union Volunteer Refreshment Saloon, 100
United Confederate Veterans, 152
UNICEF, 332
United Day of Service, 310
United Nations, 219, 221, 332
United Nations Information Technology Service (UNITeS), 304
United Seamen's Service (USS), 212, 331
United Service Organizations for National Defense (USO), 208, 213, 221, 331
U.S. Association of Museum Volunteers, 257
United States Brewers Foundation, 123
United States Chamber of Commerce, 263
United States Children's Bureau, 170
United States Junior Naval Reserve, Girls' Division, 178
U.S. Sanitary Commission, 100-2, 133
U.S. Student YMCA, 325
United Support of Artists for Africa (USA for Africa), 265
United Way (of America), 138, 306, 309, 341, 352
Universal Peace Union, 158
University Year for Action, 247
UPS Foundation, 349
Urban Institute, 349
Urban Survival, 272
USA Freedom Corps, 308-9, 310, 345, 349

V

Vaccination Institute, 61
Veterans and Reservists to End the War in Vietnam, 235
Veterans Bedside Network, 221-2
Veterans of Foreign Wars, 152, 221, 331
Veterans Vigil Society, 277
Victory Corps, 211, 212
Vietnam Veterans of America, 331
VISTA, 344

Voluntary Organizations Assisting in Disaster (VOAD), 330
VOLUNTEER: The National Center (on Citizen Involvement), 262, 265, 341, 344, 345
Volunteer Aid Societies, 150
Volunteer Corps (New York), 280
Volunteer Lawyers for the Arts, 327
VolunteerMatch, 308
Volunteers for Prosperity, 309
Volunteers in Service to America (VISTA), 237-8, 246, 280, 306
Volunteers in Technical Assistance (VITA), 332
Volunteers of America, 138-9, 199

W

War Advertising Council, 213-4, 225
War Camp Community Service, 181
War Relief and Refugee Service, 204
Weekly Society of Gentlemen, 20
Welfare Rights Association, 320
Westinghouse Company, 204-5
Western Union, 95
"What Can *I* Do?" League, 181
White Brotherhood, 117
White Caps, 148, 149
White League, 118
White Line, 118
Wilkie Clubs, 192
Woman's Christian Temperance Union, 130, 151, 193
Woman's Land Army of America, 181
Woman's War Council, 179
Women's Central Relief Association for the Sick and Wounded of the Army, 100-1
Women's Committee for Modification of the Volstead Act, 193
Women's Committee for Repeal of the Eighteenth Amendment, 193
Women's Constructive Peace Movement, 178
Women's Field Army, 197
Women's Municipal League of Boston, 166
Women's National Indian Association, 140
Women's Organization for National Prohibition Reform, 193
Women's Strike for Peace, 235
Woolworth's, 232
Working Men's Home Association, 92
Working Men's Party, 55
Working Women's Association, 131
World Federation of Friends of Museums, 257
World Peace Foundation, 178
Writers and Artists Protest Committee, 235
Wyoming Stock-Growers' Association, 128

X

Xerox, 248, 316

Y

Yale College (University), 23, 147, 324
Young Americans for Freedom (YAF), 238
Young Farmers, 189
Young Men's Christian Association (YMCA), 92-3, 134, 138, 145, 146, 170, 172, 180, 192, 195, 204, 208, 212, 251, 325, 326, 337
Young Men's Mental Improvement Society for the Discussion of Moral and Philosophical Questions of All Kinds, 59
Young Women's Christian Association (YWCA), 92-3, 121, 122, 180, 193, 195, 208, 212, 251, 326
Youth Challenge Program, 247
Youth Crime Watch of America, 330
Youth Service America, 280, 310

Z

Zero Population Growth, 328

Subject Index

A

Abolitionism, 33-4, 56, 74, 75-81, 88, 89-90
Abortion rights, 256, 331
Abuse, domestic, 139, 149, 332
ACTION, 7, 246-7, 262, 280, 306, 341
Adult education, 34, 45, 58-9, 71, 91, 122, 126,143-4, 165, 171, 199, 238, 250-1, 267-8, 298, 323
African-Americans, volunteering by, 33, 36-7, 50, 59, 60, 69-70, 77, 79-80, 89-90, 103, 115, 125-6, 130,163-4, 166, 177, 179, 196, 199, 220, 231-4, 304-5, 309, 321, 357
Aged, caring for, 19, 252-3, 283, 319
Agriculture. *See* Farming and farmers.
AIDS, 257, 274-6, 295, 322
Alcohol abuse, 65-6, 75, 130, 149, 193, 269, 271, 273, 322
Almshouses, 18-9, 61, 67
Alternative sentencing, 4, 5, 7, 281-3, 299-300, 329, 359
Amateur, as related to volunteering, 11, 347
Ambulance corps, 102, 107, 180, 207, 210, 273-4, 330
American Red Cross. *Go to* Organization Index.
"Americans Volunteer" study (1974), 247, 266
Americans with Disabilities Act of 1990, 287
Amnesty for draft evasion, 255
Animal and bird protection, 139, 208, 301, 303, 327-8
Anti-foreign activity, 141, 142, 159, 181-2, 188, 196
Arbor Day, 147
Arts, cultural, 71, 91, 95, 143-4, 166, 174, 204, 205, 225, 257, 263, 327
Asian-Americans, 141, 187, 191-2, 195-6, 259, 309, 333, 357

B

Background checks on volunteers, 346
Banking, 29-30, 54, 123, 178, 314
Barter, 202, 269, 283
Beautification programs, 147-8, 230, 336
Benevolent societies, 20, 55, 70, 115-6, 128, 141
Bicentennial celebration, U.S., 276-7
Birth control and family planning, 166, 198, 321, 328
Bloomerism, 88
Bowling Alone, 291-2
Boycotts, 34-5, 55, 123-4, 170, 205, 219, 220, 231-2, 236, 259-60, 278, 333
Brown v. Board of Education of Topeka, 219, 220
Business and industry, 54, 119, 123, 171-2, 188, 189, 192, 194, 205, 213-4, 224, 233, 236, 238-9, 247-8, 250, 278, 284, 293-4, 315-6

C

Camping, 146-7, 175, 177, 251, 326
Cause-related marketing, 263
Certification in volunteer administration, 340, 343
Chambers of commerce, 123, 165, 171-2, 224, 315
Charity, 18-20, 64-5, 123, 136-8, 164-5, 200-1, 203
Charter schools, 297-8, 358
Chautauqua movement, 143-4
Chavez Cesar Day of Service, 310
Chesapeake Bay Resolution, 72
Child welfare, 19, 56-7, 66-8, 92, 123, 129, 139-40, 146-7, 161-2, 170, 197-8, 206, 210, 228, 271-2, 276, 291, 306, 319, 326, 332

Christian Commission, 102-3, 337
Civic engagement, 292
Civil defense, 177-8, 198, 208-9, 214, 221, 337
Civil Rights Act of 1957, 233
Civil Rights Act of 1964, 219
Civil rights advocacy, 3, 78, 113, 162-4, 194-5, 220, 231-4, 256, 325, 333, 337
Civil society, 11, 292
Civil War, U.S., 87-109, 142
Classification of volunteering, 13-4
Client rights, 255
Clubs civic and social, 19, 25, 129-30, 161, 172, 179, 192, 197, 203, 207, 221, 292, 315, 324, 336
Colleges and universities, 23-4, 127-8, 144-5, 147, 224, 235-6, 252, 267, 278-9, 299, 309, 322-4, 338, 325, 343
Commemorative stamp for volunteering, 265
Commissions on National Service (state), 342
Communal life, 16-7, 27-8, 47-8, 52, 82, 141, 292; *see also* Mutual aid.
Communications, 25-6, 31-2, 44-5, 94-5, 172-3, 177, 204-5, 213-4, 225, 223, 272, 291, 316-8
Communism, fear of, 188, 219-20, 222-3
Community chest drives, 138, 164-5
Community policing, 300
Compulsory community service, 4, 5, 7, 281-3, 296, 298, 359-60
Computers, 268-9, 283, 290, 292-3, 316, 317, 323; *see also* Internet and World Wide Web.
Confederate States of America, 96, 103, 104-9, 152
Conservation, 147, 174-5, 181, 207-8, 230-1, 258, 301, 327, 336, 337
Consumer rights, 123-4, 166, 194, 239, 295, 296, 305, 316, 318, 322, 333
Corporate social responsibility, 7, 142, 172, 192, 203, 213-4, 224-5, 233, 238-9, 247-9, 250, 262-4, 265, 282, 284, 294, 316; *see also* Employee volunteer programs.
Corporation for National and Community Service, 7, 305-6, 341, 342, 349, 352
Court-ordered community service. *See* Alternative sentencing.
Courts. *See* Justice system.
Crime prevention, 28-9, 49-51, 253-5, 270-1, 272, 273, 291, 299-301, 329, 330
Cycle of organizational development, 354-5

D

Days of caring/service, 309, 359
Definition of volunteering terms, 2-14
Demographic trends, 356-7
Depression, Great, 187, 188, 190-1, 192, 200-4
Dictionary of Occupational Titles, 339
Digital divide, 290, 316
Disabilities, physical, services for people with, 63, 68, 138, 166-7, 198-9, 228, 272, 292-3, 321, 326, 331
Disability rights, 255, 296, 322
Disaster relief, 19-20, 133, 143, 180, 200, 221, 226, 278, 302, 320, 330, 361
Doctors, service by, 20-1, 38, 62, 63, 93, 100, 133, 134, 203, 212, 264, 295, 308, 336
DOVIAs, 339-40
Draft/military conscription, 11-2, 36, 97-8, 114, 176-7, 208, 210-11, 235-6, 255, 280, 331
Drug abuse, 195, 269, 270-1, 300, 322
Drunk driving, 273, 282, 322

E

Earth Day (1970), 258
Education, 21-4, 50, 56-9, 67, 91-2, 115-6, 122, 126, 137, 140-1, 143-5, 165, 167, 171, 189, 197-8, 199, 209, 229-30, 249-50, 267-8, 271, 290, 297-9, 322-4, 325, 358
Elections and political campaigns, 71, 115, 118, 127, 131, 162, 177, 188, 192, 205, 220, 234, 244, 256, 287, 332-3, 338, 347
Emergency services, 60, 139, 173, 229, 267, 273-4, 297, 302, 303, 320, 330, 336
Employee volunteer programs, 247-9, 263, 294, 316, 340

Enrollment Act of 1863, 97
Entertainers volunteering by, 105, 142, 174, 198, 208, 210, 223, 235, 257, 259, 265, 270, 327
Environmentalism, 258, 301-2, 327-8
Epidemics, 21, 60-1, 62, 67, 271, 275, 288, 336
Equal Rights Amendment, 256
Extremist groups, 196-7, 223, 234, 236, 333

F

Fair Deal, 220
Fair Labor Standards Act, 197, 347
Family Support Act of 1988, 283
Family volunteering, 251, 357
Farm Aid, 270
Farming and farmers, 16-7, 24-5, 27, 48, 53-4, 94, 124-8,168-9, 175, 189, 192, 200, 211-2, 223-4, 270, 315, 357
Feminism, 162, 244-6, 256
Firefighting, 30, 48, 124, 214, 225, 230, 267, 273-4, 278, 303, 308, 330, 336, 338
Foreign aid, 141-2, 182, 209-10, 221, 237, 264, 278, 303, 304, 325, 332
Forests and forestry, 147, 225, 230, 325, 346
Foundations, 137, 168, 178, 224-5
Fourierites, 74-5
Fraternal orders, 19, 25, 128-9, 170, 229, 310, 326
Freedmen's Bureau, 115-6, 118, 338
Freedom riders, 232
French and Indian War, 36
Fresh-air funds, 146, 337
Friendly visitors, 137, 161
Fugitive Slave Law, 89
Future of volunteering, 356-61

G

Gabriel's Rebellion, 76
Gallup Poll, 266
Gay rights, 256-7, 275, 304, 333
Gleaning projects, 269, 315
Global Youth Service Day, 309-10
Government, corruption and reform of, 92, 132, 239-40, 347
Government, role of, 47-8, 51-2, 105, 125, 135, 147, 162, 171, 174, 179, 188-9, 191, 194, 197-8, 200-1, 203, 206, 208, 214, 215, 220, 238-9, 244, 260-2, 269-70, 275, 280, 305-7, 308-9, 310, 353, 358, 360
Government sponsored volunteer programs, 189, 203, 237-8, 246-7, 251, 253, 280-9, 305-9
Gun control, 305, 326

H

Halley's Comet, 276
Ham radio operators, 173, 302, 317
Hands Across America, 270
Health benefits of volunteering, 266
Health care. *See* Medicine and medical care.
Hispanic peoples. *See* Latino peoples.
Homelessness, 100, 269-70, 297, 319
Hospices, 274, 295, 321
Hospitality to travelers, 26, 46-7, 94, 104, 212, 318
Hospitals and sanatoriums, 21, 61, 63, 100, 101, 108, 134, 167, 168, 199, 214, 221-2, 229, 271, 293, 294-5, 315, 321, 338, 346, 359
Housing, 92, 162, 199, 232-3, 269-70, 296, 297, 319
Human rights, 221
Hunger and food, 64, 104-5, 200-2, 203, 259-60, 269, 315, 320, 332

I

"I Can" program, 251
Immigrants, aid to, 66, 67, 92, 121, 141, 196, 210, 259, 277-8, 320
Intergenerational programs, 251
International service, 237-8, 264, 280, 304, 308-9, 324, 332
International Year of Disabled Persons 1981, 255
International Year of Volunteers 2001, 287, 310, 342-3, 360-1
Internet and World Wide Web, 287, 289-91, 292-3, 303, 304, 308, 316, 323, 339, 342, 357, 358

J

Join Hands Day, 310
"Just Say No" campaign, 271
Justice system, 28-9, 30, 49-51, 52-3, 139, 140, 148-9, 162, 198, 229, 281-3, 299-301, 329-30, 337
Juvenile courts, 139, 140, 162, 198, 229, 329

K

King (Martin Luther Jr.) Federal Holiday and Service Act of 1994, 309
Know Nothings, 88-9
Korean War, 219-20, 221, 222,
Ku Klux Klan. *Go to* Organization Index.

L

Labor and employment, 19-20, 55-6, 71, 91, 94, 119-24, 131, 170-2, 189, 190-2, 196, 197, 199-200, 224, 228, 249, 314, 347-8, 358-9
Lancastrian method of teaching, 57
Latino peoples, 141, 195, 234, 310, 333, 357
Lawyers, volunteering by, 159, 264
Legal liability issues, 274, 295, 307, 346
Legislation on volunteer issues, 267, 274, 279, 296
Libraries, 23, 91, 121, 125, 126, 144, 228, 323, 336
Life cycle of volunteer involvement in organizations, 370-1
Literacy programs, 122, 267-8, 298, 323
Loggers and logging camps, 122
Lotteries, 29, 49
Lyceums, 71

M

Make a Difference Day, 309
Mandated service. *See* Compulsory community service.
March on Washington for Freedom and Jobs (1963), 233
McCarthyism, 222-3
"Me decade," 243-4, 260
Medical societies, 62-3
Medicine and medical care, 12, 20-1, 38, 59-63, 93, 108-9, 133-4, 166-8, 180, 197, 212, 226-7, 274-6, 294-5, 320-2
Mentally ill, treatment of, 68, 93, 166, 227, 255, 272, 297, 323
Mergers, corporate and institutional, 293, 294-5, 358
Mexican War, 73, 87, 90, 96
Midwives, 20, 166
Migrant workers, 199-200, 228-9, 315
Military, 11-2, 35-8, 72-4, 96, 107, 120, 149-50, 175-8, 179, 208-9, 211, 212, 213, 214, 221, 236-7, 288, 290, 331, 337
Miltary personnel, service by, 140-1, 212, 237, 331
Militias, 36, 72, 96, 98, 114-5, 149-50, 209, 338
Mill workers, 105, 122, 170-2
Miners and mining camps, 52-3, 120, 121-2
Missionaries, 69, 115, 122, 141, 143, 200, 324
Modern Health Crusade, 167
"Moonlight schools," 171
Mormons, 94
Muckrakers, 164
Municipal volunteer programs, 253, 340, 352
Museums and monuments, 23, 59, 144, 257, 277, 327, 340
Mutual aid, 3, 15-7, 20, 82, 105, 120, 123, 141, 160, 196, 201-3, 204, 274, 315

N

Names Project quilt, 276
Nat Turner's Rebellion, 79-80
National and Community Service Act of 1990, 305
National Gandhi Day of Service, 309
National Guard, 149, 163, 175, 208, 209, 236
National service, 280-1, 305-6, 308, 342
National Volunteer Week, 341
Native Americans, aid to, 69, 77, 140-1, 194-5
Native Americans, service by, 177, 194-5
Neighborhood councils, 253
New Deal, 188-9, 197, 201, 206, 215
"New Frontier," 220
Newspapers and magazines, 31-2, 44-5, 92, 164, 265-6, 268, 309
Nursing and nurses, 21, 38, 52, 101, 107-8, 166, 214, 336

O

Oklahoma City bombing, 287, 302
Older people as volunteers, 238, 251-3, 283, 319, 356
Olympic Games, 276, 326

One Day's Pay, 303, 310

P
Parks and playgrounds, 145-7, 174, 203, 206, 230-1, 325, 346
Peace Corps. *Go to* Organization Index.
Peace movements and pacifism, 73, 90, 97-8, 151-2, 177-8, 209, 220, 222, 235-6, 249, 331
Persian Gulf wars, 287, 288
Physicians. *See* Doctors.
Points of Light award, 341
Points of Light Foundation (& Volunteer Center National Network), 281, 305, 306, 307-8, 310, 340, 352
Police, 28, 50, 60, 90-1, 118, 148-9, 254, 271, 272, 300-1, 330
Polio vaccine trials, 227
Political action committees (PACs), 244
Political campaigns. *See* Elections and political campaigns.
Pollution control, 258, 278, 301, 328
Pony Express, 94-5
Poor, care for the, 18-9, 64-8, 92-3, 122, 135-40, 200-4, 228, 234, 237
Posses, 28, 51, 229, 337
Postal service, 26-7, 44, 64-5, 173, 225, 265, 318
Presidents' Summit for America's Future (for Volunteering), 306
Prisoners, service by, 210, 254, 329
Prisons, 49-5, 210, 254, 329, 337, 359
Privatization, 294, 359
Pro bono publico work, 7, 263-4, 316
Professional development of volunteer management, 267, 335-52
Professional societies and associations, 124, 144-5, 171-2, 226-7, 263-4, 316, 317, 318, 319, 320, 322-3, 327, 330; in volunteerism, 340, 343
Progressivism, 135, 157-60, 161, 165, 168, 182-3
Prohibition, 187, 188, 193
Proposition 13, 244
Public health, 60-2, 93, 132-4, 322
Public/private sector initiatives. 261-2
Publicity for volunteering, mass media, 265-6, 279
Puritanism, 16, 18-9, 22, 24-5, 145

Q
Quakers, 17-8, 73, 74, 75, 235
Quality circles, 249, 314
Quality Housing and Work Responsibility Act of 1998, 296
Quarantines, 59-61

R
Radio, television, and film, 172-3, 204-5, 208, 223, 225, 265, 268, 288, 303, 317, 319
Railroads, 45-6, 94, 99, 107, 119, 120, 196, 212, 213, 265, 302, 318
Ranchers and ranching, 128, 315
Reconstruction period in the South, 113-8, 337
Recreation and leisure, 24-5, 70-2, 114, 121, 123, 128-9, 145-7, 174-5, 181, 187, 206, 208, 212-3, 229, 230-1, 318, 321, 325-7, 329, 337
Recycling, 328
Refugees, resettlement of, 259, 277-8, 332
Reinvestment funds, 297
Religion and faith communities, 8, 16, 17-8, 21-2, 24, 49, 68-70, 92-3, 102-3, 115, 121, 134, 135, 143, 145, 160, 187, 193, 196-7, 198, 200, 203-4, 205, 206, 231, 233, 256, 261, 277, 297, 324-5, 336-7, 349-50, 355
Religious Society of Friends. *See* Quakers.
Resistance to volunteers, 244-6, 347-8
Restorative justice, 301
Revolutionary War, 15, 36-9
Right to volunteer, 359-60
Risk management. *See* Legal liability issues.
Rose Bowl Parade 1983, 265
Rural life movement, 175; *see also* Farming and farmers.

S
Safety, 28-9, 47, 60, 116, 119,124, 171, 189-90, 207, 225-6, 239, 254, 258, 269, 273, 318, 330

Sanctuary movement, Latin American refugee, 277, 325
Sanitary Commission U.S., 100-2, 133
Sanitation, 27, 132-3, 148, 167, 328
Schools. *See* Education.
Scientific inquiry and exploration, 59, 95-6, 127-8, 166, 226, 258, 276, 323, 324, 331
Scientific philanthropy, 137-8
Secret societies, 88-9, 120, 128-9
Selective Service Act of 1917, 177
Self-help groups, 3, 7, 79, 82, 193, 202, 228, 233, 257, 271, 272-3, 292, 300, 317, 320, 322, 336, 355
Seneca Falls Convention, 43, 88
September 11th, xii, 287, 302-3, 310-1
Service credit. *See* Time bank.
Service-learning, 7-8, 250, 278-9, 298-9, 324
Settlement houses, 135-6, 336
Short-term volunteering, 293-4, 358-9
Sit-ins, 232
Slavery, end to. *See* Abolitionism.
Smoking prevention, 273, 321
Social Compact of 1620, 16
Social Gospel, 135, 145
Social welfare, 17-20, 64-8, 98-9,135-40, 160-2, 166-8, 228-9, 297, 319-20
Social workers, 13-4, 137, 159, 160-1, 166, 201, 337
Socially-responsible investing, 278, 316
Spanish-American War, 150-2
Sports, 71-2, 147, 196, 206-7, 265, 326
Spying and smuggling, 37, 99, 104, 105, 106, 182, 211
Stamp Act, 32, 34
Statistics and research on volunteering, 247, 266-7, 310-11, 338-9, 343, 349-50, 361
Statue of Liberty restoration, 277
Stereotypes about volunteers, viii, 6
Stipends for volunteers, 3, 238, 251, 280-1, 359
Strikes, labor, 55, 120, 121, 131, 149, 170, 192, 348
Suffrage, for freed slaves, 104, 115, 130
Suffrage, for women, 81, 129-31,162-3, 187,193
Sunday schools, 56-7
Sweat equity, 297
Synonyms for volunteer, 7-8

T

Tax Reform Act of 1986, 261
Tax work-off programs, 253
Teachers, volunteering by, 22, 56, 115-6, 122, 176, 230, 323, 324, 336
Technical assistance, international, 304, 316, 332
Telegraph, 44, 95, 180
Television. *See* Radio, television and film.
Temperance movement, 65-6, 75, 130, 193
Terrorism, 287, 302-3, 308, 330, 337
Time bank (service credit, time dollar), 281, 283
Titles for volunteer program managers, 339
Town maintenance, 27-31, 49, 132-3
Town meetings, 17-8, 52-3, 202-3, 332
Transitional volunteering, 251
Transportation, 25-6, 45-8, 90, 150, 190, 225-6, 231, 239, 273, 301-2, 318
Trends in 21st century volunteerism, 356-61
Tuberculosis, 133-4, 167-8, 229

U

Underground Railroad, 77-80, 89-90, 103, 336
Unemployment, 190-1, 200, 238-9, 262, 269, 291, 293, 296, 358
Unions. *See* Labor and employment.
United Nations, 219, 221, 222, 304, 310, 332
Universal Declaration on the Profession of Leading and Managing Volunteers, 343
Universities. *See* Colleges and universities.
Unrelated business income tax (UBIT), 261
USA Freedom Corps, 308-9, 310, 349
Utopian communities, 74-5

V
Veterans, 100, 101, 152, 198, 209, 221-2, 277, 331
Victim services, 329
Victory Corps, 211
Vietnam War, 219, 220, 234-7, 243, 259, 277, 280
Vigilantism, 28-9, 50-1, 116-8, 148-9, 159, 193, 254
Virtual volunteering, 288-9, 292, 304, 353, 358
Voluntarism and volunteerism definitions, 8-9
Voluntary associations, 9, 10, 25, 28, 39, 48, 51-2, 64, 74, 91, 119, 171, 197, 226, 320-3, 353-4
Volunteer Act of 1914, 176
Volunteer centers, 308, 340-1
"Volunteer Connection" campaign, 265
Volunteer management, profession of, 335-52; international, 339, 342-3,
Volunteer Management Capacity in America's Charities and Congregations, 349-50
Volunteer Protection Acts, 267, 305-6
Volunteer vacations, 324
Voting rights, 233, 238; *see also* Suffrage.

W
Wagon train masters, 47, 59, 338
War, homefront support of, 34-5, 37-8, 73, 98-109, 150-1, 178-2, 209-14, 336, 337
War of 1812, 67, 72-3
Weather observation, 328
Welfare Reform Law of 1966, 295-6
Welfare rights, 234, 255
Welfare-to-work, 296
Women as volunteers, perceptions of, viii, 13-4 244-6
Women, role of, 13-4, 18, 27, 34-5, 37-8, 44, 59, 75, 81, 88, 91, 98-9, 102, 105-8, 114, 123, 125, 129-31, 139-40, 145, 150, 161-2, 177, 178-80, 193-4, 197, 209, 224, 234, 244-6
Women's rights. *See* Feminism; *also see* Suffrage, for women.
Work experience through volunteering, 250-1, 267
Workers' compensation, 120, 284, 359
Workfare, 7, 281, 283
Workplace volunteering. See Employee volunteer programs.
Works Progress Administration, 204
World Hunger Year, 259
World War I, 178-82
World War II, 187, 189, 196, 200, 208-14, 221
World Wide Web. *See* Internet and World Wide Web.

Y
Yellow fever epidemic of 1793, 60, 67
Youth (children and teens), service by, 35, 38, 57, 58, 81, 101, 108, 147-8, 167, 169, 180, 189-90, 198, 200, 211, 212, 213, 226, 249-50, 277, 280, 310-1, 315, 324, 326, 329, 332, 336

9336873R0

Made in the USA
Charleston, SC
03 September 2011